THE STEPHEN BECHTEL FUND

IMPRINT IN ECOLOGY AND THE ENVIRONMENT

The Stephen Bechtel Fund has

established this imprint to promote

understanding and conservation of

our natural environment.

The press gratefully acknowledges the generous contribution to this book provided by the Stephen Bechtel Fund.

ENVIRONMENTAL FLOWS

ENVIRONMENTAL FLOWS

Saving Rivers in the Third Millennium

Angela H. Arthington

UNIVERSITY OF CALIFORNIA PRESS   Berkeley   Los Angeles   London

University of California Press, one of the most distinguished university presses in the United States,
enriches lives around the world by advancing scholarship
in the humanities, social sciences, and natural sciences.
Its activities are supported by the UC Press Foundation
and by philanthropic contributions from individuals and
institutions. For more information, visit www.ucpress.edu.

University of California Press
Berkeley and Los Angeles, California

University of California Press, Ltd.
London, England

Library of Congress Cataloging-in-Publication Data

Arthington, Angela H., 1943-
    Environmental flows : saving rivers in the third
millennium / Angela Helen Arthington.
        p.   cm. — (Freshwater ecology series ; 4)
    Includes bibliographical references and index.
    ISBN 978-0-520-27369-6 (cloth : alk. paper)
1. Stream ecology.   2. Streamflow—Environmental
aspects.   3. Stream conservation.   4. Biotic
communities.   5. Water-supply—Environmental
aspects.   I. Title.
    QH541.5.S7A78   2012
    577.6'4—dc23   2012012445

Manufactured in the United States of America

21   20   19   18   17   16   15   14   13   12
10   9   8   7   6   5   4   3   2   1

The paper used in this publication meets the minimum
requirements of ANSI/NISO Z39.48–1992 (R 2002)
(*Permanence of Paper*).

Cover image: Coomera River, southeast Queensland.
Photograph by David Sternberg, Griffith University.

For my extended family and river warriors everywhere

CONTENTS

PREFACE AND ACKNOWLEDGMENTS

Environmental Flows: Saving Rivers in the Third Millennium is a single source of information on environmental flows—"the quantity, timing and quality of water flows required to sustain freshwater and estuarine ecosystems and the human livelihoods and well-being that depend upon these ecosystems" (Brisbane Declaration 2007). Water in its standing and flowing phases, in gaseous, liquid, and solid forms, drives a global cycle of hydrological processes that underpin the biodiversity, functionality, and vitality of aquatic ecosystems. How much water does each ecosystem type need? What happens when natural seasonal flow patterns or standing-water regimes are radically altered by dams, hydropower generation, or pumping to meet the needs of humans? Can damaged ecosystems be restored by providing environmental flows? How can human societies come to grips with climate change, less water for everyone, greater impacts on aquatic biodiversity, and increasingly dysfunctional ecosystems?

These questions are the focus of this book. It is not a cookbook of recipes for estimating environmental flow requirements. It is a narrative about methodological development, from simple hydrological formulas to ecosystem perspectives informing water management at multiple spatial scales. Citations to original sources provide easy access to a wealth of additional information and case studies, from aquatic ecology and the science of environmental flows to implementation, monitoring, legislation, and policy. The book ends with recommendations for adaptation to climate change—the ultimate challenge—and the role of environmental flows as a means to sustain the benefits of freshwater biodiversity and the ecological goods and services of healthy freshwater ecosystems.

Like many books, this one had its origin in lectures and seminars. Collating readings into manuals for student reference signaled the need for a synthesis of the science and practice of water management for ecosystem protection and restoration. Several excellent texts and papers informed and inspired this volume, including Dyson et al. (2003) and Hirji and Davis (2009). Recent developments in methods, applications, and monitoring vis-à-vis environmental flows appear in a special issue of *Freshwater Biology* (Arthington et al. 2010a) and helped to shape this volume.

Environmental Flows draws heavily on the resources and publications cited throughout. Numerous colleagues have together shaped this science, applied the methods, and extended the field along many dimensions during decades of collaborative research, allied activities, and adventures. The following colleagues deserve mention, each in special measure: Robin Abell, Mike Acreman, Alexa Apro, Harry Balcombe, Anna Barnes, Ian Bayly, Barry Biggs, Andrew Birley, Stuart Blanch, David Blühdorn, Nick Bond, Paul Boon, Andrew Boulton, Anthea Brecknell, Gary Brierley, Sandra Brizga, Margaret Brock, Andrew Brooks, Cate Brown, Stuart Bunn, Jim Cambray, Samantha Capon, Hiram Caton, Tom Cech, Fiona Chandler, Bruce Chessman, Peter Cottingham, Satish Choy, Peter Cullen, Felicity Cutten, Bryan Davies, Peter Davies (Tasmania), Peter Davies (Western Australia), Jenny Davis, Jenny Day, Ben Docker, David Dole, Michael Douglas, David Dudgeon, Patrick Dugan, Mike Dunbar, Kurt Fausch, Christine Fellows, Max Finlayson, Mary Freeman, Kirstie Fryirs, Ben Gawne, Peter Gehrke, Keith Gido, Chris Gippel, Paul Godfrey, Nancy Gordon, Gary Grossman, Wade Hadwen, Ashley Halls, John Harris, Barry Hart, Gene Helfman, Tim Howell, Jane Hughes, Paul Humphries, Cassandra James, Xiaohui Jiang, Gary Jones, Ian Jowett, Fazlul Karim, Eloise Kendy, Mark Kennard, Adam Kerezsy, Alison King, Jackie King, John King, Richard Kingsford, James Knight, Louise Korsgaard,

Sam Lake, Cath Leigh, Cathy Reidy Liermann, Simon Linke, Lance Lloyd, Kai Lorenzen, Stephen Mackay, Nick Marsh, Jon Marshall, Carla Mathisen, Michael McClain, Rob McCosker, Elvio Medeiros, David Milton, David Merritt, Michael Moore, Bob Morrish, Peter Moyle, Robert Naiman, Jon Nevill, Christer Nilsson, Richard Norris, Ralph Ogden, Jay O'Keeffe, Julian Olden, Jon Olley, Ian Overton, Tim Page, Margaret Palmer, Shoni Pearce, Ben Pearson, Richard Pearson, Geoff Petts, Bill Pierson, LeRoy Poff, Carmel Pollino, Sandra Postel, Jim Puckridge, Brad Pusey, Gerry Quinn, Johannes Rall, Martin Read, Peter Reid, Birgitta Renöfält, Brian Richter, David Rissik, Ian Robinson, Kevin Rogers, Robert Rolls, Nick Schofield, Patrick Shafroth, Clayton Sharpe, Fran Sheldon, Deslie Smith, Christopher Souza, Robert Speed, David Sternberg, Mike Stewardson, Ben Stewart-Koster, David Strayer, Rebecca Tharme, Martin Thoms, Klement Tockner, Colin Townsend, Charlie Vörösmarty, Keith Walker, Jim Wallace, Robyn Watts, Angus Webb, Robin Welcomme, Gary Werren, Kirk Winemiller, Bill Young, and Yongyong Zhang. Special thanks to Sam Capon and Stephen Mackay for preparing the figures, David Sternberg for double-checking the references and for the cover photograph, and Jean Mann for preparing the index. Most of the figures have been redrawn from original publications with permission from the publisher.

Personal research underlying this book has been funded by the Australian Rivers Institute, Griffith University; the Australian Water Research Advisory Council; Land and Water Australia; the National Water Commission; the International Water Centre; the eWater Cooperative Research Centre (CRC); the Freshwater CRC; the Rainforest CRC; the Tourism CRC; the Marine and Tropical Science Research Facility; and several Queensland and Commonwealth government agencies. Thanks are due also to international agencies that provided support and experience during consultancy and advisory work in South Africa, Brazil, Cambodia, China, Korea, Laos, Thailand, Vietnam, New Zealand, Canada, the United Kingdom, the United States, Spain, and Sweden.

Last but certainly not least, members of my editorial and production team—Chuck Crumly, Ric Hauer, Lynn Meinhardt, Kate Hoffman, Julie Van Pelt, Pamela Polk, and Jean Mann, University of California Press—are thanked most warmly for their ongoing encouragement and support, keeping the spirit of the book alive and everything shipshape during its writing and production. Thanks are due also to members of the Editorial Board of the Freshwater Ecology Series for their advice on structure and content, especially Stuart Bunn, who promoted the concept of this book and supported its gestation throughout.

Grateful thanks to each and every individual named herein for your commitment to the work we do to look after rivers and wetlands across the globe. May this vitally important work continue unabated in your country and mine for as long as it takes to face the reality of the freshwater biodiversity crisis and to turn the third millennium into an era of transformation and restoration for the benefit of ecosystems and people.

Angela H. Arthington

Australian Rivers Institute
Griffith University
June 2012

I

RIVER VALUES AND THREATS

THE FRESHWATER BIODIVERSITY CRISIS

Rivers and their associated floodplains, groundwater, and wetlands are in crisis. Globally they are the world's most damaged ecosystems, losing species at a rate that far outstrips the decline of biodiversity in terrestrial and marine systems (Dudgeon et al. 2006). A new synthesis of threats to the world's rivers (Vörösmarty et al. 2010) has found that over 83% of the land surface surrounding aquatic systems has been significantly influenced by the "human footprint." The stamp of human activities is manifest as widespread catchment disturbance, deforestation, water pollution, river corridor engineering, impoundments and water diversions, irrigation, extensive wetland drainage, groundwater depletion, habitat loss, and introduced species. Impoundments and depletion of river flows are the clearest sources of biodiversity threat in that they directly degrade and reduce river and floodplain habitat, with 65% of global river discharge and aquatic habitat under moderate to high threat. This threat level exceeds past estimates of human appropriation of accessible freshwater runoff and is approaching the 70% level anticipated by 2050 (Postel et al. 1996).

The worldwide pattern of anthropogenic threats to rivers documented by Vörösmarty et al. (2010) offers the most comprehensive accounting ever undertaken to explain why freshwater biodiversity is in a state of crisis. Estimates suggest that at least 10,000–20,000 freshwater species are extinct or at risk, largely from anthropogenic factors. Loss rates for freshwater biodiversity are believed to rival those of the Pleistocene-to-Holocene transition.

In 2002, Paul Crutzen suggested that the world has entered a new epoch—the Anthropocene—because humans dominate the biosphere and largely determine environmental quality (Zalasiewicz et al. 2008). Numerous correlative studies, experiments, and meta-analysis all point to human activities as the common factor in freshwater biodiversity decline. Given escalating trends in species extinction, human population growth, water use, development pressures, and the additional stresses associated with climate change, the new global synthesis predicts that freshwater systems will remain under threat well into the future.

RIVER VALUES

River degradation and loss of freshwater biodiversity have major implications for human water security, prosperity, health, and well-being because they threaten the provision of ecosystem services—the tangible benefits people gain from ecosystems. The Millennium Ecosystem Assessment, a global synthesis and analysis of the state of the world's major ecosystems, grouped ecosystem services into four main categories: provisioning, regulating, cultural, and supporting (MEA 2005).

Provisioning services (Table 1) are the products obtained from ecosystems. Rivers and lakes hold about 100,000 km³ of freshwater globally, amounting to less than 0.01% of all water on Earth (Schwarz et al. 1990). Yet this tiny fraction of global water is absolutely vital for human life support and the provision of most other ecosystem services, including those dependent on diverse biological systems. These biologically based services include food (shrimp, fish, plants), fuel products (peat), fibers and building materials (timbers and thatch), and pharmacological products. Freshwater ecosystems underpin global food production based on artisanal and commercial fisheries, aquaculture, flood-recession agriculture, and pastoral animal husbandry (MEA 2005). Clean freshwater of low salinity is essential to grow most food and fiber crops and to drive the industries that produce food products, cooking utensils, clothing, housing, infrastructure, transport, recreation, and enter-

TABLE I   *Provisioning ecosystem services provided by
rivers, wetlands, and groundwater systems*

With examples of hydrological, geomorphic, and ecological processes
underpinning each service and some consequences if services are lost

Provisioning ecosystem services	Supporting processes and structures	Consequences of losing the service
Water supply	Transport and storage of water throughout catchments (river basins)	Loss of water for residential, commercial, urban, and irrigation use
Water storage	Intact floodplains and wetlands; vegetation increases infiltration of rainwater and enhances groundwater and deep aquifer recharge	Droughts exacerbated; loss of groundwater stores for private and public use; loss of vegetation and wildlife
Food production		
(a) Primary production	Production of new plant tissue	Reduction in food and food products derived from aquatic plants (e.g., algae, rice, tubers)
(b) Secondary production	Production of new animal tissue or microbial biomass	Shortages in fisheries including finfish, crustaceans, shellfish, and other edible biota
Wood and fuel production	Production of timber, thatch, and peat	Reduction in wood, fiber, and fuel products derived from riparian and wetland vegetation
Biodiversity	Intact freshwater systems support diverse plant and animal species; are reservoirs of genetic diversity for future human use and evolutionary potential	Reduced ecosystem resilience and limited adaptation to disturbances (e.g., climate change); species losses can reduce all other provisioning services

SOURCES: Adapted from Danielopol et al. 2004; Palmer et al. 2009; Gustavson and Kennedy 2010

tainment. Some estimates suggest that global food production must double by 2050 to meet human needs, and this must be achieved using less water; already, 70% of the world's freshwater is used in agriculture (Molden 2007).

Regulating services (Table 2) are equally vital, being the benefits obtained from the regulation of ecosystem processes such as the climate regime, hydrologic cycle, nutrient processing, and natural hazards. Rivers, lakes, wetlands, and aquifers store freshwater or slow the passage of water. Floodplains and wetlands absorb large pulses of catchment runoff and help mitigate the damaging effects of floods on landscapes and the built environment (Freitag et al. 2009). Water returning off floodplains is rich in nutrients and energy sources that fuel the food webs supporting riverine biota and dependent terrestrial species such as waterbirds and amphibians (Douglas et al. 2005). Rivers also convey freshwater to estuaries, coastal wetlands, and the nearshore environment, where flow pulses contribute to maintaining habitats of tolerable salinity for plants and animals directly used by humans. Estuarine inflows carry nutrients that stimulate primary and secondary production and support the recruitment of fish and crustaceans (Gillanders and Kingsford 2002). Mangroves, salt marshes, and seagrasses that are partly dependent on freshwater help to stabilize sediments, alter waterflow patterns, produce large quantities of organic carbon, and influence nutrient cycling and food web structure (Hemminga and Duarte 2000).

Cultural services (Table 3) are the benefits people obtain through recreation, education, and aesthetics; celebrations revolving around water and its goods and services to humans; and spiritual enrichment (MEA 2005). For many societies, rivers and lakes have profound cultural and religious significance; they are the sites for important ceremonies, the burial places of beloved family members, and the dwelling places of gods and guardian spirits. The Australian Aboriginals who lived as nomads in a very dry continent with extremely patchy freshwater resources appreciated water as few other cultures have needed to do (Bayly 1999). Caring for and protecting freshwater places and species is bound up with human perceptions of dependence on freshwater resources and species during both this life on Earth and in the afterlife. Cultural ecosystem services are made possible by supporting services such as nutrient cycling and provision of habitat and food for aquatic species.

TABLE 2   *Regulating ecosystem services provided by rivers, wetlands and groundwater systems*

With examples of hydrological, geomorphic, and ecological processes underpinning each service and some consequences if services are lost

Regulating ecosystem services	Supporting processes and structures	Consequences of losing the service
Flood control	Intact floodplains, wetlands, and riparian vegetation buffer large increases in discharge by physically slowing water flow, temporarily storing water, or removing water through plant uptake	Increase in frequency and magnitude of floods; damage from floods to infrastructure and public amenity values of landscape
Erosion/sediment control	Soil held in place or trapped by intact riparian vegetation; algae and geomorphic features reduce erosive forces on stream banks and beds and wetland shorelines; aquatic and riparian habitats are maintained	Loss and burial of aquatic habitat impacts fisheries and biodiversity; can cause increase in contaminant transport and reduction in downstream reservoir storage or can impact wetland, groundwater, and coastal ecosystems
Water purification		
(a) Nutrient processing	Retention, storage or removal of excess nitrogen and phosphorus; organic matter is decomposed (leaf litter, plant parts, animal carcasses, etc.)	Excess nutrients accumulate, making water unsuitable for drinking or supporting life; algal blooms lead to anoxic conditions and death of biota
(b) Processing of contaminants and pollutants	Plant and microbial uptake or transformation limits flux of pollutants and contaminants downstream or into groundwater; plants and geomorphic features act to reduce suspended sediment, and sediment transport downstream.	Toxic contaminants, suspended sediments, and other pollutants can kill or impair aquatic biota; highly turbid and contaminated water not potable, cannot be used in certain industries and may be aesthetically offensive

SOURCES: Adapted from Danielopol et al. 2004; Palmer et al. 2009; Gustavson and Kennedy 2010

TABLE 3   *Cultural ecosystem services provided by*
rivers, wetlands, and groundwater systems

With examples of hydrological, geomorphic, and ecological processes
underpinning each service and some consequences if services are lost

Cultural ecosystem services	Supporting processes and structures	Consequences of losing the service
Recreation, celebrations, education, aesthetics, and religious and inspirational values	Clean water, particularly water bodies with pleasant natural surroundings such as forests and natural wildlife refuges, are valued natural wonders; provide for recreation; inspire painting and poetry; support cultural and religious value systems	Lost opportunities for relaxation, enjoyment of nature, spending time with family; economic losses to various industries, particularly tourist ventures; loss of quality of life and spiritual, cultural, and religious values

SOURCES: Adapted from Danielopol et al. 2004; Palmer et al. 2009; Gustavson and Kennedy 2010

THREATS TO RIVER VALUES AND PEOPLE

Escalating human demand for freshwater is jeopardizing the very eco-system services on which millions of humans depend directly for water, food, secure housing, quality of life, health, and prosperity. River impoundment and water diversions, in particular, threaten freshwater habitats, biodiversity, and provisioning ecosystem services, while the barriers created by dam walls and large expanses of impounded water, coupled with downstream flow reduction, can sever ecological connections in aquatic systems, fragmenting rivers from their headwaters and productive floodplains and from their estuarine deltas and coastal marine environments (Nilsson et al. 2005). The regulation of river discharge by large dams can change the quantity, quality, and timing of freshwater flows and in so doing frequently disrupts life-history behaviors and most of the ecological processes on which riparian, freshwater, and estuarine ecosystems depend (Poff et al. 1997; Naiman et al. 2008).

Many other human interventions at catchment scale intercept or exacerbate overland flows and influence the hydrology of streams and rivers, wetlands, and estuaries. Not only do catchment activities alter surface and groundwater hydrology, they also alter the dynamics of other catchment resource regimes: sediments, nutrients and organic matter, temperature, and light/shade (Baron et al. 2002). Alterations to these resource regimes have many consequences for aquatic and riparian ecosystems, and they frequently interact to form damaging constellations of stressors (Ormerod et al. 2010). With escalating development of catchment land, deforestation, wetland drainage, irrigation, urbanization and commercial activities, these threats to aquatic biodiversity and human dependencies on freshwater and estuarine ecosystems will most certainly continue to rise.

In their global synthesis of threats to rivers and human freshwater resources, Vörösmarty et al. (2010) found that nearly 80% (4.8 billion people) of the world's population (for 2000) lives in areas with high threat levels for human water security and/or biodiversity. Vörösmarty et al. make the following critical points:

- Regions of intensive agriculture and dense settlement show the highest levels of threat, including much of the United States, virtually all of Europe, and large portions of central Asia, the Middle East, the Indian subcontinent, and eastern China. Water scarcity particularly threatens arid and semiarid river basins across the desert belt of all continents (e.g., Argentina, the Sahel, central Asia, and the Australian Murray-Darling Basin).

- Heavily populated and developed areas pose particularly high threats to people and biodiversity in spite of high rainfall and greater pollution dilution capacity in such areas, for example, eastern China, especially within the Yangtze Basin. More than 30 large rivers that collectively discharge half of global runoff to the oceans are threatened at the river mouth by water diversions, including the Nile in Egypt, the Colorado in the United States, the Yellow in China, as well as countless smaller rivers with flow patterns so modified that the biodiversity and productivity of their estuaries and deltas are threatened (Postel and Richter 2003).

- Only the most remote areas of the world (about 0.16% of the earth's surface area), including the high north (Siberia, Canada, Alaska) and unsettled parts of the tropical zone (Amazonia, northern Australia), show low threat levels for people and ecosystems.

Global warming and climate change are likely to intensify both historical legacies and today's threat syndromes in agricultural catchments and urbanized landscapes (Palmer et al. 2009). The Intergovernmental Panel on Climate Change (IPCC) reported that the earth's mean temperature will increase by at least 1.5°C above preindustrial times (IPCC 2007). A warmer atmosphere and higher evaporation and precipitation rates are expected to accelerate the global hydrologic cycle (Vörösmarty et al. 2004). Climate change appears to be a major factor in the increasing intensity and frequency of weather extremes such as cyclones, hurricanes, flood and drought episodes, and fires, while decreases in snow and ice cover have already been observed (IPCC 2007). Shifts in climatic regimes and associated alterations to global precipitation and runoff patterns, evapotranspiration rates, and other environmental regimes are already changing river flow and thermal regimes, producing longer and more severe drought episodes, and leading to more intense and frequent storm events followed by flooding.

These changes will affect freshwater supplies for humans and ecosystems, in particular the amount and timing of precipitation and runoff, rates of evaporation and transpiration, and sea level rise. The former of these hydrologic changes have implications for the distribution, character, and even the persistence of freshwater ecosystems, while rise in sea level is expected to impact estuaries, low-lying brackish and freshwater wetlands, and other coastal ecosystems. Changes in atmospheric temperature and hydrologic regimes will be accompanied by changes and interactions with other environmental regimes that have a strong influence on aquatic ecosystems. Together these shifts in the global water cycle and freshwater availability are certain to intensify problems of water supply in an increasingly populous world that has high expectations of better health, living standards, and prosperity (Alcamo et al. 2008). Rivers and groundwater systems will feel the most pressure because they are the main sources of water for most of the world's population.

With decreasing precipitation in many areas of the globe, and other changes to runoff and river hydrology, there is intense interest in defining the ecological water requirements of aquatic ecosystems, especially rivers, floodplains, and associated groundwater systems, but also the freshwater needs of estuaries into which many of the world's great rivers flow. Restoring biodiversity, ecosystem function, and resiliency (the capacity to respond and adjust to disturbance) are now global imperatives for river managers, scientists, and civil society (Dudgeon et al. 2006; Palmer et al. 2008). The challenge is immense and it is global. It requires deep understanding of the ecological roles of natural hydrologic and other environmental regimes, how alterations in flow regime impact aquatic and riparian ecosystems, what flow volumes (discharges) and temporal patterns of variability are most needed to sustain these ecosystems, and how to manage and share the world's finite supplies of freshwater to achieve the greatest benefits for people and for nature.

HOW MUCH WATER DOES A RIVER NEED?

This question was famously asked by Richter et al. (1997) during work by The Nature Conservancy (TNC) on rivers with highly altered flow regimes. Many scientists and water managers have provided answers to this question for thousands of streams and rivers in almost every country. The majority of "in-stream flow" methods (70%; Tharme 2003) either provide simple rules founded on the hydrologic characteristics of surface water flows, or they quantify the flow volumes needed to maintain aquatic habitat in terms of water depth, velocity, and cover for selected species, usually fish of commercial or recreational value (e.g., salmonids). Often the flow recommended to support habitat is a "minimum flow," the smallest amount of water that could maintain a wetted channel and provide opportunities for limited movement and maintenance feeding. These foundational methods, and innovations focused on two- and three-dimensional habitat modeling and other techniques, have generated many insights (e.g., Booker and Acreman 2007; Kennard et al. 2007) as well as many misgivings, because suitable habitat is only one dimension of the needs of aquatic species and the ecosystems that support them.

Around the late 1980s, river scientists working on in-stream flow methods, and a broader group interested in river ecology and restoration, drew attention to the importance of many facets of the flow regime, not just the low flows within the channel that maintain critical habitats for aquatic species. Ecologists working in very different systems and countries recognized the dynamic nature of river flows and fluxes to and from floodplain wetlands and also exchanges with groundwater systems (e.g., Gore and Nestler 1988; Statzner et al. 1988; Junk et al. 1989; Petts 1989; Stalnaker and Arnette 1976; Ward 1989; Poff and Ward 1990; Hill et al. 1991; Arthington et al. 1992; Sparks 1995; Walker et al. 1995; Poff 1996; Richter et al. 1996, 1997; Stanford et al. 1996; Naiman and Décamps 1997; King and Louw 1998).

Furthermore, it became increasingly apparent that alterations to river flow magnitudes (discharge), seasonal patterns, and temporal variability by dams and other interventions have severe consequences for aquatic species and ecosystem processes. In 1997 a seminal publication succinctly captured these ideas in a new paradigm for river restoration and conservation. This Natural Flow Regime Paradigm reflects on evidence that the structure and functions of riverine ecosystems, and many adaptations of aquatic biota, are dictated by temporal patterns of river flows (Poff et al. 1997). At the same time, papers by Richter et al. (1996, 1997) identified important facets of river flow regimes, and they set out how to estimate these facets statistically and to quantify alterations to them, to support the management of river flows for ecological purposes.

ENVIRONMENTAL FLOWS

A broad general agreement has emerged from these scientific debates: that to protect freshwater biodiversity and maintain the ecosystem services of rivers, natural flow variability, or some semblance of it, must be maintained. With this shift in thinking there arose a broader "riverine ecosystem" perspective on the assessment of in-streams flows, and this term switched almost imperceptibly to the more inclusive terms "environmental flows" (E-flows) or "environmental water allocations" (EWAs) and the related terms "ecological and environmental water requirements" (EEWRs), "ecological water demand," and "eco-environmental water consumption" (Moore 2004; Song and Yang 2003).

All of these terms refer to flows that maintain the biophysical and ecological processes of river corridors—the dynamic aquatic continuum from source areas to the sea—embracing river channels, alluvial groundwater and hyporheic zones, riparian and floodplain wetlands, estuaries, and coastal zones. A recent definition of environmental flows also makes an explicit link between healthy river and estuarine ecosystems and the livelihoods and well-being of people and societies dependent on them: "Environmental flows describe the quantity, timing and quality of water flows required to sustain freshwater and estuarine ecosystems and the human livelihoods and well-being that depend upon these ecosystems" (Brisbane Declaration 2007; see also the appendix in the present volume).

Several features of this definition have universal appeal. The description signals that the "quality" of water is an important dimension alongside water quantity and temporal flow patterns, and it also highlights the continuity of rivers and estuaries and their dependence on freshwater flows. Furthermore, it explicitly links environmental flows, river and estuarine ecosystems, and the livelihoods and well-being of people and societies.

In the narrative of this book, an "environmental flow" is an integral part of the continuity of the hydrologic cycle, managed to a greater or lesser extent by human interventions to produce outcomes beneficial to species, ecosystems, and people. All components of the hydrologic cycle "flow" from place to place and time to time, in one form or another, supplying water to aquatic ecosystems that are connected and driven by surface and groundwater flows, biogeochemical fluxes, and ecological processes. How humans influence and manage these water flows is of immense significance to the aquatic and terrestrial components of the biosphere and to human welfare. As the new global synthesis of threats to freshwater ecosystems so graphically demonstrates, rivers and freshwater biodiversity are in crisis, and 80% of the world's population lives in areas with high threat levels for human water security and/or biodiversity (Vörösmarty et al. 2010).

Environmental Flows: Saving Rivers in the Third Millennium tells the story of the global freshwater crisis: from basic hydrology to river ecology and hydroecological principles; through a litany of threatening processes and degradation syndromes: to the methods, frameworks, modeling techniques, decision support systems, and the legislation, policy, and water management strategies now available to protect the water rights of aquatic ecosystems and the people dependent on them. The book's final chapter turns to climate change—the ultimate challenge—

and what it may mean for aquatic ecosystems and the role of environmental flows as a means to sustain ecosystem resiliency and biodiversity. The book concludes by making the case for a vigorous global river and catchment restoration effort to sustain and restore the benefits of freshwater biodiversity and the ecological goods and services of healthy rivers and estuaries, wetlands, and groundwater. Given the enormous potential of human adaptive capacity, and the power of innovative science to inform and guide environmental flow management and other restoration measures, many rivers, wetlands, and estuaries can be saved. With effort, commitment and vision, the third millennium could become the era of transformation and restoration of Earth's natural resiliency and healing power for the benefit of people and the ecosystems on which so many human lives and species depend.

2

GLOBAL HYDROLOGY, CLIMATE, AND RIVER FLOW REGIMES

GLOBAL HYDROLOGY AND CLIMATE ZONES

The natural fluctuations of freshwater ecosystems and water supplies are governed by the climatic regime of the region and the prevailing hydrologic cycle—the dynamic mechanism connecting all forms of water in its liquid, solid, and vapor phases and in the cells and tissues of living organisms (Fig. 1). In a perpetual cycle driven by solar energy, the global hydrological cycle delivers an estimated 110,000 km³ of water to the land annually as precipitation. About two-thirds of this precipitation is water recycled from plants and the soil as evapotranspiration (70,000 km³ per year), while one-third is water evaporated from the oceans and transported over land (40,000 km³ per year). Groundwater holds about 15,000,000 km³ of the world's freshwater, much of which is stored in deep aquifers not in active exchange with the earth's surface (Jackson et al. 2001). Most deep groundwater represents a relic of wetter climatic conditions and melting Pleistocene ice sheets, and is sometimes termed "fossil water." Once used, this ancient water cannot readily be replenished, whereas renewable groundwater systems depend on current precipitation rates for refilling and are vulnerable to increased water use and drought. Groundwater hydrology, surface water–groundwater relationships, and processes of importance for riverine ecology are taken up in Chapters 15 and 16.

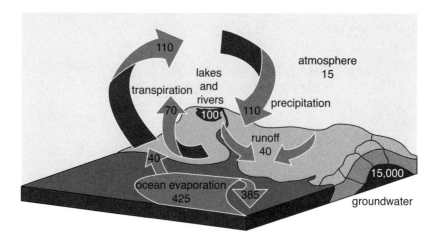

FIGURE I. Hydrologic cycle, showing the renewable freshwater cycle in thousands of km³ for pools (white numbers) and thousands of km³ per year for fluxes (black numbers). Total precipitation over land is ~110,000 km³ per year, of which two-thirds is evapotranspiration from plants and the soil (evapotranspiration is 70,000 km³ per year) and one-third is water evaporated from the oceans that is transported over land (40,000 km³ per year). Total evaporation from the oceans is 425,000 km³ per year. Groundwater holds ~15,000,000 km³ of freshwater. (Redrawn from Figure 2 in Jackson et al. 2001, with permission from the Ecological Society of America)

Lakes and rivers hold 100,000 km³ of freshwater, less than 0.01% of all water on Earth. Accessible freshwater supplies sustain freshwater and terrestrial biodiversity, water for drinking, food production, and industrial production, as well as the many direct and indirect ecological goods and services that rivers, wetlands, and estuaries provide to people (see Chapter 1).

Freshwater availability varies dramatically worldwide in response to climatic constraints that determine the amount of precipitation, its seasonal distribution, and its form as rainwater, snow, or ice. The world's main climatic zones are grouped into five broad categories based on their average annual precipitation, average monthly precipitation, and average monthly temperature (Kottek et al. 2006). The most frequently used climate classification, known as the Köppen-Geiger climate scheme, includes the equatorial zone (A), the arid zone (B), the warm temperate zone (C), the snow zone (D), and the polar zone (E). A second letter in the classification considers precipitation (e.g., Df for snow and fully humid), and a third letter denotes the air temperature (e.g., Dfc for snow, fully humid, with cool summer). The two-letter scheme produces 14 climate types (Table 4), while combinations of the three letters produce 31 climate types.

Globally the dominant climate class by land area is arid B (30.2%), followed by snow D (24.6%), equatorial A (19.0%), temperate C (13.4%), and polar E (12.8%). The most common individual climate type by land area is BWh (14.2%)—hot, desert; followed by Aw (11.5%)—equatorial savannah (Peel et al. 2007). The distribution of climate types across the major landmasses varies significantly and sets the climatic context for the development of fluvial systems and freshwater ecosystems (Table 5). These global climatic patterns also support and constrain the accessibility of freshwater for human use. Two-thirds of all precipitation falls between 30°N and 30°S in latitude as a function of high solar radiation and evaporation rates, and runoff in tropical regions is also typically higher than elsewhere. Very low rainfall and high evaporation rates translate to very little runoff in desert areas except during erratic periods of high precipitation (Young and Kingsford 2006). Average runoff in Australia is only 4 cm per year, approximately eight times less than the figure for North America and far less than in tropical South America.

The Köppen-Geiger climate classification describes average weather conditions that determine annual, monthly, and daily precipitation and transpiration/evaporation rates, which in turn directly influence landscape hydrology and water yield. Regional climatic variation translates to a similar pattern of hydrologic variation that is then modulated by interactions with basin area, topography, geology, and geomorphology. Local variations in the interaction between average weather conditions and topographic features influence the volume and timing of runoff and river flows through such factors as cloud capture and orographic forcing, vegetation cover, soil infiltration properties, levels of groundwater storage, and the influence of snowmelt (Snelder and Biggs 2002; Poff, Bledsoe, et al. 2006; Sanborn and Bledsoe 2006). While there is generally broad concordance with climatic zone (e.g., arid-zone rivers are characteristically highly variable in their river flows as a function of highly variable regional and local precipitation patterns of arid

Temperature and precipitation conditions equal
the first two letters of the classification

Type	Description	Criteria
A	Equatorial climates	$Tmin \geq +18°C$
Af	Equatorial rainforest, fully humid	$Pmin \geq 60$ mm
Am	Equatorial monsoon	$Pann \geq 25 (100 - Pmin)$
As	Equatorial savannah with dry summer	$Pmin < 60$ mm in summer
Aw	Equatorial savannah with dry winter	$Pmin < 60$ mm in winter
B	Arid climates	$Pann < 10$ Pth
BS	Steppe climate	$Pann > 5$ Pth
BW	Desert climate	$Pann \leq 5$ Pth
C	Warm temperate climates	$-3°C < Tmin < +18°C$
Cs	Warm temperate climate with dry summer	$Psmin < Pwmin,$ $Pwmax > 3$ $Psmin,$ and $Psmin < 40$ mm
Cw	Warm temperate climate with dry winter	$Pwmin < Psmin$ and $Psmax > 10$ Pwmin
Cf	Warm temperate climate, fully humid	Neither Cs nor Cw
D	Snow climates	$Tmin \leq -3°C$
Ds	Snow climate with dry summer	$Psmin < Pwmin,$ $Pwmax > 3$ $Psmin,$ and $Psmin < 40$ mm
Dw	Snow climate with dry winter	$Pwmin < Psmin$ and $Psmax > 10$ Pwmin
Df	Snow climate, fully humid	Neither Ds nor Dw

(continued)

TABLE 4 *(continued)*

Type	Description	Criteria
E	Polar climates	Tmax < +10°C
ET	Tundra climate	0°C ≤ Tmax < +10°C
EF	Frost climate	Tmax < 0°C

SOURCES: Kottek et al. 2006. For world map of this Köppen–Geiger climate classification and underlying digital data, see Global Precipitation Climatology Centre (GPCC) at the German Weather Service (http://gpcc.dwd.de) and University of Veterinary Medicine, Vienna (http://koeppengeiger.vu-wien.ac.at)

NOTES: A dryness threshold Pth in mm is introduced for the arid climates (B), which depends on Tann, the absolute measure of the annual mean temperature in °C, and on the annual cycle of precipitation

Tann = Annual mean near-surface (2 m) temperature

Tmax = Monthly mean temperatures of warmest months

Tmin = Monthly mean temperatures of coldest months

Pann = Accumulated annual precipitation

Pmin = Precipitation of the driest month

Psmin, Psmax, Pwmin, Pwmax = Lowest and highest monthly precipitation values for summer and winter half years on the hemisphere considered

TABLE 5 *Continental distribution of climate types*
by % of land area

	Climate type				
Continent	A: Equatorial climates	B: Arid climates	C: Warm temperate climates	D: Snow climates	E: Polar climates
Africa	31.0	57.2	11.8		
Asia	16.3	23.9	12.3	43.8	3.8
North America	5.9	15.3	13.4	54.5	11.0
South America	60.1	15.0	24.1		
Europe		36.3	17.0	44.4	2.3
Australia	8.3	77.8	13.9		
Greenland and Antarctica					100

SOURCE: Peel et al. 2007

climatic zones), individual arid-zone rivers have their own characteristic hydrological "signatures" (Young and Kingsford 2006). Snowmelt, equatorial, and temperate rivers all express their individuality in accordance with climate, topography, and modulating factors. Large rivers may flow through several different climatic zones before reaching their terminus. For example, the Nile Basin is comprised of eight major sub-basins, each with different physical, climatic, and hydrological characteristics; however, the Ethiopian highlands (Blue Nile and Atbara) and Lake Victoria and the Equatorial Lakes (White Nile) form the two main climatic and hydrological regions. The White Nile maintains a relatively constant river flow over the year, because seasonal variations are moderated by steady flows from the central African lakes of Victoria and Albert and from the freshwater swamps of the Sudd. The Blue Nile–Atbara system reflects the wet summer–dry winter rainfall pattern of the Ethiopian highlands, where monsoonal floods dominate the seasonal discharge pattern that persists along the Nile below the Great Bend to Aswan.

The seasonality of river flows is an important attribute, however there are several other major characteristics that together define the natural flow regimes of flowing water systems, from the smallest headwater streams to the largest floodplain river systems.

DESCRIBING FLOW REGIMES
FACETS OF RIVER FLOW REGIMES

The hydrologic signatures of individual rivers can be described in many ways using a wide range of hydrologic statistics based on measured flow data. Many years of observation from a stream-flow gauge are generally needed to describe the characteristic pattern of a river's flow regime (long-term statistical pattern of flows) and other features. Ecologists recognize five ecologically relevant characteristics, or facets, of natural stream and river flow regimes: the magnitude, frequency, timing or predictability, duration, and rate of change of hydrological conditions (Richter et al. 1996; Poff et al. 1997). These facets can be used to characterize the entire range of flows and specific hydrologic events (such as floods or low flow) that are critical to the biota and ecological functioning of river ecosystems. Furthermore, by defining river

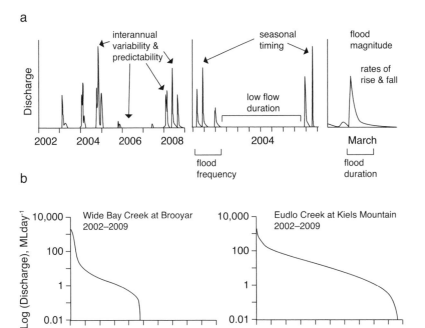

FIGURE 2. Hydrograph of the Mary River, southeast Queensland, Australia, illustrating the terms that describe facets of the flow regime (a) and showing flow duration curves (b) for sites on the Mary River. (Data provided by Department of Environment and Resource Management, Queensland, Australia)

flow regimes in terms of these ecologically relevant features, ecologists have an explicit means to quantify the hydrologic and associated ecological consequences of particular human activities that modify one or more facets of the flow regime. The five facets of river flow regimes are described here in brief, with simple examples to indicate their ecological relevance, and they are illustrated in Figures 2 and 3. More detailed treatment of the ecological roles of flow regime facets and differences is given in Chapter 4.

Flow *magnitude,* or "discharge" (volume of flow per unit of time), is the amount of water moving past a fixed location per unit of time (Fig. 2a). It can be expressed in various units (e.g., m³ per second, ML per day, GL per year, etc.) depending on conventions or purpose. Magnitude can refer to the absolute unit of discharge or the quantity of flow relative to some river property, such as the volume of water needed to provide an adequate water depth in a stream riffle important for fish passage, or to inundate an area of floodplain. Minimum, maximum, mean, and median flows vary according to the climate zone and precipitation processes and with the size of the catchment that delivers water.

The *frequency of occurrence* refers to how often a flow of a given discharge occurs over some nominated time period (Fig. 2b). The frequency of any particular flow magnitude is revealed by a flow duration curve, which shows that low flows (small discharge volumes) occur far more often than large flows and events that cause flooding (Fig. 2b). A 100-year flood event is defined as the size of flood that is equaled or exceeded once in 100 years, or has a 0.01 (1%) chance of occurring in any given year. Floods of this size may occur quite close together in time, depending on local and regional climate and rainfall, but the likelihood is that, over the long term, such a large flood will not occur more than once every 100 years. The median discharge has a 0.5 (50%) probability of occurrence. Flood frequency determines floodplain inundation regimes, how often obligate flood spawning fish can reproduce, and how often riparian trees flower and set seed.

Duration is the length (period) of time associated with a particular discharge event, such as a flood that inundates a floodplain for weeks to months, or a very low-flow period that lasts for days to several months (Fig. 2a). Ecologists need to know the number of days or months in sequence (i.e., without any breaks) that a particular flow condition, such as a period of absolutely no stream flow, persists; such a period would be called a "dry spell" of X days or months or years duration. Another useful statistic is the total number of days, spread across a year, with no surface flow or with modest flows. These figures can be read from a flow duration curve (Fig. 2b). Ironically, the term "duration" in this sense does not mean the same as "dry spell duration," because the number of days of any flow magnitude that are summed in a flow duration curve are not necessarily sequential—the plot simply presents the total number of days when each flow magnitude is equaled or exceeded, regardless of when they occurred. Flow duration curves can be used to compare different types of flow regime and to quantify changes brought about by land use, water extraction, dams, and weirs. They are also used to support environmental flow assessments.

The *timing* or *predictability* of discharge can refer to two different flow characteristics. Timing alone can mean the month or season in a year when a particular event is likely to occur, such as fish migration or spawning. Predictability means the degree to which flood or drought events are autocorrelated temporally, typically on an annual cycle. Predictable events might also be correlated with other environmental signals (e.g., seasonal thermal extremes). Floods in many tropical rivers (e.g., the Mekong River) have a predictable annual flood pulse to which many fish synchronize migration and/or spawning activities (Welcomme et al. 2006). The occurrence of flooding is typically far less predictable in arid-zone regions, where flood frequencies and timing are dependent on regional climatic factors and erratic local rainfall/runoff events (Puckridge et al. 1998).

The *rate of change,* or "flashiness," refers to the rate at which stream discharge changes from one magnitude to another (Figs. 2 and 3). *Flashy* streams have very rapid rates of rise (and often fall) in discharge; whereas *stable* streams have a very steady pattern of flows, and if flow does vary the changes take place relatively slowly. In most catchments, some precipitation percolates into the ground and reaches streams slowly over long periods, often sustaining low-level stream flows (baseflows) during periods without any rain. Depending on precipitation phenomena, such as sudden rainstorms or snowmelt, and catchment characteristics, precipitation may take a faster route to the stream channel, and this is often called quickflow or stormflow (Burt 1996). Precipitation usually contributes to high stream flows. As a result of these two sets of processes, a stream hydrograph typically presents periods of high flow separated by longer periods of low, gradually declining flow (Figs. 2a and 3). Differences in the rates and dimensions of these processes distinguish flashy hydrographs and streams from those with more stable flows.

Taken together, the five facets of a river's flow regime (magnitude, frequency, timing or predictability, duration, and rate of change) give ecologists an essential summary of the hydrological character of that system. Important features from an ecological perspective are the volumes and seasonal patterns of discharge (e.g., summer or winter floods, timing of dry spells); whether the flow is ephemeral (flowing briefly only after storm events), intermittent (flowing after storm events and

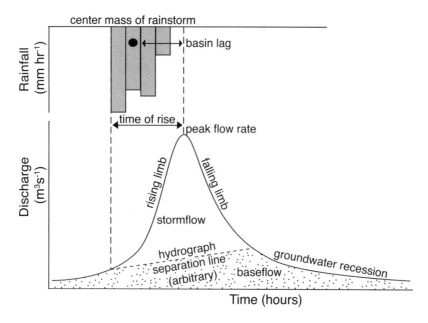

FIGURE 3. Stream hydrograph showing baseflow (groundwater), stormflow (quickflow), and the rising and falling limbs of a flow pulse generated by a rainstorm. (Adapted from Figure 2.2 in Burt 1996)

during wet seasons when fed by groundwater), or perennial (with year-round flows); and the overall variability and predictability of flows over days, months, and years.

Combinations of these flow facets determine many of the physical and biogeochemical processes of aquatic ecosystems to such an extent that flow has been called the "master variable" (Power et al. 1995), or the "maestro . . . that orchestrates pattern and process in rivers" (Walker et al. 1995). The naturally dynamic flow regime plays a critical role in sustaining native biodiversity and ecosystem integrity in streams and rivers, and this Natural Flow Regime Paradigm underpins universal principles of river conservation, restoration, and environmental flow management (Poff et al. 1997; Bunn and Arthington 2002; Naiman et al. 2008). How river biota respond to the five facets of the flow regime and what changes occur when flow regimes are altered by dams and other human interventions are discussed in Chapters 4–8.

The world's streams and rivers vary widely in flow magnitude and temporal patterns, with differences reflecting climatic settings and a host of modulating factors. Interest in the geographic diversity of river flow patterns has a long history, evidenced by many attempts to classify river flow regimes at global, continental, and regional scales (reviewed in Pusey et al. 2009; Olden et al. 2011). Hydrologic classification is the process of systematically arranging streams and rivers into groups that are most similar with respect to the characteristics of their flow regimes. Many different flow metrics (including statistical measures of the five flow facets) have been used in numerous classifications, the selection of metrics depending on the objectives of the analysis (Olden and Poff 2003). The flow metrics selected, the geographic distribution of the gauging-station datasets (within and between basins), the length of record, and the temporal overlap of compared records can all influence the outcomes of a flow classification (Kennard et al. 2010a, 2010b). In the discussion below, selected examples outline some of the dominant patterns, similarities, and differences among rivers at global, continental, and regional scales. This treatment sets the scene for discussion of the ecological roles of flow facets and the impacts of flow regime changes brought about by land-use patterns, dams, weirs, and water transfers between basins (see Chapters 4–8).

One of the earliest global classifications produced 13 seasonally distinctive flow regime types based on 969 stream gauging stations and 32,000 station years of data from 66 countries (Haines et al. 1988). An average flow regime was determined for each station by averaging flow in each month over all years of record, thus effectively ignoring year-to-year variations in flow patterns. Nevertheless, this classification identified important seasonal differences among flow regime types as well as the main climatic influences and the geographic affiliations of each category (Table 6, Fig. 4). It has informed a wide range of studies, including environmental flow assessments (e.g., the Benchmarking Methodology, see Chapter 11).

In a global river flow classification focused on flow variability, Puckridge et al. (1998) used 23 hydrological measures covering the 5 flow regime facets (and likely to be biologically significant) to distinguish

Flow regime types	Characteristics	Examples
Group 1: Uniform	Even flow regime, all months in the range 5–12% of annual flow; no seasonal flow peaks	Central Europe and a belt from southern Finland across to north of the Caspian Sea
Group 2: Mid–late spring	Pronounced flow peak in last two spring months accounting for over 40% of total annual flow	Distinctive snowmelt pattern, e.g., northwestern United States and Canada
Group 3: Late spring–early summer	Longer cold season of 5–6 months, major peak in last spring month and first summer month	Belt extending from Scandinavia across Russia to the Kamchatka Peninsula
Group 4: Extreme early summer	Delayed spring thaw produces massive flow > 60% of annual flow	Regions with 6 subzero-degree months to north of Group 3 in Europe and Asia
Group 5: Moderate early summer	Broad flow peak in early summer months declines rapidly to low flows in late autumn, winter, and early spring	Tropical to subarctic areas; may be combined with winter drought in southern Africa, South America, and East Asia
Group 6: Midsummer	Strong late summer or early autumn peak combined with winter low flow; heavy summer rains moderate and extend the summer flow peak	Tropical or subtropical areas of southern Africa, South America, and Asia; isolated examples also found at higher latitudes (e.g., Norway)
Group 7: Extreme late summer	Typical "monsoonal" flow regime derived from intense late summer rainfall; >50% of flow occurs in the peak three-month period, with prolonged low flow through winter and spring	Exclusively tropical; snowmelt may influence flow regimes in Nepal and Argentina
Group 8: Moderate late summer	Pronounced late summer peak, increasing influence of winter rainfall forming higher low-season flows, commonly a minor peak in winter	Exclusively subtropical, concentrated in southern Queensland and northern New South Wales, Australia

(continued)

TABLE 6 *(continued)*

Flow regime types	Characteristics	Examples
Group 9: Early autumn	Similar to Group 7 but with strong peak flow centered in early autumn rather than late summer	Almost exclusively tropical and subtropical, occurs widely in tropical Africa and Asia with Group 10 rivers
Group 10: Midautumn	Moderate peak flow midautumn following average flow in summer, with low flows in late winter and spring	Mainly tropical and subtropical, also found in Central America and on the southern tip of South America
Group 11: Moderate autumn	Broad autumn peak flow, often with minor peak in late spring associated with passage of the intertropical convergence zone	Tropical areas on islands and peninsulas (e.g., Panama and Malay), also eastern Australia and European Atlantic seaboard
Group 12: Moderate winter	Very broad winter and early spring peak, and distinct low summer flow	Moist temperate areas with fairly even rainfall all year
Group 13: Extreme winter	Very strong winter and early spring flow, declining to very low level over summer	Clear relation to Köppen Csa and Csb climates, also found in eastern United States
Group 14: Early spring	Related to Group 12 but less winter flow, building to a peak in early and midspring. Snowmelt forms spring thaw peak, then declines through summer	Largest regime group found in temperate regions
Group 15: Moderate spring	Closely related to Group 11, also has no distinct low-flow periods; relative importance of spring and autumn flow reversed, snowmelt forms spring peak	Mainly in temperate areas of North America, South America, and southern Africa

SOURCE: Haines et al. 1988

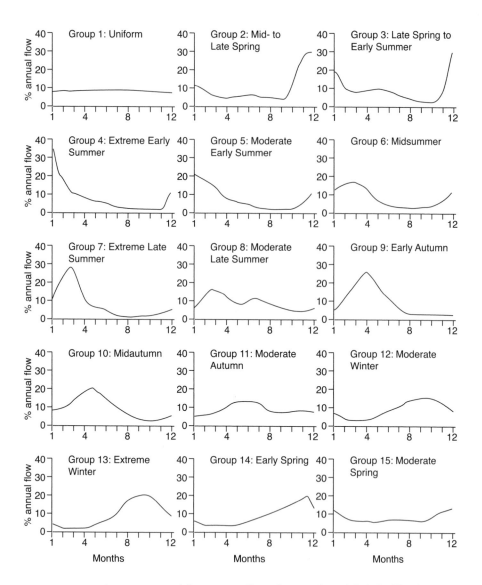

FIGURE 4. Average seasonal flow pattern for each group in a global classification of the rivers from 66 countries. (Redrawn from Figure 3 in Haines et al. 1988, with permission from Elsevier)

distinctive temporal patterns in 52 large rivers; catchments of 100,000–500,000 km² were selected to reduce the effects of catchment size on flow variability, and the earliest available 20 years of continuous records were used to minimize effects of dams and flow regulation. Hydrological measures of variability were calculated from raw monthly and annual data and expressed as range-standardized range/median. Expressed in this fashion, flow variability signatures were often correlated with global climatic zones. Arid-zone (dryland) rivers of high overall flow variability and a "tropical rainy climates" group of low overall flow variability marked the extremes of a spectrum of global river flow variability (Figs. 5 and 6). Large Australian dryland rivers (e.g., the Cooper and Diamantina in the Lake Eyre basin) were considered the most variable in this global dataset, whereas the Niger, Mekong, Ogooue, Indigirka, and Red (at Alexandria) Rivers were identified as having the least variable (most predictable) flow regimes among rivers of comparable discharge.

An intercontinental comparison of hydrologic regimes based on daily flow data for 463 stream-flow gauges has revealed further similarities and differences in rivers of Australia, New Zealand, South Africa, Europe, and the United States (Poff, Bledsoe, et al. 2006). Australian streams were characterized by large magnitudes and variation in maximum flows and rise rates, indicating relatively flashy flows both intra- and interannually. In contrast, New Zealand and European streams had high minimum flows, a high baseflow index, a high coefficient of variation (CV) in fall rate, and relatively high spring flows. South African streams were distinguished by high autumn flows and a large CV of maximum flow and rise rate. The most extreme flow regimes in this dataset, with the greatest intra- and interannual variation, were located in Australia and South Africa, with some US streams in arid landscapes also showing high variability.

US streams showed the broadest variation in flow regimes, including examples of the hydrological characteristics of the other four continents. Poff (1996) distinguished 10 distinctive flow regime types—seven permanent and three intermittent—based on 11 ecologically relevant hydrological metrics describing flow variability, predictability, and low- and high-flow extremes. Five prominent examples from this classification highlight differences between snowmelt, snow and rain, intermit-

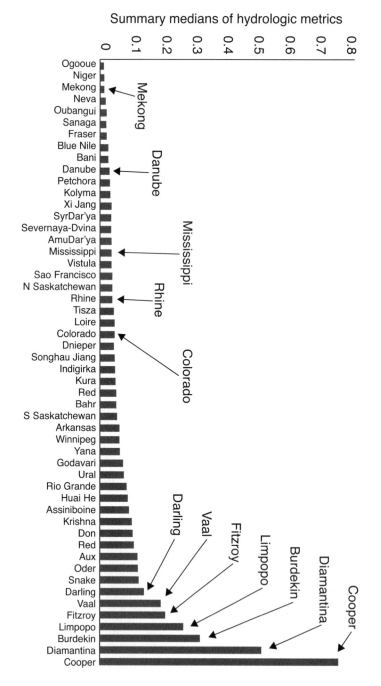

FIGURE 5. Summary medians of 23 measures of hydrologic variability for 52 gauging stations labeled by river. (Redrawn from Figure 4a in Puckridge et al. 1998, with permission from CSIRO Publishing, copyright CSIRO 1998, www.publish.csiro.au/nid/126/paper/MF94161.htm)

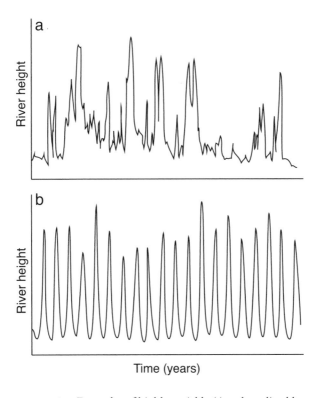

FIGURE 6. Examples of highly variable (a) and predictable (b) annual flow regimes.

tent, perennial flashy/runoff, and stable groundwater-flow regime types (Fig. 7). Ellipses reflect the natural range of variability of two of the classification flow metrics (flood predictability and baseflow index—the ratio of baseflow to total flow). Snowmelt streams were mostly restricted to the Rocky Mountains region, snow and rain streams to the Pacific Northwest and other northern states; while perennial flashy streams were mostly clustered in the Midwest along the forest-prairie transition zone. The harsh intermittent stream type was found in the northern and southern prairie zones and the far Southwest.

Classification of unregulated streams and rivers (830 stream-gauge datasets) throughout Australia using Bayesian mixture modeling produced the country's first continental scale analysis of flow regimes based on 120 ecologically relevant flow variables (Kennard et al. 2010a, 2010b).

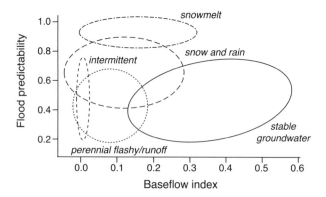

FIGURE 7. Five major river flow regime types in the United States plotted in two-dimensional space defined by flood predictability and baseflow index. Ellipses (90% confidence intervals) show natural range of variability for the two flow metrics for each of five river types. (Adapted from Figure 4 in Poff et al. 2010, with permission from John Wiley and Sons)

This study identified twelve distinctive flow regime classes differing in flow predictability and variability, seasonal discharge pattern, flow permanence (perennial versus intermittent discharge), and the magnitude and frequency of extreme flow events (floods and low-flow spells). The geographic distributions of flow regime classes varied greatly, as did differences in key hydrologic metrics (Table 7, Fig. 8). Climatic, geologic, and catchment topographic factors successfully differentiated between most of these flow regime types, providing a basis for the prediction of flow regime types and flow class membership of stream sites in ungauged catchments.

Continental flow classifications (in some cases several) are available for the United Kingdom, Europe, France, Sweden, Scandinavia, Austria, western Europe, Turkey, Russia, South Africa, Lesotho, Swaziland, Tanzania, Nepal, New Zealand, Australia, and the United States (Pusey et al. 2009). The flow classifications vary according to the types of flow data used (daily, monthly, annual), the flow facets explored (magnitude, frequency, timing, duration, rate of change), and the statistical approach employed. Explicit advice on scientifically defensible processes for river flow classification can be found in Olden et al. (2011).

TABLE 7 *Australian flow regime classes and geographic distributions*

Flow regime class	Class description	Distribution
1	Stable baseflow	Widespread, most often in Southeast Coast, Tasmanian, and Southwest Coast drainage divisions
2	Stable winter baseflow	Restricted to southern temperate half of the continent
3	Stable summer baseflow	Primarily in northern Australia, Wet Tropics region, Gulf of Carpentaria, and Timor Sea drainage divisions
4	Unpredictable baseflow	Widely distributed across southern and eastern Australia
5	Unpredictable winter rarely intermittent	Mostly in southeastern coastal streams and the headwaters of Murray-Darling drainage division
6	Predictable winter intermittent	Classic Mediterranean flow regime, primarily southwestern Australia and western portion of southeastern Australia
7	Unpredictable intermittent	Eastern coastal fringe, especially at temperate and subtropical climatic transition zone
8	Unpredictable winter intermittent	Eastern headwaters of the Murray-Darling drainage division and southeast Tasmania
9	Predictable winter highly intermittent	Inland areas in the Southwest Coast and Murray-Darling
10	Predictable summer highly intermittent	Exclusively in the Timor Sea and Gulf of Carpentaria drainages
11	Unpredictable summer highly intermittent	Northeast drainage division, large rivers discharging east to Coral Sea
12	Variable summer extremely intermittent	Arid and semiarid regions in the Indian Ocean, Lake Eyre, Murray-Darling, and southern Gulf of Carpentaria drainage divisions

SOURCE: Kennard et al. 2010b

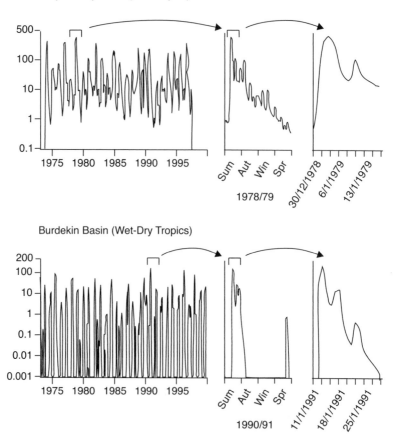

FIGURE 8. Hydrographs of daily runoff (ML per day per km²) for Australian Wet and Wet-Dry Tropics rivers at three scales of temporal resolution: the long-term record, the year record, and the three-week period encompassing the flow event with the highest peak magnitude. (Adapted from Pusey et al. 2009)

HYDROLOGICAL CLASSIFICATION AND
ENVIRONMENTAL FLOWS

Hydrological classification plays an important role in the progression toward scientifically informed water management to protect river ecosystems and sustain livelihoods in two major contexts. First, management decisions are often urgently needed for individual rivers or specific locations where there is insufficient ecological knowledge to support more advanced environmental flow assessments. In these circumstances, techniques that develop environmental flow prescriptions based on natural patterns of flow variability can be applied (e.g., Stanford et al. 1996; Richter et al. 1997). Methods of this type can be combined with a monitoring program to identify actual ecological responses to any recommended flow regime and thereby can improve understanding of the hydroecological system being managed (e.g., Bunn and Arthington 2002; Poff et al. 2003).

Second, environmental flow assessments and water management strategies are often required at broad regional or even national scales, which naturally embrace substantial spatial variation in climatic, physiographic, and ecological conditions (Arthington et al. 2006; Poff, Bledsoe, et al. 2006). Identifying hydrologically similar regions on a continental or regional scale can facilitate the development of hydroecological principles and relationships common to rivers of the same hydrological type. These relationships may then be extrapolated to other rivers of the same hydrological type that may be less well studied. Such an approach can be extended to any number of distinctive flow regime types within a user-defined geographic region to support environmental flow assessments, as well as to predict ecological responses to future flow regime alterations and possibly also as strategies for adapting to climate change (Arthington et al. 2006; Kennard et al. 2010b).

Hydrological classification forms the foundation of a new framework designed to help define sustainable levels of water usage and flow regulation for many rivers of a user-defined geographic region. Known as ELOHA (Ecological Limits of Hydrologic Alteration), this framework builds on early environmental flow methods and available ecological data to develop models of ecological response to natural flow variability and flow regime change within distinctive flow regime types, which are expected to be similar ecologically and arguably form "practical management units" (Arthington et al. 2006; Poff et al. 2010; see Chapter 13).

Although flow is widely regarded as a "master variable," many other environmental factors modulate the way that a flow regime translates into predictable habitat types and patches, and how aquatic biota respond to habitat at various spatial and temporal scales in the stream network (Bunn and Arthington 2002; Kennard et al. 2007; Stewart-

Koster et al. 2007). Geomorphic differentiation and channel network structure, substrate types, water quality, and riparian character can all influence the development of typical habitat types throughout a river basin. Understanding and subclassification of geomorphic variability within any particular flow regime type provides a means to translate reach-scale spatial patterns and disturbance regimes generated by river flows into the various habitat conditions actually experienced by aquatic biota (Poff et al. 2006a). How flow interacts with the geomorphic features and other characteristics of rivers, and the ecological implications of such interactions, is the focus of Chapter 3.

Global patterns of climatic variation provide a broad context for discussion of geographic variation in river flow regimes and their classification. However, global climates are changing and these changes will inevitably bring about changes in river flow and thermal regimes, thus shifting the baseline for environmental flow assessments and many aspects of water and environmental management. The phenomena associated with climate change and their implications for freshwater ecosystems and environmental flow management are discussed in Chapter 22.

3

CATCHMENTS, DRAINAGE NETWORKS, AND RESOURCE REGIMES

CATCHMENTS AND DRAINAGE NETWORKS

Rivers and other freshwater systems receive their water from rain, hail, sleet, and snow in the endless flow of evaporation, transpiration, precipitation, infiltration, and runoff processes of the hydrologic cycle. Water is delivered to each freshwater system from its catchment or drainage basin (watershed)—an area of land that collects precipitation and drains that water to a common point in the landscape or into another freshwater body. Larger catchments are made up of smaller subcatchments, and the familiar treelike branches of streams join to form larger tributaries and then major river channels, all of which form the drainage network of the catchment. These networks, and their associated freshwater habitats, can take very different forms as flowing water carves out a series of channels on its way downhill.

Some rivers take a relatively direct route while others develop meanders—broad looping bends shaped by the natural scouring and deposition processes of flowing water. Often when a river develops a highly sinuous form, the narrow neck of land between two meanders is breached, cutting off the meander and turning it into an isolated oxbow lake. Isolated lakes formed in this way are very common along the Rio Grande and the Missouri and Mississippi Rivers in the United States (Cech 2010) and along the Murray and other floodplain rivers in Australia, where such lakes are known as billabongs ("billy-bong" is the Australian Aboriginal name for a small creek or backwater).

Another type, the braided river, forms in coarse geologic formations such as gravels, where the power of flowing water is insufficient to move the substrates, and so the flowing water takes another, less resistant course, leaving a multitude of small islands separated by complex channels that look from a distance like plaited ropes. Rivers of this type are common on the South Island of New Zealand and in parts of the United States.

Drainage networks can be described as dendritic (branching), trellis (developed in terrain with alternating hard and soft substrates), rectangular (formed in terrain with right-angle faults or joints, often found in granitic rocks), radial (formed where streams flow outward from a dune or volcanic cone), centripetal (formed where streams converge toward the center of their basin), annular (developed around a dome or basin where concentric bands of hard and soft substrates have been exposed), parallel (formed in areas of pronounced localized slope), and distributary (diversion channels formed in deltas or alluvial river fans). Further details of drainage networks can be found in Gordon et al. (1992).

Flowing surface waters, from the smallest headwater springs and streams to the largest floodplain rivers, are prominent features of most landscapes, even deserts, and exert a significant influence on landscape form and function. Rivers are the major agents of erosion, transport, and deposition of materials from the mountains to valleys and the oceans or inland to closed wetlands and lakes. They transport sediments, chemicals, nutrients, and organic matter ranging from small particles of plant material to whole trees, logs, and organisms in various life-history stages (Nilsson and Svedmark 2002). These inorganic and organic transport functions of rivers play significant ecological roles, which are discussed in Chapters 4, 7, and 8.

GEOMORPHIC GRADIENTS

Geomorphologically, streams and rivers can be divided into three intergrading longitudinal zones (Fig. 9). Typically, the headwater areas of upland channels have coarse substrates, such as cobbles and boulders,

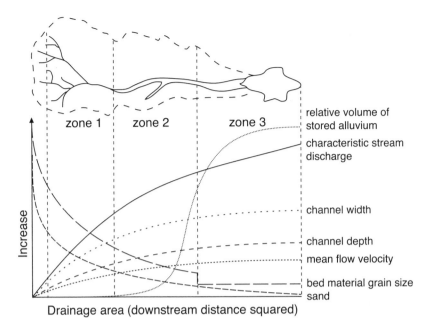

FIGURE 9. Characteristic longitudinal variations in river flow, velocity, substrate characteristics, channel width and depth, and the volume of material stored in alluvial deposits along a large river. Vertical dotted lines demark longitudinal zones 1, 2, and 3 described in the chapter. (Adapted from Figure 9.3 in Church 1996)

that the force of water cannot move very far (Church 1996). These upland areas form the erosional zone (zone 1). With increasing distance downstream, river flows increase in volume and erosive power and carve out wider, deeper, and more complex channel forms through processes of sediment erosion and deposition; this middle zone is termed the "transport" or "transfer" zone (zone 2). The downstream, low-gradient reaches of large rivers (zone 3) are comprised of finer substrates, usually sand and silt (Church 1996). These finer substrates form the depositional zone. In the flatter valleys of large rivers, processes of channel, bank, and floodplain water storage, and interactions between the river and its groundwater zones, become more important (Gustard 1996; Boulton and Hancock 2006), although groundwater may interact with surface water at intervals along the length of river corridors (see Chapter 15).

In the erosional zone the water is generally clear, well oxygenated, and turbulent, while habitats take the form of riffles (sections of relatively shallow, rapid, and turbulent flow over coarse substrates), pools (sections of relatively deep, slow flow, often with eddies), and various combinations of waterfalls, cascades, rapids, chutes, runs or glides and debris dams (Downes et al. 2002). In the transport or transfer zone, the riffle–pool sequence is maintained over larger lengths of river, and the channel may develop lateral and midchannel bars, or become braided, or develop a more complex array of physical habitats associated with large logjams, tree roots, and bank structures. In the depositional or storage zone, the river is larger, deep, and usually turbid with a distinct floodplain, and often there are pronounced meanders as the river cuts a path across fine sediments through processes of erosion and deposition. Habitat structure in this depositional zone may take the form of deep pools, shallower connecting reaches, bars, backwaters, and floodplain wetlands, with further physical diversity contributed by large logjams and persistent snags (woody debris). Longitudinal variability in physical habitat structure and the diversity of habitat types play an important part in maintaining both biodiversity and normal river ecosystem function (see Chapter 4).

The longitudinal profile of a river describes changes in bed elevation over distance, generally developing a characteristic concave shape, with the slope decreasing from the upper erosional zone, through the transport zone, to the lower depositional zone. This concave shape is associated with increasing discharge and decreasing sediment particle size downstream. However, rivers differ in longitudinal profile according to precipitation volume and source, topography, bedrock features, and changes in bed materials; and rivers may form knickpoints where the geology changes (e.g., at waterfalls) or at tributary junctions where another source of water enters the channel. Knickpoints and tributary junctions influence the hydrogeomorphic characteristics of stream segments, the physical habitat template, and the distribution patterns of riverine biota (see Chapter 4).

As water flows along the bed profile and through the three main geomorphological zones, the shape of the stream hydrograph alters. A stream with a steeper longitudinal profile will respond rapidly to precipitation events in its catchment and produce higher peak discharges

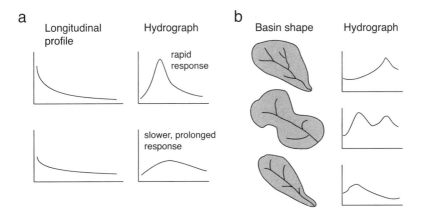

FIGURE 10.   Effects of longitudinal profile (a) and basin shape (b) on hydrograph shape. (Redrawn from Figure 4.16 in Gordon et al. 1992, with permission from John Wiley and Sons)

than one with a shallower profile (Fig. 10a). Shorter, wider stream basins will produce a faster rise and fall in stream flow than longer, narrower basins due to the shorter travel time of water down the catchment (Fig. 10b) (Gordon et al. 1992). Travel times of water down a long catchment, combined with nonsynchronous tributary inflows and downstream channel and floodplain storage capacities, collectively act to dampen flow peaks and attenuate them (Poff et al. 1997). These processes produce characteristic longitudinal variations in river flow, velocity, substrate characteristics, channel width and depth, and the volume of material stored in alluvial deposits (see Fig. 9).

Vegetation cover and land-use patterns also influence stream hydrograph shape, since vegetation affects infiltration rates. Grasslands tend to show an earlier, more rapid hydrograph than wooded catchments, and runoff rates tend to increase after wildfires until the vegetation growth becomes reestablished (Gordon et al. 1992). Complex storm patterns over a river basin—and spatial variations in catchment characteristics and drainage density (total stream length as a proportion of catchment area), as well as in drainage network structure—may lead to multipeaked hydrographs that introduce diversity into the nature of the flow regime and its influence on habitat structure and ecological properties, from stream headwaters to river mouth.

HYDROLOGICAL VARIABILITY ALONG RIVERS

Many rivers flow through different climatic, geologic, topographic, and biological zones as they increase in basin area. These differences, and the associated longitudinal gradients described above, impart spatial variability to river flow regimes within individual basins. Such variability may result in very different hydrologic signatures and associated ecological potential throughout a single river basin. Characterizing this within-basin variability is typically difficult, because many rivers have highly modified "natural" flow regimes (e.g., due to dams or land-use changes) and because smaller streams are generally sparsely gauged.

Poff et al. (2006a) addressed these issues for a sample of US river basins with a range of climatic and runoff conditions and for which historical (pre-dam) flow data were readily available. Within each of five basins, the researchers analyzed daily stream-flow records from five gauging stations representing the available sizes and associated characteristics of gauged sub-basins. The chosen river basins ranged in climatic variation from very wet (Willamette Basin) to intermediate runoff (White and Potomac Basins) to arid (Colorado and Canadian Basins). Analysis of daily stream-flow data in terms of ecologically relevant flow statistics encompassing the five flow regime facets (see Chapter 2) revealed inconsistent patterns in flow regime variation with an increase in sub-basin size (Fig. 11).

In three rivers (Willamette, Potomac, and Colorado), the five sampled sub-basins were relatively similar in flow regime, whereas others (Canadian, White) showed marked differences in flow signature along their lengths. Homogeneity of hydroclimatic settings explained the downstream similarity of flow regimes in the Willamette Basin in the US Pacific Northwest; streams of this region are generally "rain-on-snow" or "winter rain" types (see Poff 1996) characterized by a wet regional climate (see Fig. 7, Chapter 2). In the Colorado Basin, all five stream gauges along the river showed similar hydrological signatures dominated by a strong snowmelt signal derived from the river's headwater streams, even though the Colorado's main channel flows through the very arid lowlands of the American Southwest (Poff et al. 2006a). The Canadian River also flows from snowy mountain headwaters onto an arid plain, but along the way it passes through a gradient of decreas-

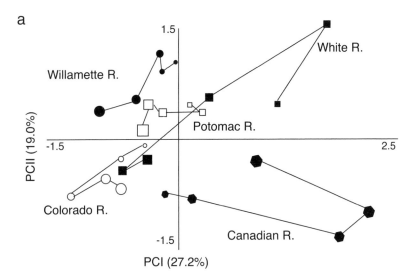

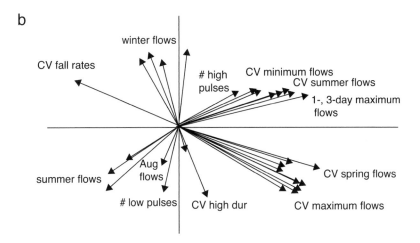

FIGURE 11. Multivariate relationship among 25 US gauges (grouped by river basin) in two-dimensional ordination space (a) and the relative loadings of flow variables that best explain site separation (b). Longitudinal position within each basin (i.e., gauge basin area) is represented by symbol size. (Redrawn from Figure 4 in Poff et al. 2006a, with permission from John Wiley and Sons)

ing and then increasing mean annual precipitation with high interannual variability; this precipitation gradient is reflected in the large differences in flow regime characteristics along the length of the Canadian River (Fig. 11).

Several important points arise from this case study and similar analyses of flow regime variability along rivers of other continents (e.g., Snelder and Biggs 2002; Pusey et al. 2009). First, the spatial extent to which the hydrologic characteristics for an individual stream gauge can be extended upstream or downstream may be highly variable, depending on variation in climate, geology, and vegetation cover among sub-basins; and furthermore, the spatial extent for valid extrapolation of flow records is usually unknown. Second, the representation of a river's hydrological character from a few available stream gauges may not capture spatial flow regime differences of ecological significance. Third, these issues have management implications when the environmental flow regimes of streams and rivers are founded largely on measured hydrologic signatures or on extrapolations of flow regime types from a few stream gauges. Pusey et al. (2009) remarked that the placement of gauges across the landscape is not random; stream gauge locations primarily address the needs of hydrographers and hydrologists rather than ecologists interested in defining hydrological and ecological variation. Olden et al. (2011) noted that all hydrological classifications are vulnerable to the limitations of gauge distribution and density, such that large regions lacking an adequate gauging network may present as having relatively few distinctive hydrological types, whereas in fact much more hydrological variability may be present within and among sub-basins. One solution to this problem is to install more stream gauges at points relevant to ecological analysis in poorly gauged catchments. Another is to develop hydrologic simulation models of rainfall-runoff and other watershed processes and to use these models to generate flow time series from which ecologically relevant hydrologic metrics can be extracted (e.g., Wagener et al. 2004; Kennen et al. 2008; Pusey et al. 2009).

HYDROGEOMORPHIC GRADIENTS OR PATCHES?

The general observation that physical features of streams and rivers change gradually from headwaters to river mouth (as depicted in Fig. 9) led to the characterization of rivers as intergrading linear networks with a continuous gradient of flow, physical conditions, and "consistent patterns of loading, transport, utilization and storage of organic matter along the length of a river" (Vannote et al. 1980). This model—known as the River Continuum Concept (RCC)—also proposed that biological populations (especially invertebrates with various feeding behaviors) responded predictably to the continuum of physical habitats and, in particular, to the major sources of energy (carbon) along the length of rivers. Ecological details of the RCC are discussed in Chapter 4, while here the intent is to discuss an alternative perspective on hydrogeomorphic variability in river basins: the proposition that rivers take the form of discontinuous patches rather than physical continua.

Building on principles from fluvial geomorphology, Thorp et al. (2006, 2008) proposed the Riverine Ecosystem Synthesis (RES) as "a conceptual marriage of eco-geomorphology (ecological aspects of fluvial geomorphology) with a terrestrial landscape model describing hierarchical patch dynamics." The RES builds from the geomorphological concepts of Montgomery (1999), who concluded that a predictable physical continuum perspective (like that inherent in the RCC) is valid only for a limited range of streams in fairly constant geomorphologic and climatic settings. Montgomery proposed the Process Domains Concept, based on the importance of local geomorphic conditions and landscape disturbances that collectively produce a mosaic of predictable areas where disturbance influences geomorphic processes and governs physical habitat type, structure, and dynamics. Poole (2002) further proposed that rivers are composed of patchy discontinua where biotic communities respond to local features of the fluvial landscape. The hierarchical framework for stream habitat classification (Frissell et al. 1986) and concepts of hierarchical patch dynamics (Wu and Loucks 1995) have also contributed to the RES.

The RES views any river system as a downstream array of large hydrogeomorphic patches (e.g., constricted, braided, and floodplain channel areas) formed by the interaction of climate, catchment geomorphology and topography, soils, rainfall–runoff characteristics, and vegetation (Fig. 12). The flow regime and physical habitat characterizing each type of hydrogeomorphic patch together provide the template for shaping each patch's biotic communities and delimiting ecosystem processes (e.g., organic matter dynamics, nutrient spiraling, system metabolism, productivity). Hydrogeomorphic patches in the riverine landscape may be present on land or in water; in the channel, slack-water areas, or floodplains; in pelagic, benthic, or hyporheic (ground-water) zones; and in estuarine deltas. At local spatial scales, patches may be formed by autotrophic (plant related) and heterotrophic (animal related) biotic processes operating within hydrogeomorphic habitat patches (Thorp et al. 2008).

The RES presents 17 tenets (propositions or hypotheses), collectively predicting how patterns of individual species distributions, community regulation, ecosystem processes, and floodplain interactions can be expected to vary over spatiotemporal scales in relation to the functional process zones formed by hydrogeomorphic differences throughout the river network (Thorp et al. 2008). Many of these tenets are relevant to the study of hydroecological relationships, environmental flow assessments, and water/catchment management more broadly.

Where there is significant geomorphological variation within individual hydrological types or classes within a river basin (or across the rivers of a region), Poff et al. (2010) propose that a geomorphic sub-classification may be necessary to adequately represent how the flow regime is translated into the hydraulic habitats available to, and experienced by, riverine biota within a given physical setting; for example, "whether a given level of flow will create a bed-moving disturbance or an overbank flow is determined by local characteristics such as channel geometry, floodplain height, and streambed composition." The same level of flow in one geomorphic setting may not translate into an important habitat condition or ecological event or process, whereas in a second setting it may (Poff et al. 2006a). Therefore, differentiating rivers on the basis of physical characteristics—such as constrained versus alluvial channels, or sand-bedded versus cobble-bedded reaches—is necessary for the development of hydroecological relationships to support environmental flow assessments and river restoration (Poole 2002; Snelder and Biggs 2002; Jacobson and Galat 2006). In essence, this physical differentiation along the longitudinal and lateral axes of rivers is what the RES is proposing, and taking account of such variability is important when estimating the flow requirements of aquatic biota and in planning river restoration.

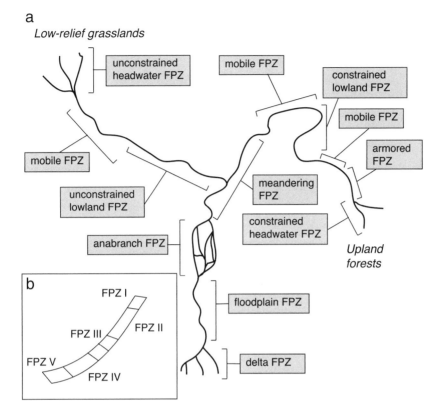

FIGURE 12. The Riverine Ecosystem Synthesis (RES). Schematic view of a complex river catchment showing various ecological functional process zones (FPZs) extending from headwaters to river delta (a). FPZs are formed by large hydrogeomorphic patches (b). (Redrawn from Figure 1 in Thorpe et al. 2006, with permission from John Wiley and Sons)

CATCHMENT RESOURCE REGIMES

All aquatic ecosystems are deeply influenced by the characteristics of the catchment (basin or watershed) in which they are situated and from which they receive their water. "In every respect, the valley rules the stream" (Hynes 1975). As water flows downhill on its way to the sea, it erodes and transports sediments and dissolved chemicals, nutrients, and particulate materials, which may pass through or accumulate in the freshwater systems through which water flows. Major cations of biological importance are sodium, potassium, calcium, and magnesium, while important anions include chloride, sulfate, and bicarbonate. Minor or trace elements present in minute quantities also perform important metabolic functions: silica is essential for the formation and growth of diatom shells (thecae), while iron, zinc, copper, molybdenum, and manganese influence plant growth and other biological processes. The major plant nutrients, nitrogen and phosphorus, are delivered from upland areas as dissolved forms in surface and subsurface flow or are associated with soil and sediment particles originating from eroded rocks. Catchment vegetation and the riparian zone, with its various vegetation formations and processes, may exert a strong influence on inputs of dissolved and particulate materials from the catchment into streams, rivers, and wetlands (Gregory et al. 1991; Naiman et al. 2005). Natural disturbances in catchments—such as storms and cyclones, landslides, fire, and defoliation by insects and mammals—influence the rates and levels of material deliveries to receiving waters. Rivers, wetlands, and estuaries are ultimately the recipients of chemicals and materials generated from their catchments. Hence they are greatly influenced by terrestrial processes, including human use and modifications of the land and landscapes, such as deforestation and logging, livestock grazing, cropping, salinization, and urbanization (Allan 2004; Dudgeon et al. 2006).

The flow, or water regime, is one of five dynamic environmental regimes that regulate much of the structure and functioning of every aquatic ecosystem. Interacting with flowing water are the environmental regimes of sediment and organic matter, chemicals and nutrients, light/shade, and temperature (Fig. 13). Each may differ in relative importance among aquatic ecosystem types, and it is the interaction of these drivers in space and time that defines the dynamic nature of all freshwater ecosystems (Baron et al. 2002) and, to a great extent, the character of estuaries and associated tidal wetlands.

A river's flow regime defines the rates and pathways by which precipitation enters and circulates within river channels, wetlands, floodplains, and interconnected groundwater systems and the residence time of water in the surface and groundwater compartments of the fluvial hydrosphere. Inputs of sediment and organic matter (plant litter, fallen timber, dissolved organic compounds), conveyed largely by water, provide raw materials to create and sustain physical habitat structure, refu-

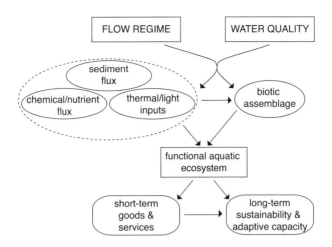

FIGURE 13.   Conceptual model of the five dynamic environmental drivers that regulate much of the structure and functioning of aquatic ecosystems. (Redrawn from Figure 1 of Baron et al. 2002, with permission from the Ecological Society of America)

gia, and connectivity pathways and to maintain nutrient storage and supply (Nilsson and Svedmark 2002; Pinay et al. 2002). Thermal and light regimes regulate organismal metabolism, activity levels, and ecosystem productivity, while chemical and nutrient characteristics regulate pH, productivity, and water-quality conditions (e.g., dissolved oxygen, turbidity, contaminants) of importance for aquatic plants, animals, and people (Baron et al. 2002; Olden and Naiman 2010).

In naturally functioning river ecosystems, unaltered in any way by human activities, each environmental driver has a natural range of variability that depends on the geomorphic character of the catchment, the climatic regime, and local factors. All five environmental drivers display natural annual variation according to seasonal changes in climatic conditions such as precipitation, temperature, and day length; and they may also display interannual and long-term variations to various degrees depending on the climatic regime, its variability, and climate change (Baron et al. 2002). Natural historical variations in river flows, sediment and chemical levels and fluxes, and thermal and light conditions have set the stage for the evolution of life-forms adapted to conditions in running and standing waters, floodplains, wetlands, ground-water systems, and interconnected estuaries or terminal lakes (Lytle and Poff 2004). The ecosystems of which aquatic and semiaquatic organisms form the living component are highly attuned to the variability of their physical and chemical milieu in catchment space and over time.

Given that each environmental driver has a natural range of variability, excessive stress (e.g., prolonged low flows in regulated rivers, nutrient enrichment), habitat loss, and impaired riparian functions have the potential to shift functionally intact freshwater ecosystems beyond the limits of their natural short-term seasonal cycles and interannual fluctuations (Baron et al. 2002). Shifted too far beyond these limits, ecosystems lose their natural resiliency, eventually becoming degraded and unable to support their biological assemblages and to provide important ecological goods and services in the short term, and potentially forever once a critical threshold or tipping point has been reached (Gladwell 2000). How much change from the natural hydrological regime is too much to sustain particular aquatic ecosystems and their biota is a central theme in environmental flow assessment and the management of freshwater to sustain aquatic ecosystems (see Chapters 9–13). Furthermore, climate change is expected to influence existing natural resource regimes that sustain freshwater and estuarine ecosystems, and this must be accommodated in environmental water and catchment management (see Chapter 22). In the next chapter, concepts of running-water ecosystems establish a context for understanding how alterations to natural resource regimes, especially freshwater flows from catchment areas to and through streams, can affect biological diversity, community patterns, and ecological processes.

4

RIVER ECOLOGY, THE NATURAL FLOW REGIME PARADIGM, AND HYDROECOLOGICAL PRINCIPLES

CONCEPTS OF RIVER ECOLOGY

THE FOUR DIMENSIONS OF RIVERS

The directionality of flowing water is so vital to running waters that physical system structure and ecological linkages within a river system are generally divided into longitudinal, lateral, and vertical vectors (Poole 2002). River ecosystems have also been visualized as four-dimensional systems made up of longitudinal, lateral, and vertical components, relationships, and processes, with temporal vectors adding the fourth dimension (Ward 1989; Ward and Stanford 1995). The differentiation of rivers into major geomorphological zones (see Chapter 3) led to biologically based schemes of longitudinal zonation. Early schemes classified rivers into three or four zones along the upland-floodplain transition, each characterized by distinctive invertebrate and/or fish faunas (e.g., Illies and Botosaneanu 1963; Hawkes 1975). Zonation schemes for fish are occasionally employed in Europe and elsewhere (e.g., Santoul et al. 2005), however in many river systems the evidence of such distinctive biological zonation patterns is poor, and the concept gave way to different thinking about riverine organization from headwaters to terminus.

Stream ecologists have long recognized gradual rather than abrupt changes in physical and biological processes along the downstream gradient of running-water systems from small headwater streams to wide lowland reaches. These longitudinal patterns have been interpreted as a continuum rather than a series of distinctive river zones and were formalized in the River Continuum Concept, or RCC (Vannote et al. 1980). The continuum (simplified in Fig. 14) starts in headwater areas where streams are overhung and shaded by riparian vegetation that periodically sheds leaves and other plant parts. These materials enter the stream in the form of coarse particulate organic matter (CPOM), which is processed (i.e., physically broken down) by chewing invertebrates (shredders) and biologically decomposed by aquatic microbes (bacteria, fungi, algae). Processed leaf and other plant fragments are released downstream as finer pieces of organic matter that, in turn, are consumed by another suite of invertebrates, until very fine particulate organic matter (FPOM) is produced and utilized by filter-feeding and suspension-feeding aquatic invertebrates (e.g., caddisflies and black-flies). In this model, invertebrate communities that process organic matter of riparian origin along the river continuum have a predictable composition in terms of their feeding behaviors (traits). Shredders dominate in the upland CPOM-processing zone, and filter feeders are more prominent in the lowland FPOM-processing zone (Vannote et al. 1980). Although the multiple roles of the flow regime were not given particular attention in the RCC, downstream flows are integral to this model, since flow is the primary agent of material and energy transfers along the river continuum.

The River Continuum Concept has been considered by many ecologists to be a central organizing paradigm in running-water ecology, applicable to many rivers, even though local modifiers such as tributaries and impoundments require special consideration (Ward 1989). For example, Winterbourn et al. (1981) showed that streams running off treeless montane slopes in New Zealand are fed by FPOM, not CPOM. Ecologists also emphasized that the RCC would need considerable modification before it can be applied to large rivers (Davies and Walker 1986; Sedell et al. 1989). Townsend (1989) suggested that

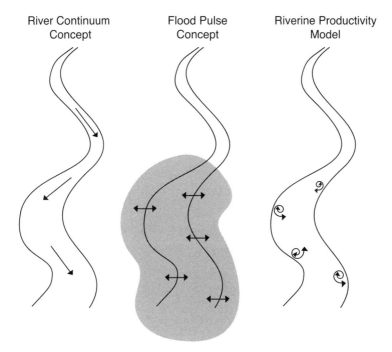

River Continuum   Flood Pulse   Riverine Productivity
Concept   Concept   Model

FIGURE 14.   Comparison of the main spatial arrangements and ecological processes of the River Continuum Concept, the Flood Pulse Concept,
and the Riverine Productivity Model. Straight arrows represent longitudinal (River Continuum) and lateral (Flood Pulse) biophysical exchanges
in river systems, while curled arrows represent local processes of primary
production (Riverine Productivity).

the concept of patch dynamics may have greater general applicability
in running-water systems, whereas Pringle et al. (1988) felt that patch
dynamics could be accommodated by the RCC and nutrient-spiraling
paradigms. Ideas centered on the concept of patchy physical templates
and associated ecological processes, rather than a predictable continuum, form the foundations of the Riverine Ecosystem Synthesis (Thorp
et al. 2008) discussed in Chapter 3.

The RCC developed from an appreciation of terrestrial-aquatic interactions, especially those governed by the riparian zone, as well as the
primary influences of geomorphology and physical conditions in flowing river channels on stream invertebrate communities, energy sources,

and energy flow through food webs. The concept was less concerned with aquatic vertebrates. Ideas about ecological processes that influence riverine fish communities were advanced by quite different studies that placed more emphasis on the lateral dimensions of rivers and riparian zones.

THE FLOOD PULSE CONCEPT

Many studies of tropical fisheries and more recent work on temperate and arid-zone floodplain rivers have confirmed the importance of physical and ecological linkages between rivers and their floodplains, and the vital roles of floods (Walker et al. 1995; Winemiller 2004; Tockner et al. 2008). From studies in tropical floodplain rivers with a predictable annual flood of long duration, Junk et al. (1989) formalized the Flood Pulse Concept (FPC) (Fig. 14).

According to the FPC, the ecology of unmodified floodplain rivers is governed almost entirely by the pulsing of the predictable annual flood cycle. These pulses maintain the system in a state of dynamic equilibrium in which organisms and processes respond to the rate of rise and fall and the amplitude, duration, frequency, and regularity of the flood pulses. During flooding, high habitat diversity on the inundated floodplain is coupled with massive increases in the area of aquatic habitat, nutrient regeneration, and increased primary and secondary productivity. Reproductive cycles and associated migrations of many fish species are timed to place juveniles on the floodplain at this time of maximum food availability and shelter (Welcomme 1985; Lowe-McConnell 1985). The predictable annual flood pulse of long duration, and associated primary and secondary productivity on the floodplain, underpin massive "booms" of fish biomass in some of the world's most productive freshwater fisheries (Craig et al. 2004; Welcomme et al. 2006). In the FPC, the main function of the river channel was thought to be the provision of a migration route and dispersal system (i.e., a highway) that allows aquatic biota to access resources and refuges up and down the river system.

The FPC was developed for tropical floodplain rivers with a predictable annual flood pulse; however, the concept has broadened to embrace the ecological roles of flow pulses within river channels and large floods that may not occur on a predictable annual cycle (e.g., Puckridge et al. 1998; Walker et al. 1995). Studies in arid and semiarid floodplain river systems increasingly reveal the importance of floods that occur infrequently and with low predictability, interspersed between long periods (months to years) of low or no flow and increasing dehydration of channel habitats. During occasional large floods, isolated drying water bodies become filled and reconnected, nutrients are replenished, fish reproduction and dispersal become possible on a grand scale, and fisheries productivity of inundated floodplains reaches "boom" proportions (Bunn et al. 2006; Balcombe et al. 2007). These floodplain processes maximize the chances of floodplain and channel water bodies starting the dry season with a diverse, abundant, and healthy fish assemblage immediately after flood recession, and this ultimately enhances the survival of fish and other biota through prolonged periods of adverse conditions—the "bust" (Walker et al. 1995; Arthington and Balcombe 2011).

THE FLUVIAL HYDROSYSTEM

The combination of the River Continuum Concept (with its emphasis on linkages between catchments, riparian zones, and upstream-downstream connections) and the Flood Pulse Concept (focused on the two-way exchanges between river channels and their floodplains) gave rise to the concept that river ecosystems are strongly dependent on maintaining hydrological connectivity in longitudinal and lateral dimensions (e.g., Heiler et al. 1995). A further development was the welding of these ideas together in the Fluvial Hydrosystem Concept (Petts and Amoros 1996)—a three-dimensional system dependent on the dynamic interactions of hydrological, geomorphological, and ecological processes over a range of time scales. This concept focused on river corridors and their adjacent floodplains—with their diversity of aquatic, wetland, and terrestrial habitats—and the underlying alluvial aquifer. In this concept, biota are seen to be distributed according to predictable environmental gradients modified by biological processes (competition, predation, colonization, succession, extinction), while the primary environmental drivers are those related to the character of the catchment—discharge, sediment, and water-quality regimes.

VERTICAL DIMENSIONS

The vertical dimensions of rivers include the relationships of surface water and groundwater, the movement of dissolved and particulate materials in water, and the dynamics of hyporheic (subsurface) biological communities (Boulton et al. 1998). Upwelling hyporheic water can influence surface water quality, primary productivity, sediment microbial activity, and decomposition of organic matter. The differing degrees to which rivers and riparian corridors depend on groundwater mediate all of these interactions, which also vary along the length of river corridors (Boulton and Hancock 2006). Further detail on the nature, ecology, and importance of subsurface waters is given in Chapter 15, together with a discussion of how these dynamic systems may change over time and in response to human activities such as groundwater pumping, extraction, and pollution. The water requirements of subsurface biological communities are discussed in Chapter 16.

TEMPORAL DIMENSIONS

The fourth, or temporal, dimension of rivers proposed by Ward (1989) "superimposes a temporal hierarchy on the three spatial dimensions." Ward felt that ecological research, environmental impact studies, hydraulic engineering, and the management of regulated rivers all require an appreciation of past environmental conditions, the time scales of ecological processes, and changes brought about by human activities. Understanding historical and recent temporal patterns of flow, temperature, and other environmental drivers is central to the development of river management and environmental flow strategies (Petts and Amoros 1996). Appreciation of the dynamic nature of river flows in spatial dimensions and over different times scales was one of the ideas that sparked the next conceptual development.

THE NATURAL FLOW REGIME PARADIGM

The overriding importance of dynamic flow patterns in streams and rivers is captured in the Natural Flow Regime Paradigm (Poff et al. 1997), which states that "the integrity of flowing water systems depends on their natural dynamic character" and "streamflow, which is strongly correlated with many critical physicochemical characteristics of rivers, such as water temperature, channel geomorphology and habitat diversity, can be considered a 'master variable' . . . that limits the distribution and abundance of riverine species and regulates the ecological integrity of flowing waters." One of the main ideas in this paradigm is that "naturally variable flows create and maintain the dynamics of in-channel and floodplain conditions and habitats that are essential to aquatic and riparian species" and that the "predictable diversity of in-channel and floodplain habitat types has promoted the evolution of species that exploit the habitat mosaic created and maintained by hydrologic variability" (Poff et al. 1997). Adaptation of riverine species to this environmental dynamism "allows aquatic and floodplain species to persist in the face of seemingly harsh conditions, such as floods and droughts, that regularly destroy and re-create habitat elements" (Poff et al. 1997).

A river's flow regime can be described in terms of five flow facets: the magnitude, frequency, duration, timing, and rate of change of flows (see Chapter 2). To appreciate the diverse ecological roles of these characteristics is no mean feat, for they can interact in many different ways and present as a wide range of individual flow signatures. Nevertheless it is convenient to consider each facet individually as a first step toward appreciating the ecological significance of flow facets in various configurations. Poff et al. (1997) focused on low and high-flow events, since these often present ecological bottlenecks that act as critical stresses and opportunities for a wide array of riverine species. Tables 8–12 summarize the ecological functions of flow magnitudes from normal and drought-level low flows to channel flows (channel pulses or freshes) and high flows that break out of the channel onto the floodplain; followed by the importance of the frequency of particular flow events and their duration, seasonal timing, and the significance of the rate of change in flow conditions.

TABLE 8 *Facets of the flow regime*

Low- and high-flow magnitude and their ecological functions

Flow facets	Ecological functions
Low (base) flows	Normal level
	Maintain suitable water temperatures, dissolved oxygen, and water chemistry
	Provide adequate habitat space for aquatic organisms
	Keep fish and amphibian eggs suspended
	Enable fish to move to feeding and spawning areas
	Maintain water table levels in riverbanks and floodplain, soil moisture for plants
	Support hyporheic organisms (living in saturated sediments)
	Provide drinking water for terrestrial animals
	Drought level
	Provide refuge habitat in pools after riffles and runs dry out
	Concentrate prey into limited areas to benefit predators
	Enable recruitment of certain floodplain plants
	Enable limited invertebrate and fish recruitment
	Purge invasive, introduced species from aquatic and riparian communities
High flows within channel	Shape physical character of river channel, including pools, riffles, runs
	Determine size of streambed substrates (sand, gravel, cobble)
	Prevent riparian vegetation from encroaching into channel
	Restore normal water-quality conditions after prolonged low flows, flushing away waste products and pollutants
	Aerate eggs in spawning gravels, prevent siltation
	Provide suitable habitats for invertebrates and fish
	Maintain suitable salinity conditions in estuaries
Large floods	Shape physical habitats in channels and on floodplain (e.g., lateral channels, oxbow lakes)
	Provide migration and spawning cues for fish, trigger invertebrate life-history phases
	Enable fish to spawn on floodplain, provide nursery habitat for juvenile fish
	Provide new feeding opportunities for fish, amphibians, waterbirds
	Distribute life stages of fish and invertebrates among channel habitats
	Create sites for recruitment of colonizing plants
	Provide plant seedlings with prolonged access to soil moisture

(continued)

TABLE 8 *(continued)*

Flow facets	Ecological functions
Large floods *(continued)*	Maintain diversity in floodplain plant and forest types through differential inundation
	Disburse seeds and fruits of riparian plants
	Flush organic materials (food) and woody debris (habitat structures) into channel
	Purge invasive, introduced species from aquatic and riparian communities
	Maintain suitable salinity conditions in estuaries
	Provide nutrients and organic matter to estuaries
	Stimulate spawning of estuarine biota and support recruitment

SOURCE: Adapted from Postel and Richter 2003 and references therein

TABLE 9 *Facets of the flow regime*

Ecological significance of the frequency of flows

Flow facets	Ecological functions
Frequency of flows	The timing, or predictability, of flow events is critical ecologically because the life cycles of many aquatic and riparian species are timed to either avoid or exploit flows of variable magnitudes
	Natural timing of high or low stream flows provides environmental cues for initiating life-cycle transitions in fish, e.g., spawning, egg hatching, rearing, movement onto the floodplain for feeding or reproduction, or migration upstream or downstream
	Match of reproductive period and floodplain or wetland access explains some of the yearly variation in stream fish community composition
	Many riparian plants have life cycles that are adapted to the seasonal timing components of natural flow regimes through their "emergence phenologies"—the seasonal sequence of flowering, seed dispersal, germination, and seedling growth
	Interaction of emergence phenologies with temporally varying environmental stress from flooding or drought helps to maintain high species diversity in floodplain forests
	Productivity of riparian forests is influenced by flow timing and can increase when short-duration flooding occurs in the growing season

SOURCE: Adapted from Poff et al. 1997 and references therein

TABLE 10 *Facets of the flow regime*

Ecological significance of the duration of flows

Flow facets	Ecological functions
Duration of flows	The duration of a specific flow condition often determines its ecological significance
	Differences in tolerance to prolonged flooding in riparian plants and to prolonged low flow in aquatic invertebrates and fish allow these species to persist in locations from which they might otherwise be displaced by dominant, but less tolerant, species
	Seasonal access to floodplain wetlands is essential for the recruitment of certain river fishes; the duration of floodplain inundation can influence the growth potential and recruitment of fish and other biota that need to use floodplain habitats and food resources
	Duration of dry periods in arid-zone rivers can influence the survival of fish to the point that isolated water bodies may lose their entire fish assemblage unless replenished by flow

SOURCE: Adapted from Poff et al. 1997 and references therein

TABLE 11 *Facets of the flow regime*

Ecological significance of the seasonal timing of flows

Flow facets	Ecological functions
Seasonal timing of flows	Natural timing of high or low stream flows provides environmental cues for initiating life-cycle transitions in fish, e.g., spawning, egg hatching, rearing, movement onto the floodplain for feeding or reproduction, or migration upstream or downstream
	Match of reproductive period and floodplain or wetland access explains some of the yearly variation in stream fish community composition
	Many riparian plants have life cycles that are adapted to the seasonal timing components of natural flow regimes through their "emergence phenologies"—the seasonal sequence of flowering, seed dispersal, germination, and seedling growth
	Interaction of emergence phenologies with temporally varying environmental stress from flooding or drought helps to maintain high species diversity in floodplain forests
	Productivity of riparian forests is influenced by flow timing and can increase when short-duration flooding occurs in the growing season
	Natural seasonal variation in flow conditions can prevent the successful establishment of nonnative species with flow-dependent spawning and egg incubation requirements, such as striped bass *(Morone saxatilis)* and brown trout *(Salmo trutta)*

SOURCE: Adapted from Poff et al. 1997 and references therein

TABLE 12   *Facets of the flow regime*

Ecological significance of the rate of change in flow conditions

Flow facets	Ecological functions
Rate of change in flow conditions	The rate of change, or flashiness, in flow conditions due to heavy storms can influence species persistence and coexistence
	Rapid flow increases in streams of the central and southwestern United States serve as spawning cues for native minnow species, whose rapidly developing eggs are either broadcast into the water column or attached to submerged structures as floodwaters recede
	More gradual, seasonal rates of change in flow conditions regulate the persistence of many aquatic and riparian species
	Cottonwoods (*Populus* spp.) are disturbance species that establish after winter–spring flood flows, during a narrow "window of opportunity" when competition-free alluvial substrates and wet soils are available for germination
	A certain rate of floodwater recession is critical to cottonwood seedling germination because seedling roots must remain connected to a receding water table as they grow downward
	Nonnative fish generally lack the behavioral adaptations to avoid being displaced downstream by sudden flood, e.g., the introduced predatory mosquitofish *(Gambusia affinis)* can extirpate the native Gila topminnow *(Poeciliopsis occidentalis)* in locations where natural flash floods are regulated by upstream dams, but the native species persists in naturally flashy stream

SOURCE: Adapted from Poff et al. 1997 and references therein

HYDROECOLOGICAL PRINCIPLES

The Natural Flow Regime Paradigm and numerous place-based studies illustrate the many ecological roles of flow magnitude, flood frequency, timing and duration, low flows, and other facets of flow regimes. More general hydroecological principles help to conceptualize and quantify the ecological roles of flow and thereby contribute to frameworks and methods for the assessment of environmental flows. Explicit hydroecological principles and conceptual models start with a series of papers published in 2002 in *Environmental Management.* In-stream biodiversity (aquatic plants, invertebrates, and fish), riparian vegetation, and nitrogen dynamics were the primary themes, with a fourth paper providing a synthesis and forward viewpoint (Naiman et al. 2002). The following sections of this chapter present hydroecological principles common to most stream and river ecosystems, even though the particulars can be expected to vary with climate, biome, topography, catchment vegetation, and flow regime type. These first principles have provided the foundations for a number of environmental flow guidelines and field studies (e.g., Arthington et al. 2003; Forslund et al. 2009; Hirji and Davis 2009; Jiang et al. 2010).

FLOW REGIMES AND AQUATIC BIODIVERSITY

Bunn and Arthington (2002) proposed four guiding hydroecological principles driving freshwater biodiversity in unaltered rivers and their floodplains, and they linked these to the effects of altered flow regimes on aquatic biodiversity. The four principles are set out in Table 13 and illustrated in Figure 15, while the physical and ecological impacts of flow alterations are taken up in Chapters 7 and 8.

Three simplified annual hydrographs (Figure 15) represent how river flows can vary in magnitude and hydrograph shape from year to year. Many more attributes of flow regime variability can be incorporated into this conceptual model, to which the particular ecological responses of any river system can be added by expanding and filling out the four boxes with known details for the river and species under investigation. Such a process is one of the fundamental preparatory steps in several environmental flow assessment methods (e.g., the Building Block Methodology, the Benchmarking Methodology, DRIFT; see Chapter 11).

TABLE 13   *Principles that govern the relationship of*
flow regime and aquatic biodiversity

Principle	Description
1	Flow is a major determinant of physical habitat in streams, which in turn is a major determinant of biotic composition. Modified flow regimes alter habitat at varying spatial scales and influence the distribution and abundance of species and the composition and diversity of aquatic communities.
2	Aquatic species have evolved life-history strategies primarily in direct response to the natural flow regime. Flow pattern has a major influence on shaping the life-history strategies of aquatic species, and alteration of flow regimes can lead to recruitment failure and loss of biodiversity of native species.
3	Maintaining natural patterns of longitudinal and lateral connectivity is essential to the vitality of populations of many riverine species. Loss of longitudinal and lateral connectivity through construction of barriers can lead to isolation of populations, failed recruitment, and local extinction of fish and other aquatic biota.
4	The invasion and success of exotic and translocated species in rivers is facilitated by the alteration of flow regimes. Flow regulation and the creation of large man-made lakes can affect the establishment, spread, and persistence of both types of introduced species. Interbasin transfers of water can act as a major mechanism for the transfer of exotic and pest species between catchments.

SOURCE: Bunn and Arthington 2002

FLOW, PHYSICAL HABITAT, AND BIODIVERSITY

It is no coincidence that the first hydroecological principle for rivers concerns aquatic habitat—that range of places and physical/chemical resources used by aquatic species from birth/germination and through the entire life cycle to death. A good understanding of how physical habitats are created and maintained, and how habitat varies across the spatial and temporal dimensions of river corridors, is fundamental to environmental flow management and river restoration (Bovee 1982; Bond and Lake 2003).

Physical habitat structure is largely a function of the movement of water across the landscape and the influence of moving water on the shape, size, and complexity of river channels; the formation of anabranches and deltas; the distribution of riffle, run, pool, and backwater habitats; the diversity and stability of small-scale patches of substrate; and the nature of interactions between the main channel, its riparian and hyporheic (sub-

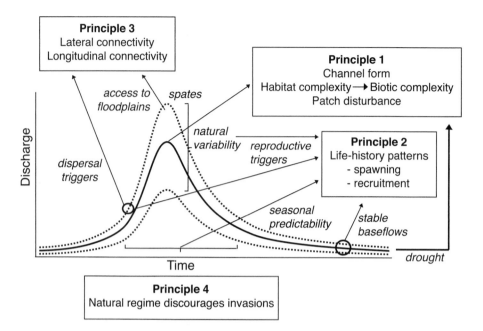

FIGURE 15. Conceptual model of four hydroecological principles illustrating how facets of the natural flow regime govern aquatic biodiversity in rivers and floodplains. (Redrawn from Figure 1 in Bunn and Arthington 2002, with permission from Springer-Verlag)

surface) zones, and the floodplain. Physical processes in streams and rivers are driven by flow magnitude (baseflows, channel flows, floods), and the frequency, duration, and variability of these discharges of water interacting with the catchment's geomorphology and the streamside (riparian) vegetation. Riverine and floodplain biota have evolved and adapted to this complex, shifting spatial and temporal mosaic of physical habitats in river systems (Lytle and Poff 2004). In turn, this complex interaction between flows and physical habitat is a major determinant of the distribution, abundance, and diversity of stream and river organisms, ranging from microorganisms, algae, and aquatic plants to invertebrates and fish and other vertebrates (Table 14).

FLOW AND LIFE-HISTORY STRATEGIES

The seasonal timing and predictability of the natural flow regime is critical because the life cycles of many aquatic species are timed to

TABLE 14   *Principle 1: Flow, habitat, and biodiversity*
With examples for aquatic plants, invertebrates, and fish

Ecological components	Description of relationships with flow
Aquatic plants	Aquatic plant assemblages are influenced by stream hydraulics, substrate composition and stability, disturbance intensity and frequency, water velocity, turbulence, shear stress, and scouring. They typically have patchy distributions as a result of spatial variations in these factors as well as water quality, light, and the colonization success and growth rates of species in response to habitat factors. The scouring action of floodwaters on floodplain soils rejuvenates habitat for aquatic plants that germinate only on barren, wetted soils free of competitors or species that require shallow water tables.
Invertebrates	Physical disturbances wrought by floods and low flow periods are major determinants of the diversity, spatial patterns, and temporal dynamics of benthic invertebrate communities in streams. Rivers with unstable substrates tend to be characterized by low species diversity, and the biota often have life-history or behavioral characteristics suited to life in frequently disturbed environments. Natural flow disturbance can cause catastrophic downstream drift of invertebrates, while colonization patterns and rates are determined by small-scale substrate and velocity characteristics.
Fish	Many steam fish species prefer particular habitat types (pools, runs, riffles) and are likely to occur at particular locations in a river basin. Typically, fish species richness increases with distance downstream in response to increasing habitat diversity associated with stream/river discharge, width, depth, etc. Streams with high flow variability support species with generalized feeding strategies and preference for low water velocity, silt, and general substrates. In more stable streams, with high predictability of daily flows and stable baseflows, fish assemblages contain more specialized species; and in some rivers, silt-intolerant trophic specialists may dominate.

SOURCE: Adapted from Bunn and Arthington 2002 and references therein

avoid or take advantage of particular flow conditions (Poff et al. 1997). Furthermore, specific components of the thermal regime have ecological relevance for particular freshwater organisms throughout their life histories (Olden and Naiman 2010). Many life-cycle processes are synchronized with temperature and day length such that the availability of suitable habitats and food resources present windows of opportunity for the sensitive early developmental stages. Examples of the importance of

TABLE 15   *Principle 2: Flow and life-history processes*
With examples for aquatic plants, invertebrates, and fish

Ecological components	Description of relationships with flow
Aquatic plants	River flows and wetland water regimes influence seed establishment, recruitment, and growth of submerged aquatic plants. Rates of water-level fluctuation, disturbance frequency (floods and spates), and intensity (velocity and shear stress) can affect seedling survival as well as plant growth rates.
Invertebrates	Stream invertebrates have flexible life-history patterns in highly variable and unpredictable discharge regimes, whereas tighter synchrony of invertebrate development is found only in regions with a more predictable flow regime. In large floodplain rivers, many aquatic species (e.g., benthic microorganisms, invertebrates, and zooplankton) are cued to rising flood levels, emerging from resting stages or spawning in response to the cue of rising water levels and inundation.
Fish	Critical life-history events of fish are linked to flow regime (timing of reproduction, spawning behavior, larval survival, growth patterns, and recruitment). Fish life-history strategies have been grouped as opportunistic, periodic and equilibrium, each adapted to the variability patterns of flows and to the thermal regime. Many river fishes are cued and respond to increases in river channel flows or the timing of large floods in floodplain rivers. Others breed opportunistically within the channel at any time of year, but may take advantage of floodplain resources as and when they become available.

SOURCE: Adapted from Bunn and Arthington 2002 and references therein

flow to the life-history processes and strategies of aquatic plants, invertebrates, and fish are given in Table 15.

FLOW AND CONNECTIVITY

Bunn and Arthington (2002) suggest that the viability of populations of many species of fully aquatic organisms depends on their ability to move freely through the stream network. Migration has evolved as an adaptive response to natural environmental variation on a daily, seasonal, and multiannual basis, with the biomes and habitats visited during the life cycle, and distance traveled, being essential characteristics of the migration patterns of invertebrates and fish and other vertebrates (Pringle 2001; Fausch et al. 2002; Lucas and Baras 2001). Aquatic species from shrimp to fish and river dolphins use different habitats at different times, and longitudinal migrations may be an obligatory component of life histories—particularly when migration is associated with breeding (Welcomme et al. 2006). Longitudinal migrations may occur at various spatial scales within the stream and river network, or from river to lake or sea and back, or from sea or lake to river and back (Dudgeon et al. 2006). Salmonid migrations upstream for breeding purposes are among the most famous and well-studied ecological movement phenomena (e.g., Enders et al. 2009).

Hydrological connectivity between the river channel, backwaters, the floodplain, and groundwater governs the spatial and temporal heterogeneity of floodplain habitats, contributing to their characteristic high biodiversity (Tockner et al. 2008). In large tropical floodplain rivers, the lateral expansion of floodplain habitats during the predictable annual flood pulse creates important spawning, nursery, and foraging areas for invertebrates and for many fish species and a variety of other vertebrates (Junk et al. 1989). Lateral connections and exchanges between a river channel and its inundated floodplain underpin vital life-history processes of aquatic invertebrates, and fish and other vertebrates (e.g., turtles, waterbirds) that utilize floodplains to feed and grow (e.g., AJ King et al. 2003). Lateral connectivity also drives processes of nutrient and organic-matter transfer that contribute to the feeding relationships and interactions in a biological community—the food web. Examples of the importance of hydrological connectivity for aquatic plants, invertebrates, and fish are given in Table 16.

The fourth principle relates to changes in flow regimes and the propensity for flow alterations of various types to favor exotic species (or alien, i.e., species originating from another country) over native species. These and other consequences of flow alterations and river impoundments for native aquatic biodiversity are discussed in Chapter 8.

FLOW AND NITROGEN CYCLING

In-stream, riparian, and floodplain zones contribute to shaping and maintaining water quality in aquatic ecosystems, and the natural water regime has a profound influence on the biogeochemical processes of these zones as well as their ability to cycle and mitigate nutrients fluxes

TABLE 16 *Principle 3: Flow and the ecological roles of connectivity*
With examples for aquatic plants, invertebrates, and fish

Ecological components	Description of relationships with flow
Aquatic plants	Longitudinal and later connections throughout rivers are affected by channel flow and flood-driven passive transfers of plant parts and their propagules. Hydrochory—the dissemination of seeds or plants by water—can involve whole plants; propagules such as rhizomes, stolons, tubers, and turions; and live seeds of many plant species.
Invertebrates	Large migratory invertebrates such as shrimps and crabs are an important component of the biota in tropical and subtropical streams, because they directly influence ecosystem level processes and the composition of benthic algal and invertebrate communities. Lateral connections and exchanges between a river channel and its inundated floodplain underpin vital life history processes of aquatic invertebrates that utilize floodplains to feed and grow. Lateral connectivity also drives processes of nutrient and organic matter transfer that contribute to the feeding relationships and interactions (the food web) in a biological community.
Fish	In large floodplain river systems like the Mekong the separation of major fish habitats and spawning areas in time and space forces most fish to migrate, often upstream. After monsoonal flood waters inundate the Tonlé Sap river and lake system in Cambodia, there is a massive dry season (November–March) migration downstream from Cambodian floodplains into Vietnam, during which many migrating fish are caught by the Dai fishery. The frequency and duration of lateral hydrological connectivity, and the periodic isolation of floodplain water bodies from the main river channel, are critical in determining spatial variation in the composition of fish assemblages in floodplain rivers.

SOURCE: Adapted from Bunn and Arthington 2002 and references therein

originating upstream and upslope (Pinay et al. 2002). The nitrogen cycle is of particular interest in freshwater ecosystems. Pinay et al. (2002) define three guiding principles driving the nitrogen cycle in river systems that, in general, should apply to other nutrients. Principles that regulate the cycling and transfer of nitrogen in rivers are presented in Table 17, with the pathways and processing of nitrogen at the catchment scale depicted in Figure 16.

TABLE 17   *Principles that regulate the cycling and transfer of nitrogen in rivers at the catchment scale*

Principle	Processes governed by the flow regime
Principle 1: The mode of nitrogen delivery affects ecosystem functioning	In forested catchments, particulate organic nitrogen is transferred to aquatic systems mainly as litter fall from nitrogen-fixing and other plants in riparian zones. After degradation and recycling, particulate inputs contribute to export of dissolved organic nitrogen via surface and subsurface pathways. Riparian forests also receive, recycle, and transfer large amounts of sediments and nutrients to streams (as nitrate in subsurface flow) from upslope. Riparian zones utilize and retain nitrogen moving upstream in the bodies of migrating animals such as salmonids. Flood duration, frequency, and magnitude regulate delivery of nutrients and create a mosaic of nutrient-enriched geomorphic surfaces that influence successional development of riparian vegetation.
Principle 2: Increasing contact between water and soil or sediment increases nitrogen retention and processing	The area of water-substrate interface is positively correlated with the efficiency of nitrogen retention and use in river ecosystems, both in-stream and in the riparian and floodplain zone. Hyporheic zones are highly reactive sites for nutrient cycling because they expand the surface of contact between water and sediments. Riparian wetlands provide a large contact area between water and soils, which promotes nitrogen retention and processing, thereby regulating fluxes from uplands to streams.
Principle 3: Floods and droughts are natural events that strongly influence pathways of nitrogen cycling	The water regime directly affects nitrogen cycling in alluvial soils by controlling the duration of oxic and anoxic phases and the processes of ammonification and denitrification. The flood regime also indirectly affects nutrient cycling in flood-plain soils by influencing soil structure and texture through the patchy deposition of sediment. Floodplains contribute to the regulation of nitrogen fluxes by sorting sediments mobilized during floods and recycling nitrogen deposited during floods.

SOURCE: Adapted from Pinay et al. 2002 and references therein

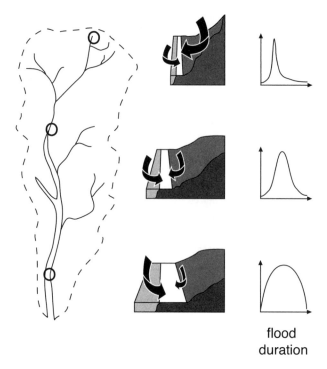

flood
duration

FIGURE 16. Preferential water and nutrient movements (arrows) through the riparian zones (white) of rivers (light gray) as a function of their location within a drainage basin (darker gray). Along small streams, most of the water and associated nutrients flow from upland catchments via the riparian zone, while along larger streams the main flow direction is from the stream toward the floodplain, mainly during flood events. (Redrawn from Figure 1 in Pinay et al. 2002, with permission from Springer-Verlag)

Nitrogen processing rates vary among climates. For example, nitrate fluxes are rather constant in temperate and wet tropical areas, and allochthonous nitrate seems to be completely removed within a few meters of travel in the riparian zone. In contrast, "the riparian zone is rather ineffective in initial retention of upland nitrogen inputs in continental and arid climates, in part because overland flow rapidly transports water and nitrogen across the riparian surface during storms" (Pinay et al. 2002). However, the three basic principles driving nitrogen regulation in rivers and riparian zones remain relevant and universally applicable in land and water management. Sustainable management practices should be "assessed according their impact on: (1) the delivery mode of nitrogen to river ecosystems; (2) the length of contact between water, soil, and sediment; and (3) the timing, intensity, and duration of floods and drought" (Pinay et al. 2002). The consequences of altered flow regimes for the processing of nitrogen are discussed in Chapter 5.

FLOW REGIMES AND RIPARIAN VEGETATION

Riparian systems represent transition zones between terrestrial and aquatic ecosystems, organized in networks across landscapes and riverscapes. Riparian zones encompass the stream channel between the low- and high-water marks and the terrestrial landscape above the high-water mark, where vegetation may be influenced by elevated water tables or flooding and by the ability of the soils to hold water (Nilsson and Svedmark 2002). Streams and their riparian zones provide habitat for a wide range of plants that have a variety of adaptations and can be grouped into four major categories: invaders (produce large numbers of wind- and water-disseminated propagules that colonize alluvial habitats), endurers (resprout after breakage or burial of either the stem or roots from floods or after being partially eaten), resisters (withstand flooding for weeks during the growing season, moderate fires, or epidemics), and avoiders (lack adaptations to specific disturbance types; individuals germinating in an unfavorable habitat do not survive) (Naiman and Décamps 1997). Catchment characteristics (climate, topography, geology, soils, etc.) set the context for development of riparian vegetation systems, while linkages and connectivity along streams and rivers and with adjacent wetland and floodplain systems regulate what is imported or exported.

The flow regime of a river, and especially floods, determine local riparian communities and the corridor functions and biodiversity of the riparian zone. Nilsson and Svedmark (2002) proposed three basic principles that determine the important qualities of riparian vegetation and the processes governed by the flow regime (Table 18). The processes embedded in each principle are summarized in Tables 19–21, while Figure 17 depicts a simple model of the relationship between flood

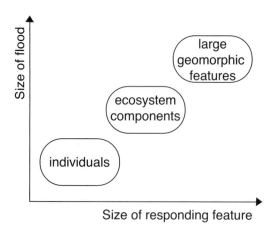

FIGURE 17. Simplified model showing the relationship between flood magnitude and the size of the physical and biological variables that are affected in rivers and their riparian zones. High-magnitude, infrequent floods influence large geomorphic features, whereas small, frequent floods have effects at the level of individual plants. (Redrawn from Figure 2 in Nilsson and Svedmark 2002, with permission from Springer-Verlag)

magnitude and the size of the physical and biological variables that are affected in rivers and their riparian zones. High-magnitude, infrequent floods influence large geomorphic features, whereas small, frequent floods have effects at the level of individual plants.

The three fundamental characteristics and processes of riparian zones outlined above can all be affected by changing hydrologic regimes and all require specific management efforts to sustain their vital functions. Management strategies may involve protection, restoration, rehabilitation, and substitution (Naiman et al. 2000). These issues are taken up in Chapters 11–13.

TABLE 18   *Principles that govern the relationship of flow regime and riparian vegetation*

Principle	Processes governed by the flow regime
1	The flow regime determines the ecological processes and the successional evolution of riparian plant communities and ecological processes.
2	The riparian zone serves as a pathway for redistribution of organic and inorganic material that influences plant communities along rivers.
3	The riparian system is a transition zone between land and water ecosystems and is disproportionately rich in plant species compared to surrounding ecosystems.

SOURCE: Nilsson and Svedmark 2002

TABLE 19   *Principle 1: Flow regime and riparian vegetation communities*

Definition	Processes governed by the flow regime
The flow regime determines the ecological processes and the successional evolution of riparian plant communities and ecological processes	Riparian plant communities are generally arranged along elevation gradients into more or less distinct zones with various plant growth forms (forest, shrub, and herbaceous plants). Lateral and vertical gradients of water availability and fluvial disturbance control the distribution, abundance, and diversity of plants on banks. Patterns of succession and rate of species turnover are governed by the frequency and magnitude of physical disturbances, especially high-magnitude floods that influence the formation of large geomorphic features (e.g., new channels or deltas). Floods of intermediate size determine riparian components at the patch scale, and more frequent minor floods have effects at the species level.

SOURCE: Adapted from Nilsson and Svedmark 2002 and references therein

TABLE 20   *Principle 2: Flow and the riparian zone as a pathway*

Definition	*Processes governed by the flow regime*
The riparian zone serves as a pathway for redistribution of organic and inorganic material that influences plant communities along rivers	Water movements redistribute virtually all fractions of soil within riparian zones, but fine particles dominate by mass. Sediment redistribution in a river represents the interplay between processes of erosion and deposition. Dense riparian vegetation helps to minimize soil erosion by covering the soil, by reducing current velocity during periods of high discharge, and by stabilizing the underlying soils through root growth. Disturbance and colonization episodes wrought by flowing water produce temporal and spatial patchiness in riparian communities. Partial smothering or burial of plants by waterborne silt can disturb the normal establishment, growth, and survival processes in riparian zones. Flow is a key factor in hydrochory, and both the mean and maximum dispersal distances of seeds increase with increasing discharge. The seasonal timing of propagule dispersal is also partly dependent on flow conditions but is moderated by the timing of propagule release by plants and the length of time propagules remain buoyant. Large woody debris (LWD) moved about in streams and rivers by flowing water can influence stream morphology by accumulating and sometimes blocking entire channels, creating pools and waterfalls and affecting channel width and depth. The presence of LWD facilitates accumulation of finer sediments and organic matter that provide a substrate for early-succession plant species; these processes influence riparian successional patterns. The structure and diversity of aquatic habitats for stream organisms is also substantially influenced by the spatial patterns of LWD and its effects on stream hydraulics and cover.

SOURCE: Adapted from Nilsson and Svedmark 2002 and references therein

TABLE 21   *Principle 3: Hydroecological principles and the species richness of riparian vegetation*

Definition	*Processes governed by the flow regime*
The riparian system is a transition zone between land and water ecosystems and is disproportionately rich in plant species compared to surrounding ecosystems	Riparian communities contribute to the biodiversity of river ecosystems because they are disproportionately rich in plant species compared to their surroundings. Hydroecological principles explain this richness of plant forms. Floods of varying intensity and frequency interact with geomorphic features to form a mosaic of landforms with different disturbance history and different stages of vegetation succession and plant diversity. In addition, a large proportion of a region's flora may be captured in the riparian zones of river systems that cross climatic zones and biomes. Various disturbance regimes are imposed on the riparian corridor, including fire, landslides, mudflows, and herbivory, creating further opportunities for species diversification and turnover in space and time. Riparian plants have efficient mechanisms that spread their propagules along riparian corridors; hydrochory is the most important means of dispersal, followed by dispersal of propagules by wind and animals. Finally, riparian communities are easily invaded by exotic plants, and such invasion is further promoted by flow alterations, either adding to the diversity of indigenous vegetation or detracting from it.

SOURCE: Nilsson and Svedmark 2002

5

EFFECTS OF CATCHMENT CHANGE
AND RIVER-CORRIDOR ENGINEERING

THE HUMAN FOOTPRINT

Every environmental flow assessment has a catchment context with a particular "human footprint" (Sanderson et al. 2002). Environmental flow assessments are most often focused on the geomorphic and ecological implications of flow alterations below large dams, but many other human interventions at the catchment scale intercept or exacerbate overland flows and influence the hydrology of streams and rivers, wetlands, and estuaries. Not only do catchment activities alter surface and groundwater hydrology, they also alter the dynamics of other catchment resource regimes—sediments, nutrients and organic matter, temperature, and light. Alterations to these regimes have many consequences for aquatic and riparian ecosystems, and they frequently interact to form damaging combinations of stressors.

Human transformation of the global water cycle through interference with hydrologic processes and indirectly through widespread land-cover change, engineering of river channels, wetland drainage, aquatic habitat loss, and pollution inevitably necessitates integrated management of land and water resources. A recent perspective is that environmental flow practitioners should take a whole water-cycle approach merged with a multiple driver approach (Baron et al. 2002; Hirji and Davis 2009); and this should be done with full recognition that aquatic ecosystems are the victims of many disturbances, not just hydrologic alteration. This ultimately is the goal of integrated water resource management—"the coordinated development and management of water, land and related resources in order to maximize economic and social welfare without compromising the sustainability of vital environmental systems" (Global Water Partnership 2011).

This chapter is concerned with the scope and diversity of multiple interacting stressors, how they affect rivers individually and interact to degrade all aquatic ecosystems. A rich litany of examples adds weight to the proposition that environmental flow assessments and water management may be ineffective in isolation from efforts to mitigate other threats within a catchment.

THREAT CATEGORIES

The biota and processes of aquatic ecosystems have varied naturally over millennia in accord with climatic cycles, changing environmental regimes, and catastrophic extinction events (e.g., the Cretaceous apocalypse that wiped out the dinosaurs and up to 85% of all species living 65 million years ago). Species flocks have evolved and declined only to be replaced by new species and genetic strains and different kinds of ecosystems (Dudgeon et al. 2006). Superimposed on these natural historical processes and legacies are the activities of humans, now the dominant species on Earth (Vitousek et al. 1997). With the rise of human societies around the globe, aquatic ecosystems and the five natural drivers of aquatic ecosystems have been altered—originally very little, but over about 10,000 years, more and more intrusively (Worster 1985). Soil erosion from agricultural lands "began when the first heavy rains struck the first furrow turned by a crude implement of tillage in the hands of prehistoric man" (Bennett and Lowdermilk 1938). Now, on a global scale, more than 83% of the land surface has been significantly influenced by the human footprint, and this percentage is even higher in some countries and regions (Sanderson et al. 2002; Vörösmarty et al. 2010).

Threats to aquatic ecosystems and biodiversity start in their catchments with alterations to the hydrologic cycle and the materials carried by water, and threats ramify through riparian and river corridors to the smallest scales of habitat in surface water and groundwater sys-

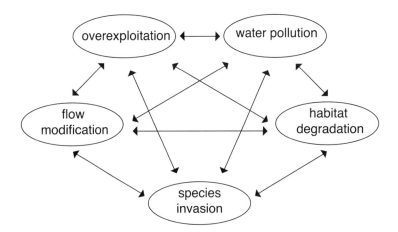

FIGURE 18. The five major threat categories and their established or potential interactive impacts on aquatic biodiversity. (Redrawn from Figure 1 in Dudgeon et al. 2006, with permission from John Wiley and Sons)

tems (Hynes 1975; Naiman et al. 2008). Water is such an effective vector for the many physical, chemical, and biological effects of stressors that freshwater and estuarine networks have been highly modified in many parts of the world. There is ample evidence that very few water bodies have *not* been irreversibly altered from their original state by human activities (Lévêque and Balian 2005). Their position in the landscape makes lakes, wetlands, and rivers the inevitable recipients of wastes, sediments, and pollutants carried in runoff, and "while this is also true of estuaries and oceans, inland water bodies typically lack the volume of open marine waters, limiting their capacity to dilute contaminants or mitigate other impacts" (Dudgeon et al. 2006).

At the catchment scale, the main threats to aquatic ecosystems arise from land-use change (deforestation and afforestation, agricultural development, land and wetland drainage, flood protection, and urbanization). Activities at the scale of river and floodplain corridors, loosely termed "corridor engineering," are just as intrusive, if not more so. Interventions in river corridors involve the removal of riparian vegetation, channelization, dredging and mining, floodplain engineering, channel modifications for navigation and transport, recreational activities, barrier effects of dams and weirs, flow regulation by dams, water abstraction and groundwater pumping, and the mass transfer of water within and between catchments (Boon et al. 1992; Vörösmarty et al. 2004).

Modifications to the natural functioning of catchments and aquatic ecosystems can be distilled down to five interacting threat categories (Fig. 18): water pollution, flow modification, destruction or degradation of habitat, invasion by exotic species, and overexploitation (Dudgeon et al. 2006). Of these, habitat degradation and the presence of nonnative species are often cited as the major contributors to loss of freshwater biodiversity, for example, fish diversity (Jelks et al. 2008; Magurran 2009).

EFFECTS OF CATCHMENT LAND-USE CHANGE

CATCHMENT DISTURBANCE SYNDROMES

The cumulative geomorphological, hydrological, and ecological impacts of deforestation, timber harvesting, agricultural development, urbanization, land drainage, and flood protection on rivers and wetlands have been widely documented (Welcomme 1985, Davies and Walker 1986; Allan 2004). Agricultural land use alone may adversely affect freshwater ecosystems by removal or reduction of catchment and riparian vegetation, altered patterns of runoff and groundwater recharge, increased soil erosion and sedimentation, elevated nutrient levels, and influx of agricultural chemicals (Gregory et al. 1991; Matson et al. 1997; Allan 2004). Because this suite of impacts tends to arise in irrigated agricultural landscapes where dams guarantee water supply, it has been dubbed the "irrigation syndrome" (Petts and Calow 1996). For many unimpounded rivers and wetlands, it is these land-use activities, rather than dams, that are the primary causes of altered flow regimes and their effects on ecosystems (Poff et al. 1997).

DEFORESTATION AND AGRICULTURE

Removal of natural forest vegetation and the conversion of forests or grasslands to agricultural lands generally decrease soil infiltration and often result in increased overland flow, channel incision, and headward erosion of stream channels (Poff et al. 2006a). Combined with extensive draining of wetlands or overgrazing, these land-use practices reduce retention of water in catchment soils and, instead, route it quickly downstream, increasing the size and frequency of floods and reducing baseflow levels during dry periods (Leopold 1968; Poff et al. 1997). These changes increase temporal variation of abiotic factors and often degrade water and stream habitat quality (Campbell and Doeg 1989). More unpredictable and flashy flood regimes, faster rise and fall of water levels, and lower dry-season flows are potentially detrimental to many species of invertebrates and fish adapted to particular patterns of flow variability (Welcomme 1985; Pusey et al. 1993).

Following timber harvesting, dissolved nutrients leached from organic debris and soils usually increase, and dissolved oxygen depletion may also result from the decay of slash vegetation and other organic debris (Campbell and Doeg 1989). Over time, these effects degrade channel habitats for aquatic species, particularly when riparian functions are also lost through vegetation clearance or damage caused by grazing animals. High silt loads characterize many rivers that drain heavily populated areas and regions where agricultural malpractice and deforestation have denuded land, increasing runoff and soil loss.

Increased sediment loads tend to accelerate the natural erosion/deposition processes that normally conserve the dynamic equilibrium of floodplain systems, and this increased instability can be detrimental for aquatic plant communities, invertebrates, and fish (Welcomme 1985). Suspended sediments (turbidity) directly interfere with light penetration and may reduce the depth to which phytoplankton can develop or may shade out floating and submerged aquatic plants and filamentous algae; losses of primary producers and plant biomass may result in less shelter and food for aquatic biota (Bruton 1985; Wood and Armitage 1997). Decreases in plant biomass can bring about reductions in abundance of herbivorous fish and other species (Henley et al. 2000). Suspended matter may also reduce the visibility of pelagic food resources to fish and may influence the feeding efficiency and assemblage structure of predatory species, particularly visual piscivores (Rodriguez and Lewis 1997).

Settled sediments may smother productive benthic substrates and spawning sites and may clog fine structures such as fish gill rakers and filaments. These impacts generally affect fish breeding success, egg and larval survival, growth, population size, and age structure (Bruton 1985) and the diversity and composition of fish assemblages.

Urban development associated with human population expansion across catchment landscapes creates vast areas of impermeable surfaces that direct water away from subsurface pathways to overland flow, into drains and often into the nearest stream or wetland. Extensive use of storm drains and pipes is a feature of many urbanizing catchments, and such conduits often completely bypass riparian zones by channeling large amounts of water from impervious surfaces directly into streams. Consequently, stream flows increase in velocity and become more flashy and unpredictable; and floods increase in frequency and intensity (Walsh et al. 2005). Stream incision, or "downcutting" (Fig. 19), results from large volumes of water scouring out sediment that has accumulated during agricultural activity and/or residential construction in the catchment (Groffman et al. 2003).

Stream incision and reduced infiltration in impervious urban uplands can reduce riparian groundwater levels and disturb soil moisture levels, soil type, organic-matter content, and the structure and functions of the riparian ecosystem, for example, the role of the riparian zone in regulating nitrogen fluxes from upland catchments to streams (Pinay et al. 2002; see also Chapter 4). Groffman et al. (2002) observed high levels of NO_3^- and nitrification and low rates of denitrification in aerobic, urban riparian soil profiles with deep water tables compared to forested riparian soils with shallow water tables. Changes in surface water and groundwater hydrology in turn influence the vegetation of the riparian zone and its roles in regulating light, shade, and stream temperature; inputs of food resources (leaf litter, flowers and pollen, insects) to the stream food web; and provision of woody debris to create stream habitat (Bunn et al. 1997; Pusey and Arthington 2003).

The riparian corridors of many urban streams have become infested with exotic grasses, shrubs, vines, and trees discarded by homeowners or escaped from gardens and parklands (Werren and Arthington 2002). Increased biomass of exotic aquatic vegetation (such as ponded pasture grasses and floating-leaved plants) can alter stream flows, channel morphology, and water quality; degrade the open water and littoral habitats of fish and invertebrates; and disrupt the entire aquatic food web (Arthington et al. 1983; Bunn et al. 1997). Animals and avifauna associ-

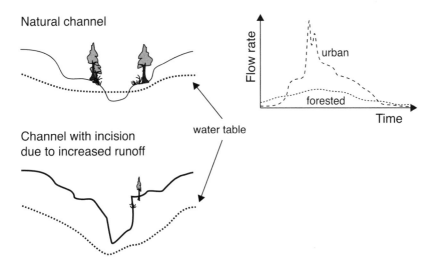

Natural channel

Channel with incision
due to increased runoff

water table

FIGURE 19. Conceptual diagram showing incised stream channel and reduced riparian groundwater levels in an urban catchment compared to a forested catchment. (Adapted from Figure 3 in Groffman et al. 2003, with permission from the Ecological Society of America)

ated with riparian zones can also be affected by riparian loss, fragmentation, and compositional changes (Groom and Grubb 2002; Marzliff and Ewing 2008).

Some of the ecological consequences of more flashy stream flows are likely to be enhanced rates of invertebrate drift and decline in benthic diversity and also the food resources of fish. The cumulative effects of urban development are particularly apparent in the lower reaches of rivers and their floodplains, often the prime sites for urban, metropolitan, and industrial development (e.g., Davie et al. 1990). Increased runoff from hardened surfaces, and the conveyance of diffuse urban pollutants from properties, streets, fuel stations, and industries, can severely degrade urban streams, rivers, and receiving estuaries. The combined effects of toxicants (salt, nutrients, metals, pesticides, other organic compounds) and secondarily treated (or untreated) sewage have severe effects on the diversity and abundance of stream biota (Arthington et al. 1983; Allan 2004).

Changes in catchment land use, channelization, and urbanization can alter the energy budget and thermal capacity of a stream or river and also its flow regime, and these two processes may have synergistic effects. Streams and rivers are generally well mixed and turbulent, so they respond readily to changes in atmospheric temperature conditions and can become warmer (Kaushal et al. 2010). Loss of catchment vegetation and riparian cover can expose streams to sunlight and heating, and high summer temperatures combined with low summer flows tend to exacerbate increases in water temperature (Nelson et al. 2009). Changes outside the natural range of flow or temperature variability may have severe consequences for aquatic species and ecosystem functions, depending on the rate of change in temperature or discharge relative to the adaptive capacity of species (Olden and Naiman 2010).

EFFECTS OF RIVER-CORRIDOR ENGINEERING

DISTURBANCE SYNDROMES

Direct physical interventions in river corridors are undertaken to provide flood control; to improve drainage, navigation, and access (bridge building and walkways); to offer opportunities for various industrial and economic pursuits; and to create recreation opportunities (motorized boating, swimming, angling). Corridor engineering implies a degree of control over stream flows and channel and bank form; such alteration may involve the barring of the channel, either transversely by weirs and dams or longitudinally by levees, bank revetments, dikes, and other structures (Welcomme 1985). Widening, straightening, and deepening as well as clearing and removal of large woody debris may also be involved (Brookes 1988).

CHANNELIZATION

Dams and water diversions affect rivers of virtually all sizes; land-use impacts are particularly evident in upper catchment areas and stream headwaters, whereas lowland rivers are far more influenced by activities that sever channel-floodplain linkages (Poff et al. 1997). Flood-control projects have shortened, narrowed, straightened, and leveed many river systems and have cut the main channels off from their floodplains (Welcomme 1985). There is a long history of river channelization throughout the world, extending back at least 2,000 years in Britain and longer for early societies established along rivers.

Channels of the Mississippi River and its tributaries, for example, have been modified by at least 27 locks and dams, as well as dikes, bank revetments, and dredging, largely to facilitate navigation (Smart et al. 1986). Loss of gravel deposits and slow-moving side channels used for spawning has been a major factor in the decline of the pallid sturgeon *(Scaphirhynchus albus)*, the first fish species in the Mississippi River drainage to be listed as endangered. Channelization of the Kissimmee River above Lake Okeechobee, Florida, by the US Army Corps of Engineers is another prominent example, not least because a major restoration program has restored wetland habitat and ecosystem values. The original 166 km meandering river with floodplains that were 1.5 to 3 km wide was turned into a 90 km long canal flowing through a series of five impoundments, resulting in great loss of river channel habitat and adjacent floodplain wetlands (Toth 1995).

LEVEE BANKS

Levees are designed to prevent increases in the lateral expansion of river flows onto their natural floodplains, so rivers constrained to narrower flow paths typically respond by cutting deeper channels, reaching higher velocities, or both. Rivers with levees are vulnerable to occasional but inevitable large floods that cannot be held back and that eventually inundate floodplains reclaimed for agriculture and human settlement. Large floods impose enormous damage and disaster costs on society (Freitag et al. 2009). For example, the main stem of the Mississippi River and many of its tributaries are narrowly confined by levees, and much of the damage caused by extensive flooding along the river in 1993 resulted from levee failure. In 2008, another massive flood in the Upper Mississippi Basin caused US$2 billion in flood damage. Even though buildings were removed from tens of thousand of acres of floodplain after the 1993 flood, creating open space for floodwaters to spread and wetlands to rejuvenate, new levees were constructed, new developments went ahead, and the levees failed again (Freitag et al. 2009).

The severing of floodplains from rivers curtails the processes of sediment erosion and deposition that regulate the topographic diversity of floodplains. Floods of varying intensity and frequency interact with geomorphic features to form a diversity of landforms with different disturbance histories (Nilsson and Svedmark 2002). This diversity is essential for maintaining species diversity on floodplains, where relatively small differences in land elevation result in large differences in annual inundation and soil moisture regimes, which regulate different stages of vegetation succession and plant diversity, distribution, and abundance.

In large tropical floodplain rivers, the lateral expansion of floodplain habitats during the predictable annual flood pulse of long duration creates important spawning, nursery, and foraging areas for invertebrates and many fish species and a variety of other vertebrates (Junk et al. 1989). Reducing the extent and duration of river flooding, or cutting off floodplain access completely, has major implications for the diversity and productivity of riparian vegetation, fish, and wildlife in tropical, temperate, and arid-zone rivers (Welcomme 1985; Kingsford et al. 2006).

DEGRADATION OF RIPARIAN CORRIDORS

A healthy, diverse riparian vegetation corridor is universally recognized as a key factor in stream and river functioning (Cummins 1993; Naiman and Décamps 1997; Nilsson and Svedmark 2002). The loss of the riparian vegetation corridor, with its highly diverse plant communities, can result in loss of its buffering role and increased bank instability, followed by erosion and interference in vital ecological processes of energy flow and food web dynamics (Bunn et al. 1997). Overgrazing in riparian corridors, involving high densities of animals over prolonged periods, may degrade streamside vegetation, particularly ground cover, and cause trampling and soil compaction instability, and erosion of riverbanks; high nutrient and soil inputs; and the introduction and spread of exotic weeds. Impacts on rivers frequently involve degraded water quality, increased sedimentation, silting of water holes and infilling of coarse stream substrates, reduced water quantity, and loss of habitat both in the channel and within the riparian zone (King and Warburton 2007).

Riparian vegetation and wetland areas naturally provide a large contact area between water and soils that promotes nitrogen retention and processing, thereby regulating fluxes from upland catchments to streams (Pinay et al. 2002). The efficiency of a riparian zone in regulating nitrogen fluxes is not simply a function of the surface area of the riparian zone, but rather a function of the hydrological length of contact between the riparian zone and the upland drainage basin (Haycock and Pinay 1993). During high water periods, the extension of the wetted area increases laterally from the stream and extends farther upstream, while during low water periods, the wetted area shrinks in width and decreases in length upstream. Riparian zones associated with small upland streams develop a more intimate wetland-upland interface than riparian zones along larger rivers and better contribute to mitigating diffuse pollution from the catchment (Peterson et al. 2001).

Vegetation clearing in upland catchments, removal of riparian vegetation, and channelization reduce the spatial extent of wetted areas, infiltration rates, and the duration of riparian soil saturation (Worrall and Burt 1998). Straightening river channels, dredging riverbeds, and the clogging of interstitial spaces by fine sediments also reduce the size of the hyporheic zone and its exchange rates with surface water, thereby affecting the nutrient recycling capacity of the stream and many other processes associated with the hyporheic zone (Boulton and Hancock 2006). As a consequence, these human-driven alterations reduce the ability of the river network to efficiently mitigate diffuse nutrient pollution (Pinay et al. 2002).

Alterations to the amount and type of riparian vegetation can affect shading, water temperature, the light environment, and in-stream primary production (Bunn 1993). In forested headwater catchments, riparian litter inputs provide energy to aquatic food webs through the biological processing of terrestrial energy sources by microbes and invertebrates (reducing coarse particulate organic matter to fine). The loss of riparian energy sources will rebound on stream invertebrate and fish communities along the river continuum (Vannote et al. 1980). Farther downstream, the food web is usually more dependent on in-stream primary production by algae and plants; these too are vulnerable to altered flows, sedimentation, shading, and nutrient enrichment (Bunn et al. 1997; Groffman et al. 2003).

LARGE WOODY DEBRIS

Changes in deposition rates of large woody debris (LWD) derived from riparian trees and shrubs affect invertebrates and fish that depend on logs and litter for refuge from thermal extremes and protection from predators and also as safe spawning sites (Pusey and Arthington 2003). Fish and aquatic invertebrates often decline after LWD removal and increase locally in response to LWD additions (Lyon et al. 2009; Howell et al. 2012). Removal of LWD from rivers to improve navigation for river transport and trade has a long and devastating history for the riverine ecosystems of many countries. For example, more than 5,500 drifted trees ranging from 5 to 9 ft in diameter and 90 to 120 ft in length were removed from a 55 mi stretch of the Willamette River, Oregon; the river was later confined to one channel by engineers (Maser and Sedell 1994). Today, salmon-enhancement programs in much of the western United States and Canada are replacing wood by direct reintroduction or by leaving large trees growing alongside streams for future supply of timber to waterways.

In Australia between 1870 and 1970, millions of pieces of LWD were removed from the Murray-Darling river system to facilitate navigation of riverboats (Phillips 1972). Toward the end of this period, water authorities removed submerged wood in the expectation that this would improve water conveyance and the efficiency of rivers as the source of water for irrigation (Gippel et al. 1996). The reintroduction of woody debris to restore fish and invertebrate habitat is becoming common practice in Australian rivers that were "de-snagged" in the past (Erskine and Webb 2003; Brooks et al. 2006).

6

HISTORY OF WATER CONTROL
AND DAM IMPACTS

HISTORY OF WATER CONTROL

Human activities have modified the natural hydrologic and ecological processes of catchments and rivers, wetlands, floodplains, and estuaries for thousands of years (Boon et al. 1992). Early hunter-gatherer societies drew upon the natural resources of rivers and floodplains, their riparian corridors, and the surrounding areas for water, food, and shelter (Freitag et al. 2009). Fishing and hunting activities were closely attuned to the seasonal cycles of climate and river flows and to the plants and animals adapted to those natural cycles. Various devices were used to catch fish (nets, stone traps, fish wheels, spears, and hooks) and to capture wildlife for food, hides, and bones.

Hunter-gatherer societies also used fire to herd animals while hunting and to open up and convert forest and shrubland to grassland habitats used by grazing animals. One of the effects of this was undoubtedly to reduce riparian forests and floodplain vegetation (Di Stefano 2001). Some societies constructed simple bark canoes and used the rivers and estuaries for transport, hunting, communication, and trade with other groups. Apart from these activities, impacts on river catchments and their riparian and aquatic resources were relatively minor (Freitag et al. 2009). In some parts of the world, large reptiles, mammals, and birds disappeared at about the same time that humans settled and hunted for food. Whether these declines were partly due to climatic events (e.g., retreat of the last continental ice sheets between 10,000 and 12,000 years ago) and disease as well as hunting pressure is still debated (Stringer and McKie 1996).

Among the species eliminated in North America were large beavers (Freitag et al. 2009). These animals cut down riparian trees and large branches with their teeth, gnaw sticks for food, build dams across streams, and excavate canals and banks into bank dens. The barriers formed by beaver dams change surface water and groundwater levels, affect water quality, and influence the local evolution of rivers and their floodplains (Andersen and Shafroth 2010). The presence of beavers, and their demise in many areas, undoubtedly affected channel properties and the riverine landscape, so much so that attempts are being made to restore beaver populations and provide for their environmental flow requirements (Shafroth et al. 2010).

The earliest forms of human civilization emerged around 6,000–8,000 years ago along river valleys and on floodplains of the Tigris, Euphrates, Nile, and Indus Rivers. Access to water and the skills to manipulate and control water resources for human benefit were essential to cultivate food and fiber crops for large groups of people. These "hydraulic societies" (Worster 1985) began to develop social and political organizations that eventually led to the first settled cities, such as Ur on the Euphrates River. Along with the Tigris River, the Euphrates provided much of the water that supported the cultures of ancient Mesopotamia ("the land between the rivers"). Low rainfall and high temperatures in the floodplains of southern Mesopotamia made irrigation systems essential for crop production. The earliest form was probably not the irrigation canal but floodwater dammed up in basins near to crop fields. Canals were later built to transport river water when land and crops produced in the vicinity of the river could no longer supply the needs of growing populations. Remnants of those ancient canal systems can still be seen today.

Historians believe that Mesopotamian irrigation systems were also the downfall of that early era of human civilization, because constant irrigation brought salts to the surface of alluvial soils, and soil salinities rose until crop production was no longer possible. Wheat was replaced with more salt-tolerant barley until that too could no longer be cultivated. Similar problems with soil salinization abound today in many irrigated landscapes (Ghassemi and White 2007).

Small communities living in arid regions of the Middle East, central Asia and North Africa developed a system for conveying water from underground springs in distant, wetter hill regions to their lowland villages and fields (Pearce 2007). These *qanats* (from the Semitic word "to dig") consisted of a series of wells dug by hand and connected at their base to underground tunnels leading straight to a mother well that collected water from a groundwater spring in the foothills. Some tunnels were up to 45 km long, sloping gently so that gravity provided conveyance of water from the spring source to cultivated fields and villages. In modern Iran there are 22,000 *qanats*, representing more than 250,000 km of underground tunnels and supplying 75% of the nation's fresh water (Cech 2010). Similar tunnel and well systems developed in Afghanistan, Pakistan, and western China, where they are called *karez*.

The Romans constructed water-delivery systems made from baked clay and lead piping leading from underground storage cisterns at higher elevations near their cities; the water was delivered to public fountains and baths and the homes of a few private citizens (Cech 2010). Aqueducts were first built around 312 BC and provided water to Rome; water was also used to flush sewage into the Tiber River. Romans built immense canals to drain lakes and wetlands and provide fertile soils for cultivation.

In China, drought and severe flooding drove the development of water-engineering technologies along the Yellow River, so named for its very high silt loads carried down from the Qinghai-Tibetan plateau. Devastating floods have killed tens of thousands of people living along rivers, so preventing catastrophic floods has been a major concern throughout Chinese history (Jiang et al. 2010). Levees were constructed on smaller tributaries of the Yellow River more than 2,500 years ago to control floods, and some were used to divert water into enemy villages, a kind of water warfare (Cech 2010). Repeated efforts to control flooding by raising the height of levee banks have contributed to a "suspended" river in which the channel bottom is above ground level, sometimes by more than 10 m (Leung 1996).

Early water-engineering technologies involved simple wells, tunnels, pipes, cisterns, *qanats*, canals of ever-increasing width and length, and aqueducts. Early civilizations also constructed dikes and levee banks and barriers made of earth, rocks, logs, and weeds to redirect water for flood control and provide water for irrigation. Larger dams eventually became a fundamental water-management technology to control, regulate, and deliver water collected during wet cycles for use during dry cycles; to provide water for a multitude of human uses; to generate electricity; for flood control; to store mine tailings; to foster fish and wildlife; and for recreation (WCD 2000).

DAMS AND DAM STATISTICS

While the contribution of dams to human development has been enormous, their effects on biodiversity, ecosystems, and the ecological goods and services provided to people and societies are of growing concern (WCD 2000; MEA 2005). In 1935, the Hoover Dam in Black Canyon on the Colorado River near Las Vegas, Nevada, became the world's first megadam. Lake Mead, behind the dam, is the largest artificial lake in the United States. It has an enormous catchment (drainage basin), with almost 10% of the entire land area of the United States draining into Lake Mead. The dam rises 221 m above bedrock and is capable of storing 36.7 billion m^3 of water, more then twice the Colorado River's annual flow (Cech 2010). Many more large dams soon followed on almost every continent. In 1989, river scientists reported that 500 high dams (>15 m) were being built every year, and in Europe alone large dams greater than 150 m high were built at a rate of 1 every 1.65 years (Gore and Petts 1989). In 1992, there were twenty-eight dams over 200 m high and as many were planned or under construction (Boon et al. 1992). Most of the world's big river systems, including the 20 largest and the 8 with highest biological diversity—the Amazon, Orinoco, Ganges, Brahmaputra, Zambezi, Amur, Yenisei, and Indus—have dams on them, with most of the dam-free rivers located in the empty Arctic tundra and northern boreal forests (Pearce 2007). Some of the world's largest rivers—such as the Nile in Egypt, the Colorado in the United States, the Yellow in China, and the Murray-Darling River system in Australia—as well as countless smaller ones, barely reach the sea now or have flow patterns so modified that the productivity of their estuaries and deltas has been severely reduced (Postel and Richter 2003; Pearce 2007).

In the second half of the twentieth century, the World Bank spent US\$75 billion on building large dams in 92 countries. Recent estimates suggest 50,000 high dams are in operation worldwide (Berga et al. 2006). These impoundments are estimated to have a cumulative storage capacity somewhere between 7,000 and 10,000 km³, the equivalent of five times the total volume of all the world's rivers (Vörösmarty et al. 2003; Chao et al. 2008). In addition, many smaller impoundments and farm dams are used for capturing and supplying water in grazing lands and irrigated areas, including several million small dams in the United States alone. Water impoundment by dams in the Northern Hemisphere is now so great that it has caused measurable geodynamic changes in the earth's rotation and gravitational field (Chao 1995).

Postel et al. (1996) predicted that by 2025, 70% of the available runoff from rivers will be appropriated for human use. When that was written in 1996, the figure for human use of river water was 54%, but the projected increase to 70% is staggering and may rise further under the pressure of increasing human populations, rising living standards, and expanding urbanization. Added to these increasing demands for freshwater are the effects of global climate change. Shifts in amounts and patterns of precipitation, evapotranspiration, and runoff, accompanied by more variable and extreme floods and drought, are expected to generate yet more water-engineering responses to ensure water security (Vörösmarty et al. 2004; Palmer et al. 2009). Some authorities believe it inevitable that more dams will be built or existing ones enlarged, even though there are many alternative options for water capture, storage, and management (see Chapters 19 and 20).

CATEGORIES OF DAM IMPACTS

The construction of a dam, weir, or barrage on a stream or river has three major types of impact on the river's biota and the functioning of the aquatic ecosystem: upstream, barrier, and downstream impacts. General concepts of the physical, chemical, and biological changes associated with dams are well established from historical compilations (e.g., Ward and Stanford 1979, 1983; Davies and Walker 1986; Craig and Kemper 1987; Petts et al. 1989), reviews (Boon et al. 1992; Poff et al. 1997; Naiman et al. 1995, 2008), global data analyses (Nilsson et al. 2005; Poff and Zimmerman 2010), and many accounts of individual dam-related changes. In the following sections of this chapter, the upstream and barrier effects of dams are described and illustrated, drawing on the hydroecological principles discussed in Chapter 4. The downstream impacts of dams are discussed in Chapters 7 and 8.

UPSTREAM EFFECTS OF DAMS

Dams and modified flow regimes alter habitat at varying spatial scales and influence the distribution and abundance of species and the composition and diversity of aquatic communities (Bunn and Arthington 2002). Upstream effects on natural riverine habitat represent one of the major habitat impacts of dams. In these newly inundated upstream areas, riverine habitat is replaced by lake-like habitat, with lake area, volume, basin shape, and other features depending on valley morphology, dam height, and storage characteristics.

It is often argued that the loss of riverine habitat associated with dams is balanced by the creation of lacustrine habitat; however, natural lakes and wetlands often function in a very different way than river impoundments (Bunn and Arthington 2002). In lakes and wetlands, much of the carbon and nutrient flux associated with primary production occurs in the littoral margins (Wetzel 1990). Large impoundments are generally not operated at a constant water level. They fluctuate daily, seasonally, or annually depending largely on the reservoir's purpose and therefore diverse, productive littoral areas are rarely sustained. Furthermore, impoundment water levels are usually significantly elevated above natural streambed levels, flooding part of the terrestrial-aquatic interface and creating a new littoral zone with steeper banks, less complex aquatic habitat, and different physicochemical conditions for aquatic plants and animals (Walker et al. 1992). Water levels have a direct effect on benthos, periphyton, and aquatic plant abundance; increases in water level that inundate lush vegetation temporarily increase the supply of food and cover for fish whereas extensive drawdown concentrates fish and can increase the foraging efficiency of predators.

Weirs have transformed the Lower River Murray in southern Australia into a chain of cascading locks and elongated pools, supplanting most of the riverine environment with pool habitats (Walker et al. 1992). This massive loss of river habitat has affected the distribution of the Murray crayfish *(Euastacus armatus),* now listed as endangered, and several species of riverine and wetland snails have declined, one possibly near to extinction. Relatively stable water levels have encouraged the invasion of bulrushes (*Typha* spp.), water hyacinth *(Eichhornia crassipes)* and other exotic plants in rivers and wetlands lacking their normal wet–dry cycles (Kingsford 2000).

New impoundments are frequently stocked with fish to support subsistence as well as recreational fishing. Fish introductions are not always beneficial in the long term because often the species stocked are exotic and have damaging effects on the riverine ecosystem and its native fauna (Canonico et al. 2005; Strayer 2010). Exotic fish and invertebrate species introduced for other purposes, and escapees from the aquarium industry, can also colonize impoundments. For example, the introduced Mozambique mouthbrooder, or tilapia *(Oreochromis mossambicus),* thrives in the impoundments behind large dams in Africa, Sri Lanka, and Australia (Arthington and Blühdorn 1994). This tilapia has flexible habitat and dietary requirements and an ability to breed early at small body sizes under harsh environmental conditions; it employs parental care of eggs and young; and introduced populations tend to increase and spread to other waterways (Canonico et al. 2005). Concern about the potential impacts of *O. mossambicus* on the vulnerable Australian lungfish (*Neoceratodus forsteri*) contributed to the recent decision not to proceed with the proposed Traveston Dam on the Mary River, Queensland (Arthington 2009).

There are many examples of large-scale and dramatic effects of exotic species on indigenous species (e.g., Nile perch, *Lates niloticus,* in Lake Victoria; the crayfish plague in Europe; salmonids in Southern Hemisphere lakes and streams). The impact of exotics on indigenous species and ecosystem processes, and their interactions with other stressors in aquatic ecosystems, are projected to increase further (Strayer 2010). As an example, the Colorado River is regulated by hundreds of impoundments varying in area from less than 1 ha in high-altitude headwaters to more than 650 km² in lowland channel segments (Stanford and Ward 1986a). Conversion of one-quarter of the Colorado River to lake-like habitat has resulted in the loss of fish adapted to turbid riverine habitats. In addition, numerous introductions of highly competitive exotic fishes (more than 50 species), many thriving in impoundments and regulated river reaches, have contributed to the extirpation of native fishes in the Colorado River; most of the native big-river fish face extinction (Stanford and Ward 1986b). In the headwaters of the upper basin, the range of the Colorado River cutthroat trout *(Oncorhynchus clarkii pleuriticus)* is limited to a few isolated populations, and nearly all of the endemic desert-stream fish are in severe decline.

Emissions of greenhouse gases—carbon dioxide (CO_2) and methane (CH_4)—from impoundments as a result of the immersion and decay of biomass and soil organic matter have recently received attention. Rates of emission depend on water depth, residence times, temperature, influx of organic matter from the catchment, primary productivity within the water body, age of the impoundment, and its operating regime (McCartney 2009).

BARRIER EFFECTS OF DAMS ON FISH

The construction of barriers across streams and rivers to create water storage results in discontinuities in the river continuum (Ward and Stanford 1995) and leads inevitably to loss of longitudinal (and often also lateral) connectivity in flowing waters (Bunn and Arthington 2002). Although there are engineering solutions to the barrier effects of dams (fish-bypass facilities, locks, ladders, and elevators), they seldom restore the original capacity of a river system to allow free movement of biota through the basin network (Lucas and Baras 2001). Dams in tropical regions are generally constructed without appropriate fishways or fish passes; or fishways are based on designs that are suitable only for salmonids, and thus they obstruct the migrations of fish with different swimming speeds and other behavioral capacities (Roberts 2001).

Fish and other animals (from shrimp to river dolphins) use different habitats at different times, and longitudinal migrations may be an obligatory component of life histories, especially if migration is associated with breeding. Longitudinal migrations may occur within a river, or from river to sea or lake and back, or from sea or lake to river and back (Dudgeon et al. 2006). Long-lived species with low reproductive rates are likely to be the most vulnerable to barriers (Carolsfeld et al. 2004). For example, the Yangtze sturgeon *(Acipenser dabryanus)* and the Mekong River's giant catfish *(Pangasianodon gigas)* are threatened by barriers to movement as well as overfishing (Hogan et al. 2004; Wei et al.

2004). The presence of an impassable barrier can lead to isolation of populations, failed recruitment, reduced gene flow, and local extinction of fish and other aquatic biota (Hughes et al. 2009; Northcote 2010). Diadromous fishes, which migrate long distances within the main channels and larger tributaries of rivers (and to and from oceans), are particularly sensitive to barriers to longitudinal passage, because obstruction of their migratory pathways may interfere with the completion of the life cycle (McDowall 2006). The introduction of barriers to migration has caused population declines in important commercial and recreational species worldwide (e.g., salmonids, sturgeon, paddlefish, and clupeids). Migratory species such as shad, lamprey, and eels have disappeared from the Rhone River in France and the Guadalquivir River in Spain (Reyes-Gavilan et al. 1996). Two examples of the effects of dams on fish migrations are given in Table 22.

The effects of dams on migratory fish vary with the position of an impoundment within the river system's catchment. Barriers to movement situated in low-lying parts of catchments may cause isolation or extirpation of all or most upstream migratory species. The prevention of species with an obligate marine phase in their life cycles from moving to and from the sea has the potential to impact upstream portions of the river by, for example, disrupting the nutrient transmission that occurs during spawning migrations of anadromous salmon, which gain more than 95% of their biomass in the open ocean (e.g., Naiman et al. 2002; Pringle 2001).

A series of barrages and dams starting at the estuary-freshwater interface and built at intervals along the lower reaches of a large river may progressively filter out migratory species. A large dam in the headwaters of a river system can affect the flow regime of the entire river and disrupt dispersal right to the dam wall by altering cues to movement and the availability of suitable depths and velocities for fish passage. In highly fragmented rivers with many dams, only small portions of previously large, viable populations may remain. Isolating fish in short stream fragments increases the chances that random environmental events such as a severe drought will extirpate these populations from the basin (Rieman and McIntyre 1995). Thus, even if a species is still present after river regulation, it may be more vulnerable to local extinction events (Renöfält et al. 2010), and its isolation because of

TABLE 22 *Effects of dams on migratory pathways of North American fish*

Species	Effects
American shad	The anadromous American shad *(Alosa sapidissima)* ranges from the St. Lawrence River, Canada, to the St. Johns River, Florida (Limburg et al. 2003). From their overwintering grounds on the Scotian Shelf, the St. Lawrence population undertakes an annual spring migration of approximately 2,000 km to reach its spawning grounds in the vicinity of Montreal, Quebec. This population has suffered severe reductions since the late nineteenth century, mainly from exploitation during the spring migration and the construction of multiple hydroelectric dams in the vicinity of Montreal and in the Ottawa River. Given the low abundance of the population through much of the twentieth century, the loss of potentially significant spawning grounds upstream of contemporary dams, and the fact that only two spawning areas are presently known (Daigle et al. 2010), American shad is one of eleven species listed as vulnerable under Quebec legislation on threatened and endangered species.
Chinook salmon and steelhead	Snake River spring and summer chinook salmon *(Oncorhynchus tshawytscha)* and steelhead *(Oncorhynchus mykiss)* populations declined dramatically in the 1970s, coinciding with development and operation of the Federal Columbia River Power System (FCRPS). Both species are listed as threatened under the US Endangered Species Act. Juvenile salmon and steelhead migrating from Snake River spawning streams to the ocean must pass through eight large hydroelectric dams and 522 km of slack water. Dams slow flow velocities and the outmigration rate of smolts to the estuary, with a range of consequences: exposure to predation and higher temperatures during migration, increasing energetic costs, and poorly timed entry to the estuary relative to a smolt's physiological state and to the environmental conditions during early ocean residence. Recommendations to enhance smolt migrations involve several mechanisms (spills from dams, higher water velocity) to reduce fish travel time through the FCRPS (Petrosky and Schaller 2010).

habitat fragmentation may inhibit recolonization from previously connected river basins (Falke et al. 2010).

The impact of barriers on mobile organisms is not confined to very large structures. Even small in-stream barriers, such as v-notch gauging weirs, can impede the movement of fish, for example, the western minnow *(Galaxias occidentalis)* in forest streams in southwestern Australia (Pusey et al. 1989).

BARRIER EFFECTS OF DAMS ON INVERTEBRATES

Invertebrates as well as fish can be affected by barriers to upstream movement. For example, damming of the lower reaches of one of the main drainages of the Caribbean National Forest in Puerto Rico has had a major impact on shrimp recruitment. More than 50% of migrating larvae were drawn into water intakes for municipal supplies, and juvenile shrimp returning upstream faced severe predation below the dam (Pringle and Scatena 1999). Cessation of water abstraction during evening periods of peak nocturnal larval drift, upkeep of a functional fish ladder, and maintenance of a minimum flow could significantly reduce impacts of the dam and its operations.

The dispersal of unionid (pearly) mussels is likely to be affected by the many barriers to fish movement in freshwater systems, since these mussels produce specialized larvae (glochidia) that become obligate more-or-less species-specific parasites of fish (Strayer 2008). Once attached to the fish host, the larvae encyst and transform into juveniles; they persist in this parasitic phase for days to months, this period providing their main opportunity to disperse as passengers on their mobile hosts. Barriers to fish movement, and fish movements beyond their native range by human activities (stocking, interbasin transfers of water; see Chapter 8), probably greatly affect the dispersal of unionid mussels with particular host dependencies (Strayer 2008). For these and many other reasons, unionid mussels are believed to be much more threatened than most other freshwater organisms (Strayer et al. 2004).

BARRIER EFFECTS OF DAMS ON RIVER
TRANSPORT MECHANISMS

Rivers play important roles as corridors for the transport of water, sediments, organic matter, chemicals, and living organisms, from seeds to large woody debris and even whole trees (Nilsson and Svedmark 2002). In free-flowing rivers, floating plant propagules are rapidly transported far downstream during floods. When dams disrupt the longitudinal pathway of normal river flows, plant dispersal by hydrochory is reduced and plant communities can become fragmented (Nilsson et al. 2010). In Sweden, for example, 9 of 13 major river channels have been converted to stairs of lake-like water bodies interrupted by dams and underground passages (Jansson et al. 2000b). In river reaches between dams, the regulated riparian zones harbor fewer vascular plant species than free-flowing rivers, and the dispersal process is difficult to restore without opening or removing the dams.

In impounded rivers, current velocity is often low and floating plant propagules either sink or become swept ashore by winds (Jansson et al. 2000a); this reduces the normal travel distances of seeds and alters the distribution of species along the riparian zone. Very few plant propagules pass dams through turbines or spillways because openings to passageways are usually missed; however, seeds with long floating times have a greater probability of successful passage downstream. Given that dams regulate most of the world's rivers, floristic disruptions of riparian corridors may be a global phenomenon (Nilsson and Svedmark 2002), with many ecological consequences for river biota and ecosystem functions (e.g., Pusey and Arthington 2003).

7

EFFECTS OF DAMS ON SEDIMENT, THERMAL, AND CHEMICAL REGIMES

DAM OPERATIONS AND DOWNSTREAM EFFECTS

Dams are the most obvious direct modifiers of river flow because they capture both low and high flows and can alter the entire flow regime in many different ways. Modification of the natural flow regime dramatically affects sediment dynamics and channel morphology, nutrient transformations and other chemical conditions, thermal regime, habitat structure, and recruitment of both aquatic and riparian species in streams and rivers worldwide (Poff et al. 1997; Naiman et al. 2008). Ecological responses to altered flow regimes in a specific stream or river depend on how the five basic components of a flow regime have changed relative to the natural flow regime for that particular stream or river (Poff and Ward 1990) and how specific geomorphic and ecological processes respond to this relative change (Arthington et al. 2006; Graf 2006). As a result of variation in flow regime within and among rivers (see Chapters 2 and 3), the same human activity in different locations may cause different degrees of change relative to unaltered conditions and, therefore, have different ecological consequences (Poff and Zimmerman 2010).

DAM OPERATIONS

Every dam captures, stores and releases water in its own particular way depending on its climatic and catchment setting, purpose, design, and mode of operation. Just under 50% of the 50,000 large dams constructed globally since the 1950s support irrigation. Many others provide domestic and industrial water supply as well as flood protection, while many more generate hydropower and a great many are used for recreation (boating, fishing). In many cases a single dam supports many of these functions (ICOLD 2003).

For example, the Aswan High Dam, built on the River Nile in the early 1960s, provides water for Egypt's agriculture (approximately 2.5 million ha) and from 1979 to 1988 protected Egypt from prolonged drought, as well as greatly reducing the impact of severe flooding in 1973 and 1988. The reservoir also supplies the domestic and industrial water requirements of most of Egypt's 80 million people, generates electricity, and supports a fishing industry.

In the United States, more than 75,000 dams 2 m high or higher impound portions of every river basin in the country, and 137 of the very large dams (each storing 1.2 km³ of water or more) alter the flows of every large river (Graf 2006). On average, these very large dams reduce annual peak discharges by 67% (and up to 90% for some dams), decrease the ratio of the annual maximum to mean daily flow (a measure of flow variability) by 60%, decrease the range of daily flows by 64%, and increase the number of reversals of discharge by 34%. Daily rates of rise in water level are 60% less than for unregulated rivers on a national basis, probably reflecting the damping of natural flashy increases in discharge. The same dams also alter the seasonal timing of annual maximum and minimum flows by up to six months (Graf 2006).

Geographic differences in the effects of dams on river flow regimes reflect storage capacity relative to the mean annual water yield for the catchment, and therefore the degree of control of each impoundment over river hydrology. When the storage/yield ratio is greater than one, the dam can store the incoming flow for more than one year and will have a far greater impact on downstream flows than a storage with a ratio of less than one, exerting far less control over the annual inflow to the reservoir. In the latter case, even though such dams have little downstream hydrologic impact, they still trap sediments and influence downstream geomorphology, channel characteristics, and aquatic/floodplain habitats (Graf 2006).

The Flaming Gorge Dam on the Green River, a major tributary of the Colorado River in Utah, is one of the largest dams in the American

West. The dam stores water for the Colorado River Storage Project, which distributes water in the Upper Colorado Basin and also generates hydropower. The reservoir at Flaming Gorge is a popular recreation spot for fishing and also scuba diving, and below the dam the Green River is used for whitewater rafting. Before the Flaming Gorge Dam was completed in 1963 (see Fig. 1 in Lytle and Poff 2004), the river experienced floods from spring snowmelt and droughts during autumn and winter (October to March). Damming the river truncated these flow extremes, causing both floods and droughts to become less frequent and smaller in magnitude (Lytle and Poff 2004). The Colorado River presents almost every conceivable example of the ecological consequences of dams and flow regime alterations.

Dams built mainly for flood control are designed to hold the probable maximum flood for a region (Cech 2010). The water level in a flood-control dam is usually kept as low as possible (given other functions) in order to retain enough space to capture that probable maximum flood, or the lesser amounts of inflow generated by surface runoff during storm events or snowmelt. This stored water is released according to predetermined schedules, depending on the other purposes of the dam.

Irrigation dams are usually kept as full as possible until irrigation supplies are needed for the crops being grown downstream. When water is stored and released largely for irrigation purposes, the common outcome is disruption of the seasonal patterns of the natural flow regime, such that, in extreme cases, almost all high flows and potential floods are captured during the high-flow season and released downstream during the former low-flow season when there is little precipitation and crops need water. During the first part of the twentieth century, increasing demand for water for human settlements in Australia's Murray Valley led to the construction of the Hume Dam in 1934, Yarrawonga Weir in 1939, and Dartmouth Dam in 1978. These impoundments store winter and spring flows for release during summer and autumn (Maheshwari et al. 1995), effectively inverting the natural seasonal distribution of river flows (Fig. 20). This often results in elevated low flows and, in many instances, far more stable flow levels. The phenomenon of artificially elevated flows during the dry season in many agricultural catchments has been termed "anti-drought" (McMahon and Finlayson 2003). For a river to receive more water dur-

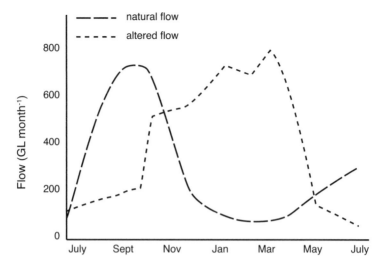

FIGURE 20. Seasonally inverted flow regime of the River Murray at Albury. (Adapted from MDBMC 1995)

ing a formerly dry period might sound like a beneficial outcome, but it generally has a range of adverse effects on aquatic and riparian species and ecosystem function (Poff et al. 1997; Bond et al. 2010).

Dams built to generate hydropower bring a different set of alterations to the natural flow regimes of rivers. Renöfält et al. (2010) review the main operational issues as follows:

> The purpose of hydroelectric dams and reservoirs is to provide hydraulic head and release water through turbines on a schedule that matches energy demands. Storage reservoirs help provide a better match between flow availability and power demand by storing water between seasons and years, and run-of-river impoundments serve to meet variation in electricity demand between days and nights. . . . Many rivers have storage reservoirs and hydropower stations in steep headwater reaches but no dams in flat downstream sections [Fig. 21b and d], leaving long reaches affected only by upstream dams. Rivers with a continuous slope from headwaters to coast can have cascades of hydropower installations all along their course, with no rapids remaining [Fig. 21a and c]. As a consequence, most of the river's length is made up of impoundments with slow flow and artificial water-level variation.

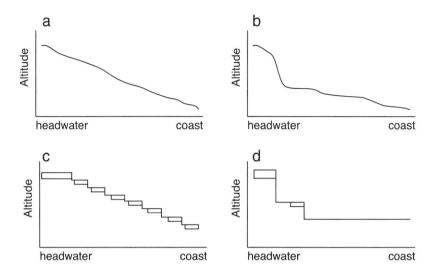

FIGURE 21. Schematic diagrams showing two types of river profile (a and b) and their development for hydropower (c and d). (Redrawn from Figure 1 in Renöfält et al. 2010, with permission from John Wiley and Sons).

Hydropower dams have their own unique suite of downstream consequences for river biota and ecosystem processes determined by operational procedures that can result in rapid daily flow fluctuations occurring at completely unnatural rates (Poff et al. 1997; Bunn and Arthington 2002).

CHANNEL PROCESSES AND SEDIMENT DYNAMICS BELOW DAMS

Geomorphic adjustments to channel shape and substrate characteristics in response to flow modification by dams usually involve contraction and degradation of the channel, planform adjustments, and the development of in-stream bars, benches, and islands accompanied by bed stabilization and bed armoring. Responses vary widely, depending on dam location, size and purpose, geomorphological context and river characteristics, dam release strategies and type of flow regulation, valley sediment characteristics and sediment availability, sediment transport post-impoundment, and specific stream power (Gregory 2006). The effects of dams may be complicated by channel responses to other geomorphic disturbances in catchments and river channels, such as deforestation, clearance of riparian vegetation, removal of timber from river beds (de-snagging), grazing, urbanization, channelization, levees, ditches and drainage schemes, sediment removal and addition, bridge crossings and culverts, motorized boating, invasion of exotic riparian and aquatic plants, and beaver removal (Gregory 2006).

Dams capture all but the finest sediments moving down a river and eventually start to infill impoundments with sediment. Sediment capture behind dams was recognized as a problem in the 1920s but was not addressed until the 1960s, when dams were designed with dead space to store sediments, thereby increasing their life expectancy (Petts and Gurnell 2005). For example, the lower 78 m of Lake Mead behind the Hoover Dam is allocated as dead storage for the containment of sediment (Cech 2010). In many cases the reduction in sediment load is greater than 70%; for example, in the Nile River 100% of the pre-dam sediment discharge has been lost to the river because of dams (Vörösmarty et al. 2003).

The amount of sediment-laden water released downstream varies with dam type and purpose: flood-control and hydropower dams release most of their stored water downstream and so retain their capacity to transport sediment, although the actual load is reduced by settlement in the impoundment. Below most irrigation and urban water-supply dams, the flow of the river is typically much reduced and so too is the sediment load, for example, by 100% for the Colorado River and by 96% for the Rio Grande in the United States (Walling 2006).

Storage of sediment-laden water within dams has many severe consequences for downstream river reaches and habitat structure, and these can extend all the way to the river mouth at its delta or estuary (Vörösmarty et al. 2003; Walling 2006). Sediment-depleted water released from dams can erode finer sediments from the receiving channel (clear-water erosion), causing channel incision and bed lowering (degradation); the process reflects an excess in flow energy, shear stress, or stream power (sediment-transporting capacity) relative to the amount of sediment supplied to the river (Simon and Rinaldi 2006). Degradation results in systematic lowering of the riverbed over a period of years and can affect long stream reaches, entire lengths of single streams, or the whole stream network; it is a "quintessential feature of a disequilibrated fluvial system" (Simon and Rinaldi 2006).

As river channels below dams erode and downcut, tributary erosion may be triggered and eroding tributaries may migrate headward, contributing an additional load of fine sediments downstream of a dam. As an example, channel degradation below the Missouri River's mainstem dams has caused the average bed elevation to drop by 10 ft or more for many miles downstream of Garrison Dam, and downward incision is occurring along many of the Missouri's tributaries. Tributary incision occurs because the slope of the tributary increases in order to meet the lowered elevation of the main channel.

Channel degradation below dams also disconnects the river from its floodplains because downcutting prevents river flows from reaching the elevation needed to overflow the banks and flood out of the channel. Lack of flooding also removes a source of periodic recharge water for infiltration to the groundwater table, and the lowered riverbed and flow level reduces the degree of recharge of the alluvial aquifer. This effectively drains water from oxbow lakes and wetlands. More stable water levels below dams alter the natural fluctuations in floodplain water-table depth that promote plant diversity on floodplains, because some species do best where the water table is high and others where it is low (Nilsson and Svedmark 2002).

Another effect of degradation by channel incision is to reduce the migration and meandering rate of the channel in its alluvial corridor. When a river can no longer migrate to its original extent, this restricts the development of meanders, oxbow lakes, and other side-channel and off-channel habitats that sustain riverine biodiversity. For example, with less flow in the river and with channel armoring, the mean annual meandering rate has been reduced from 25 ft per year to 6 ft just below Fort Peck Dam in the Missouri River basin (Shields et al. 2000). Reduced meandering rates in tributaries of the Missouri River have reduced the regeneration rate of cottonwoods (*Populus* spp.) (Johnson 1992).

Whether sediments released by downcutting below dams and from eroded tributaries are deposited or exported depends on the size of the sediment particles moving into channels and the volume of peak flows (i.e., stream competency). Substrate particle size and hydraulic forces are major determinants of the biodiversity and composition of stream algae, invertebrates, and fish. The coarsening of a degraded streambed alters aquatic habitat structure and this in turn can affect many aquatic species that use the bottom substrates and interstitial spaces as habitat, for foraging, and as spawning sites (Benke and Cushing 2005). Excessive channel erosion is known to decrease abundances and lead to dominance by a few taxa (Allan and Castillo 2007).

Storage of flood waters and high flows deprives the river below a dam of its flushing flows that would normally have the capacity to scour out accumulated sediments and rejuvenate stream habitat. If sediment deposition fills interstitial spaces, this can reduce hyporheic habitat availability for invertebrates and spawning areas for benthic fish (Nelson et al. 2009). In the absence of adequate flushing flows, species with life stages that are sensitive to sedimentation, such as the eggs and larvae of many invertebrates and fish, can suffer high mortality rates (Poff et al. 1997). Aquatic plant diversity and vegetation distribution and abundance can be affected by enhanced sedimentation in preferred habitats. Hyporheic habitat structure and inhabitants can also be affected by accumulations of silt, and the reduced flow of water through the hyporheic zone can influence water quality, temperature, and ecological functions (Boulton and Hancock 2006).

Sediment transport and redistribution along rivers represents the interplay between processes of erosion and deposition, both of which may affect riparian vegetation, either by disturbing established plants or favoring colonization of deposition patches by young and productive stages of vegetation (Nilsson and Svedmark 2002). Waterborne sediments may be deposited as a thin veneer on plant leaves and stems, reducing photosynthesis and growth, or sediment may be deposited in larger quantities that partially or completely bury plants and cause stress or mortality). Plants able to root adventitiously and spread vegetatively are most likely to recover from silt burial. Partial smothering or burial of plants by waterborne silt can disturb the normal establishment, growth, and survival processes of vegetation in riparian zones (Nilsson and Svedmark 2002).

TEMPERATURE CHANGES BELOW DAMS

Specific components of the thermal regime have ecological relevance for particular freshwater organisms throughout their life histories, and the integrity of the thermal regime is just as important as the integrity of the natural flow regime (Olden and Naiman 2010). Thermal effects of river regulation by dams vary depending on the landscape position of the dam, mode of dam management and operation, the mechanisms and depth of water release, and the climatic and geomorphologic setting (e.g., Johnson et al. 2004). Changes in thermal regime can extend for relatively short or extremely long distances below dams, depending on heat exchange with the atmosphere, hydrologic inputs from tributaries and groundwater recharge, and the characteristics of dam discharges (Palmer and O'Keeffe 1989). In many instances there are major shifts in the thermal regimes below dams, especially where vertically stratified dams release cold water from below the thermocline of the impoundment (i.e., the deep hypolimnetic layer), which is often oxygen deficient as well as colder than normal for the receiving system. Cold-water thermal regimes are established by releasing water from a single deep hypolimnetic exit valve or portal (often associated with hydroelectric generation) or by selectively withdrawing water from different reservoir depths, termed "multiple offtakes" (Olden and Naiman 2010).

Depression of the normal thermal regime of a river is often termed "thermal" or "cold-water pollution" because water temperatures are typically much lower during the spring and summer months compared to free-flowing rivers. However, during the winter months, dam operations typically have the opposite effect—they elevate water temperatures in relation to natural river conditions by releasing water from the upper or epilimnetic layer of the impoundment (above the thermocline). For example, Lessard and Hayes (2003) found that summer temperature below dams increased an average of 2.7°C, ranging from a 1.0°C cooling to a 5.5°C warming. For a range of examples of thermal alterations below dams from across the world, see Olden and Naiman (2010).

Since aquatic insects and fish use the combined cue of day length and the sum of day degrees to synchronize emergence as adults, the release of cooler water downstream of impoundments can influence the life-history processes of invertebrates and the spawning behavior and success of fish. Modified thermal patterns and day-length cues have been shown not only to disrupt insect emergence patterns but also to reduce population success. Cold-water releases associated with hydro-

TABLE 23   *Effects of thermally altered flow releases from dams on fish*

Altered flows	Effects
Olifants River	In the Olifants River, South Africa, differences in the temperature of water released from Clanwilliam Dam are critical to spawning success of the Clanwilliam yellowfish *(Barbus capensis)*. Experimental water releases from the dam have shown that warm epilimnetic freshes (19–21°C) triggered fish spawning behavior and the movement of individuals onto spawning beds, whereas cool hypolimnetic baseflows (16–18°C) released immediately after the experimental freshets caused fish to abort their spawning activities. This study indicated that water temperatures must be maintained at the warmer levels for an extended period after spawning to support the development and recruitment of yellowfish embryos and larvae. The implication is that in the long-term, hypolimnetic releases could cause selective disappearance of susceptible species from considerable lengths of river channel below dams (King et al. 1998).
Murray-Darling Basin	In the Murray-Darling Basin, southeastern Australia, depressed summer temperatures extend up to several hundred kilometers downstream of dams on a number of major rivers, including the Murrumbidgee, Marquarie, Mitta Mitta, Namoi, and Murray. Cooling and delayed timing of maximum temperatures in the Namoi River below Keepit Dam have reduced the spawning success of silver perch *(Bidyanus bidyanus)* by 25–70%, and of golden perch *(Macquaria ambigua)* by 44–87% relative to pre-dam years. From similar studies it has been predicted that cold-water releases downstream of Dartmouth Dam on the Mitta Mitta River would significantly threaten the postspawning survival of Murray cod *(Maccullochella peelii)* by reducing the average minimum female population size by 76% (Preece and Jones 2002; Todd et al. 2005).

electric dams can delay spawning by up to thirty days in some fish species (Zhong and Power 1996). Two examples of the effects of thermally altered flow releases from dams are given in Table 23; the effects on fish breeding in rivers of New South Wales, Australia, are illustrated in Figure 22.

Olden and Naiman (2010) concluded that characterizing thermal regimes and assessing the downstream impacts of dams "will be challenging for many of the same reasons that assessing hydrologic vari-

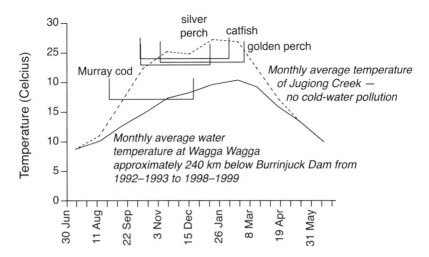

FIGURE 22. Implications of cold-water pollution for fish breeding in an impounded Australian river. (Redrawn from a figure in NSW Department of Primary Industries, Fishing and Aquaculture 2012).

ability and alteration continues to be difficult—perhaps even more so." Very few studies have attempted to explore the potential individual and interactive effects of flow and thermal modifications on fish assemblages downstream from dams (Haxton and Findlay 2008; Murchie et al. 2008).

OXYGEN DEPLETION AND GAS SUPERSATURATION BELOW DAMS

As well as disrupting the thermal regime of a river by lowering water temperatures over considerable distances along impounded rivers, dams can affect the chemical constituents and dynamics of water released downstream. Vertical thermal stratification of a large impoundment can produce oxygen-depleted hypolimnetic water. Oxygen stratification is undesirable because anoxic conditions in the hypolimnion limit habitat availability and can degrade water quality throughout the reservoir and downstream. Major fish kills have been attributed to the release of oxygen-depleted hypolimnetic water downstream from dams.

Fish mortality may also be caused by gas supersaturation (especially nitrogen) and fatal gas bubble disease below hydroelectric power dams. Total dissolved gas supersaturation commonly occurs at hydropower facilities when large volumes of spilled water entrain significant volumes of atmospheric gases that are forced into solution by the increased pressure at depth in the stilling basins. Gas supersaturation conditions persist where relatively deep impoundments or nonturbulent river reaches offer less effective gas dissipation than shallow, more turbulent river reaches that naturally facilitate degassing (Weitkamp and Katz 1980). Many efforts have been made to rectify this problem below hydropower dams. The US Environmental Protection Agency (1977) established a water-quality standard for dissolved gases at 110% saturation. Deflectors and other devices have been designed to alter flow dynamics and lower gas supersaturation levels to meet this standard (Orlins and Gulliver 2000; Muir et al. 2001).

Although this is an old and well-resolved problem in many places, it continues to arise with new dams. With the implementation of the West-East Power Transmission Strategy in China, a number of high-dam hydropower projects, such as Zipingpu, Xiluodu, Xiangjiaba, and Jinping, have been constructed or are under construction, and a large number of high dams (>200 m, e.g., Shuangjiangkou and Baihetan) are planned (Ran et al. 2009). These developments have renewed research into the causes and amelioration of gas supersaturation problems to protect the many endemic fish species in China's western rivers.

NUTRIENT TRANSFORMATIONS BELOW DAMS

Human activities in rivers and their catchments often overwhelm natural nitrogen fluxes and transformations. When dams significantly reduce the magnitude and frequency of flood events and change their periods of occurrence, there are implications for the natural character and soil fertility of floodplains (Pinay et al. 2002). Impoundments accumulate sediments, and the lack of sediment limits the lateral migration and meandering of channels downstream and erodes and depletes floodplain soils for hundreds of kilometers farther downstream. As a result, river floodplains shift from being a sink for sediment and nutrients to a source, reducing the river ecosystem's capacity to retain nutrients and its overall fertility (Pinay et al. 2002). The effects of sediment trapping in large dams can extend far downstream of the impoundment. For example, because the Aswan High Dam traps so much sediment, silt deposition on the Nile floodplain is greatly reduced, and the resulting loss of soil fertility on the floodplain requires the addition of some 13,000 tonnes of nitrate fertilizer each year (Nixon 2003).

Changes to the water regime through alterations in the frequency, duration, and timing of occurrence, or through the volume and intensity of flows and floods, directly affect nitrogen cycling in alluvial soils by controlling the duration of aerobic and anaerobic phases. Alternating aerobic and anaerobic conditions enhance organic-matter decomposition and nitrogen loss through denitrification (Groffman and Tiedje 1988). The flood regime also indirectly affects nutrient cycling in floodplain soils by influencing soil structure and texture through the deposition of sediment, with the fastest denitrification rates measured in soils with fine texture. Thus floodplains contribute to the regulation of nitrogen fluxes by sorting sediments mobilized during floods and recycling nitrogen deposited during floods (Pinay et al. 2002). Overall, natural water-table fluctuations in floodplains are key drivers of soil fertility, with changes to the natural flood regime often decreasing floodplain productivity.

8

EFFECTS OF DAMS ON HABITAT AND AQUATIC BIODIVERSITY

HABITAT ALTERATIONS BELOW DAMS

Flowing water creates and maintains a variety of habitats, reflecting channel planform and variation in hydraulic conditions across the stream, modified by habitat elements such as fallen timber, fine vegetable litter, overhanging and in-stream vegetation, rocky outcrops, undercut banks, and root masses (Pusey et al. 1993). These elements and the distribution patterns of flow velocities and depths create diverse hydraulic habitat patches across and along streams and rivers. This diversity of habitat (and associated chemical conditions) is important for maintaining various ecological functions: resting and refuge, foraging, spawning and nesting, seedling establishment, plant germination, local movement patterns of invertebrates and fish, and achievement of passage for long-distance migratory fishes (Matthews 1998; Nilsson and Svedmark 2002; Chessman 2009).

Habitat alterations and loss caused by dams and flow regulation take many forms (Bunn and Arthington 2002). Some of them are discussed in Chapter 5, for example, those caused by clear-water erosion, channel degradation, tributary erosion, and migration below impoundments. At any point along a river, channel morphology and habitat configurations are constantly adjusting to supplies of water and sediment from upstream, modified by local conditions (Petts and Calow

1996). Changes in water flows and sediment regimes can have devastating effects on benthic and hyporheic organisms, from algae and plants to invertebrates, fish, and riparian/floodplain vegetation.

EFFECTS OF STABLE FLOWS

Flow regulation by dams often disrupts the patchiness and diversity of stream and river habitats in particular ways relative to the position of a site or reach along the river continuum and the way the regime is altered. With elevated and more stable low-flow rates below dams, as well as loss of flushing flows and sediment accumulation, a few well-adapted species of plants typically survive and spread, and their enlarging stem and root systems trap more sediment, further stabilizing the embedded sediments and increasing their resistance to scour (Allan and Castillo 2007; Mackay et al. 2003). In circumstances where natural (or regulated) low flows and sediment accumulation coincide, aquatic vegetation may colonize previously fast-flowing areas and eventually choke the entire streambed; terrestrial plants also colonize the channel. Suren and Riis (2010) suggest that under these habitat conditions, aquatic invertebrates would decline and the system could slowly revert to one typical of slow-flowing pool-type environments. Furthermore, large diurnal fluctuations in dissolved oxygen, ranging from 40% to 130% air saturation in plant-rich lowland streams (Wilcock et al. 1998), may also stress invertebrates.

Flow modifications to Scandinavian rivers (Rørslett et al. 1989) and many rivers in the United States, Britain, France, southern Africa, India, Canada, and Australia are responsible for increases in macrophyte abundance. Reduced summer floods and increased winter flows (i.e., a relatively stable flow throughout the year) have caused excessive growths of submerged aquatic macrophytes such as the submerged phenotype of the bulbous rush *(Juncus bulbosus)* in Norwegian rivers regulated by hydropower stations. In its pristine state, the flow regime of the Otra River featured low winter flows and spring/summer floods, conditions that exposed plants to extreme stress caused by frost and ice scouring, followed by the deleterious scouring effects of spring floods (Rørslett et al. 1989). The regulated regime ameliorates all of these conditions and the more benign environment enables plants to accumulate massive biomass in the reaches below dams. Prolonged periods of stabilized flows at particular water levels can result in dominance of competitive plant species and loss of poor competitors (Rørslett et al. 1989), as well as reduced productivity and litter decomposition rate (Ellis et al. 1999).

Invasion of exotic species is common in rivers with stabilized flow regimes that match the flow environments of introduced species in their native range, forcing out less competitive native species adapted to more variable and patchy aquatic habitats and resources. Indirect impacts can also arise from exotic terrestrial plants such as tamarisk (*Tamarix* spp), which alter the water regime of riparian soils and affect stream flows in Australia and North America (Tickner et al. 2001). The presence of exotic plants can also have significant effects on native vertebrate inhabitants of streamside vegetation. For example, Mazzotti et al. (1981) observed reduced abundance of three native mammal species in areas of southern Florida occupied by the Australian swamp paperbark *(Melaleuca quinquenervia)* and the she-oak *(Casuarina equisetifolia)*. The exotic rubber vine *(Cryptostegia grandiflora)*, a vigorous invasive species along river valleys in northern Australia, is avoided by insectivorous skinks because rubber vine litter contains significantly different arthropod taxa with fewer preferred prey items (Valentine 2006). In addition, rubber vine leaves have a different shape than the elongate native leaf litter, providing less suitable cover with potentially decreased camouflage for foraging animals.

Prolonged flows of particular levels can be damaging to fish. In the regulated Pecos River of New Mexico, artificially prolonged high summer flows for irrigation displace the floating eggs of the threatened Pecos bluntnose shiner *(Notropis sinius pecosensis)* into unfavorable habitat, where none survive (Poff et al. 1997).

The humpback chub *(Gila cypha)* once ranged throughout the Colorado River system in the arid American Southwest. Peak flows are considered important to the chub for habitat maintenance (via sediment transport) and perhaps as spawning cues, but baseflows, which occur through the Grand Canyon for seven to ten months of the year, are also important. Operations of the Glen Canyon Dam directly affect the Colorado River through changes in flow, temperature, sediment transport, and vegetation dynamics. Elevated baseflows now occur a greater proportion of the time in the regulated flow regime. These changes have reduced habitat quality to such an extent that subadult humpback chub have become more numerous in the modified shoreline habitat provided by the exotic tamarisk *(Tamarix chinensis)* than in natural habitats (Converse et al. 1998). In addition, the dam has altered the thermal regime such that the growth, reproduction, and survival of native fishes have almost certainly been affected (e.g., Bulkley et al. 1981).

In the southwestern catchments of the United States, virtually all native river fish fauna are listed as threatened under the Endangered Species Act, largely as a consequence of water withdrawal, flow stabilization, and proliferation of exotic species. The last remaining strongholds of native river fish are in dynamic, free-flowing rivers, where exotic fish are periodically reduced by natural flash floods (Minckley and Meffe 1987; and see Chapter 4).

Long-term success (integration) of an invading fish species is much more likely in an aquatic system permanently altered by human activity than in a lightly disturbed system (Moyle and Light 1996a), and the most successful invaders are those adapted to the modified flow regime (Moyle and Light 1996b). Regulation of flows in many Australian rivers and streams is thought to favor exotic fish species such as carp *(Cyprinus carpio)* and mosquitofish *(Gambusia holbrooki)*. These species appear to benefit from seasonally stable low flows and may displace native species adapted to more variable flows and heterogeneous habitat conditions. Regulated rivers of the Murray-Darling system have a lower diversity of fish than relatively undisturbed rivers farther inland, with the reduction in diversity largely due to greatly increased numbers of carp in regulated reaches (Gehrke et al. 1995).

EFFECTS OF HYDROELECTRIC DAMS

Rather than stabilizing flows downstream, hydroelectric dams cause extreme daily variations in water level that have no natural analogue in freshwater systems and represent an extremely harsh environment of frequent, unpredictable flow disturbance (Poff et al. 1997). Bottom-dwelling aquatic species adapted to permanently inundated stream habitats can suffer physiological stress and high mortality when frequently exposed to the atmosphere, especially in shallow shoreline habitats

(Weisberg et al. 1990). Regulated river reaches below some hydroelectric dams with high daily variations in water level are typically characterized by species-poor macroinvertebrate communities containing a few small sensitive species, small individuals, and immature stages (De Jalon et al. 1994). In some cases, flow regulation may favor the proliferation of specific, more tolerant taxa such as orthoclad chironomids (Munn and Brusven 1991). Regulation of the formerly sporadic winter flow regime of the Lower Vaal River, South Africa, has allowed large populations of blackfly (Simuliidae) larvae to survive the winter and form periodic plague outbreaks of adults in spring (De Moor 1986). It has been suggested that this pest species, which poses a health risk in the region, can be controlled to some extent by careful water-level manipulations.

Pulsed reservoir discharges associated with hydroelectric power generation can leave fish stranded on gravel bars or trapped in off-channel habitats during rapidly declining flow levels. Susceptibility to stranding is a function of behavioral response to changing flows, and this varies with species, body size, water temperature, time of year and day, substrate characteristics, and the rate of flow reductions (Nagrodski et al. 2012). Fish populations and species diversity may decline when the rearing and refuge functions of shallow shoreline or backwater areas (inhabited by small fish species and the young of large species) are impaired by frequent flow fluctuations. In these artificially fluctuating environments, specialized stream or river species are often replaced by generalist species that tolerate frequent and large variations in flow. Although production of a few species may increase greatly, it is usually at the expense of other native species and of system-wide species diversity (Ward and Stanford 1979).

ALTERED FLOWS AND LIFE-HISTORY IMPACTS

Life-history strategies are the underlying determinants of population responses to environmental variability and change, such as hydrologic alterations brought about by dams and other causes of flow regulation. The timing, or predictability, of flow events is critical ecologically because the life cycles of many aquatic and riparian species are timed to either avoid or exploit flows of variable magnitudes (Lytle and Poff

2004). Some aquatic plant species are unable to regenerate under modified conditions, while changes in rates of water-level fluctuation and disturbance frequency (floods and spates) and intensity (velocity and shear stress) can affect seedling survival as well as plant growth rates (Sand-Jensen and Madsen 1992; Blanch et al. 1999). Conversely, bulrushes (*Typha* spp.) have proliferated in numerous artificial and altered aquatic habitats throughout southern Australia; their success under altered water regimes is a function of several life-history traits. These include high dispersal capabilities (production of large numbers of small seeds dispersed by wind over long distances), a high capacity to germinate while submerged, high seedling density, and, once established, rapid growth rates (Finlayson et al. 1983).

Many riparian plants have life cycles adapted to the seasonal timing of natural flow regimes through their seasonal sequence of flowering, seed dispersal, germination, and seedling growth (collectively called "emergence phenologies"). Interactions of emergence phenologies with temporally varying environmental stress from flooding or drought help to maintain high species diversity in Southern US floodplain forests (Streng et al. 1989). Productivity of riparian forests is also influenced by flow timing and can increase when short-duration flooding occurs in the growing season (Molles et al. 1995). Cottonwoods (*Populus* spp.) establish after winter–spring flood flows, during a narrow window of opportunity when wet soils and competition-free alluvial substrates are available for germination of seeds. A certain rate of floodwater recession is critical to seedling germination because seedling roots must remain connected to a receding water table as they grow downward (Rood and Mahoney 1990). When impoundments are managed to supply irrigation water, there is often a shift in timing of peak flows from spring to summer. This shift has prevented reestablishment of the Fremont cottonwood *(Populus fremontii)*, the dominant plant species in Arizona, because flow peaks now occur after, rather than before, its germination period (Fenner et al. 1985).

Changes to the extent, frequency, timing, and duration of floods in the Murray-Darling Basin have adversely affected the health and recruitment of the river red gum *(Eucalyptus camaldulensis)* (Di Stefano 2001). Impoundments store winter and spring flows for release during summer and autumn (Maheshwari et al. 1995), effectively inverting the natural seasonal distribution of river flows (Fig. 20, Chapter 7). The normal winter and spring floods usually aid the survival and establishment of red gum seedlings by providing moisture before the hot, dry summers; prolonged summer flooding has an adverse effect on seedlings and depresses recruitment (Di Stefano 2001). Drought and flow regulation are also placing severe stress on mature trees in some stands. The primary cause is salinization of the floodplain soils caused by increased rates of groundwater discharge and increased movement of salt up into the plant root zone (Overton et al. 2006). River regulation has reduced the frequency and duration of the floods that leach salt from the plant root zone and supply freshwater for transpiration. There is widespread evidence of deterioration and failed recruitment of river red gums throughout Australia's Murray-Darling river system.

Natural hydrologic variability and predictability have acted as landscape filters for the selection of fish life-history traits (Olden et al. 2006). Critical life-history events linked to the characteristics of river flow regimes range from the phenology of reproduction, spawning behavior, fecundity, larval survival, and growth patterns to recruitment success (Junk et al. 1989; Winemiller and Rose 1992). Many of these life events are also synchronized with temperature and day length, such that changes in flow regime that are not in natural harmony with these seasonal cycles may have a negative impact on aquatic biota. Dam management practices that alter flow and thermal regimes can have persistent effects on fish faunas at local and regional scales (Olden and Naiman 2010).

Modification of natural flow timing, or predictability, can affect aquatic organisms both directly and indirectly. For example, some native fishes in Norway use seasonal flow peaks as a cue for egg hatching, and river regulation that eliminates these peaks can directly reduce local populations of these species (Næsje et al. 1995). Furthermore, entire food webs, not just single species, may be modified by altered flow timing. In regulated rivers of Northern California, the seasonal shifting of scouring flows from winter to summer indirectly reduces the growth rate of juvenile steelhead trout *(Oncorhynchus mykiss)* by increasing the relative abundance of predator-resistant invertebrates that divert energy away from the food chain that leads to trout (Wootton et al. 1996). In unregulated rivers, high winter flows reduce these predator-resistant insects and favor species that are more palatable to fish (Bunn and Arthington 2002).

Many aquatic species are cued and respond to increases in river flows or the timing of large floods (Lowe-McConnell 1985; Welcomme et al. 2006). For example, the timing of rising river flows may serve as a cue, or trigger, to the spawning of certain river fishes; examples are the Colorado River squawfish *(Ptychocheilus lucius)* in the Yampa River (Nesler et al. 1988) and the Clanwilliam yellowfish *(Barbus capensis)* in the Western Cape, South Africa (King et al. 1998). For the yellowfish, turning off the flow release from an upstream dam during a controlled experiment inhibited spawning behavior downstream (King et al. 1998).

Flooding, rather than rising river flows, may act as the spawning trigger for fishes in large floodplain rivers with a predictable annual flood (Junk et al. 1989; Welcomme et al. 2006). Studies of the effects of both extensive and limited floodplain inundation on stream fish indicate that some species are adapted to exploiting floodplain habitats, and these species decline in abundance when floodplain use is restricted or floods fail (Welcomme and Hagborg 1977; Arthington and Balcombe 2011). The timing of floodplain inundation is also important for some fish species because migratory and reproductive behaviors must coincide with access to floodplain habitats.

Extensive regulation of the Mississippi River by levees has reduced floodplain area in some locations by 90%, influencing the normal ecological functioning of the river–floodplain system. Rutherford et al. (1995) found that growth rates of several fish species were positively correlated with the duration of the "growing season" (period with water temperature >15°C) rather than with flooding in the channelized river. Gutreuter et al. (1999) concluded that "the Lower Mississippi River is no longer an ecologically functional floodplain river in the sense of Junk et al. (1989)."

In alluvial valleys, the loss of overbank flows can greatly modify riparian communities by causing plant desiccation, reduced growth, competitive exclusion, ineffective seed dispersal, or failure of seedling establishment. When riparian communities are disconnected from the rivers, they no longer receive and release plant propagules as during natural conditions. They thus become more isolated in a landscape context and overall diversity declines (Bravard et al. 1997). Changes in the duration of flow conditions also have significant biological consequences. Riparian plant species respond dramatically to channel dewatering, which occurs frequently in arid regions due to surface water diversion and groundwater pumping. These biological and ecological responses range from altered leaf morphology to total loss of riparian vegetation cover.

The elimination of flooding may also affect animal species that depend on terrestrial habitats. Poff et al. (1997) described effects on several birds in the flow-stabilized Platte River of the US Great Plains, where the channel has narrowed dramatically (up to 85%) over a period of decades: "This narrowing has been facilitated by vegetative colonization of sandbars that formerly provided nesting habitat for the threatened piping plover *(Charadrius melodus)* and endangered least tern (*Sterna antillarum;* Sidle et al. 1992). Sandhill cranes *(Grus canadensis),* which made the Platte River famous, have abandoned river segments that have narrowed the most (Krapu et al. 1984)."

Floodplains support high biodiversity and provide valued ecological goods and services that have attracted human use and occupancy of floodplains, often to the detriment of the very processes that generate valued ecosystem benefits (Tockner et al. 2008, 2010). Floodplain rivers in arid and semiarid regions with low annual rainfall (mean <500 mm) and high annual evaporation rates (collectively termed "drylands") cover more than 50% of the world's land surface (Tooth 2000). They are perhaps the most threatened of all river systems because their defining hydrological characteristic is extreme flow variability (Walker et al. 1995), whereas humans want flow stability to secure reliable water supplies.

In the natural state, most dryland rivers alternate between long, harsh dry periods relieved by occasional channel flows and/or large floods (Puckridge et al. 1998). The associated ecological systems of floodplain rivers track hydrological patterns, varying between periods of high productivity (the "boom") associated with flooding and habitat expansion and periods of low productivity (the "bust") following flood recession, channel drying, and habitat contraction (Bunn et al. 2006). Floods also enhance recruitment of invertebrates, fish, frogs, turtles, and waterbirds and support the high levels of pasture production that underpin the vitality and viability of the livestock industry in dryland catchments of western Queensland (Kingsford et al. 2006; Ogden et al. 2002).

The boom and bust productivity phenomenon is easily disrupted by human activities, especially water resource developments, for example, river impoundment, flow diversion, or interbasin transfers that alter the natural hydrologic regime of arid-zone floodplain rivers (Wishart 2006). Dramatic ecological impacts and fish losses have been observed in many regulated dryland floodplain river systems, for example, the Aral Sea in Uzbekistan and Kazakhstan, the Mesopotamian Marshes, Mono Lake in California, and the Macquarie Marshes and floodplain wetlands along the Lower River Murray in Australia (Kingsford et al. 2006).

EFFECTS OF ALTERED CONNECTIVITY
BETWEEN CATCHMENTS

Historical patterns of species distribution, local endemism, and meta-population structure of aquatic organisms are largely determined by catchment boundaries and the presence of natural in-stream barriers, such as waterfalls, and saltwater barriers (Hughes et al. 2009). As a result, low gene flow and local radiation lead—in the absence of human disturbance—to considerable variation in biodiversity among drainages and high levels of endemism (Dudgeon et al. 2006). Aquatic species and genetic strains have been moved across catchment boundaries to other drainage systems by accidental or deliberate movement of propagules—seeds, plant fragments, eggs, fingerlings (e.g., by fish stocking)—and by natural locomotion (e.g., flying insects). However, alteration of flow regimes and the infrastructure associated with water-engineering schemes are also major contributors to the spread of both native and exotic aquatic species between drainages.

Interbasin transfers (IBTs) of water have taken place in most countries to provide improved water supplies in areas of water deficit; to support household, irrigation, industrial, and mining activities; and to supply hydropower generation and flood control (Ghassemi and White 2007). Infrastructure schemes transferring large quantities of water between natural river basins may present serious problems in terms of water balance, water temperature and chemistry, erosion and sedimentation, groundwater levels, the spread of pests and diseases, alterations to natural biotic distribution patterns, and the disruption of significant ecological processes dependent on the original natural flow regime of the donor and receiving aquatic systems.

Ghassemi and White (2007) provide a global catalog and analysis of the costs and benefits of numerous IBT projects on every continent and indicate the potential for more and far larger (megascale) IBTs involving transfer across and between countries (e.g., from Canada to the United States and Mexico).

The South African Orange-Vaal River Project, the Orange-Fish-Sundays River Intercatchment Transfer Scheme, and the Tugela-Vaal Water Transfer Scheme provide examples of river engineering at the national scale, where significant human benefits can be measured against potentially severe environmental consequences (Cambray et al. 1986). Major problems of soil erosion, turbidity, salinization, nutrient enrichment, algal blooms, urban impacts, and industrial pollution are anticipated or already apparent, while the transfer of endemic flora and fauna between catchments began well over a decade ago (Skelton 1986), with a variety of consequences both biogeographical and practical. The catfish *(Clarias gariepinus)* has invaded the Great Fish River through the intercatchment transfer tunnel from Lake Verwoerd and has become established in the Sundays River system. Four species of fish have been introduced from the Orange River drainage to the Great Fish River drainage via IBTs. There is concern that the transmission of schistosomes may be enhanced by temperature changes below large dams, where the altered thermal regime affects the dynamics of snail host and parasite populations. Interbasin transfers of these parasites into rivers previously free of schistosomiasis are also of concern. Since the construction of impoundments there have been outbreaks of pest simuliid blackflies (De Moor 1986).

Interbasin transfers can take place between rivers in separate catchments or within the same river basin (intrabasin transfer), for example from an upland water source to lowland river reaches. Given that the headwater, middle, and lower reaches of rivers operate ecologically much as predicted by the River Continuum Concept (Vannote et al. 1980; and see Chapter 4), there are many possible ecological consequences of inter- and intrabasin water transfers. Davies et al. (1992)

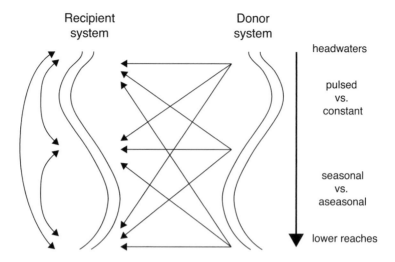

Recipient
system

Donor
system

headwaters

pulsed
vs.
constant

seasonal
vs.
aseasonal

lower reaches

FIGURE 23.   Diagram representing possible impacts of inter- and intrabasin transfers of water along the continuum of a river. (Redrawn from
Figure 1 in Davies et al. 1992, with permission from John Wiley and Sons)

proposed a conceptual model depicting 15 basic forms of IBT (Fig. 23). These can be elaborated to produce about 60 potential scenarios, depending on the spatial arrangements of water movement and the mode of water delivery (constant, pulsed, seasonal flow, etc.). If an IBT is sourced from a dam or series of dams in the donor catchment, the downstream river system can be expected to deteriorate according to the release patterns, temperature, sediment loading, and the fundamental character of the river. The consequences of "unwitting experiments in genetics" (Davies and Day 1998), when species previously separated in different catchments are brought together, are perhaps the most difficult to predict. Biodiversity decline and the loss of future evolutionary potential are likely outcomes in many instances.

9

INTRODUCTION TO
ENVIRONMENTAL FLOW METHODS

CONTEXTS OF ENVIRONMENTAL FLOW ASSESSMENTS

Environmental flow assessments (EFAs) take place in many different management contexts, at various spatial scales, within different biophysical systems, and in contrasting socioeconomic contexts and political settings. These settings and circumstances have a strong bearing on the methods most suited to achieving desired ecological outcomes. As many reviews of methods have noted, there is no single best approach to determining an environmental flow regime. Nevertheless, it is possible to set out some parameters for selecting a suitable method. More than 200 methods are available, and variations continue to be developed to accommodate particular issues and special circumstances (Tharme 2003; Acreman and Dunbar 2004; Arthington et al. 2010a).

Ecologists tend to use the term "unregulated" for systems with a near to natural flow regime, while "regulated" means any type of change to a flow regime regardless of its cause. In regulated systems, the natural flow quantities and seasonal patterns may be altered by major structural interventions—interbasin transfers, major dams, large weirs, major surface and subsurface diversion channels, and associated water-management infrastructure. Water flows in these types of regulated rivers can truly be managed in quantity, timing of flows, frequency, duration, and hydrograph shape. Furthermore, water may be drawn from a designated depth in stratified impoundments to reduce water-quality problems (e.g., deoxygenation or temperature differential in the downstream river reach). In regulated systems without water-management infrastructure, the flow regime may be variously modified from its natural state by changes in land use, farm dams, levee systems, minor water diversions, water harvesting from channel flow pulses and floodplain flows, wetland modifications (infilling, drainage, diversion), and groundwater pumping. The effects of these types of flow regime alterations can be mitigated to improve ecological outcomes (e.g., by removal of levee banks or by instituting groundwater recharge processes, etc.). All such strategies can help to reinstate some of the characteristics of the original flow regime for the ecological benefit of rivers, groundwater systems, or floodplain wetlands (Dyson et al. 2003).

Environmental flow assessments may vary greatly in scale, from relatively simple flow restoration projects in a single reach of a regulated river to whole-of-catchment water-resource planning in large basins with a mix of regulated and unregulated tributaries (Tharme 2003). Assessments can be extended to consider even larger spatial scales, for example, several large catchments, bioclimatic regions, political provinces, or countries (Poff et al. 2010). The larger the spatial scale the more complex the assessment is likely to become.

At the scale of an entire large catchment, levels of development and commitment of existing water resources to consumptive use may vary from one subcatchment to another, and so will the human footprint. There may be opportunities for improving existing system management strategies to foster environmental flow provisions, or the management objective may be to greatly expand water-resource development in a catchment, a scenario likely to allow for less generous environmental flow provisions. Existing water uses and infrastructure also place constraints on providing environmental flows (e.g., outlet valves or gateways may be too small to release large flow volumes; or there may not be a multilevel offtake system); and such constraints often limit the effectiveness of environmental flows. All infrastructure constraints must be realistically considered as part of the assessment process, and ways to mitigate them should become part of the implementation phase (see Chapter 20).

Other significant variables in making EFAs are the size of the river basin, its geomorphic variability, and the characteristics of the flow regime, which may vary from intermittent to perennial and from seasonally predictable to highly unpredictable in temporal variability patterns. Flow regimes may differ considerably in the subcatchments of very large river basins and almost certainly across broader biogeographic regions (see Chapters 2 and 3). Understanding the differences in flow regime type within a river basin or across a large study area, and how each regime has been modified by existing water infrastructure or land use, or how each might be altered if new water-resource developments are planned, are fundamental aspects of every EFA (Poff et al. 1997; Arthington et al. 2006; Richter et al. 2006).

Biophysical knowledge systems have a significant bearing on the methods and approaches used during an EFA. Many different skills and tools can be applied from the disciplinary fields of hydrological and hydraulic modeling, fluvial geomorphology, sedimentology, water chemistry, aquatic and terrestrial ecology, genetics, and evolutionary biology, as well as the multidisciplinary skills required for complex decision making and integrated river basin management. Where these skills, tools, and decision processes are less well developed, EFAs have drawn upon a more limited knowledge base for the study area, backed up by general knowledge from the literature, simpler tools, expert opinion/judgments, and a range of risk assessment methods (King and Brown 2010; Poff et al. 2010). Socioeconomic contexts and political settings establish the potential and scope for knowledge generation, acquisition of skills, and the willingness to undertake and to pay for complex assessments versus simpler methods (Dyson et al. 2003).

The assessment of environmental flows originated in freshwater systems about fifty years ago, whereas assessments that consider the influence of river flows on downstream tidal systems (estuaries, coastal wetlands, coastal lagoons, and nearshore waters) are relatively recent (Estevez 2002). Although attention to the water requirements of subsurface ecosystems associated with rivers and their floodplains is increasing (Tomlinson and Boulton 2010), this too is a relatively recent development. Formal and acceptable procedures to integrate the hydrologic and biogeochemical connectivity of surface and groundwater compartments of rivers, wetlands, and estuaries present one of the main scientific challenges for the future of environmental flows (see Chapter 16).

Environmental flow studies have been criticized by participating scientists and the broader community for their focus solely on flow-related

issues and management strategies, to the virtual exclusion of other factors that may influence the condition of riverine and groundwater ecosystems (see Baron et al. 2002). Catchment disturbances and threats associated with corridor engineering are typically not considered in most
EFAs. A focus solely on river discharge can ignore water-quality problems of catchment origin (Nilsson and Renöfält 2008), the effects of
riparian degradation and loss caused by catchment activities and land use
(Pinay et al. 2002), or the ecological impacts associated with exotic species (fish, invertebrates, and aquatic and riparian plants). Frequently the
failure to address such issues arises because responsibility for each domain
lies with a different management agency that may or may not be willing,
or able, or allowed to participate in an EFA. Hirji and Davis (2009) call
for methods and frameworks that can accommodate the problems arising from multiple stressor syndromes at the scale of entire catchments.

Every environmental flow study has a time frame for completion, and
often the time allowed is relatively short, even though plans for new
developments typically have long gestation periods. There are no hard
and fast rules about how long to spend on each assessment; however, the
methods available generally dictate their duration. Simple hydrological
methods may involve little more than looking up an index value from
a reference database, while several years may be spent on hydrological
analysis, field data collection and complex modeling of hydroecological
relationships in an individual or multiple-river restoration study (e.g.,
Shafroth et al. 2010). The greater the effort expended to understand
and quantify how a riverine ecosystem functions and to model how it
may respond to hydrologic alteration, the more defensible the eventual
environmental flow recommendations, and the more likely they are to
generate anticipated ecological and other benefits. Brown and Watson
(2007) point out that the cost of an EFA is typically less than 0.5% of the
cost of engineering and other water-resource investigations for major
developments.

ORIGINS OF ENVIRONMENTAL FLOW ASSESSMENT
Tharme (2003) traced the development of environmental flow methods worldwide, observing that historically the United States was at the
forefront of research, with the first ad hoc methods appearing in the

late 1940s. Rapid progress was achieved during the 1970s, primarily as a result of new environmental legislation and demands from the water-planning community for quantitative documentation of environmental flows, coinciding with the peak of the dam-building era (WCD 2000). In many countries, the concept and practice of EFAs began to attract interest and practitioners in the 1980s (e.g., in Australia, the United Kingdom, New Zealand, and South Africa) and later elsewhere (e.g., in Brazil, Japan, and Portugal) (Tharme 2003). Other parts of the world, including eastern Europe and much of Latin America, Africa, and Asia, are now advancing rapidly with application of existing EFA methods and their own unique innovations. The Water Framework Directive of the European Union is the driving policy framework for environmental management, designed to achieve "good ecological status" of freshwater systems throughout Europe (Acreman and Ferguson 2010). China is developing an asset-based, holistic EFA approach adapted from Australian ecosystem frameworks (Gippel et al. 2009; Jiang et al. 2010).

In early studies, the focus of environmental flow assessment was to maintain economically important freshwater fisheries, especially salmonids, in snowmelt streams and rivers of the Pacific Northwest of the United States. The main objective was to define a minimum acceptable flow based almost entirely on predictions of in-stream habitat availability matched against the habitat preferences of one or a few species of fish (see reviews in Jowett 1997; Acreman and Dunbar 2004). It was assumed, although not always explicitly stated, that flow recommendations designed to protect target fish populations, habitats, and food resources would ensure maintenance of other communities and the river ecosystem. These foundational methods, and sophisticated innovations focused around two- and three-dimensional habitat modeling, supported by spatially referenced habitat mapping techniques, have generated many insights as well as many misgivings. While protection of aquatic habitats for valued species is undoubtedly important, many other facets of the flow regime and ecosystem requirements need to be considered (e.g., Poff et al. 1997; Bunn and Arthington 2002).

During the early years, while environmental flow methods were developing, a broader group of river ecologists, particularly those interested in river restoration, increasingly drew attention to the importance of many facets of the flow regime, not just the low flows that maintain habitat for fish and other biota. With publication of the Natural Flow Regime Paradigm as a template for river restoration and conservation (Poff et al. 1997), scientists and practitioners increasingly recognized the importance of flow variability and the many dimensions of the flow regime of every river system. By the late 1990s, there was growing agreement among scientists and many water managers that to protect freshwater biodiversity and maintain the ecosystem services provided by rivers, natural flow variability—or some semblance of it—must be maintained (e.g., Arthington et al. 1992; King and Louw 1998). The emerging field of environmental flow science soon shifted from a species to an ecosystem and source-to-sea perspective. Postel and Richter (2003) trace these developments in *Rivers for Life: Managing Water for People and Nature*. A recent special issue of *Freshwater Biology* devoted to the science and management of environmental flows offers new insights (Arthington et al. 2010a), while contributions from the broader fields of stream and river ecology, restoration ecology, and ecosystem science have helped to shape this review of methods.

CLASSIFICATION OF METHODS

Techniques for assessing environmental flow requirements range from simplistic use of available hydrologic records to establish minimum and flushing flows, to sophisticated modeling procedures linking changes in river discharge with geomorphological and ecological responses at species, community, and ecosystem scales. The various approaches have advantages and disadvantages, depending on the situational factors discussed above and the desired outcomes of the study.

Tharme (2003) recognized four relatively discrete categories of methods—namely, hydrological, hydraulic rating, habitat simulation, and holistic (or ecosystem)—while noting that combinations of methods are frequently applied during more demanding EFAs, and many statistical techniques (category "other") are used to analyze data for input to EFAs (Table 24). Dyson et al. (2003) give alternative terms for the categories recognized by Tharme (2003). Hydrological methods are described below. Chapter 10 covers hydraulic rating and habitat simulation methods, and Chapters 11–13 describe features and examples of holistic (ecosystem) methods.

TABLE 24   *Categories of environmental flow methods*

Category	Tharme (2003)	Dyson et al. (2003)
1	Hydrological	Lookup tables
2	Hydraulic rating	Desktop analysis
3	Habitat simulation	Habitat modeling
4	Holistic	Functional analysis
5	Combined	
6	Other	

SOURCES: Tharme 2003; Dyson et al. 2003

The intent of reviewing these EFA methods is not to present recipes but to highlight the strengths and weaknesses of each type of method and to indicate how each has been applied and has progressed. Citations from older literature demonstrate how soon each method was subjected to scrutiny and criticism, yet the simplest and oldest methods (categories 1–3 in Table 24) continue to be applied and still constitute around 70% of available environmental flow methods. Readers looking for manuals setting out the details of each method will be disappointed, as only three have been produced: the Instream Flow Incremental Methodology (IFIM) and the physical habitat modeling platform known as PHABSIM (Bovee and Milhous 1978; Bovee 1982; Stalnaker et al. 1995), the Building Block Methodology (King et al. 2000), and the biophysical module of DRIFT (Brown et al. 2005). There is a massive gray literature of informal and unpublished case studies and other valuable supporting documents held in agency and client libraries, university offices, and with catchment-care groups. Many reports and journal papers present step-by-step accounts of actual EFAs, with comments on their strengths and limitations, and should serve to guide new studies just as informatively as manuals.

HYDROLOGICAL METHODS

Every environmental flow assessment is founded on hydrology and is delivered to water managers as hydrological recommendations in some quantitative form, often with some specified degree of certainty about

the anticipated geomorphic and ecological outcomes of water allocations for the environment. Differences among methods lie in the degree
to which hydrological prescriptions are founded on theoretical, empirical, or experimental evidence of hydroecological relationships or represent a summation of expert opinion or risk analysis. Hydrological
methods sensu Tharme (2003) are also known as "rule of thumb,"
"threshold," or "standard setting" methods. Hydrological methods
constituted 30% of all methods applied globally at the time of Tharme's
2003 review, and she recorded 61 different hydrological indices or techniques used in 51 countries.

MONTANA METHOD

The Montana (or Tennant) Method (Tennant 1976) is the most frequently used hydrological method throughout the world (Tharme 2003).
Tennant (1976) considered three factors as crucial for fish well-being:
wetted width, depth, and velocity. In developing the method, Tennant
measured physical, biological, and chemical parameters along 58 transects from 11 different streams at 38 different discharges in three states
of the northwestern United States, augmented with data collected from
a further 21 states. He proposed that certain baseflows maintain particular qualitative fish-habitat conditions that range from "optimum"
habitat (60–100% of the average annual flow) to "poor or minimum"
and "severe degradation" (10% of average flow to zero flow) (Table 25).
Tennant recognized that the flat allocation of a single discharge to a
modified flow regime effectively ignored the pattern of seasonality, and
so he proposed different baseflows for two 6-month seasonal blocks.
He also recommended a "flushing or maximum" flow to help maintain
habitat quality.

Advantages of the Montana Method include that it is rapid, cheap,
and easy to apply; has moderate data requirements; and can be executed
in the office but has the potential for field calibration. Tennant believed
it to have wide applicability in the United States and elsewhere but
thought it most applicable for mountain streams with "virgin" flow.
Obviously, if the flow regime is already partly regulated then suggested
allocations may be too low to maintain the desired habitat conditions
(Pusey 1998).

The Montana Method has several limitations that should be rec-

TABLE 25   *Temporal variation in proportion of mean annual flow (MAF) allocated to maintain differing levels of habitat quality*

	Recommended flows (% of MAF)	
Flow category / habitat quality	October to March	April to September
Flushing or maximum	200	200
Optimum	60–100	60–100
Outstanding	40	60
Excellent	30	50
Good	20	40
Fair or degrading	10	30
Poor or minimum	10	10
Severe degradation	10% of average flow to zero flow	

SOURCE: Tennant 1976

ognized before attempting to apply it; often they are not taken into account, leading to weaker environmental flow recommendations. First, the method is absolutely dependent on the provision of extensive stream-flow data for the rivers of interest. Lengthy flow records are not available in many regions of the world, and furthermore, where long time series of data are available, choices must be made as to which temporal segment of stream-flow data should be used. Where the natural variability of flows is high from month to month and year to year, and flow sequences cycle through wetter and drier periods of several years, such choices are critical (Pusey 1998). In its original form, the Montana Method offered only two "seasonal" flow profiles although there is the potential to develop different flow provisions for wet and dry years (Stalnaker and Arnette 1976). Although flushing flows were included in Tennant's original recommendations, they may not achieve all the desirable benefits of a wider range of high-flow events.

The Montana Method's major limitation is that its application in streams other than those where it was developed may introduce unknown error into environmental flow estimates, particularly for streams that are morphologically dissimilar to those originally examined (Stalnaker and Arnette 1976). Without undertaking a calibration exercise for new geographic regions and different stream types, the use of Tennant's original flow levels has no theoretical or empirical basis (Pusey 1998). Moreover, in regions with variable flows (i.e., the mean flow is substantially different from the median flow), application of the Montana Method may result in water allocations more generous than required (Richardson 1986). In spite of these constraints and accumulated wisdom, the Montana Method is still being applied without any form of calibration to local conditions.

FLOW DURATION CURVE ANALYSIS

Another suite of hydrological methods makes direct use of the flow duration curve (see Chapter 2) and are frequently referred to as "flow duration curve analysis," or FDC methods. Stalnaker and Arnette (1976) recommended that certain percentile flows be maintained to support specified ecological processes. The 80th percentile exceedance flow was recommended to maintain food production, the 40th percentile to maintain conditions necessary for salmonid spawning and migration, and the 17th percentile to provide a "flushing flow." The choice of these flow percentiles was based on empirical data related to flow and salmonid habitat in the southwestern United States.

A consistent criticism and limitation of this approach is that it requires calibration when used outside of the original geographic region. In the United States, several methods have been devised that modify the FDC approach to account for differences in stream size and region (Tharme 2003), and other countries have elaborated on the method as well. The Texas Method uses variable percentages of the monthly median flow based on the known requirements of fish (Matthews and Bao 1991). Other rules of thumb based on flow duration curves include 25% of the mean annual flow (MAF), the 7Q10 (i.e., 10-year low of 7-day average flows), the 7Q2 (2-year low of 7-day average), the Q_{95} (95th percentile exceedance flow), and the 10th percentile of monthly flows (Kilgour et al. 2005). The 7Q10 flow and Q_{95} are the most commonly used low flow indices (Tharme 2003).

Flow duration curve analysis has an important advantage in that it can be elaborated to include flows of any volume and frequency of occurrence to accommodate different ecological processes linked to particular flow magnitudes. Several Australian studies have recommended incorporation of variable monthly percentile flows as well as different percentiles for dry, normal, and wet years to allow for maintenance of the natural temporal pattern of intra- and interannual variation.

The UK Environment Agency applies a flow duration curve in the water-allocation method known as CAMS (Catchment Abstraction Management Strategies). This approach defines a target FDC that guides the setting of limits on water abstraction (Petts et al. 2006), based on the sensitivity of four riverine elements: physical characteristics, fisheries, aquatic macrophytes, and macroinvertebrates. A naturalized FDC is produced, and a set of simple tabulated rules is used to determine the percentage of natural low flow that can be abstracted, depending on the environmental sensitivity of the particular stream. A low flow is defined as the flow exceeded 95% of the time (Q_{95}); other exceedance flows are also recommended based largely on the professional judgment of specialists, since critical levels have not been defined empirically for a great many UK streams. These first-level estimates of flow requirements may be subject to more detailed analysis using habitat simulation models (e.g., PHABSIM to assess fisheries) or other more detailed methods such as River Flow Indexing using benthic macroinvertebrates (Extence et al. 1999; Dunbar et al. 2010).

In a pilot assessment of environmental flow requirements for Indian river basins, Smakhtin and Anputhas (2006) developed a series of FDCs, each intended to achieve a particular level of aquatic ecosystem protection. These curves are accomplished by shifting the original "natural" FDC to the left along the probability axis, to achieve an overall reduction in flow volumes across the full spectrum of the flow regime and progressive loss of flow variability with each decreasing level of ecosystem protection. Different categories of environmental protection are assigned to each river basin depending on the presumed sensitivity to flow alteration. The output is presented as an environmental FDC and a corresponding environmental monthly flow time series.

RANGE OF VARIABILITY APPROACH

Hydrological methods took a giant leap forward with the Range of Variability Approach (RVA) and software package (Richter et al. 1996, 1997). This approach provides a comprehensive statistical characterization of ecologically relevant features of a flow regime as recommended in the Natural Flow Regime Paradigm. The natural range of hydro-logical variation is described using 32 different hydrological indices derived from long-term daily-flow records. Natural and altered flow regimes can be compared to produce Indicators of Hydrologic Alter-ation (IHAs), grouped into five categories that represent major regime characteristics (monthly flow variations; the magnitude, frequency, and timing of high- and low-flow spells; and rates of rise and fall in flow). The natural ranges of these flow statistics are identified for a period of unregulated flows, and environmental flow rules are set to provide a modified flow regime with statistical parameters that lie mostly within this natural range of values.

A limitation of the RVA is that there is no ecologically grounded pro-cedure for deciding how much any particular flow parameter should be allowed to vary beyond the natural range of variability characteristic for the river under investigation. Simple rules are likely to be mislead-ing. For example, providing half of the natural magnitude of the peak discharge will not move half of the accumulated sediment, nor will half of an overbank flow necessarily inundate half of the floodplain (Poff et al. 1997). Hydrologic targets must be monitored, calibrated to partic-ular circumstances, and refined to produce improved ecological out-comes over time (Richter et al. 1996, 1997).

The RVA has been used often in trend analysis of pre- and postregu-lation flow scenarios to characterize the flow-related changes in regu-lated rivers. In many recent instances, hydrologic variability has been correlated with ecological factors, such as fish populations and assem-blage structure, aquatic vegetation, water quality, geomorphological processes, and species' habitat (e.g., Pusey et al. 2000; Mackay et al. 2003; Kennard et al. 2007), and to supplement the results of physical microhabitat modeling. Tharme (2003) recommended further dem-onstration of the ecological relevance of the IHAs, a point soon fol-lowed up in several ecosystem frameworks (e.g., the Benchmarking Methodology; Brizga et al. 2002). Scruton et al. (2004) commented that further research is required to determine the relevant components of the natural flow regime and what magnitudes of flow are necessary to maintain the essential character of a river, while allowing some modi-fication to the flow regime.

A somewhat similar hydrological approach originating in Australia is also based on the representation of hydrological attributes captured in the Natural Flow Regime Paradigm. Known as the Flow Translucency Approach (Gippel 2001), it scales down the various seasonal magnitudes of flow (using various functions), while maintaining similar levels of temporal flow variability, to produce a recommended regulated flow regime. Gippel (2001) felt that the approach held promise but recommended more adequate incorporation of ecological and geomorphological considerations into the methodology. Jacobson and Galat (2008) describe a similar approach designed to develop a more naturalized flow regime to support reproduction and survival of the pallid sturgeon along the Lower Missouri River.

Tharme (2003) considered that methods based on historical flow records have substantial value during the early reconnaissance phase of the water-allocation process, as rapid, simple, and low-resource means of "block booking" quantities of water for environmental purposes. As a result of the rapid and cheap provision of low-resolution flow estimates, hydrological methods are generally used mainly at the planning stage of water-resource developments, or in situations where preliminary flow targets and exploratory water allocation trade-offs are required, or in low-controversy situations (Dyson et al. 2003).

IO

HYDRAULIC RATING AND
HABITAT SIMULATION METHODS

HYDRAULIC RATING METHODS

Both the Montana Method (Tennant 1976) and the FDC approach (Stalnaker and Arnette 1976) are based on the premise that the amount and quality of habitat in a stream is related to the amount of water transported down its channel. Hydraulic rating methods seek to define the relationship between flow volume (discharge) and the amount and type of habitat provided during the passage of flow along a stream channel. Once this relationship is known, a modified flow regime can be defined that either maintains that habitat at maximum suitability or at lesser levels of suitability (Pusey 1998). More than 20 hydraulic rating methods represent around 11% of the global total of environmental flow assessment (EFA) methods (Tharme 2003).

The most simple and historically most commonly used of the hydraulic rating approaches is the "wetted perimeter or area" method. This procedure usually involves placing a single transect at a river location most likely to be responsive to changes in flow. The relationship between wetted perimeter and discharge is then determined from measurements taken at several different water-level (stage) heights, with the environmental flow generally identified as the discharge near to the curve's breakpoint (Fig. 24), which is assumed to represent the optimal flow for habitat protection below which habitat is rapidly lost. Riffles or runs are usually the focus of analysis because they are most responsive to changes in discharge. It is also assumed that consideration of one habitat type only is sufficient to satisfy the requirements of other biotopes or habitat types, and, further, that wetted perimeter is a useful surrogate for many other factors or processes that govern overall stream integrity.

Multiple transect methods offer a means to rectify the limitations associated with reliance on a single transect, on the assumption that more cross-sections will provide a more reliable description of hydraulic conditions along a river. An analysis of survey data from 100 river reaches in Europe, Australia, New Zealand, and South Africa suggested to Stewardson and Howes (2002) that 15 cross-sections are adequate in most cases, with fewer required in more uniform channels. Further information on the wetted perimeter method can be found in Gippel and Stewardson (1998), who argue that the breakpoint on the curve is almost universally, but incorrectly, termed an "inflection" point and determined by eye from a graph, whereas it should be defined objectively using mathematical techniques.

Davies et al. (1995) used the wetted perimeter method when assessing the environmental flow requirements of fish in the Esk River, Tasmania. One of the target species in that investigation was the southern pygmy perch *(Nannoperca australis)* restricted to and dependent on aquatic macrophyte beds found in pools. Wetted perimeter analysis was used to determine the flow required to maintain inundation of macrophyte beds in test reaches, as a surrogate for direct measurement of the flow requirements of the fish. In Colorado, the R-2 cross method has been used to set environmental flows in the region's cold-water streams (Espegren 1998); it relies on a hydraulic model (R-2 cross) to generate relationships between stream discharge and channel hydraulics, from which an environmental flow for fish is derived using hydraulic parameters and expert opinion.

Relatively low-resolution hydraulic habitat techniques have their uses, especially when more advanced methods cannot be employed for want of resources or data. However, in many countries they have been superseded by more advanced habitat modeling or assimilated into frameworks with a broader ecosystem focus. For example, Stewardson and Gippel (2003) incorporated wetted perimeter analysis into their

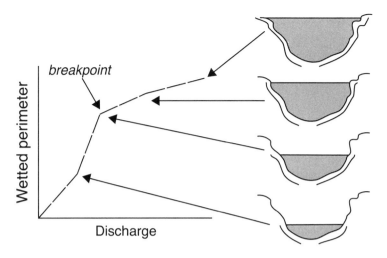

FIGURE 24. Plot of wetted perimeter, measured at a stream cross-section, versus changes in discharge. The breakpoint represents a threshold water depth below which wetted habitat decreases rapidly.

proposed Flow Events Method (FEM) designed to capture ecologically important flow events and the temporal variability of those events within environmental flow regimes. They suggested that environmental flow targets can be specified as the maximum allowable change in recurrence interval or some other criterion relevant to the influence of flow on stream hydraulics (e.g., drying of the streambed, inundation of floodplain wetlands, or an ecological process). Stewardson and Cottingham (2002) applied the FEM to assessment of environmental flows in the regulated Broken River, Victoria. A scientific panel developed conceptual models to identify ecological targets that could be restored by environmental flows (e.g., sufficient shallow-water habitat for fish and aquatic macrophytes), while HEC-RAS was used to generate relevant hydraulic parameters (e.g., wetted perimeter, area of shallow streambed) to meet those targets at representative reaches. The FEM recommends that the maximum allowable change in any ecologically relevant flow variable identified from wetted perimeter analysis, or any other technique, should be developed in consultation with relevant specialists, with the general objective to maintain the level of change in recurrence interval at a low level of risk for specified ecological targets (Stewardson and Cottingham 2002).

HABITAT SIMULATION METHODS

This category of methods represents a major advance on hydrologic and habitat rating techniques. Tharme (2003) identified 58 variants representing 28% of the global total of EFA methods. The Instream Flow Incremental Methodology (IFIM) holds center stage in this category. The IFIM was developed in North America by the Cooperative Instream Flow Service Group of the US Fish and Wildlife Service, Colorado, in the late 1970s, and is still considered by many practitioners to be the most scientifically and legally defensible suite of methods available for assessing environmental flows (Gore and Nestler 1988; Dunbar et al. 1998). The IFIM was originally concerned primarily with the protection of salmonid species in snowmelt streams (Bovee and Milhous 1978; Bovee 1982) but has since been implemented in many other regions and many other types of stream. A primer is available for the IFIM (Stalnaker et al. 1995), and there is a commercial package of software programs (TRPA n.d.).

The core component of the IFIM—the physical habitat modeling platform known as PHABSIM—has been used in at least 20 countries, while several more countries use the equivalent riverine hydraulic habitat simulation program called RHYHABSIM (Jowett 1989). In their essential features and utility, the two software packages are identical. However, Gan and McMahon (1990) compared PHABSIM II and RHYHABSIM and noted that the latter is more limited in its application (e.g., it does not contain anywhere near the number of programs or options as PHABSIM II), and it has some hydraulic modeling limitations. PHABSIM forms only one component of the IFIM in its entirety; the full package includes legal/institutional analysis, problem diagnosis, study objective design, multiparameter modeling, linkage of habitat with hydrology, alternatives analysis, and negotiation and resolution.

There are six main steps in the application of PHABSIM within the IFIM framework.

Step 1 defines study objectives, the river sectors to be modeled, and the target species (usually fish or invertebrates) likely to be found in those sectors. Then it evaluates the availability of habitat preference data suitable for use in the PHABSIM modeling procedure (Fig. 25). Bovee and Milhous (1978) recognized three different categories of habi-

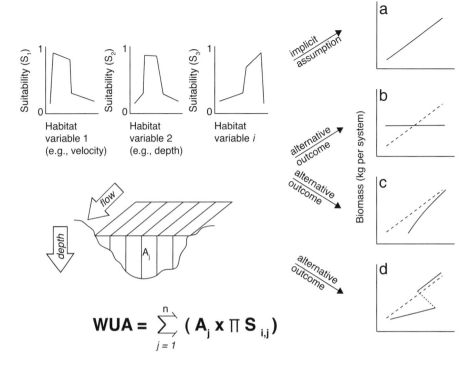

$$\text{WUA} = \sum_{j=1}^{n} (A_j \times \prod S_{i,j})$$

FIGURE 25. Main features of the PHABSIM module of IFIM. Habitat suitabilities (S_i) represent organism tolerances to different habitat variables (velocity, depth, and substrate characteristics). Suitability values are assigned to stream subsections with area (A_j) to determine the weighted usable area (WUA) available to fish. The relationship of fish biomass to WUA is often assumed to be linear (a), but it may take different forms, e.g., be nonexistent (b), be nonlinear (c), or involve rapid transitions between alternative states (d). (Redrawn from Figure 3 in Anderson et al. 2006, with permission from the Ecological Society of America)

tat suitability criteria. Category 1 criteria are derived from information in the literature or from professional experience and are considered the least valuable, often used as a last resort when site-specific or general habitat information is unavailable for the target species (Jowett 1989). Category 2 criteria are based on empirical data and are usually termed "utilization" functions. Category 3 criteria take utilization functions and scale them to reflect the availability of each habitat type for a target species, hence the term "preference" functions. Moyle and Baltz (1985) emphasized the importance of using system-specific data to generate preference curves rather than data from a number of rivers that may have different habitat characteristics. Tharme (2003) recommended that species from a wide array of trophic levels should be included to improve the generality of the predictions made by PHABSIM.

Step 2 considers whether the catchment to be studied is in equilibrium and whether macrohabitat conditions are suitable for implementation of IFIM procedures focused on particular target species. Pusey (1998) drew attention to the need to consider macrohabitat conditions before commencing an IFIM study, because there would be little point if target species are unlikely to occur in the river reaches to be modeled (e.g., if study reaches are located above barriers to fish movement).

Step 3 involves selection of study, or "reference," sites. As with the multiple transect method for wetted perimeter analysis, the location of study sites in a river is critical in determining the outcome and utility of the PHABSIM procedure. In selecting reference sites (usually riffles or runs), it is assumed that they actually do represent other parts of the river and therefore that discharge-related changes in habitat at a few reference sites can be extrapolated to elsewhere in the catchment with confidence. This focus on riffle/run habitat may overlook other habitat types (pools, backwaters) that are important to many other species in the system. Halleraker et al. (2007) suggested that seasonal variations in availability of mesohabitat types, such as deeper areas, and the flow conditions that maintain suitable pool habitat or that generate deteriorating pool habitat, need further investigation as part of sustainable environmental flows.

At step 4, stream transects (cross-sections) are selected within each reference site to characterize and measure stream habitat as required by the PHABSIM hydraulic and habitat models (Fig. 25). King and Tharme (1994) recommended that an experienced hydraulics expert be involved in the initial phase to advise on the placement of transects and measurement procedures, a recommendation followed up in numerous instances. Simulating the changes in suitability of a river reach for a particular species involves two separate procedures: hydraulic simulation and habitat simulation. The PHABSIM II module consists of 240 separate programs covering depth, velocity, substrate, and cover. Simulations are usually based on transect data collected on one occasion (i.e., at one discharge) and a series of measurements relating discharge to river-stage height. However, many studies have collected habitat data across the full range of discharge conditions to characterize seasonal variability in habitat availability.

The accuracy of execution of each procedure largely determines the utility of the subsequent outcomes for environmental flow assessment. Gan and McMahon (1990) stressed that good reliability (90%) can only be obtained with very accurate survey data and calibration. Pusey et al. (1993) argued for greater attention to more complex habitat elements such as woody debris, macrophyte beds, and leaf litter that are not readily modeled by PHABSIM, even though a cover component is usually included in the habitat preference curves. Elliott et al. (1999) noted that seasonal macrophyte growth presents problems when calibrating PHABSIM, since it increases water-surface levels at given discharges and also changes the velocity pattern within the river. Hearne et al. (1994) suggested that this issue may be minimized by ensuring that the principal PHABSIM hydraulic model calibration dataset is collected when macrophyte growth is at a maximum, or at a level consistent with the study's period of interest.

Step 5 is the main prediction phase of the IFIM. It combines information derived from the hydraulic simulation phase with data on the preferred physical microhabitat of the target species to assess how much of the preferred microhabitat is available at different discharges; habitat is expressed as weighted usable area (WUA) (Fig. 25). Physical cells within a stream reach are given suitability ratings, expressed as the area of each cell suitable for use by the target species (Gan and McMahon 1990) or as a cell that is 76.5% suitable (King and Tharme 1994). For a detailed discussion of WUA concepts and interpretation, see Payne (2003), who proposed a different term—"relative suitability index."

As in wetted perimeter analysis, interpretations of PHABSIM outputs rely on identifying breakpoints at which the rate of change in WUA shifts abruptly with decreasing stream discharge. Experiences with RHYHABSIM have shown that species-rich fish assemblages generate multiple and not necessarily compatible flow recommendations based on WUA analysis, because habitat requirements differ among species and also between juvenile and mature individuals. One solution is to recommend a range of flows rather than a single discharge. Davies et al. (1995) recognized this problem but dealt with it using risk analysis, where various levels of risk can be assigned to different possible environmental flow levels based on the amount of habitat lost for a proportion of all target species, in this case invertebrates.

Step 6 forms a final step in many IFIM studies. It involves generating a WUA time-series plot and analyzing changes in WUA over time as a consequence of water abstraction or some other process altering the river's flow regime. Monthly discharge records for the study reaches are converted to WUA and plotted for the "natural" (unregulated) flow regime and for several scenarios of water abstraction (i.e., regulated scenarios). The results can be plotted and compared as habitat duration curves. Habitat time-series analysis has been applied to individual species, life-history stages, and multiple species.

Using habitat time-series analysis, Elliott et al. (1999) found that for 30% of the time in the years 1970–92, water abstraction reduced the natural level of trout habitat in a representative reach of the River Allen, United Kingdom, by more than 50%. Navarro et al. (2007) applied time-series analysis of physical habitat generated by PHABSIM to identify habitat bottleneck periods that threaten the endangered Júcar dace *(Chondrostoma arrigonis)* in the Júcar River basin, Spain. Based on the Continuous Under Threshold Curves Methodology (Capra et al. 1995), habitat was considered "critically impacted" when the area suitable for this species was reduced by 50% or more, while habitat reductions of up to 50% were termed "stress situations." Flow regulation reduced suitable habitat for young and adult stages of the Júcar dace 60–77% of the time in two major tributaries, while habitat suitable for spawning was reduced by 73%. This study also demonstrated greatly extended and more frequent periods of time (spells) without suitable adult and young-of-the-year habitat. Habitat Spell Analysis (Marsh 2003) was used to quantify the changes in low-flow spell duration between naturalized flows and regulation scenarios.

OTHER HABITAT SIMULATION MODELS

Since the IFIM and PHABSIM came into wide usage, several other habitat simulation models based on linking hydraulic attributes of streams and habitat suitability for fish or invertebrates have become available. For example, RIVER2D developed in Alberta contains much the same processes as IFIM (Katopodis 2003). In Europe, CASIMIR (Computer-Aided Simulation Model for Instream Flow Requirements) is a popular toolbox for habitat simulation in rivers, developed at the Stuttgart Institute of Hydraulic Engineering since the beginning of the 1990s. CASIMIR has been applied to examine the consequences of various types of human activity on natural processes in river systems; for example, to model relationships between flow-related temporal and spatial patterns in river-bottom shear stress and habitat suitability for invertebrates (Jorde et al. 2000). The Riverine Community Habitat Assessment and Restoration Concept (RCHARC; Nestler et al. 1998) has been applied in river-flow restoration planning and impact analysis for the main stem Missouri River and a number of rivers in the southeastern United States.

Innovations in habitat assessment include three-dimensional (3D) habitat-measurement techniques and models to calculate usable volume (UV) as a more realistic representation of habitat availability in streams than usable area (UA). Mouton et al. (2007) describe a UV approach using HaMoSOFT (habitat-modeling software) embedded in Microsoft Excel, which generates cross-sectional velocity contour plots for different stream discharges. HaMoSOFT offers a trade-off between complex 3D hydraulic modeling and the practical need for physical habitat quantification (including depth and velocity distributions and interactions) in river-flow management and habitat restoration.

A Functional Flows Model (FFM) has been proposed to integrate hydrogeomorphic processes and ecological functions into physical habitat evaluations, where "functional flows are defined as discharge values that interact with the river bed morphology through hydraulic processes providing shear stress conditions that serve ecological purposes" (Escobar-Arias and Pasternack 2010). Shear stress represents the force available to scour the riverbed and transport sediments, thereby delimiting physical habitat conditions and dynamics that underpin particular ecological functions at selected habitat units. A test case applied the FFM to assessments of the physical habitat used during the spawning stage of fall-run chinook salmon *(Oncorhynchus tshawytscha),* an endangered Pacific Northwest salmon species that is considered an indicator of ecosystem functionality. Application of the FFM enabled a series of flow scenarios to be interpreted in terms of their effects on shear stress and streambed characteristics that are important for spawning, incubation, and rearing of salmon and for bed preparation for redds. This contribution provides advice on model formulation, scenarios generation and testing, and interpretation of outcomes. A subsequent study (Escobar-Arias and Pasternack 2011) used the FFM to evaluate gravel-bed riffle functionality for fall-run chinook salmon with respect to river rehabilitation on the Mokelumne River and flood-induced channel change on the Yuba River, California.

MESOHABITAT METHODS

A special issue of *River Research and Applications* reported recent developments through collaborative research activities of the European Aquatic Modelling Network (EAMN) between 2000 and 2005 (Harby 2007). This volume consistently called for methods to scale up flow-habitat suitability models and biotic response models from the reach (PHABSIM) scale to meso- and macrohabitat and basin scales. Harby et al. (2007) described a robust, cost-efficient mesohabitat assessment method applied in Norwegian rivers to map habitat types and describe hydraulic variability based on depth, velocity, and substrate measurements. Lamouroux et al. (1995) and Booker and Acreman (2007) have developed generalized models for predicting depth and velocity at the stream-reach scale. Parasiewicz (2001) developed a PHABSIM derivative, meso-HABSIM, to map habitat conditions (e.g., channel shape, substrate, depth of water, flow rate, etc.) at different flows along extensive sections of rivers in order to establish the suitability of each mesohabitat for the dominant members of the fish community. These methods enable development of rating curves to describe changes in relative areas of suitable habitat in response to flow at large spatial scales appropriate for water-resource planning (Jacobson 2008).

Despite these developments, much remains to be done to link habitat-based methods such as PHABSIM and new landscape-level analyses of hydraulic processes and other features of the physical environment with ecological responses. Anderson et al. (2006) discuss the further research required to integrate models of population dynamics with large-scale physical habitat and bioenergetic processes in streams and rivers (see Chapter 14).

11

FLOW PROTECTION METHODS

ORIGINS OF ECOSYSTEM APPROACHES

A major shift in thinking about environmental flows emerged in the early 1990s, when river scientists concerned about the limitations of existing water-allocation methods (then termed "in-stream flow methods") increasingly made the case for a broader approach to sustain and conserve river ecosystems rather than just a few target species. Conceptual foundations were laid by several contributors, for example Hill et al. (1991) outlined ecological and geomorphological concepts for in-stream and out-of-channel flow requirements. Holistic approaches incorporating ecologically relevant features of the natural hydrologic regime to protect the entire riverine ecosystem emerged through parallel developments and collaboration in Australia and South Africa (Arthington et al. 1992; King and Tharme 1994; King and Louw 1998). Likewise, Sparks (1995) suggested that rather than optimizing water regimes for one or a few species, a better approach would be to try to approximate the natural flow regime that maintained the "entire panoply of species." These early holistic (ecosystem) methods were formulated around hydroecological principles later articulated as the Natural Flow Regime Paradigm (Poff et al. 1997), and they also drew upon general principles guiding river restoration (e.g., Stanford et al. 1996).

Holistic ecosystem approaches share a common objective: to protect or restore the flow-related biophysical components and ecological processes of in-stream and groundwater systems, floodplains, and downstream receiving waters (e.g., terminal lakes and wetlands, estuaries, and nearshore marine ecosystems). Ecosystem components commonly considered in holistic assessments include geomorphology and channel morphology, hydraulic habitat, water quality, riparian and aquatic vegetation, macroinvertebrates, and fish, and other vertebrates with some dependency on the river/riparian ecosystem (i.e., amphibians, reptiles, birds, mammals); estuarine water requirements and fisheries issues may also be included (e.g., Loneragan and Bunn 1999). The flow requirements of each of these ecosystem components can be evaluated using a range of field and desktop techniques (e.g., Arthington and Zalucki 1998; Dunbar et al. 1998; King et al. 2000; Tharme 2003), modeling, risk analysis, theoretical principles, and/or expert opinion when there is little quantitative data available and insufficient resources to collect new data or undertake long-term research.

Scientific panels and workshop procedures are typically employed to compare and contrast recommendations from individual specialists, and together the panel members reach agreement on the flows to be incorporated into a modified flow regime for a number of reaches within the river system under investigation. The use of scientific panels has precedents in medical risk assessment, ecological impact assessment, and natural resource management and has become standard practice in ecosystem-level environmental flow assessments (Cottingham et al. 2002; Richter et al. 2006).

In her global review of methods, Tharme (2003) grouped similar approaches and broader frameworks into the category "holistic methodologies," whereas Dyson et al. (2003) referred to them as "functional analysis" methods because they "build on an understanding of the functional links between all aspect of the hydrology and ecology of the river system." For the purposes of this review, they are called "ecosystem frameworks" (Arthington et al. 2010a) to reinforce their intent to address hydroecological relationships along the full continuum of the riverine ecosystem, from source to sea or other terminus. Ecosystem frameworks proliferated rapidly in the 1990s, such that after a decade of trial and error 16 were formulated, representing around 8% of the global total of methods (Tharme 2003). These methods spread rapidly beyond South Africa and Australia to both developed and developing regions of the world, with strong expressions of interest from Canada, Europe, Latin America, Asia, and Africa.

CONTEXTS OF ECOSYSTEM FRAMEWORKS

Two major contextual applications of ecosystem frameworks emerged in the late 1990s, here termed river "protection" and river "restoration" frameworks. Strictly speaking, the term "rehabilitation" is more appropriate, but it seems to have faded from use in recent years, while "restoration" has generally come to mean partial return of some features of the ecosystem toward its previous relatively undisturbed state, not full ecological restoration of a pristine ecosystem (Arthington and Pusey 2003).

The first ecosystem frameworks developed in South Africa and Australia were designed to define and quantify the volumes and temporal patterns of stream discharge that should be preserved to flow downstream below new dams and thus to sustain particular ecological and societal values. These "proactive" methods helped to advise water managers and dam designers at the planning stage of new water-infrastructure developments, as a means to "block book" water for the environment and forestall overallocation to off-stream uses of river water (King and Louw 1998) and to set constraints on new developments in large catchments (Arthington 1998). River restoration science was already employing somewhat similar ecosystem approaches around this time (see Chapter 12).

FLOW PROTECTION METHODS

Two different proactive frameworks emerged, often termed "bottom-up" and "top-down" approaches (Arthington et al. 1998). Bottom-up methods were the first to appear as expert and scientific-panel methods developed through collaborative research in South Africa and Australia. Top-down methods soon followed once the limitations of bottom-up methods became obvious. Bottom-up methods aim to construct a modified flow regime from a starting point of zero flow, thereafter adding various quantities of flow, such as baseflows, freshes, and floods of various frequency, timing, and duration. These "constructed" environmental flow regimes are intended to maintain the river–floodplain eco-system in a particular target condition or "desired future state" (King and Louw 1998).

Methods of this type are demanding to implement and vulnerable to knowledge gaps about flow–ecology relationships, so there is poten-tial to leave out critical flow characteristics (Bunn 1999; Tharme 2003), possibly resulting in implementation of modified flow regimes that will not achieve the desired ecological objectives. Top-down methods helped to resolve this difficulty. Top-down methods define environ-mental flows in terms of acceptable levels of change from the natural flow regime and the natural (before alteration) structure/functioning of the riverine ecosystem. They enable consideration of many scenarios vis-à-vis the relationships between flow regime alteration and ecologi-cal consequences, while associated decision-making processes are able to select a final recommended flow regime for implementation (JM King et al. 2003). Bottom-up and top-down approaches are beginning to merge in several of the broader environmental flow frameworks that address both contexts (see Chapter 12).

BUILDING BLOCK METHODOLOGY

One of the first bottom-up frameworks to elaborate concepts from the ecosystem approach, and similar thinking from earlier studies in South Africa (e.g., Ferrar 1989), became known as the Building Block Methodology (BBM) (King and Louw 1998). In this method, an envi-ronmental flow assessment (EFA) is developed for a number of sites within representative and/or critical river reaches and comprises three phases:

1. Preparation for an EFA workshop, including stakeholder consultation, desktop and field studies for site selection, geo-morphological reach analysis, river habitat integrity and social surveys, objective setting for future river condition, assessment of river importance and ecological condition, and hydrological and hydraulic analyses.

2. Multidisciplinary workshop-based construction of modified flow regime through identification of ecologically essential flow

features on a month by month (or shorter time scale) and flow element by flow element basis, for maintenance and drought years, based on best available scientific data.

3. Use of scenario modeling and hydrological yield analysis to link the environmental flow regime with a water-resource-development engineering phase.

In more recent iterations of the BBM, the modified environmental flow regime is designed to achieve a specific predefined river condition that may vary from class A (negligible modification from natural conditions and negligible risk to sensitive species) to class D (high degree of modification from natural conditions and the expectation that intolerant biota are unlikely to be present) (DWAF 1999). In a workshop setting, flow components are added to a baseline of zero flows, and each component is defined as a flow magnitude and the timing of its occurrence. Monthly baseflows are established first, allowing for different flows in the wet and dry months of the hydrologic year; several channel pulses (e.g., for fish migration or as spawning triggers) or seasonal floods may be added to the monthly baseflows (Fig. 26). Each specialist contributes whatever data and hydroecological relationships are at hand or uses expert judgment to advocate for a particular flow component. The process is dynamic, challenging, and time-consuming; first attempts can take a full day to complete the EFA for a single river site. The final product is typically a single environmental flow prescription to sustain aquatic communities and ecological functions in "normal" years, and usually one for drought years, at several river sites.

Tharme (2003) points out the strengths of the BBM, including its comprehensive assessment of ecosystem components, its focus on a desired future state for the river sites under study (or for the entire river), its high potential for application to other aquatic ecosystems (e.g., wetlands, estuaries), its flexibly and adaptability to circumstance (e.g., regulated or unregulated rivers), and its amenability to simplification for more rapid assessments.

The BBM now incorporates the Habitat Flow Stressor-Response Method (HFSR) (O'Keeffe and Hughes 2002; Hughes 2004), facilitating top-down, scenario-based assessments of alternative flow regimes,

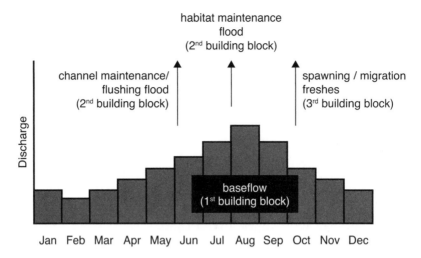

FIGURE 26. Diagram representing the process of developing a modified flow regime to protect the desired future state of a river using the Building Block Methodology. (Copyright 1998 from "Instream flow assessments for regulated rivers in South Africa using the Building Block Methodology," by King and Louw 1998. Reproduced by permission of Taylor & Francis Group LLC., www.taylorandfrancis.com.)

each with an expression of the potential risk of change in a river's ecological condition. In this modified form, the BBM is legally required for intermediate (2-month) and comprehensive (1- to 2-year) determinations for the South African Ecological Reserve—the water set aside for ecosystem protection and basic human needs (DWAF 1999). The HFSR has been applied to about 10 large reserve studies. An integrated software framework SPATSIM (spatial and time series information-modeling software) was used for many of the major environmental flow assessments (Hughes 2004). Another development has seen the BBM environmental flow prescriptions from many comprehensive EFAs grouped according to river hydrology, to extract more general hydroecological principles that may guide EFAs in rivers of contrasting hydrological character. This EFA method is known as the Desktop Reserve Model (Hughes and Hannart 2003).

An Australian–South African trial of the BBM in the Logan River, Queensland, identified several limitations of the bottom-up approach, particularly the absence of a formal process for deciding the target condition or desired future state of the river system. A balance between aquatic conservation and off-stream water use was deemed desirable, but the team wondered what balance would be appropriate, given existing river uses, conservation values, fisheries issues, future plans for urban development, and minor industries: who should decide? In this BBM trial, knowledge constraints bedeviled the formulation of the "normal year" and "drought year" environmental flow regimes, especially in the larger lowland river reaches near the freshwater-tidal interface, where previous studies were lacking and where the flow requirements of estuaries were unknown.

Following this trial, officers from the participating water-management agency put new requests to the river scientists: How much can a river's natural flow regime be modified before the aquatic ecosystem begins to noticeably change or becomes seriously degraded? Could there be a critical threshold flow regime to maintain ecosystem health and, if so, how different would it be from the natural flow regime? Can such thresholds be identified? Queensland water planners wanted a methodology to facilitate evaluation of many different options for water-resource development in large catchments (e.g., Fitzroy Basin, 143,000 km²; Burdekin Basin, 130,000 km²; Burnett Basin, 33,000 km²), and they were especially keen on the concept of a threshold ("edge of cliff") flow regime that could signal the limits to further hydrologic alteration. Faced with these challenges, river scientists proposed the Benchmarking Methodology (Brizga et al. 2002).

BENCHMARKING METHODOLOGY

The Benchmarking Methodology provides a top-down risk assessment framework to evaluate the ecological implications of potential hydrologic alterations at whole-of-catchment scale. This EFA method involves making comparisons between near-natural "reference" reaches and a set of "benchmark" reaches subject to varying levels of impact resulting from existing water-resource development (e.g., dams, weirs, water abstraction by pumping or via intra- or interbasin water transfer). The benchmark reaches are selected to cover a range of levels and types of flow regime change typical of the study catchment.

Benchmarking is comprised of four main phases:

1. Formation of multidisciplinary technical advisory panel and development of daily time-step hydrological model for the catchment: this model simulates predevelopment flows, estimates flow alterations at each benchmark site, and runs future flow management scenarios.

2. Ecological condition and trend assessment: development of spatial reference framework (multiple river sites within representative and critical river reaches), assessment of ecological condition for a suite of ecosystem components (using three-point rating of degree of change from reference condition and appropriate methods for assessing each component). Generic models (conceptual, empirical) are developed to define links between flow regime components and ecological processes, using a selection of hydrologic indicators and statistics to represent existing facets of flow regimes.

3. Development of risk assessment framework to guide evaluation of potential impacts of water-resource plans and management scenarios: benchmark models are developed for all or some key hydrologic indicators, showing levels of risk of geomorphological and ecological impacts associated with different degrees of flow regime change. Risk levels are defined by association with benchmark sites that have undergone different degrees of flow-related change in condition.

4. Evaluation of future water-resource development scenarios, using risk assessment and conceptual/empirical models: ecological implications of scenarios and associated levels of risk are expressed in graphical form, showing predicted change in ecological condition with particular hydrologic alterations (e.g., change from moderate to major ecological impact).

Selection of the key flow characteristics (indicators) is an important step in the benchmarking process. To provide a workable framework, a limited set of hydrologic indicators represents the natural flow regime. Hydrological indicators include estimates of flow quantity, seasonal timing, frequency and duration of flood events, and patterns of flow variability. In addition, flow hydrographs (plots of discharge over time) are examined to identify changes not apparent from the summary statistics (e.g., hydrograph rise and recession rates). Assessment of ecological condition involves accessing and interpreting existing datasets (e.g., vegetation lists from herbarium collections, fish distribution patterns and species composition from prior studies, invertebrate monitoring data, water-quality data); most benchmark sites are visited once by the full study team to gather observational data and supplement other information (Brizga et al. 2002).

Risk assessment models may vary in complexity depending on the size of the catchment, the range of existing water infrastructure and other options for benchmarking hydrologic impacts, and the complexity of future water-management scenarios. The EFA for the Barron River (north Queensland) evaluated the ecological condition of three river sites, each with a different level of flow regime change from natural (Brizga et al. 2000b, 2001). These benchmark sites were situated at Tinaroo Falls (very major change from natural flow regime), Mareeba township (major change from natural flow regime), and Myola township (minor to moderate change from natural flow regime). The risk assessment model for the 1.5-year daily flow volume, an indicator of minor flood events, is shown in Figure 27 as an example of the risk assessment framework.

To indicate the likely level of ecological risk, flow statistics describing potential water-resource management scenarios for other sites in the catchment can be overlaid onto these graphs (called traffic-light diagrams and colored accordingly from green—ecologically healthy—to orange to red—ecologically degraded). For example, if the flow regime at a future development site changed from reference condition to the same degree as had occurred in the regulated Barron River at Tinaroo Falls, the risk assessment models would suggest that this hydrologic change would be associated with a very high risk of ecological degradation.

More refined risk assessment models were developed for the Burnett Basin study area (central Queensland), which has a more complex pattern of water-resource development, including five major dams, managed flow releases, and water extraction by pumping (Brizga, Arthington, et al. 2000). Two risk levels were identified from the relationships between each hydrologic indicator and the ecological condition of

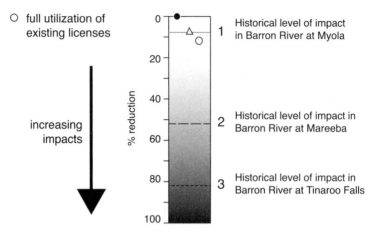

- ● no development case
- △ historical flows
- ○ full utilization of existing licenses

increasing impacts

% reduction

0
20
40
60
80
100

1 — Historical level of impact in Barron River at Myola

2 — Historical level of impact in Barron River at Mareeba

3 — Historical level of impact in Barron River at Tinaroo Falls

FIGURE 27. Risk assessment model for a hypothetical flow variable developed using the Benchmarking Methodology in the Barron River, north Queensland, Australia. Three benchmark sites were assessed for ecological condition: Myola, Mareeba, and Tinaroo Falls below Tinaroo Dam. (Redrawn from a figure in Brizga et al. 2001, with permission from the Department of Environment and Resource Management, Queensland, Australia)

more than 20 benchmark sites. Table 26 presents the hydrologic indicators and risk levels applied in the risk assessment framework for the Burnett and Barron waster-resource plans and environmental flows. A key point about these risk levels is the inference that a substantial proportion of the natural flow in these river systems (e.g., 84–87% of mean annual flow, 86–92% of the 1.5-year average return interval daily flow) needs to be retained in order to maintain ecological values at a low level of risk (i.e., within the green zone). Furthermore, these examples demonstrate the importance of maintaining the natural seasonal flow regime and close-to-natural levels of daily flow variability and dry spells in the two river systems.

The Benchmarking Methodology offers a framework to make the best use of available data and limited field sampling/surveys in a simple but robust risk assessment approach. It can be applied in any catchment

TABLE 26. *Percentage change from natural for selected hydrologic indicators associated with each risk level for the Barron Basin and Burnett Basin water resource plans*

| Hydrologic indicators | Barron River change from natural | | | Burnett River change from natural | |
	Myola (minor to moderate impact)	Mareeba (major impact)	Mareeba (very major impact)	Risk level 1	Risk level 2
Mean annual flow	87%	69%	62%	84%	79%
CV of mean annual flow	NA	NA	NA	+/−0.17	+/−0.25
Flow regime class	NA	NA	NA	no change from natural class	no change from natural class
1.5-year ARI daily flow	92%	49%	18%	86%	72%
5-year ARI daily flow	85%	49%	25%	89%	69%
20-year ARI daily flow	87%	54%	36%	91%	80%
Duration of zero flow	NA	NA	NA	+/−10%	+/−20%
Length and frequency of zero-flow spells	NA	NA	NA	+/−10%	+/−50%

SOURCES: Brizga et al. 2000a, 2001

NOTES: Different hydrologic metrics were assessed in the two river studies (NA); CV = coefficient of variation; ARI = average return interval.

with an array of existing water infrastructure and/or water abstraction. Tharme (2003) considered the approach potentially useful for developing countries and for application to other aquatic ecosystems (e.g., wetlands, estuaries). Unlike the BBM, any number of altered flow scenarios can be assessed using the benchmarking risk models. The benchmarking framework includes the option of providing recommendations to guide a monitoring program and suggesting additional research to refine empirical relationships and generate a deeper understanding of important issues, as part of environmental flow implementation through a resource operations plan (ROP) and subsequent adaptive monitoring and adjustment of environmental flow rules. The resulting water resource plans are reviewed after the recommended environmental flows have been implemented for 10 years.

Several features of the Benchmarking Method have stimulated further work, especially the applicability and sensitivity of key hydrologic indicators in different river types (Tharme 2003) and the degree to which negative benchmarks in a single river basin can be transferred to other sites within large basins, or even to other river basins. An EFA framework to achieve interbasin comparisons and to validate models across several basins—known as ELOHA (Ecological Limits of Hydrologic Alteration)—has since been proposed (Poff et al. 2010) and is discussed in Chapter 13.

Benchmarking has provided environmental flow recommendations for many coastal river basins in Queensland and has helped to inform water resource plans for inland arid-zone rivers such as Cooper Creek. Monitoring of the ecological outcomes of benchmark guidance has validated several recommendations, such as the delivery of the first postwinter flow down the Fitzroy River, central Queensland, to stimulate spawning of the golden perch *(Macquaria ambigua oriens)* and support ecosystem recovery after dry months. Experiences from benchmarking studies have contributed to EFAs in regulated rivers of the Murray-Darling Basin, where there are numerous dams and weirs to provide negative benchmark sites (Kingsford 2000). New top-down frameworks for EFAs have followed benchmarking principles, particularly DRIFT (Downstream Response to Imposed Flow Transformation) and ELOHA.

DOWNSTREAM RESPONSE TO IMPOSED FLOW TRANSFORMATION

The Benchmarking Methodology cannot be applied in rivers and catchments where there are very few existing water-infrastructure developments to provide the negative benchmarks and ecological-condition ratings that underpin risk assessment of future flow regime changes. In these circumstances, an alternative top-down approach is needed to be able to forecast the likely ecological consequences of different scenarios of hydrologic alteration. J. M. King et al. (2003) developed DRIFT to meet the demand for a rigorous and transparent top-down EFA with the capacity to evaluate alternative scenarios of water management in data-limited situations. Working in the montane rivers of the Lesotho Highlands, southern Africa, an international team, led by the originators of the Building Block Methodology, worked out the parameters of DRIFT—a robust collection of field and desktop procedures, database systems, and decision support tools for proactive planning of environmental flow provisions for rivers (JM King et al. 2003). In its original formulation, DRIFT is comprised of four modules (Fig. 28):

1. A biophysical module describes present ecosystem condition and predicts how biophysical river components will change under a range of specified flow alterations, with each prediction and the direction and severity of change accompanied by a confidence rating and subsequently recorded in a customized database.

2. A sociological module identifies subsistence users of river resources who would be at risk from flow alterations and quantifies their relationships/uses of river goods and services, including their river-dependent health profiles.

3. A scenario development module links the first two modules through querying of the biophysical database, to extract predicted consequences of altered flows (with potential for presentation at several levels of resolution); this process is used to create flow alteration scenarios (typically four or five of them).

4. An economic module: generates a description of the costs of mitigation and compensation for each flow alteration scenario.

During scenario generation in the Lesotho DRIFT application, emphasis was given to progressive reductions in wet- and dry-season low-flow volumes, reduced frequency of occurrence of flow pulses confined to channels, and altered flood frequency. The fish component of DRIFT described how the participating ecologists judged and rated the likely effects of these quantitative flow regime alterations (Arthington et al. 2003). A literature review and lists of the possible ecological responses of fish to low- and high-flow volume alterations helped to focus these evaluations and gave rise to "generic lists" for each component of the EFA. For fish, it was important to first judge how habitat would change with each flow scenario, and this was achieved in two ways:

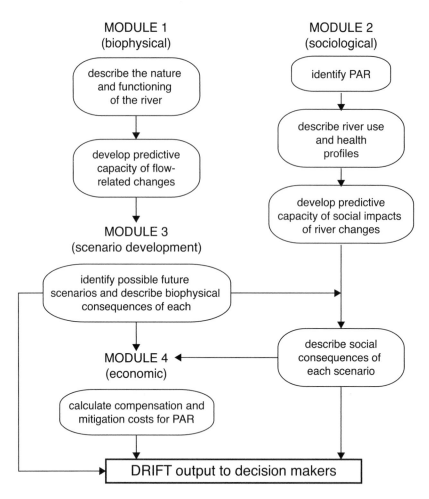

MODULE 1
(biophysical)

describe the nature
and functioning
of the river

develop predictive
capacity of flow-
related changes

MODULE 3
(scenario development)

identify possible future
scenarios and describe biophysical
consequences of each

MODULE 4
(economic)

calculate compensation and
mitigation costs for PAR

MODULE 2
(sociological)

identify PAR

describe river use
and health
profiles

develop predictive
capacity of social impacts
of river changes

describe social
consequences of
each scenario

DRIFT output to decision makers

FIGURE 28. The four modules of DRIFT (Downstream Response to Imposed Flow Transformation). PAR = people at risk from the ecological and social consequences of flow regime alterations. (Redrawn from Figure 2 in JM King et al. 2003, with permission from John Wiley and Sons)

first, by consulting with the geomorphologist and sedimentologist as to how channel morphology, habitat structures, and substrate characteristics might be altered; and second, by superimposing a form of wetted perimeter analysis on modeled scenarios of hydraulic habitat alteration in study reaches, and comparing habitat availability with fish habitat use curves generated for each species in Lesotho rivers.

Once the implications of habitat alterations were rated, evaluation turned to possible life-history consequences, a far more difficult task given the limited knowledge about most of the montane fish fauna. Information sources to support the fish assessment included published data for the same species in other catchments, field survey data collected over several seasons, statistical analysis of survey data using techniques applied in Australian studies, and professional judgment (Arthington et al. 2003). Other ecologists (e.g., plant and wildlife ecologists) working on DRIFT developed their own EFA methods (e.g., lateral gradient analysis of riparian vegetation), and a confidence rating scheme was applied to all EFAs. The DRIFT database and a protocol for multicriteria analysis allowed various scenarios to be tested and the least damaging flow regime changes to be identified (Brown and Joubert 2003). The overall DRIFT analysis for rivers of the Lesotho Highlands produced a curve (with confidence bands) that relates declining ecological condition to scenarios of decreasing flow volume below particular dams (Brown et al. 2005).

In summing up the Lesotho Highlands EFA project, King and Brown (2010) recounted how the environmental flow and socioeconomic scenarios generated by DRIFT formed the basis for negotiations between the Lesotho Highlands Development Authority (LHDA), the World Bank, and the governments of Lesotho and South Africa, eventually resulting in changes to the design of dam outlet valves and dam operating rules to allow flow releases for river ecosystem maintenance. Downstream releases increased by 300–400% compared to those that were originally specified for the Katse and Mohale Dams before the flow assessment. To compensate for loses associated with altered flow regimes (e.g., lower catches of edible fish species), compensation payments were made to villagers living along river reaches downstream of dams; approximately 7,000 households received (or will receive) compensation based on predicted resource losses over the life of the project (50 years), with the first tranche payments totaling about US$3 million made in 2004 (King and Brown 2010).

Many applications have generated refinements of DRIFT and several supporting software packages: DRIFT-SOLVER for optimization of flow regimes for ecosystem maintenance (Brown and Joubert 2003); DRIFT-HYDRO for converting hydrological series into ecologically relevant summary statistics (Brown et al. 2005); the Pangani Flows Decision Support System (DSS) links hydrological systems model outputs with ecological consequences of flow regimes and socioeconomic outcomes for multiple scenarios. A DSS for integrated basin flow assessment is under construction (Beuster et al. 2008).

12

FLOW RESTORATION METHODS

NEED FOR FLOW REGIME RESTORATION

River fragmentation and flow regulation by dams are the most pervasive and destructive changes wrought by humans in rivers worldwide (Dynesius and Nilsson 1994; Vörösmarty et al. 2010). Dams sever dynamic, interconnected surface-water and groundwater pathways of the river continuum, and they disrupt the natural flow regimes that create environmental heterogeneity and maintain biodiversity. Typically, biodiversity and biological productivity are reduced or altered in regulated rivers, and nonnative species proliferate (Poff et al. 1997; Bunn and Arthington 2002). Awareness of these impacts has generated practical efforts to recover the ecological properties of rivers by adjusting flow regimes (e.g., Petts 1989; Stanford et al. 1996; Arthington and Pusey 2003; Richter et al. 2006).

Numerous methods and modeling techniques have been applied in river restoration studies (Tharme 2003; Postel and Richter 2003). This chapter presents broad principles that inform the restoration of river flow regimes and ecosystems. Frameworks designed to cope with limited technical knowledge and capacity are presented, as well as advanced developments, including dam removal.

PROTOCOL FOR RESTORATION OF REGULATED RIVERS

Stanford et al. (1996) developed a general protocol for the restoration of regulated rivers founded on theoretical principles of river ecology, in particular the four-dimensional organization of riverine ecosystems (Ward 1989), the River Continuum Concept, and the Serial Discontinuity Concept (Ward and Stanford 1983). The latter concept explicitly recognizes the inherent connectivity within rivers (i.e., their longitudinal, lateral, vertical, and temporal components) and predicts that adverse effects of dams and flow regulation will be ameliorated downstream as a natural consequence of changes to the regulated flow regime and the longitudinal biophysical processes of rivers. Thus, at some point downstream from a dam or large weir, river conditions will be "reset" by restoration of a more natural flow regime and will come to resemble the structure and functions elsewhere in the continuum.

Although recognizing the potential for variations in this serial pattern of discontinuity and eventual ecosystem resetting below dams, Stanford et al. (1996) maintained that the ecological consequences of specific flow regulation schemes are largely predictable and therefore that environmental degradation associated with flow regulation can be ameliorated. The main goal of this restoration protocol is to reduce the range of human disturbances so that riverine habitats normally interconnected by flow can continue to support diverse and productive food webs and biodiversity, while other management practices address sources of biotic mortality from pollution and overharvest of species. Restoration of "normative habitat conditions" (Stanford et al. 1996) governed by flow and thermal regimes forms the core of the protocol, to be achieved by adjustments to dam flow release schedules and water offtake depths in particular.

Since complete removal of dams is often not possible or desirable, an additional aim of the protocol is to maximize passage efficiency for migratory biota, with the objective of reconnecting the longitudinal dimensions and processes of the river continuum, especially natural gene flow and biotic exchanges among fragmented populations (see Chapter 4). Stanford et al. (1996) noted that the entire catchment from headwaters to ocean is relevant in any river restoration program and, in particular, that the functional connectivity of freshwater and estuarine/

oceanic systems should be maintained to protect anadromous fisheries. The protocol is richly supported by practical suggestions and case studies of river restoration. It offers a flexible framework for planning comprehensive river restoration projects that embrace ecological concepts of river ecosystems at the catchment scale, the entire source-to-sea continuum, and multiple stressors.

Stanford et al. (1996) recommend an adaptive management approach to achieve "an iterative, step-wise approach that involves synthesis of available information in an ecosystem context to define the problem, public participation in goal setting (e.g., protection and restoration of native biodiversity), research and peer review to define science-based management actions (e.g., reregulation), effective monitoring and evaluation of management actions and adaptive revision of actions based on new information from scientific research." Numerous river restoration studies and several environmental flow assessment (EFA) frameworks have made similar recommendations. Some of these frameworks are discussed below.

FLOW RESTORATION METHODOLOGY

Several frameworks for river flow restoration have emerged in Australia, where many rivers in the southeastern states have been modified and significantly degraded by dams and flow regulation (Kingsford 2000; Arthington and Pusey 2003). The main frameworks have been reviewed elsewhere (Arthington 1998; Postel and Richter 2003; Tharme 2003). Here the Flow Restoration Methodology is outlined to highlight generic features of relevance to any EFA aimed at restoring, at least in part, the flow regime below a dam but also flexible enough to incorporate restoration of other river features modified by human activities (e.g., channel modifications, restoration of large woody debris, etc.). As Stanford et al. (1996) emphasized, many regulated rivers are affected by more than just flow regime changes (see Chapters 5–8).

The Flow Restoration Methodology was developed during an assessment of the environmental flow requirements of the Brisbane River downstream from Wivenhoe Dam, Queensland (Arthington et al. 1999; Greer et al. 1999). This dam was constructed primarily to impound floodwaters generated in the Upper Brisbane Valley (following a disastrous flood in 1974), but it also provides the major source of potable water to the city of Brisbane by delivering a steady flow of water (averaging 650 ML per day in 1999) to a water-treatment station; flows from Lake Wivenhoe also generate a small amount of electricity. The study involved several concurrent evaluations: environmental flow options to achieve several scenarios of ecological recovery from present-day flow regulation, a review of the operations of all water-release rules (e.g., daily flow releases and flood management), advice on restoring an inefficient fish ladder, and an assessment of the potential environmental impacts of electricity generation using the daily flow releases from Lake Wivenhoe.

The Flow Restoration Methodology is applied in two major stages: Stage 1 is an information-gathering and review phase to determine what is known about the catchment area and river system so that knowledge gaps and new field-data requirements for the EFA can be identified. A report is prepared at the end of stage 1 and "terms of reference" are developed for the detailed stage 2 studies. In the Brisbane River study, stage 2 involved seven main steps (Table 27) that are sufficiently generic to adapt to any flow restoration study. In essence, five questions must be addressed: (1) How has the original unregulated regime of the river been altered? (2) How has the riverine ecosystem responded to those hydrological changes? (3) Given the observed impacts of flow regulation, what flows should be restored to improve the flow-related functions of the riverine ecosystem? (4) Can these flows be achieved given constraints on dam operations and off-stream users of the impounded water? (5) What are the opportunities for improving river health in other ways, for example, habitat reconstruction or elimination of exotic species?

The hydrological effects of Wivenhoe Dam were estimated using statistics to compare the modeled pre-dam flow regime of the Brisbane River and the present-day status based on gauged data at several study sites (Greer et al. 1999). For example, Figure 29 demonstrates the effects of regulation on monthly discharge levels and variability (coefficient of variation, or CV) within and between years. Artificially elevated low flows that supply water for treatment, and loss of daily, monthly, and interannual variability, were major factors in the deterioration of the ecosystem below the dam (Arthington et al. 1999).

TABLE 27   *Steps in the Flow Restoration Methodology based on the Brisbane River case study*

Step	Process	Outcomes
1	Development of a daily time-step simulation model (Integrated Quantity Quality Model, or IQQM) of the river's unregulated flow regime at selected well-gauged river locations below the dam	Description of the regulated flow regime compared to the pre-dam flow regime, as a basis for assessment of ecological impacts associated with flow regulation
2	Fieldwork and research to compile and evaluate the environmental impacts of past and present flow regulation at selected reaches	Technical reports detailing the flow-ecology relationships of the river system before and after flow regulation
3	EFA workshop to define options for provision of environmental flows downstream from dam; the Brisbane River study used the Building Block Methodology to reconstruct hydroecological relationships of pre-dam river ecosystem using best available science	Expert summaries of the necessary restored flows to achieve ecological outcomes for each river component (water quality, habitat structure, invertebrates, fish, and aquatic and riparian vegetation)
4	Development of alternative environmental flow (E-flow) scenarios and modeling of scenarios using IQQM; Brisbane River scenarios included the full range of flow quantities but modified the frequency of their occurrence	Assessment of implications of each scenario for historical no-failure yield of the impoundment and for the ecological character and health of the riverine ecosystem and its biota and processes
5	Review of options for provision of E-flows given existing and future constraints on the system; consideration of alternative approaches and infrastructure arrangements to allow E-flows	Recommended E-flows for each ecological component, advice on implications of inability to deliver those flows due to system constraints (e.g., flooding of roads)
6	Identification of nonflow factors that may have influenced the condition of the river; review of remedial actions to improve ecological health	Possible remedial actions, e.g., restoration of habitat structure (benches, bars, and large woody debris); eradication of exotic vegetation
7	Development of a monitoring strategy to assess ecological benefits of E-flows	Indicators and protocols for monitoring; advice on adaptive management; research needs

SOURCE: Arthington et al. 1999

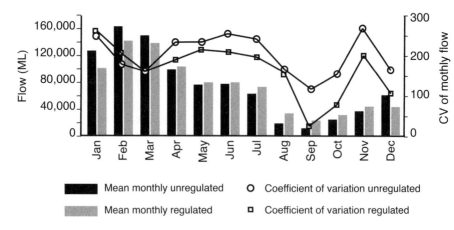

FIGURE 29. Comparison of mean monthly modeled pre-dam and present-day gauged flow data and coefficient of variation (CV) for a site on the Brisbane River downstream from Wivenhoe Dam, Queensland, Australia. (Redrawn from Arthington et al. 1999; discharge data provided by Department of Environment and Resource Management, Queensland, Australia)

Stage-discharge relationships were used to convert levels of inundation of shallow riffle areas, stream banks, riparian vegetation zones, and floodplain features to discharge magnitudes at several study sites downstream from Wivenhoe Dam. Each participating scientist identified the stage heights and related discharge levels and bands relevant to their component, starting with low flows and moving to maximum discharges at each site. Flow recommendations from each participant were collated for each flow band. For example, low flows (5.17–11.57 m³ per second = >500–1,000 ML per day) were required to maintain the physical distinctiveness of riffle, run, and pool habitats and a variety of in-stream habitats for aquatic macrophytes, invertebrates, and fish; to provide invertebrate food resources for fish and other vertebrates; and to provide low-flow conditions required for fish spawning and larval development. The maximum flow band (>1157.4 m³ per second and >100,000 ML per day) was recommended to entrain gravel substrates and retard aquatic macrophyte growth at flooded riffles and runs; to provide habitat suitable for recruitment of riparian vegetation at higher channel elevations; to maintain ongoing geomorphological processes and channel structure; to maintain coastal water quality dependent on the flushing effects of high-volume freshwater plumes; and to maintain estuarine fisheries dependent on seasonal flow pulses. The process involved reconstructing the ecological roles of the entire pre-dam flow regime using bottom-up procedures derived from the Building Block Methodology. Once the hydroecological relationships of the original pre-dam flow regime were articulated, the next step reviewed the geomorphic and ecological impacts of flow regulation and considered which particular features of the flow regime should be restored to mitigate those impacts.

One of the main lessons of the Brisbane River case study was that water managers need to be presented with many flow restoration options, not simply one or a few demanding ones that they may not be able to accommodate in full, if at all. With many scenarios on the table, a compromise flow recommendation can be reached by modeling the implications of each scenario for other users of stored water, for dam safety, and so on, and by discussing alternatives linked to their ecological implications. Scenarios were created by considering Lake Wivenhoe as a "translucent dam" (i.e., allowing different selections of incoming flows to pass through as and when they occurred in the modeled pre-dam flow regime), starting with the lowest flow threshold and band of flows and assuming that all incoming flows above that threshold in each month of every year would be released downstream to form the environmental flow regime. Not surprisingly, this first scenario drastically reduced the no-failure yield of the dam (i.e., over time this scenario would almost completely empty the storage behind Wivenhoe Dam) and was unacceptable to the client agency. The next scenario repeated this process but allowed only the first inflow volume within each flow band above the first critical threshold in each month of the year to pass through Wivenhoe Dam. More water would be stored under this scenario but it still depleted storage significantly. This process was continued by progressively reducing the frequency of inflows in each month and year that would be allowed to flow downstream; each reduction scenario increased the level of water storage in the reservoir for human uses. The resulting "trade-off" plot is presented in Figure 30.

Hydrological simulations showed clearly which environmental flows could and could not be achieved with the dam operating as flood-mitigation storage and as a major source of water for Brisbane. For

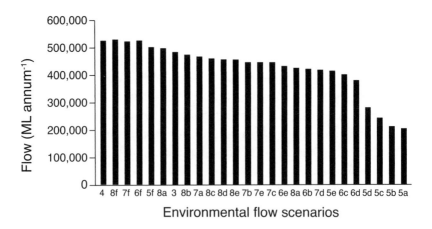

FIGURE 30.   Plot of environmental flow scenarios versus no-failure yield of Wivenhoe Dam, Brisbane River. (Redrawn from Arthington et al. 1999; discharge data provided by Department of Environment and Resource Management, Queensland, Australia)

example, a steady daily discharge of around 650 ML per day had to be delivered to the Mount Crosby water-treatment plant to meet the demands of much of Brisbane's urban population; it was not feasible to request lower, more natural low flows in dry months without severely compromising the city's major source of freshwater in those periods. At the opposite end of the flow spectrum, the highest flows, which would translate into lateral flooding downstream, could not be provided by releases of high-volume inflows without drowning out several bridges and roads in the Upper Brisbane Valley and endangering other infrastructure. A compromise seasonal flow regime was recommended to achieve more or less natural discharges and temporal variability within these twin constraints (i.e., higher low flows and lower high flows than natural but still resembling the natural monthly pattern of flows). In addition, the scientists requested greater variability of flows on a daily basis, to allow some of the drowned riffles to vary in depth and exposure and thereby to provide greater habitat heterogeneity for aquatic vegetation, invertebrates, and fish, and variability cues to stimulate other ecological processes. Even so, the restoration of this urban river was difficult to achieve without also considering options to improve river health in other ways. These included physical channel rehabilitation to replace riffle habitats drowned out by elevated low flows; floodplain reconstruction where historical gravel mining had damaged bench and bar structures; and reconstruction of the fish ladder at Mount Crosby Weir.

Experience from this study and related research generated a best practice framework for ecosystem EFAs in Australia (Arthington et al. 1998; Cottingham et al. 2002) and contributed to development of a water resource plan for the Brisbane catchment and other basins of the Moreton Bay region, southeast Queensland, a decade later.

ADAPTIVE EXPERIMENTAL RIVER RESTORATION

Flow restoration projects that are established at the outset as long-term scientific experiments—with ambitious goals, multimillion-dollar budgets, and complex governance and management structures—offer a contrast. Many scientists have called for flow restoration projects to be viewed as experiments that can generate sound understanding of hydro-ecological relationships in rivers and other aquatic ecosystems (Stanford et al. 1996; Bunn and Arthington 2002; Poff et al. 2003; Shafroth et al. 2010). Impressive examples of flow restoration experiments established within the broader framework of adaptive environmental management include programs in the Columbia River basin, the Colorado River and Grand Canyon, the Florida Everglades, the Murray-Darling Basin, and the Sacramento–San Joaquin river basin and delta in California (CALFED). The CALFED Bay-Delta Program is a unique collaboration among 25 state and federal agencies that came together in 1995 with a mission to improve California's water supply and the ecological health of the San Francisco Bay/Sacramento–San Joaquin river delta. In 2000, CALFED released a Record of Decision (ROD) that outlined a 30-year plan to improve the delta's ecosystem, water-supply reliability, water quality, and levee stability (CALFED 2000).

In an appeal for greater efforts to establish flow restoration studies as scientific experiments, Poff et al. (2003) proposed a strategy to strengthen the roles of science and society in restoring and managing rivers (and other freshwater bodies) to meet human and ecosystem needs (Fig. 31). The experimental river restoration strategy envisioned by Poff et al. (2003) is a collaborative process involving scientists, managers, and other stakeholders from the earliest stages of each project. Poff and colleagues suggest that social scientists with knowledge of human values, perceptions, behaviors, and institutional culture need to be involved from the outset and integrated into the knowledge-generation processes that guide river restoration and management. Working together in a transparent, shared problem-solving context can produce a more democratic decision-making process wherein science and social science can together better inform river restoration and management (Rogers 2006).

Individual flow restoration projects add to the knowledge base about how rivers function when modified and after more normative flow regimes are restored, along with other actions to ameliorate stressors in rivers and their catchments. What can be learned from such projects? The protocol of Poff et al. (2003) suggests that case-specific contextual knowledge should be integrated into broader scientific understanding drawn out of well-designed ecosystem experiments. However, the particulars of individual restoration case histories, and the individuality of the local human footprint, may constrain translation of individual examples into broader ecological and management generalizations. New techniques hold promise for integrating the findings of disconnected case studies to guide ecosystem management, for example, fuzzy cognitive mapping (Hobbs et al. 2002).

Another approach involves the development of Bayesian belief networks designed to capture the complexities of ecosystem and human-nature behaviors probabilistically and thus to facilitate predictive modeling based on scientific knowledge and expert judgment. Such approaches can enhance basic understanding without requiring prohibitive amounts of ecological detail (Reckhow 1999). Their application in the development of environmental flow strategies and decision making is increasing (Hart and Pollino 2009; Webb et al. 2010), as discussed in Chapter 14.

The final challenge set out by Poff et al. (2003) involves gathering the funding and institutional support for large-scale ecosystem experiments. Who should pay for them? Innovative funding partnerships include, for example, hydropower revenues generated at the main dams of the Colorado River Storage Project (Richter et al. 2003) that support both the Grand Canyon Monitoring and Research Center and

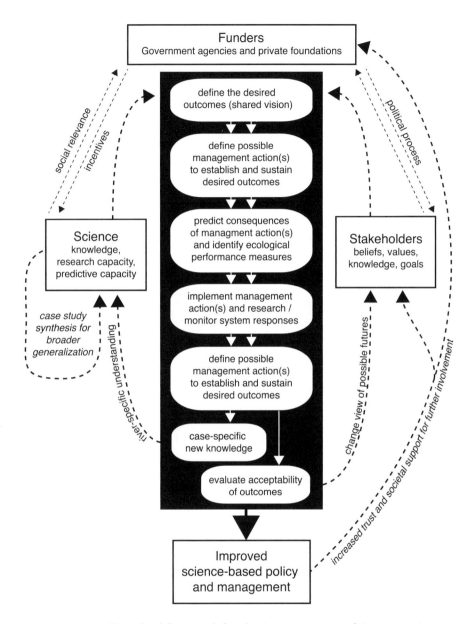

FIGURE 31. Procedural framework for adaptive management of river restoration studies and large-scale learning experiments, illustrating interactions and feedback loops between scientists, stakeholders, and funders in the pursuit of improved science-based policy and management of river ecosystems. (Redrawn from Figure 3 in Poff et al. 2003, with permission from the Ecological Society of America)

the monitoring element of the Recovery Implementation Program for Endangered Fish Species in the Upper Colorado River basin. Scientists from The Nature Conservancy are working with the US Army Corps of Engineers in a set of adaptive management experiments to modify dam operations to enhance ecological conditions on a number of rivers, including the Green River in Kentucky (Richter et al. 2003). In South Africa, the federal Water Research Commission receives all of its revenue from a tariff on national water consumption and these funds are then distributed to the research community. Poff et al. (2003) comment that although these examples are encouraging, relatively few river restoration projects are being designed and managed as experiments, and much more effort is required to set up and maintain restoration experiments for the necessary number of years.

COLLABORATIVE RIVER RESTORATION PROJECTS

Extending the theme of experimental river restoration, Richter et al. (2006) justifiably point out that costly and time-consuming restoration projects are typically far beyond the capacity of many countries, water authorities, or local community groups that want to improve the ecological health of their river systems. Richter and colleagues instead offer an adaptive, interdisciplinary, and collaborative science-based process for river restoration studies that can be adjusted to meet available knowledge as well as time and resource constraints.

This generic process mirrors most elements of the Flow Restoration Methodology and the protocol of Poff et al. (2003). It proposes an orientation meeting; literature review and summary report; a flow recommendations workshop; implementation of environmental flows; and a data-collection and research program, with a feedback loop to another flow recommendations workshop and adjustments to the environmental flow strategy. These are the fundamental steps of any adaptive management program (Walters 1986).

Elements of this generic process of particular interest to anyone setting out to conduct a river restoration project include the following: advice on the orientation meeting and scope of literature reviews and summary reports; questions to be addressed in the summary report; a table of ecological functions provided by different flow levels (see,

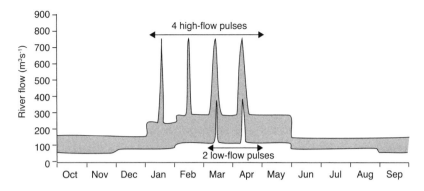

FIGURE 32. Environmental flow recommendations for the Augusta Shoals reach of the Savannah River, Georgia, specified for three different water years (dry, average, wet). The shaded band represents a synthesis of the flow recommendations across all three year types for the Augusta Shoals reach. In dry years, water managers would follow the lower band range; during wet years, flows would be closer to the upper band limit. (Redrawn from Figure 4 in Richter et al. 2006, with permission from John Wiley and Sons)

e.g., Table 8, Chapter 4 in the present volume); a detailed conceptual ecological model (flow chart) portraying the main linkages between river flows and ecological responses; and a table and summary diagram presenting the ecological objectives of the flow recommendations. These ecological objectives are presented as specific flow components (low flows, high-flow pulses within channels, and floods), time of year, and water-year type (dry, average, and wet years) following the common approach in ecosystem EFAs. The final environmental flow recommendations for the Savannah River are depicted in Figure 32.

Richter et al. (2006) note that "initially, it was quite difficult to get the participants in the flow recommendations workshop to suggest any quantitative flow targets. We found it very important to remind them that their recommendations were a first approximation that would be refined over time through an adaptive management process. Rather than allowing uncertainties to paralyse their selection of flow targets, they recorded these uncertainties in the form of data collection and research needs that would be addressed in the future to enable refinement of the flow recommendations."

DAM REMOVAL

Flow restoration strategies discussed thus far relate largely to making changes to water-release patterns below dams. A far more radical process is to remove the barrier structure altogether and allow the river system to recover some of its original characteristics and functions over time as processes governed by flow, sediment, and thermal regimes are gradually reinstated (Stanford et al. 1996). In the twentieth century, 467 dams were completely or partially removed in the United States (Poff and Hart 2002). A recent database of dam removals with details of 54 dams removed (or to be removed) in the United States in 2007 can be found at the American Rivers website (American Rivers 2007). The Ohio Department of Natural Resources has produced a video to demonstrate the rationale and ecological benefits of small dam removal (Ohio DNR n.d.).

Dam removals mostly involve very small dams less than 5 m in wall height, and several factors suggest that small dams (those that create reservoirs with a storage of 123,000 m³ or less) will continue to be removed more often than large dams; to date, few structures larger than 20 m high have been removed (Poff and Hart 2002). Small dams are often older than large dams and are more likely to be deteriorating or even unsafe. Every dam has a finite life span related to the deterioration rate of construction materials and the accumulation of sediment within the dam's impoundment, which reduces storage capacity, functionality, and utility. Sedimentation processes vary widely according to catchment climate, geology, slope, drainage density, vegetation cover, and land use; thus every impoundment has a different sediment accumulation profile and effective life span. Accordingly, sediment quantity and quality are major factors in the likelihood that a management agency or the public will consent to dam removal.

Many dams accumulate toxic sediments that can cause physical and ecological damage when released (Shuman 1995). The removal of the Fort Edwards Dam on the Hudson River, New York, in 1973 released large quantities of oils and sediments rich in polychlorinated biphenyls (PCBs) into the river (Stanley and Doyle 2003). When the remaining structure was removed in 1991, a second wave of contaminated sediments was mobilized; and the following year, average PCB concentrations in striped bass *(Morone saxatilis)* doubled (HRF 2002). Nutrients accumulated in reservoir sediments also pose threats to water quality and ecological systems far downstream, even to lakes and estuaries. For example, flushing of sediments from the Guernsey Reservoir on the North Platte River, Wyoming, caused a sixfold increase in downstream phosphorus concentrations and stimulated the growth of large filamentous green algal mats.

Mechanized sediment removal before dam breaching is an alternative to wholesale sediment release, but this can be very expensive for a large dam; however, small dams with limited sediment storage can be allowed to breach and transport their load downstream under the influence of stream discharge. Uncertainty about the probable patterns and rates of sediment transport following dam removal is a major concern (Pizzuto 2002; Stanley and Doyle 2002). These and many other environmental considerations influence the rationale, appeal, and practicality of completely removing a small dam or weir and limit the removal of much larger dams. Poff and Hart (2002) and others call for a scientific framework for making well-considered decisions about dam removal and managing such projects as scientific disturbance experiments.

The World Commission on Dams (WCD 2005) concluded that decommissioning should always be considered an option when the operations and management of a dam are being evaluated. Dam removals are increasing in many countries in spite of the threats and uncertainties outlined above (Postel and Richter 2003). The largest dam removal project in US history will reopen more than 100 km of spawning and rearing habitat for five species of salmon in the Elwha River and its tributaries, Olympic National Park, Washington State (Brenkman et al. 2012). This historic dam removal project will also restore cultural, spiritual, and economic healing for the Lower Elwha Klallam Tribe as salmon runs return and flooded sacred sites are restored.

13

ECOLOGICAL LIMITS OF
HYDROLOGIC ALTERATION
(ELOHA)

FLOW ALTERATION–ECOLOGICAL RESPONSE RELATIONSHIPS

All existing environmental flow assessment (EFA) methods—from hydrological to habitat simulation and ecosystem approaches—necessarily involve significant use of risk assessment, professional judgment, and expert opinion. How can environmental flow methods and the underlying science be enhanced to shift away from expert advice and risk assessment toward more quantitative and predictive methods?

The Natural Flow Regime Paradigm, the River Continuum Concept, the Flood Pulse Concept, and other hydroecological principles confirm that numerous hydroecological processes are common to unregulated rivers. However, these concepts do not provide immediately applicable quantitative models from which to predict how regulated rivers or any of their component biota might respond to flow regime alteration by dams and weirs, nor how impounded and regulated rivers might respond to flow regime restoration. Several general principles inform these issues; for example, the Serial Discontinuity Concept (Ward and Stanford 1983) proposes that changes downstream from dams play out in a predictable sequence and that restoration of the flow and thermal regimes of rivers should produce predictable beneficial outcomes (e.g., Stanford et al. 1996). However, at this time there are neither comprehensive compendiums of the relationships between flow restoration and ecological response nor between flow alteration and ecological response. Empirical response models of both types are required: the former to inform flow regime restoration, the latter to help predict the likely ecological outcomes when new dams and other water infrastructure are to be developed.

In light of this deficit, Poff et al. (2003) recommend integrating the findings of individual river restoration case studies to guide ecosystem management, using new tools such as fuzzy cognitive mapping and Bayesian Belief Networks to collate data from individual flow restoration experiments.

META-ANALYSIS

Two recent meta-analyses have attempted to collate flow alteration–ecological response relationships from the published literature (Lloyd et al. 2003; Poff and Zimmerman 2010). In their analysis, Lloyd et al. (2003) examined 70 studies and reported that 87% documented changes in either geomorphic or ecological variables, or both, in response to reduced flow volumes. However, it proved impossible to identify any simple linear or threshold relationship between the size of ecological change and the size of the hydrologic alteration—volumetric change being one of the most basic relationships in the definition and quantification of environmental flows (but not, of course, the only one of interest). Several constraints limited this attempt to derive quantitative relationships from a review of disparate literature, including lack of control or reference sites for unaltered conditions, other environmental changes occurring in the ecosystem (e.g., sediment flux, temperature change), and no possibility of comparing ecological conditions before and after most of the hydrologic alterations took place. Given that alteration of flow regimes is typically confounded with changes in the other environmental drivers of aquatic ecosystems, unambiguous relationships between single measures of flow alteration and ecological response may be difficult to extract (Konrad et al. 2008). Ecological responses can also be unclear because of the presence of exotic species that generate direct and indirect impacts on native species and ecosystems (Bunn and Arthington 2002). In concluding their study, Lloyd et al. (2003)

suggested that a larger dataset spanning a broader range of hydrologic alterations (i.e., not just flow volume) and types of ecosystem response might be able to detect more robust relationships.

Poff and Zimmerman (2010) conducted a comprehensive review of the literature on ecological responses to alteration of natural flow regimes, focused primarily on publications over the past decade. In particular, they sought evidence of the nature of any quantitative relationships (e.g., linear, curvilinear, or "thresholds" of response to flow alteration). Threshold relationships may be especially useful in a management context. They may signal when an ecosystem or valued ecological attribute has been shifted to the limits of resiliency and when collapse or a shift to an alternative and often undesirable ecological state is likely to occur (Folke et al. 2004).

Across a total of 165 papers that reported either aquatic (in-channel) or riparian responses to flow regime alteration, most (145) reported ecological responses to flow regime alteration in terms of population or community change of riparian vegetation, aquatic primary producers, macroinvertebrates, fish, birds, and amphibians; 99 papers reported flow alteration primarily in terms of some metric of flow magnitude. Changes in duration (25), timing (16), frequency (16), and rate of change (5) were also reported, while 4 papers did not specify a flow component.

Of the 165 studies reviewed, 70% focused only on flow modification, but some papers also mentioned alterations in other environmental drivers, including sediment (14%) and temperature (11%), and 5% mentioned sediment-temperature interactions (Poff and Zimmerman 2010). The source of flow regime change was usually a dam (88% of studies), but some alterations resulted from water diversions (17), groundwater abstraction (6), and levees (7), while a few studies reported flow alterations from weirs, road construction, or channelization; many either did not report a source (32) or reported unspecified multiple factors affecting the flow regime. Among papers reviewed, 92% reported negative ecological changes in response to a variety of types of flow alteration, and the rest reported an increased value for ecological response metrics, such as increase in nonnative species or nonwoody plant cover on dewatered floodplains. Larger changes in flow alteration were associated with greater risk of ecological change from premanagement conditions.

Fish were the only taxonomic group to consistently respond negatively to changes in flow magnitude, irrespective of whether the flows increased or decreased (Poff and Zimmerman 2010). Under reduced flows, fish responses were consistently negative, and 8 of 10 studies reported more than 50% reduction in diversity where flow magnitudes exceeded 50% change. Together, these observations suggest that fish are sensitive indicators of flow alteration.

No consistent patterns emerged for the responses of macroinvertebrates or riparian species to changes in flow magnitude. Riparian species responded to decreases in peak flows with increased nonwoody vegetation cover on the floodplain or an increase in upland species. This global review did not capture the known negative response of riparian cottonwoods (*Populus* spp.) following peak flow reductions compared to invasive salt cedar (*Tamarix* sp.) in flow-altered rivers of the American West (Stromberg et al. 2007); nor did the literature review capture the effect of a shift in timing of peak flows from spring to summer, which has prevented reestablishment of the Fremont cottonwood *(Populus fremontii)* in rivers where flow peaks now occur after, rather than before, its germination period (Fenner et al. 1985). None of the reviewed studies reported ecosystem function responses (e.g., riparian production, nutrient transformations and retention, food web processes), even though such ecological responses are clearly flow-dependent (Nilsson and Svedmark 2002; Pinay et al. 2002; Douglas et al. 2005).

Poff and Zimmerman (2010) suggested several factors that could constrain such a meta-analysis: the wide variety of ecological metrics and types of flow alteration reported; the different measures of flow alteration; different ways of measuring ecological response (e.g., upstream-downstream comparisons versus site-specific change relative to historical records); the problem of multiple hydrologic alterations (such as magnitude and seasonal timing); and interactions of flow change with other environmental characteristics, such as temperature regime, sedimentary processes, hydraulic habitat structure and dynamics, life-history processes, and the like (Konrad et al. 2008; Olden and Naiman 2010; Stewart-Koster et al. 2010).

An overriding problem for both analyses (Lloyd et al. 2003; Poff and Zimmerman 2010) was that few of the studies reviewed actually set out to relate flow regime alteration and ecological response as explicitly as is necessary to advance quantification of hydroecological relationships in undisturbed and regulated river systems. Poff and Zimmerman (2010) have called for far greater efforts to develop hydrologic alteration–eco-logical response relationships through targeted monitoring along gradients of flow regime change and before-after dam construction as well as through flow release experiments (e.g., King et al. 2010) and analysis of existing datasets.

A final and critical constraint to the meta-analyses of Lloyd et al. (2003) and Poff and Zimmerman (2010) was that the studies reviewed ranged across river types, bioregions, and climatic zones, and the number of reported studies was insufficient to stratify the data to take into account these geographic and climatic influences on flow regime and ecosystem characteristics (see Chapter 2).

FLOW-ECOLOGY RELATIONSHIPS FOR RIVER TYPES

In an attempt to address the latter constraint in particular, Arthington et al. (2006) suggested a process to quantify flow alteration–ecological response relationships for different types of river systems classified according to their natural hydrological characteristics (magnitude, timing, frequency, duration, and variability). This process extends the Benchmarking Methodology by proposing development of quantitative flow alteration–ecological response relationships determined by empirical measurement along gradients of flow regime alteration (Fig. 33), rather than ranking the ecological condition of regulated river sites into categories based on the severity of their alteration from the natural ("reference") ecological condition. Methods that rank ecological condition have fundamental limitations and are generally too coarse to identify thresholds of ecological response to flow alterations.

Arthington et al. (2006) wanted to study how streams of different hydrological character might differ in their responses to flow alteration (or to restoration of a regulated flow regime). Such an approach could address the needs of water managers for transferable hydroecological relationships and environmental flow guidelines rather than managing for the "uniqueness" of each river's flow regime. Within a region, the ecological characteristics of streams and rivers of different hydrological types are expected to be relatively similar compared to the ecological characteristics between types; therefore, these different types of rivers

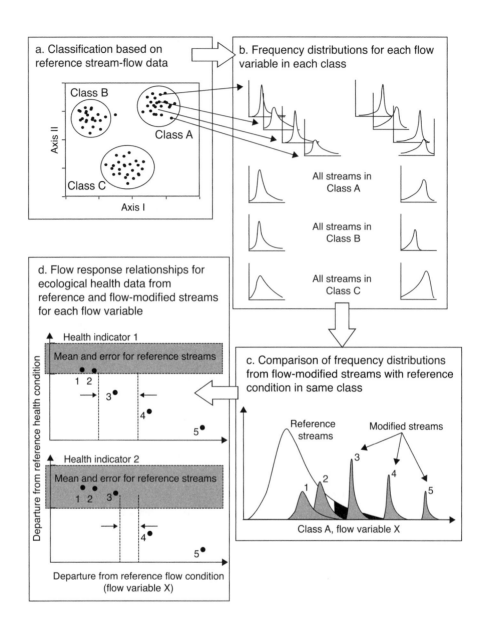

a. Classification based on reference stream-flow data

Class B

Class A

Class C

Axis II

Axis I

b. Frequency distributions for each flow variable in each class

All streams in Class A

All streams in Class B

All streams in Class C

d. Flow response relationships for ecological health data from reference and flow-modified streams for each flow variable

Departure from reference health condition

Health indicator 1

Mean and error for reference streams

1 2

3

4

5

Health indicator 2

Mean and error for reference streams

1 2 3

4

5

Departure from reference flow condition (flow variable X)

c. Comparison of frequency distributions from flow-modified streams with reference condition in same class

Reference streams

Modified streams

1 2 3 4 5

Class A, flow variable X

may represent distinct "management units." By comparing ecological condition along flow–alteration gradients, ecologically relevant flow standards can be developed and calibrated for each hydrologic stream or river type (Fig. 33). The aim is to develop empirical flow response curves for each natural asset of interest (e.g., habitat, aquatic and ripar-

FIGURE 33. *(opposite)* Steps of a framework to develop flow alteration–ecological response relationships for rivers of different hydrological character. Reference streams are classified into hydrologically similar groups according to particular combinations of ecologically important flow variables extracted from the long-term hydrograph (a). Frequency distributions are developed for each flow variable in each class and are combined to represent the natural range of spatial and temporal variation in each flow variable across all streams in the class (b). Frequency distributions from flow-modified streams are compared with the reference condition frequency distribution for the particular stream class (c). Flow–ecological response relationships are developed for each ecological health metric across the gradient of natural (or "reference") to modified flow regimes for each stream flow variable and stream class (d). Two critical risk levels or benchmarks (indicated by dotted vertical lines and small horizontal arrows) guide the setting of environmental flow standards. (Redrawn from Figure 1 in Arthington et al. 2006, with permission from the Ecological Society of America)

ian vegetation, invertebrates, and fish) and each ecologically relevant flow variable defining the stream type (e.g., low-flow discharge; the magnitude, timing, and frequency of flood flows; duration of low-flow spells; etc.).

THE ELOHA FRAMEWORK

In response to these suggestions The Nature Conservancy (TNC) invited 19 river scientists to develop a fully-fledged working framework now known as ELOHA—Ecological Limits of Hydrologic Alteration (Poff et al. 2010). The ELOHA process consists of a biophysical and a social science module, following the major scientific steps set out in Figure 33 but significantly elaborated as shown in Figure 34.

These are the ELOHA steps. (1) Hydrologic modeling is used to build a hydrologic foundation of baseline and current hydrographs for stream and river segments throughout the chosen study region. (2) Using a set of ecologically relevant flow variables based on the five facets of river flow regimes (see Olden and Poff 2003), river segments within the region are classified into a few distinctive flow regime types that are expected to have different ecological characteristics. These river types can be further subclassified according to important geomorphic features that define hydraulic habitat conditions for biota.

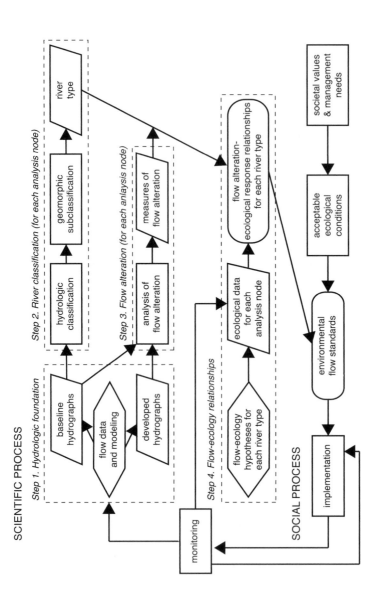

FIGURE 34. The ELOHA (Ecological Limits of Hydrologic Alteration) framework for setting environmental flow guidelines for the rivers of several distinctive hydrological classes in a user-defined region. In a scientific process, hydrologic analysis and classification (steps 1, 2, and 3) are developed in parallel with flow alteration–ecological response relationships (step 4). These response relationships provide scientific input into a social process that balances environmental values with societal values and goals. (Redrawn from Figure 1 in Poff et al. 2010, with permission from John Wiley and Sons)

(3) The deviation of current-condition flows from baseline-condition flow is determined for a suitable length of flow records. (4) Flow alteration–ecological response relationships are developed for each river type, based on a combination of existing hydroecological literature, field studies across gradients of hydrologic alteration, and expert knowledge. Ideally, a parsimonious suite of flow variables will emerge that collectively depict the major facets of the flow regime and explain much of the observed variation in ecological response to particular kinds of flow alteration in each river flow type.

After these four steps, interpretation of these hydroecological relationships and thresholds occurs in a consensus context where stakeholders and decision makers explicitly evaluate acceptable risk as a balance between the perceived value of the ecological goals (and ecosystem services), the economic costs involved, and the scientific uncertainties in functional relationships between ecological responses and flow alteration (Poff et al. 2010). The ELOHA framework is envisaged as proceeding in an adaptive management context where the objective is to formalize ongoing collection of monitoring data, or targeted field sampling, to test and fine-tune the hypothesized flow alteration–ecological response relationships.

In the science module of the ELOHA framework, the exploration of relationships between flow alteration and ecological responses begins by posing a series of plausible hypotheses that are based on expert knowledge and understanding of the hydroecological literature. Hypotheses describing expected trajectories of ecological change associated with specific types of flow alteration are then generated during the ELOHA workshop and subsequently (Table 28). Hypotheses must be tailored to the river type (e.g., largely small headwater streams or mostly large rivers with well-developed floodplains) and other relevant features of the study area and to the types of ecological data already available for analysis.

A guiding principle of ELOHA is that ecological responses to particular components of the altered flow regime can be interpreted most robustly, and usefully, when there is some mechanistic or process-based relationship between the ecological response and the particular flow regime component. Poff et al. (2010) suggest a wide range of potential ecological indicators (Table 29) that may be grouped according to taxo-

TABLE 28   *Examples of hypotheses to describe expected ecological responses to flow alteration, formulated by the authors of ELOHA*

Flow characteristic	Hypothesis
Extreme low flows	Depletion of extreme low flows in perennial streams and subsequent drying will lead to rapid loss of invertebrate and fish diversity and biomass due to declines in wetted riffle habitat, lowered residual pool area depth when riffles stop flowing, loss of connectivity between viable habitat patches, and poor water quality.
Low flows	Depletion of low flows will lead to progressive reduction in total secondary production as habitat area becomes marginal in quality or is lost.
	Augmentation of low flows will cause a decline in richness and abundance of species with preferences for slow-flowing, shallow habitats.
Small floods and high-flow pulses	Lessened frequency of substrate-disturbing flow events will lead to reduced benthic invertebrate species richness as fine sediments accumulate, blocking substratum interstitial spaces.
Large floods	Increases in floodplain inundation frequency will enhance productivity in riparian vegetation species through increased microbial activity and nutrient availability, up to a point of waterlogging, after which productivity will decline due to anaerobic soil conditions.

SOURCE: Adapted from Poff et al. 2010

nomic identity, level of biological organization, structural or functional contribution, or species' traits that reflect adaptation to a dynamic environment (e.g., life-history characteristics or morphological features). The rate of response to temporal change is an important factor in the selection of ecological indicators, to ensure that anticipated response times are captured. For example, species and communities that respond to environmental change quickly, such as algae and invertebrates, versus species or community indicators that have much longer response times, such as riparian trees, should be considered. In addition, biota and ecological processes may respond to flow alteration either directly (e.g., a spawning response to a flow threshold such as a rapid rise in flow or a flood) or indirectly (e.g., a water-quality or habitat-mediated

TABLE 29   *Ecological indicators useful in developing flow alteration–ecological response relationships*

Criteria	Indicator
Mode of response	Direct response to flow (e.g., spawning or migration).
	Indirect response to flow (e.g., habitat-mediated)
Habitat responses linked to biological changes	Changes in physical (hydraulic) habitat (width–depth ratio, wetted perimeter, pool volume, bed substrate).
	Changes in flow-mediated water quality (sediment transport, dissolved oxygen, temperature).
	Changes to in-stream cover (e.g., bank undercuts, root masses, woody debris, fallen timber, overhanging vegetation).
Rate of response	*Fast versus slow*
	Fast: appropriate for small, rapidly reproducing, or highly mobile organisms. Slow: long life span.
	Transient versus equilibrial
	Transient: establishment of tree seedlings, return of long-lived adult fish to spawning habitat. Equilibrial: reflecting an end-point of recovery to some equilibrium state.
Taxonomic groupings	Algae and aquatic vegetation; riparian vegetation; macro-invertebrates; amphibians; fish; terrestrial species (arthropods, birds, water-dependent mammals, etc.).
	Composite measures, such as species diversity; Index of Biotic Integrity.
Functional attributes	Production; trophic guilds; morphological, behavioral, life-history adaptations (e.g., short-lived versus long-lived, reproductive guilds); habitat requirements and guilds; functional diversity and complementarity.
Biological level of response (process)	Genetic; individual (energy budget, growth rates, behavior, traits); population (biomass, recruitment success, mortality rate, abundance, age-class distribution); community (composition, dominance, indicator species, species richness, assemblage structure); ecosystem function (production, respiration, trophic complexity).
Social value	Fisheries production; clean water and other ecosystem services or economic values; protection of endangered species.
	Recreational opportunities (e.g., rafting, swimming, scenic amenity); indigenous cultural and spiritual values.

SOURCE: Adapted from Poff et al. 2010

response). Bunn and Arthington (2002), Nilsson and Svedmark (2002), and Pinay et al. (2002) set out principles to guide understanding of the direct and indirect roles of flow components and flow alterations for aquatic biodiversity and nutrient processing (see Chapter 4). These and other principles, as well as local knowledge of the rivers to be studied, can guide the selection of ecological indicators.

Ecological responses to flow alteration may vary from no change to linear or to a threshold response (Anderson et al. 2006; Arthington et al. 2006), and the response may be positive or negative, depending on the selected ecological variable(s), the specific flow metric(s), and the degree of alteration for a given river type. Examples for three river types—snowmelt, groundwater-fed, and flashy—are illustrated in Figure 35. Flow alteration–ecological response relationships can be compiled from existing or new data arrayed along a flow regulation gradient; and the relationships can be tested statistically to determine the form and degree of ecological change associated with a particular type of flow regime change. One important reason for developing a flow regime classification is that the form and direction of an ecological response to flow alteration are hypothesized to be similar within river types and to vary among distinctive river types.

In the final stages of the ELOHA framework, scientists, stakeholders, and managers consider a suite of flow alteration–ecological response relationships, preferably including the response of aquatic and riparian vegetation, fish, and water-quality variables to specific types of flow alteration. Where there are clear threshold responses (e.g., overbank flows needed to support riparian vegetation or provide fish access to backwater and floodplain habitat), a "low-risk" environmental flow would be one that does not cross the threshold of hydrological alteration for overbank flows. For a linear response where there is no clear threshold for demarcating low from high risk, a consensus stakeholder process may be needed to determine acceptable risk to a valued ecological asset, such an estuarine fishery dependent on freshwater inflows (e.g., Loneragan and Bunn 1999). The ELOHA framework allows for expert panels and expert judgment to be used to identify "benchmarks" (Brizga et al. 2002), "thresholds of potential concern" (Biggs and Rogers 2003), or risk levels, as commonly occurs during river-specific environmental flow assessments.

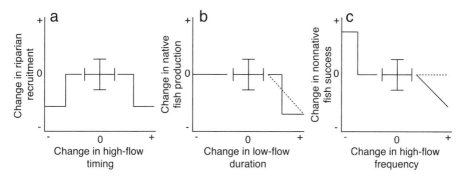

FIGURE 35. Flow alteration–ecological response relationships for three river types: snowmelt (a), groundwater-fed (b), and flashy (c). Change in the flow metric (x-axis) ranges from negative to positive, with no change representing the reference condition. The response of the ecological variable (y-axis) to the flow alteration measured across a number of altered sites ranges from low to high. The bracketed space in the center of the graph represents the natural range of variation in the flow variable and ecological variable at the reference sites. (Redrawn from Figure 3 in Poff et al. 2010, with permission from John Wiley and Sons)

The ELOHA framework is sufficiently flexible to provide inputs to several spatial scales of environmental flow assessment, ranging from river types (derived from a hydrological classification of waterways in a user-defined region) to subcatchments of large river basins, individual rivers, and river segments. While the original ELOHA concept was to predict future ecological condition should new dams and other water infrastructure, or abstractions by other means, be put into place (Arthington et al. 2006), the hydroecological relationships established along flow alteration gradients (most often below dams) can also provide the foundation for planning the restoration of flow regimes in regulated rivers within a broad region. When many different rivers of differing hydrological character with altered flow regimes have been studied systematically using an ELOHA framework, hydroecological relationships will be available to suggest how individual rivers or tributaries could be restored by returning a more natural type of flow regime to watercourses of a particular hydrological class. Opportunities might include restoring some important flow characteristics, such as a more natural level of baseflow in a water-deprived stream or an occasional flood below a storage reservoir to stimulate fish spawning or riparian recruitment. While flow restoration alone may not be sufficient to achieve desirable objectives in a restored river, or the existing legacies of past flow and catchment disturbances may be too pervasive to allow significant restoration success, an ELOHA database should nevertheless provide a useful resource for planning river restoration works in a regional water plan.

Additionally, an ELOHA database of hydroecological relationships for regulated and unregulated (reference) streams essentially provides a condition assessment, and even a conservation ranking, provided that suitable indicators (e.g., endangered species and other valued assets) have been monitored during the process. From this information it may be possible to establish broad conservation priorities and also restoration priorities specifically for rivers or river subcatchments from among a suite of possibilities. Methods and frameworks that consider each river as a separate entity for an individual environmental flow assessment cannot make these judgments, which may help to achieve a more acceptable balance between conservation of water resources for people and for ecosystem support. Not every regulated river or stream can be restored, and decisions must be made as to where to invest in river protection and restoration. ELOHA is sufficiently flexible to support both types of decision making over spatial scales that range from river reaches and tributaries, subcatchments, and several rivers to the many rivers and streams of large bioclimatic regions or political jurisdictions.

APPLICATIONS OF ELOHA

ELOHA applications are under way in several jurisdictions of the United States and in Australia, Brazil, and China. A selection of these projects is described below. Further details on progress for each application can be found at The Nature Conservancy's ELOHA website (TNC 2009).

An ELOHA study in Washington State has commenced with a statewide classification of river types based on 99 hydrologic metrics that describe ecologically relevant characteristics of the natural flow regime (Reidy Liermann et al. 2011). This analysis has identified distinctive flow regime types that differ in their seasonal patterns of discharge, variation in low flow and flood magnitude and frequency, and other aspects of flow predictability and variability. Future studies will examine interactions between hydrology and ecology in rivers of the Pacific Northwest, United States.

The Colorado Water Conservation Board has developed flow-ecology curves embedded in a watershed flow evaluation tool (WFET), a specific application within the broader ELOHA framework (Camp Dresser et al. 2009). The WFET is designed to help basin stakeholders assess nonconsumptive flow needs by associating flow regime change with ecological response by stream type. In the Roaring Fork watershed, baseline (predevelopment) conditions and existing flow conditions resulting from current water management were compared for 47 nodes (basin locations). The Indicators of Hydrologic Alteration software (Richter et al. 1996) was used to calculate flow metrics that relate to ecological and recreational conditions in the watershed for the baseline and existing hydrologic datasets. To develop the flow-ecology relationships underlying the WFET, Wilding and Poff (2008) mined diverse data from 149 sources (journal articles, technical reports, and theses). They quantified relationships between stream flow conditions and riparian vegetation, cold water and warm water fish, aquatic macroinvertebrates, and recreation (kayaking, rafting) in three steam types. Comparison of measured ecosystem parameters across varying levels of flow alteration allowed patterns to emerge that provided a basis for quantifying ecosystem response. For example, August and September flows were estimated at each node, and if the average of these summer low flows divided by the mean annual flow was between 26 and 55 percent, the ecological risk for trout was considered minimal. This information was displayed on watershed maps using different color schemes to represent ecological risk at each node.

The Nature Conservancy and the World Wildlife Fund are participating in Mexico's national multiagency technical working group to formulate a national technical standard (Norma PROY-NMX-AA-000-SCFI-2010) for setting environmental flows for the country's rivers. The Norma standard proposes a four-level hierarchy of methods for determining environmental flows, from planning levels using simple desktop hydrologic methods to detailed interdisciplinary assessments. The standard incorporates locally tailored procedures to apply the ELOHA framework for regional assessment at a basin or suprabasin scale.

A program has commenced in China to develop a framework for

evaluating river health, environmental flows, and water allocation based around the concepts of ELOHA (Gippel et al. 2009; Gippel 2010). Individual river case studies are under way to test fundamental steps in the methodology before committing to regional-scale environmental flow assessments. A trial study of the hydrologic foundation of ELOHA has explored using monthly flow records to classify rivers into hydrologic types in the many situations where daily flow data are not available (Zhang et al. 2011). Studies in the Yellow River have applied concepts from other ecosystem methodologies and hydroecological principles to estimate the flow requirements of fish in lowland reaches (Jiang et al. 2010).

The scientific module of the ELOHA framework has been tested in southeast Queensland, Australia, where coastal rivers and streams have been impounded for urban and irrigation water supply for up to 50 years, and river ecosystem integrity has declined to "poor" condition in recent stream-health assessments. In this study, data for riparian vegetation, aquatic vegetation, and fish were collected at 40 steam sites on one or several sampling occasions across two years (Arthington et al. 2012). The major ELOHA concepts tested and the results obtained are summarized in Table 30.

This study demonstrated the importance of flow versus other environmental gradients (climate, catchment characteristics, land-use patterns, stream habitat structure, and water quality) as drivers of riparian and in-stream biotic assemblage structure. Significant linear biotic responses to flow regime variability across the study area were evident for all three ecological components—riparian and aquatic vegetation and fish. Most of the responses quantified have a mechanistic basis. Different responses to flow regime alteration were apparent within flow classes because each dam altered the downstream flow regime in a different way, and there was limited opportunity for replication of each flow alteration type in the study region. Moreover, when all sites across the study area were included in a single gradient of flow alteration, the different flow classes and biotic relationships within them confounded the anticipated linear response. Nevertheless, useful flow alteration–ecological response relationships were established; they are being used to inform environmental flow management and in an assessment of the potential for climate change impacts in southeast Queensland.

TABLE 30 *ELOHA concepts tested and results obtained during a trial application in southeast Queensland, Australia*

ELOHA concept	Results
Rivers of the chosen region can be grouped into distinctive flow regime classes based on ecologically relevant flow metrics (measures of flow magnitude, seasonal timing and frequency of low flows and flooding, and overall flow variability).	Classification of unregulated flow regimes based on modeled predevelopment flow data derived from an Integrated Quantity Quality Model (IQQM) identified six flow classes that separated flow regimes along a gradient of discharge magnitude (per unit of catchment area) and discharge variability.
Within a defined geographic region, the ecological characteristics of rivers in each flow regime class are expected to be relatively similar compared to the ecological characteristics between the classes.	There were significant differences in bankfull riparian metrics across flow classes but few differences in near-stream and aquatic vegetation. Fish assemblages were significantly different across flow classes in species richness, total fish density, native density, exotic density, and assemblage composition.
Ecological responses to flow regime change by dams or other factors will vary according to the type of flow regime and the particulars of how the flow regime has been altered.	Dams and flow regulation had significant impacts on riparian and aquatic vegetation and fish in the study area streams/rivers. Impacts varied from one flow class to another and reflected the particular changes in flow brought about by each dam.
Increasing degrees of change in selected flow metrics will have increasing impacts on ecological response variables.	Riparian vegetation, aquatic vegetation, and fish showed both positive and negative responses to alteration of individual flow metrics (e.g., duration of low-flow spells, CV of daily flows).

SOURCE: Arthington et al. 2012

Elements of the ELOHA framework are being tested in a research program designed to support the Murray-Darling Basin Plan (MDBP), which has set out scenarios of environmental flows to restore the ecological condition of overallocated rivers. The MDBP is discussed in more detail in Chapters 19 and 21.

14

ENVIRONMENTAL FLOW RELATIONSHIPS, MODELS, AND APPLICATIONS

RELATIONSHIPS AND MODELS

Environmental flow assessment (EFA) and effective management require the capacity to predict the future ecological condition of a river ecosystem after its flow regime has been altered. Proactive (river protection) methods aim to predict ecological consequences after proposed dams are constructed and formerly "natural" flow regimes are changed in ways that reflect dam characteristics such as water storage and release procedures (see Chapter 11). Reactive (river restoration) methods aim to predict ecological outcomes after a regulated flow regime is restored to some degree, although flow manipulations are rarely expected to completely restore former pre-dam ecological characteristics (see Chapter 12). This chapter is devoted to recent developments in modeling ecological responses to flow in natural, regulated, and restored river systems.

FLOW AND THERMAL REGIMES

Olden and Naiman (2010) present a synthesis around the concept of the thermal regime of a river system and the ecological implications of natural and modified water-temperature regimes. A stream's thermal regime can be described using terms familiar from the description of river flow regimes: the magnitude, frequency, duration, timing, and variability in water temperatures at different spatial and temporal scales. Yet very few studies have attempted to explore the individual and interactive effects of flow and thermal modifications on biotic assemblages downstream from dams (Murchie et al. 2008). Coupled thermal and flow regimes are an assumed feature of the original Flood Pulse Concept, however they do not necessarily coincide in temperate rivers; this disjunction has implications for the evolution of life-history strategies (e.g., AJ King et al. 2003), the impacts of dams, and the design and management of environmental flows (King et al. 2010).

A number of management options exist for mitigating the thermal impacts of dams. Landscape drivers of riverine thermal regimes (e.g., riparian vegetation and tributary confluence zones) can be manipulated to promote thermal integrity (e.g., Preece and Jones 2002). The thermal impacts from dams can be managed in two main ways: exploit the temperature stratification of the reservoir by selective withdrawal of water of the desired temperature, or artificially break up the stratification prior to discharging water from the dam. Seven general strategies for mitigating thermal pollution have been promoted: multilevel water-intake structures, trunnions (floating intakes), bubble plume destratification systems, surface pumps on floating platforms, draft tubes, submerged weirs, and stilling basins (Sherman et al. 2007).

Given the complexities and trade-offs regarding alternative dam strategies for meeting both downstream flow and thermal standards, particularly in the absence of a temperature control device, Olden and Naiman (2010) suggest that environmental flow assessments would benefit from the use of formal optimization frameworks and pragmatic models incorporated into adaptive management strategies. The projected impacts of climate change and rising temperatures over the next century intensify the need for environmental flow strategies that incorporate the dynamics of water temperature (see Chapter 22).

FLOW AND WATER CHEMISTRY

As well as thermal regime, many additional aspects of water quality influence stream ecosystems (e.g., contaminants, salt, nutrients, organic matter, sediments, and dissolved oxygen) and interact with water temperature and discharge in complex syndromes. Chapters 5–7 reviewed some of the many ways that human activities in catchments and river corridors can interfere with freshwater ecosystems and water quality. A useful review of relationships between flow regime characteristics and water chemistry (Nilsson and Renöfält 2008) suggests that many problems of impaired water quality are associated with highly unnatural episodes of low flow within the channel. At these times, the concentration of at least some in-stream chemical components (e.g., dissolved salts) and contaminants is likely to increase and become stressful for aquatic biota. Several suites of models are available to link water constituents with stream discharge; for example, flow-concentration modeling can be used to predict the water quality likely to result from a given, prescribed flow regime, while concentration time-series modeling supports the ranking of complex flow scenarios in relation to potential consequences for water quality (Malan et al. 2003). These modeling approaches and a framework incorporating predictions of water quality and the implications for aquatic biota have informed the determination of the "ecological reserve" for South African rivers under the National Water Act (NWA) of 1998 (see Chapter 21). The reserve is the amount of water and timing of flow required to maintain a given level of ecosystem functioning. A guiding principle for estimating the reserve is that environmental flows should not normally be used to dilute contaminants.

Catchment and point-source management offer strategies to improve water-quality problems originating outside of streams. They include reduction of surface runoff, proper scheduling of fertilizer inputs to agricultural land, proper timing of irrigation and of wastewater release, development of riparian buffers and wetland habitats for water cleansing, and flow regimes designed to avoid extended periods of low water (Nilsson and Renöfält 2008). Numerous models support these strategies. Mitsch et al. (2005) proposed the construction of riparian wetlands to clean polluted river water before it reaches the ocean; they estimated that 22,000 km^2 of wetland creation and restoration could remove 40% of the nitrogen estimated to discharge from the Mississippi River into the Gulf of Mexico. A general management strategy to remove nitrate could be to increase the structural complexity of riverine systems, because the area of water-substrate interface is positively correlated with the efficiency of nitrogen retention and uptake both in streams and in riparian and floodplain zones (Pinay et al. 2002). Water-retentive structures, such as algal mats, aquatic vegetation, coarse woody debris, and baffles, help to promote biological processing of nitrogen. Expanding riparian wetlands and setting aside certain areas for flooding not only reduces nutrient loading into rivers but also protects other areas from being flooded (Scholz 2007).

FLOW AND AQUATIC VEGETATION

Physical determinants of aquatic macrophyte assemblage and population structure are all tightly related to flow factors such as flow extremes, stream hydraulics, substrate composition and stability, disturbance intensity and frequency, localized variations in water velocity, turbulence, shear stress, and scouring (Biggs 1996; French and Chambers 1996). Pronounced spatial variations in these factors, and in water quality and the light environment, usually generate highly patchy plant distributions in streams and rivers (Sand-Jensen and Madsen 1992). Despite their variability, these patterns are to some extent predictable based on given changes in disturbance regimes and resource availability (e.g., Riis and Biggs 2001; Mackay et al. 2003). Aquatic macrophytes are frequently affected by flow regulation, indicating that better understanding of the flow-related drivers of aquatic vegetation patterns and processes can inform the design of river regulation schemes to minimize impacts and support river restoration strategies. Development of models of wider applicability based on species traits or community attributes is one of the current challenges in macrophyte community ecology (Bernez et al. 2004).

From a management perspective, Champion and Tanner (2000) highlighted the ecological benefits of maintaining moderate levels of submerged macrophytes interspersed with shaded areas to enhance the health of degraded lowland streams. Humphries (1996) suggested that water allocations for in-stream purposes must meet the requirements of all species of aquatic macrophytes, because maintaining the heterogeneity of this type of habitat may be vital in ensuring aquatic biodiversity (particularly invertebrate diversity) and riverine health. Multivariate models and gradient analysis of native and exotic aquatic macrophyte distribution patterns continue to inform river condition and environmental flow assessments (e.g., Mackay et al. 2003, 2010). Several ecosystem EFA methods (e.g., benchmarking and flow restoration) routinely consider the ecological relationships of submerged aquatic macrophytes with characteristic patterns of river flow regimes and hydraulic habitat structure.

FLOW AND RIPARIAN VEGETATION

Determining hydrologic requirements for survival from germination to reproductive age and senescence, as well as interactions with physical and biotic factors such as channel change processes and competition, are necessary steps for specifying the flow requirements of riparian vegetation (e.g., Nilsson and Svedmark 2002). In a recent contribution, Merritt et al. (2010) reviewed models linking riparian vegetation and attributes of flow regime at individual, population, and community levels. The recruitment box model has been widely used to aid in the design of flow regimes to enhance recruitment for riparian forest restoration (Rood et al. 2005). Integration of dynamic numerical modeling and spatial mapping of site and stand dynamics has proved useful for predicting the extent and characteristics of change under various simulated flow regimes, enabling evaluation of trade-offs associated with various flow scenarios (e.g., Pearlstine et al. 1985). Matrix population modeling can be useful but has rarely been applied in developing flow standards to manage plant populations along rivers. Lytle and Merritt (2004) developed a structured population model for riparian *Populus* trees by incorporating stochastic processes (flooding, drought, and rates of river-stage decline) that are tightly linked to *Populus* vital rates (stage-specific births and deaths). At the community level, attributes used to characterize vegetation (e.g., biomass, vegetation volume, growth rates, and stand physical structure) can be regressed against flow variables, enabling an evaluation of trade-offs between managed flow scenarios and measurable riparian conditions.

A disadvantage of these techniques is that responses to flow are often river- and site-specific, limiting transferability of relationships to other rivers even in the same hydroclimatic region. To overcome these limitations Merritt et al. (2010) proposed a general framework for grouping riparian plant species into "riparian vegetation–flow response guilds," within which the members are expected to respond in similar ways to quantifiable flow attributes. Five guild categories can be recognized based on life history, reproductive strategy, morphology, fluvial disturbance, and water balance. Riparian flow response guilds can be broken down to the species level for individual projects or used to develop flow-management guidelines for regional water-management plans (Merritt et al. 2010). Similar studies on the reproductive traits of submerged macrophytes have informed response trajectories following flood disturbance.

A restoration study of the Bill Williams River, a significant tributary to the lower Colorado River in Arizona, western United States, has employed models linking hydrology and hydraulics, groundwater-surface water dynamics, and reservoir operations to estimate key hydrological and geomorphic conditions and processes that can be linked to biotic responses through other models, software, and field data collection (Shafroth et al. 2010). Riparian models are integral to this comprehensive study. Modeling of local-scale hydraulic forces integrated with field data on tree seedling monitoring is being used to evaluate the response of *Populus* seedlings to floods. The Hydrologic Engineering Center's Ecosystem Functions Model (HEC-EFM) predicted various ecological response functions along the river, including locations and substrates suitable for riparian tree seedling establishment and recruitment under specific flow scenarios. The model applies time series of daily mean flow and stage height to compute statistics relevant to any ecological response, for example, the season, duration, rate of change, and frequency of occurrence of floods.

In their appraisal of these modeling capabilities, Shafroth et al. (2010) stressed the importance of accounting for geomorphic processes that can influence ecological responses. Escobar-Arias and Pasternack (2010, 2011) make the same plea for attention to geomorphic thresholds governed by flow dynamics. Their Functional Flows Model (FFM) relates discharge values to shear-stress conditions that serve ecological purposes such as creation and maintenance of fish spawning and rearing habitat. Shear stress is also an important variable governing the establishment and survival of aquatic macrophytes in streams (Biggs 1996; Mackay et al. 2003) and is relevant to most benthic invertebrates.

FLOW AND INVERTEBRATES

The concept of riparian flow response guilds has parallels in recent studies of invertebrate functional trait niches (Poff et al. 2006b). In England and Wales, a Lotic Invertebrate Index for Flow Evaluation (LIFE) has been developed from ecological survey data to assess biotic responses to flow based on species- and family-level preferences for velocity conditions (Extence et al. 1999). LIFE is used to identify sites subject to stress, such as from water abstraction. Monk et al. (2007) showed LIFE scores to be particularly sensitive to changes in runoff (mean annual discharge per unit catchment area) within two of the three flow regime types identified for England and Wales. Using time series of river biomonitoring data from wadable lowland streams in England and Denmark, Dunbar et al. (2010) showed how local-scale habitat features mediate the response of this macroinvertebrate community index to changing river discharge. Their study also examined how habitat modification can affect invertebrate communities in streams, thereby potentially extending the idea of flow response guilds to habitat response guilds. This approach may have broad applicability for developing regional flow alteration–ecological response models in natural and engineered stream channels.

FLOW, HABITAT, AND FISH

Practitioners of PHABSIM and similar models tend to assume a linear relationship between habitat area (or volume) and population biomass and that a minimum area of suitable habitat is required to achieve a population target (Fig. 25, Chapter 10). Anderson et al. (2006) argue that habitat preference models alone are insufficient to predict the responses of fish or other organisms to flow alteration, whereas models based on individual bioenergetics or behavior can "incorporate organism responses to biotic components of the environment such as food provision rates, the costs of maintaining swimming position, competition for territories, and mortality risk." The thrust of this contribution is the need to shift from simplistic assumptions about habitat preferences to population- and community-level responses to flow regime alterations in time and in space.

Rosenfeld and Hatfield (2006) consider the effects of habitat on population limitation scale from "*(i)* effects on performance of individuals (growth, survival, fecundity) within a life history stage, to (*ii*) limitation of populations by habitats associated with specific life history stages, and (*iii*) larger-scale habitat structure required for metapopulation persistence."

Habitat models range from simple models that generate population estimates by extrapolating densities of animals in different habitat types to larger areas, to habitat-explicit, size-structured population models. Fish living in streams and rivers often persist as a metapopulation (a group of spatially disjunct populations linked by migration), and some populations may be more important than others for persistence of the species. The most important subset of populations (e.g., source populations) must be identified and protected (e.g., through habitat restoration or environmental flows). That subset may include a combination of "source and sink" populations if sink habitats are corridors for dispersal or refuges for recolonizing source populations vulnerable to stochastic extinction (Rosenfeld and Hatfield 2006). These possibilities require a strong appreciation of spatial patterns of population distribution in river networks (Labbe and Fausch 2000), linked to understanding of the factors that seems most likely to guarantee habitat and population persistence. Precisely where in catchment space and in the river network to provide an environmental flow for all dimensions of fish habitat and passage is an important consideration that must be informed by an understanding of natural patterns of biotic connectivity in space and in time. A better understanding of metapopulation processes in dendritic and fragmented river systems deprived of their natural flows seems imperative.

FLOW AND FISH ASSEMBLAGE STRUCTURE

A challenging aspect of the search for hydroecological relationships to inform environmental flow management is the potentially confounding influence of multiple hydrological variables, hydrologic alterations, and other stressors. For example, the literature contains many instances of the confounding effects of interactions between flow regime alteration and the presence of exotic species (e.g., Bunn and Arthington

2002; and see Chapters 4 and 8). To address this challenge requires sophistication of field study designs and use of the wide range of statistical tools available to address complexity in ecological systems, including historical legacies, time lags, nonlinearities, interactions, and feedback loops that vary in both time and space. Olden et al. (2008) discuss machine-learning techniques (classification and regression trees, artificial neural networks, and evolutionary computation) that model the relationship between a set of environmental input variables and known ecological outputs. They remark that "the growing use of these methods in recent years is the direct result of their ability to model complex, nonlinear relationships in ecological data without having to satisfy the restrictive assumptions required by conventional, parametric approaches." The researchers reference user-friendly software throughout their informative paper.

In a recent synthesis of fish assemblage studies, Grossman and Sabo (2010) note that "a lasting challenge for stream fish assemblage ecology is the fact that even with sophisticated statistical techniques, it is not uncommon for large amounts (~40–50%) of the variation in our data sets to remain unexplained. This is particularly common in habitat-density studies." They also comment that "recent statistical developments may aid us in resolving these problems such as information theoretic statistics, multimodel inference (Burnham and Anderson 2002), and Bayesian analyses."

FISH POPULATION MODELS

River fisheries models have received attention in recent reviews of environmental flow methods. In considering the flow requirements of fish and fisheries in large rivers, Arthington et al. (2007) reviewed useful models, including empirical, population dynamics, Bayesian, and other categories. One of the simplest empirical models describes the linear relationship between log-transformed floodplain area and fish catch (for many examples, see Welcomme et al. 2006) and the response of fish yield to the quantity of freshwater discharged into estuaries (e.g., Loneragan and Bunn 1999). In many of these models, the extent and duration of flooding during the flood phases of the hydrological cycle are the most important variables driving fish production.

Fish population dynamics models describe the response of fish populations to exploitation and environmental variation based on established theories of population regulation and recent advances in understanding of floodplain-river fisheries ecology and biology. Biomass dynamics models treat the whole fish stock as a pool of biomass subject to production, that is, the net result of growth, reproduction, natural mortality, and harvesting (e.g., Lorenzen and Enberg 2002). The age-structured dynamic pool model described by Halls et al. (2001) has been used to quantify the impacts of modified hydrological regimes on floodplain fish production in Bangladesh and to identify mitigating measures. In the field of inland and floodplain fisheries, holistic methods address fish production or yield in the broader context of environmental management and therefore integrate hydrological, environmental, and social processes such as fishing effort and the adaptive behavior of fishers (Lorenzen et al. 2007). Holistic models can be broadly classified into ecological models, multiagent models, and Bayesian networks.

BAYESIAN METHODS

Bayesian network (BN) models offer a solution to the common problem of data scarcity by making use of very basic data, empirical models, and expert knowledge. They are easy to compute and are intuitive and visually explicit, and thus they are good tools for communicating summaries of complex information beyond the reach of individual experts or decision makers. The essence of Bayesian networks consists in defining the system studied as a network of variables linked by probabilistic interactions (Jensen 1996). Bayesian networks (also called Bayes nets or Bayesian belief networks) were developed in the mid-1990s as decision support systems for medical diagnostic and financial risk assessment (Charniak 1991). They have since proven to be applicable to a wide range of problems.

The use of BN models in environmental flow assessment and evaluation of scenarios for water management is increasing (e.g., Hart and Pollino 2009; Stewart-Koster et al. 2010; Webb et al. 2010). In a recent example, Chan et al. (2010) describe the development and application of BN models that link important flow components with an ecological model to predict the abundance of two native fish species of social, cultural, and economic importance in the Daly River, Northern Territory, Australia. The BN models incorporated information on modeled changes in dry-season flow regimes under various water-extraction scenarios, combined with outputs from two-dimensional habitat simulation models of fish hydraulic habitat requirements and other ecologically important processes, such as migration, feeding, growth, reproduction, and survival (see Figs. 8 and 9 in Chan et al. 2010). If current water-extraction entitlements were fully utilized, the models showed that there would be significant impacts on the populations of two important fish species.

A framework has been proposed to incorporate BNs within DRIFT to capture expert knowledge of the flow requirements of biota, supported by age-structured population models (Arthington et al. 2007). The objective is to develop a single integrated framework and suite of models with optional components so that users can select the appropriate components, models, and parameters, depending on location in a river system, the ecological and fisheries issues under analysis, and the available data (Fig. 36). Bayesian approaches incorporated with age-structured fish population models would give estimates of risk and the possibility of error, potentially replacing the weighting system applied within DRIFT to rank levels of uncertainty in the flow response relationships (see JM King et al. 2003).

Webb et al. (2010) explored the utility of a Bayesian hierarchical approach to improve detection of important associations between stream flows, including managed environmental flows, and biophysical responses in rivers. Properties unique to the Bayesian hierarchical approach termed "borrowing strength" and "shrinkage" mean that conclusions can be greatly strengthened in data-poor situations but will be almost unaffected when data are plentiful. Webb et al. (2010) stressed that the flexibility of Bayesian modeling allows formulation of realistic models, which can be tested for generality using all available data from any source (e.g., routine river health monitoring data or a particular flow experiment). Models can be updated as new knowledge and data become available via an iterative cycle of development, monitoring, and evaluation.

Stewart-Koster et al. (2010) tested a different use of BNs in a study that modeled relationships between flow and other environmental driv-

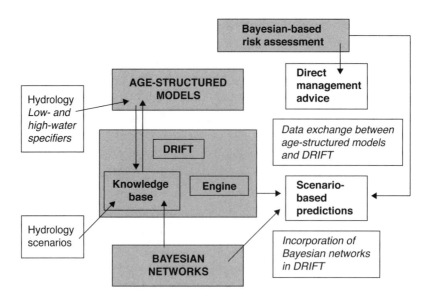

FIGURE 36.   Integration of the DRIFT methodology, Bayesian networks, and age-structured fish population models within an environmental flow assessment framework for fish. Age-structured population models can provide specific advice on flows required to sustain particular floodplain fish species, either independently or as input to the fish component of DRIFT, which draws upon empirical flow-ecology relationships and expert knowledge to assess ecological consequences of many flow alteration scenarios. (Redrawn from Figure 18 in Arthington et al. 2007, with permission from the International Water Management Institute)

ers of stream ecosystem health expressed as ecological response variables. They showed how BNs can be modified to provide Bayesian decision networks (BDNs) that incorporate not only the fundamental environmental relationships but also the relative costs and benefits of potential management actions. The idea is that inclusion of BDNs within existing river restoration and environmental flow frameworks would enhance the capacity to evaluate the influence of multiple stressors in aquatic ecosystems and the relative benefits of various restoration options.

ECOSYSTEM RESPONSE MODELS
In their meta-analysis of hydroecological relationships in regulated rivers, Poff and Zimmerman (2010) found very few examples of ecologi-

cal process rates (e.g., metabolism, production) or trophic relationships and food web dynamics that could inform environmental flow assessment and management. This seems surprising given that ideas about energy sources and aquatic food web structure have dominated river ecosystem models such as the River Continuum Concept and the Flood Pulse Concept since the 1980s. Building from these models, Douglas et al. (2005) proposed a conceptual framework and six general principles describing food webs and related ecosystem processes that have important implications for catchment and river flow management.

Thorp et al. (2006, 2008) proposed the Riverine Ecosystem Synthesis (RES; see Fig. 12, Chapter 3) as a way for ecologists (and managers) to frame research questions and management strategies at multiple spatial and temporal scales in riverine landscapes (see Chapter 3). The RES presents 17 tenets, collectively predicting how patterns of individual species distributions, community regulation, ecosystem processes, and floodplain interactions can be expected to vary over hydrogeomorphic zones (Thorp et al. 2008). For example, tenet 11 predicts that in-stream primary production, through an algal-grazer food web, provides the trophic basis for most animal productivity in many river systems. The algal-grazer pathway is well-supported in food web studies for large tropical and arid-zone floodplain rivers (Bunn et al. 2003; Douglas et al. 2005; Winemiller 2004), while the partial reliance of some fish species on carbon of riparian origin has been documented in other dryland floodplain rivers (Medeiros and Arthington 2010). How effectively RES tenets will contribute to the development of environmental flow prescriptions for river protection and restoration remains to be seen as the various tenets are tested, refined, and applied.

15

GROUNDWATER-DEPENDENT
ECOSYSTEMS AND THREATS

GROUNDWATER SYSTEMS

All water that occurs beneath the earth's surface can be termed "sub-surface" (or underground) water. Precipitation, flowing surface water, ice, wind, and tectonic forces create opportunities for surface water to penetrate into underground materials. This downward movement of water (termed "groundwater recharge" or "percolation") through soils and the root zone of plants may continue until the water meets an impenetrable layer of clay, shale, rock, or other impervious or semiwatertight barrier, such as organically cemented sand. Once such a barrier is encountered, subsurface water can accumulate and completely saturate the underground materials. The top of the saturated zone is known as the "groundwater table," and the water in the saturated zone below the water table is termed "groundwater" (Fig. 37). Any water held in the ground above the water table is termed "vadose" (shallow) water, and the zone extending from the water table to the land surface forms the unsaturated zone. Variations in precipitation between seasons and during wet or dry cycles affect the elevation of shallow groundwater tables and may bring this water to the land surface. Groundwater that accumulates right to the land surface may enable a spring, pond, lake or wetland, and riparian vegetation to establish, or it may form the base-flow of a stream or river (Fig. 37). The dependencies of these ecological systems on groundwater and the impacts of groundwater withdraw-

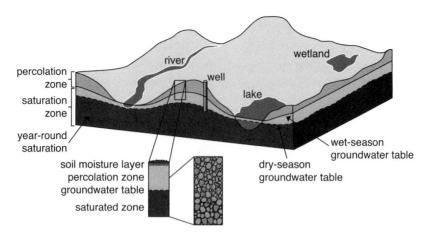

FIGURE 37. Groundwater systems, saturated and unsaturated zones, and groundwater tables in relation to topography and freshwater systems such as rivers, wetlands, and lakes. (Redrawn from Figure 4.8 in Cech 2010, with permission from John Wiley and Sons)

als on freshwater ecosystems are the subject of this chapter. Protocols, methods, and decision support tools to assess and manage groundwater-dependent ecosystems, especially rivers, are discussed in Chapter 16.

Large stores of groundwater are termed "aquifers." They occur in geologic formations such as sand, gravel, sandstone, chalk, limestone, and fractured rocks (e.g., granite) with large pore spaces or fissures that can store and yield usable amounts of water (Cech 2010). The amount of water held in an aquifer varies with the characteristics of the void space (also known as pore space, interstices, or fissures) between geologic materials. Interconnected void spaces provide opportunities for water to move under gravitational forces and to accumulate, and in sufficient quantity this accumulated water forms an aquifer. The saturated thickness of an aquifer may vary from 1 to more than 100 m thick and extend from a few meters to hundreds of kilometers across local, state, provincial, or international boundaries (Cech 2010). Where an impermeable rock, clay, or shale layer (i.e., an aquiclude) overlies an aquifer, water cannot move vertically up or down and the aquifer is said to be confined. The pressure created by the confinement of groundwater below a geologic barrier can be sufficient to force water to the surface through cracks and fissures, forming an artesian spring, which by definition does not require pumping to bring the water to the surface. Where there is no overlying low-permeability stratum (aquitard or aquiclude), the aquifer is said to be unconfined and may flow from a higher to a lower elevation to emerge on the land surface as a spring or may feed water to a wetland or stream.

Mound springs form when tectonic action and fractures allow groundwater rich in calcium and bicarbonate to escape to the surface, where precipitation of carbonates and sediment builds up a characteristic mound or small hill or water seeps into shallow marshy hollows. Several large concentrations of mound springs have formed along the southwestern edge of the Great Artesian Basin in Queensland and south Australia (Habermehl 1982). These isolated water bodies support unique aquatic invertebrates (especially snails) and fish (desert gobies, catfish, and hardyheads).

Slightly acid waters flowing through underground rock formations such as limestone (a type of sedimentary rock composed of mineral calcite) create dissolution fissures, underground caves, and collapsed areas called "sinkholes." In karst (limestone) terrain, continued dissolution of calcite in contact with moving groundwater creates unique subsurface cave systems and distinctive surface landforms. The world's longest cave—Kentucky's Mammoth Cave—has more than 240 km of accessible underground passages. The Waitomo Caves (from the Maori *wai*, which means "water," and *tomo*, "hole" or "shaft") comprise 300 known caves in the Waitomo area south of Hamilton, New Zealand. These caves are famous for a bioluminescent species of cave-dwelling Diptera, the native glowworm *(Arachnocampa luminosa).* Cave systems support unique assemblages of obligate groundwater inhabitants, largely crustaceans, but also insects, worms, gastropods, mites, and fish. Obligate groundwater faunas live in the void spaces in karst, alluvial, and fractured-rock aquifers (Humphreys 2006).

Wetlands, rivers, riparian zones, alluvial floodplains, and estuaries have various dependencies on groundwater and on water derived from the unsaturated zone and surface runoff from land (see Fig. 37). Groundwater-dependent ecosystems (GDEs) comprise a diverse, complex, and often biologically rich subset of the world's ecosystems. They can be differentiated by their varying degrees of dependency on groundwater to maintain water chemistry, thermal properties, biological composition, and ecological function (Boulton and Hancock 2006).

RIVERS AS GROUNDWATER-DEPENDENT ECOSYSTEMS

River flow may derive from direct precipitation, springs, overland flow, and from underground flow of water moving directly to the river channel. Part of this underground flow is "interflow," that is, the portion of infiltration that moves through the unsaturated zone without penetrating to the main water table. Interflow also includes water that flows from any perched water tables in the unsaturated zone. Below the water table (the top of the deeper saturated zone; see Fig. 37), groundwater can discharge directly into a river, forming the baseflow.

As the component of total stream flow that is derived from groundwater, baseflow reflects aquifer permeability, local and regional geology, bank and floodplain storage, and the topography of the water table (Newson 1994). In a catchment of impermeable rocks, where rainfall infiltrates slowly, the baseflow contribution to total stream flow is typically low, and the overland flow component is consequently high. In catchments of permeable geologic formations, overland flow may be minimal and most of the river flow will be derived from baseflow. Groundwater provides river flow during periods when there is no precipitation and surface runoff into the channel. In many rivers draining arid and semiarid regions, stream flow is solely from the baseflow most of the time, unless the system is "losing" surface water to the underlying groundwater zone. Losing, or "influent," streams are frequently intermittent or episodic (Boulton and Hancock 2006). In rivers of more temperate and wet tropical climatic zones with higher precipitation, interflow continues after rain eases and provides a river's flow most of the time, so that many of these gaining, or "effluent," systems flow permanently through the combination of interflow and groundwater contributions. Boulton and Hancock (2006) argue that apart from ephemeral rills and streams that run only after rain and surface runoff, all other streams and rivers are fully or partially dependent on groundwater.

The water visible in a river channel is almost always directly in contact with subsurface water that fills up the spaces between bed sands, gravels, and rocks lining the channel bed. This wet underground zone may extend for some meters beneath the visible river channel and for several kilometers on either side of it, forming hidden habitats for aquatic life called the "hyporheic" ("below the flow" or "the flow

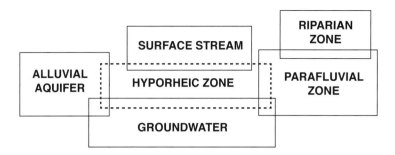

FIGURE 38. Simplified schematic diagram of the hydrological compartments that can interact with the hyporheic zone of a river. Alluvial aquifers typify floodplain rivers with coarse alluvium and are often considered synonymous with groundwater. The parafluvial zone lies under the active channel, which lacks surface water, and it can interact with subsurface water of the riparian zone. (Redrawn from Figure 1 in Boulton et al. 1998, with permission from Annual Reviews Inc.)

below") and "parafluvial" zones (Boulton and Hancock 2006). The relationships of the hyporheic and parafluvial zones with the surface-flowing stream, groundwater, alluvial aquifer, and riparian zone are depicted in Figure 38. The hyporheic zone is defined as the saturated sediments below and alongside the river channel where the stream and groundwater exchange. Most baseflow derives from groundwater that seeps in from the channel margins and floodplains via the parafluvial zone or enters from below via the hyporheic zone. The riparian zone and its ecology are also intimately linked to groundwater in most rivers via the parafluvial zone.

The functional dependency of river baseflow systems on groundwater can be viewed at three spatial scales: "the sediment scale at which microbial and chemical processes generate fine-scale environmental gradients; the reach scale where groundwater–surface water exchanges and variable hyporheic residence time of water produce gradients evident along riffles, bars and stream segments; and the catchment scale that integrates the gradients in relative sizes of the hyporheic zone, sediments and hydrologic retention along a river from its headwaters to its lowland sections" (Boulton and Hancock 2006). The hydrological, physical, chemical, and biological characteristics of river reaches with groundwater dependencies are summarized in Table 31.

TABLE 31   *The hydrological, physical, chemical, and biological characteristics of river reaches and their groundwater dependencies*

Habitat	Groundwater dependencies
Springs and seeps	
Hydrological	Typically stable flows, although seepages may be seasonal; total reliance on groundwater
Physical	Dampened thermal regime; often biota with a narrow tolerance of water temperature (stenothermal)
Chemical	Although variable at catchment scale, reach-scale water chemistry is typically stable over time and frequently enriched with particular ions (e.g., Ca, Mg) or nutrients (e.g., N)
Biological	Specialized biota near source but often lower diversity than farther downstream; generally low tolerance to variable water regime, temperature, or chemical composition
Hyporheic/parafluvial zones	
Hydrological	Upwelling and outwelling zones may vary in response to variation in sediment composition, groundwater pressure, and river flow; generally a reliable source of water; groundwater pressure maintains pore spaces free of silt through hydrological filtration; maintains mesohabitat diversity in groundwater-dominated rivers
Physical	Water-temperature variation dampened by increasing residence time in hyporheic zone; often generating a thermal refuge for biota (e.g., fish)
Chemical	Upwelling or outwelling water can supply nutrients that limit primary productivity in surface river; contribute dissolved ions and salts; exchanges in hyporheic zone can transform dissolved organic matter and nutrients
Biological	Enhanced primary productivity and macrophyte growth in upwelling and outwelling zones; invertebrate responses to groundwater inputs; fish spawning and nesting patterns; microbial activity and leaf decomposition rates

SOURCE: Boulton and Hancock 2006 and references therein

Springs and Seeps   At the scale of a river reach, the baseflow of a river is derived from springs and seeps in headwater zones and through inputs from the parafluvial and hyporheic zones in the midreaches of rivers where water upwelling and downwelling are most common (Fig. 39). Most permanent springs typically have very stable flows, water chemistry, and water temperatures, although swampy seepages may be seasonal. These freshwater systems are totally reliant on groundwater, and their biota may include obligate and endemic groundwater invertebrates (stygofauna) that lack pigmentation or eyes. With increasing distance downstream and greater diversity of habitats, the numbers of species typically increase and community composition starts to resemble that of nearby permanent streams (Boulton and Hancock 2006).

Hyporheic and Parafluvial Zones   In the midreaches of rivers with porous beds, and depending on the profile of the groundwater table, baseflow is generated by groundwater entering the stream channel from the hyporheic zone below the bed and from the parafluvial zone alongside the active channel (Figs. 38 and 39). In these upwelling or outwelling zones, various ecological processes are set in motion in response to the inflowing groundwater. Nutrients such as dissolved nitrogen in the groundwater subsidize benthic algal production, and some aquatic plants also respond to upwelling or outwelling groundwater (White et al. 1992). Subsurface microbes and invertebrates show distinctive patterns of distribution in response to the spatial patterns and degree of hydrological exchange between groundwater and stream channels. The activities of these microbes and invertebrates influence ecosystem processes such as leaf decomposition in the surface stream (Dent et al. 2000), thereby contributing to the organic-matter breakdown processes represented in the River Continuum Concept.

Upwelling groundwater in the hyporheic zone can benefit fish in several ways. Some salmonid fish prefer to lay their eggs in the sediments of upwelling zones because the groundwater prevents freezing of the eggs in winter (Benson 1953). Upwelling zones can provide oxygenated water in the sediments where fish spawn, and these enriched zones may also offer enhanced food availability (Dent et al. 2000). For freshwater

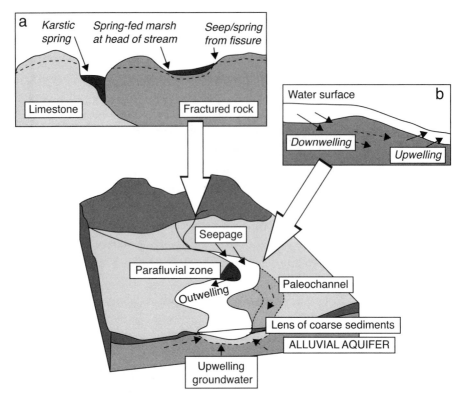

FIGURE 39. Common river baseflow system in a typical catchment, showing bedrock-controlled reaches of the headwaters, seeps, springs, and spring-fed marshes (a) and parafluvial and hyporheic zones (b) where water upwells and downwells during its passage downstream. Lateral paleochannels may carry water in lenses of coarser sediments in the lower reaches. (Redrawn from Figure 1 in Boulton and Hancock 2006, with permission from CSIRO Publishing, copyright CSIRO 2006, www.publish.csiro.au/nid/65/paper/BT05074.htm)

fish such as the cobbler *(Tandanus bostocki),* groundwater intrusion maintains habitat connectivity and migratory routes through riffles during prolonged annual dry periods characteristic of Mediterranean climatic zones (Beatty et al. 2010). Groundwater recharge and hyporheic flow can provide the only refuge for fish and invertebrates during dry spells and drought in perennial streams and are absolutely essential to sustain isolated aquatic refugia in intermittent rivers with unpredictable surface flows and extended dry periods (Arthington et al. 2010b; Larned et al. 2010). On an evolutionary time scale, aquifers have provided refugia from changing environmental conditions on the surface, including, for example, during the onset of aridity in Australia (Finston et al. 2007).

Boulton and Hancock (2006) remark that "the functional dependency of the surface river ecosystem on the additive effects of groundwater contributions from springs, seeps, hyporheic zones and parafluvial zones has never been assessed at the catchment scale." The Hyporheic Corridor Concept, or HCC (Stanford and Ward 1993) goes partway toward a catchment-scale perspective by envisaging a subsurface continuum of groundwater processes that varies along a river according to geomorphic formations and constraints that can limit the potential for groundwater to penetrate into the channel (see Fig. 39). This subsurface continuum formed by the hyporheic corridor has a lateral component connecting riparian zones, anabranches, paleochannels, and floodplain aquifers (which may extend up to 3 km from the main channel). The lateral component generates a wide array of landscape features, each with spatial and temporal degrees of connection to the surface discharge regime in the river. Alternating constrained and unconstrained reaches occur longitudinally down most rivers, and these geomorphic constraints govern the extent of groundwater contributions to river baseflows and the hyporheic and parafluvial zones. The result is that subsurface groundwater habitats expand and contract along the river corridor "like beads along a string" (Stanford and Ward 1993).

At the scale of an entire catchment, the Hyporheic Corridor Concept helps to explain several features of river and riparian systems (Boulton et al. 1998). One is the structure and dynamics of the riparian zone, which can reflect hyporheic flow patterns and areas of upwelling and down-welling (Nilsson and Svedmark 2002). Another feature is the distribution of patches of aquatic productivity within a stream or river influenced by biogeochemical exchanges and nutrient-rich water upwelling from the hyporheic zone (e.g., Dahm et al. 1998). At the broadest scale, the spatial and temporal variability in hydrological exchange processes and groundwater linkages promote biodiversity within the landscape (Boulton et al. 1998; Tockner et al. 2008).

As well as having marked spatial patterns, the volume and timing of groundwater inputs to streams and rivers also vary. As an example, cool groundwater provides a thermal refuge for fish during hot dry periods and this may enable fish stocks to persist in a subcatchment (Power et al. 1999). In arid-zone rivers such as Cooper Creek in Australia, benthic algal production is depressed after flooding but recovers once the perched groundwater level in isolated water holes stabilizes and the shallow productive littoral zone can reestablish (Fellows et al. 2009). This productive band of algae forms the basis of the water-hole food chain and directly influences the survival of a number of fish species in refuge water holes during cool dry months (Arthington et al. 2010b). Refuge water holes maintain the brood stocks that confer resilience on dryland ecosystems through massive "booms" of reproduction and recruitment when wet conditions and floods again prevail (Leigh et al. 2010).

OTHER GROUNDWATER-DEPENDENT ECOSYSTEMS

Rivers are not the only groundwater-dependent ecosystems. Tomlinson and Boulton (2010) present a conceptual framework depicting how subsurface groundwater-dependent ecosystems (SGDEs) can be linked not only to each other by groundwater flows but also to surface aquatic, riparian, terrestrial, estuarine, and oceanic ecosystems through transition zones, including the hyporheic zone, vadose zone, marine upwelling and intrusion zones, and psammolittoral zone (Fig. 40). There may also be direct connections between SGDEs, for example, where an alluvial aquifer overlies or interdigitates with another aquifer type such as calcrete or fractured rock (Eberhard et al. 2009). These dynamic ecotones are zones of exchange of materials and energy and are potential pathways for faunal dispersal and transmission of nutrients and contaminants. Tomlinson and Boulton (2010) promote an "ecohydrogeological approach" to understanding the implications of anthropogenic disturbance on SGDEs that focuses on comprehending aquifer permeability and connectivity pathways from groundwater (e.g., terrestrial, wetland, estuarine) ecosystems. Their approach offers enormous promise as an overarching model for evaluating ecological water requirements by transcending the usual compartmentalization into rivers, wetlands, estuaries, and groundwater systems.

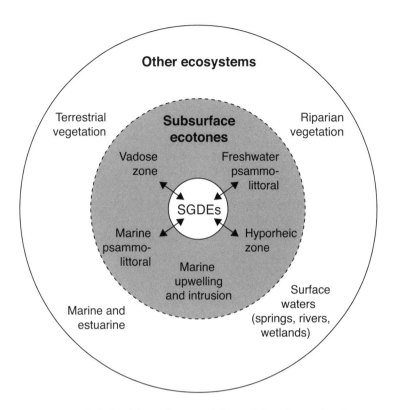

FIGURE 40.   Relationships and connectivities of subsurface and surface
aquatic ecosystems. Subsurface groundwater-dependent ecosystems
(SGDEs) (center) are linked through ecotones (shaded area) to each other
and to surface aquatic ecosystems (streams and wetlands), as well as to
riparian and terrestrial ecosystems and to estuarine and marine ecosystems.
(Redrawn from Figure 2 in Tomlinson and Boulton 2010, with permission
from CSIRO Publishing, copyright CSIRO 2010, www.publish.csiro.au/
nid/126/paper/MF09267.htm)

HYDROLOGIC ALTERATIONS AND THREATS TO
GROUNDWATER ECOSYSTEMS

Deep aquifers acquire their water stores extremely slowly; only about
1% of the freshwater in the world's aquifers is replenished by rain each
year, yet aquifers store an enormous amount of freshwater accumulated over decades to millennia. It is estimated that 4.2 million km³ of
groundwater exists within 0.8 km of the earth's surface, representing

25.6% of all freshwater; but about 90% of this groundwater is inaccessible with current technology (Cech 2010; Pearce 2007). Nonetheless, humans have accessed groundwater for domestic and agricultural use for more than 8,000 years, and at least one-third of the world's population draws its water from aquifers (Vörösmarty et al. 2005).

In the United States, approximately 85% of water consumed goes to irrigated agriculture, and more than a third of that comes from groundwater (Postel and Richter 2003). Across much of Australia, North Africa, the Middle East, South and Central Asia, Europe, and North America, excessive groundwater extraction has reduced surface-stream discharge, dried up groundwater-fed springs, and altered river flow regimes (Konikow and Kendy 2005). In the arid Middle East and North Africa, mined groundwater is mainly used for irrigation; for example, Saudi Arabia meets nearly all its irrigation requirements through non-renewable groundwater. The Great Man-Made River Project in Libya transports more than 2 km³ per annum of groundwater through a 1,600 km pipeline to huge coastal storage reservoirs that support 135,000 ha of irrigable cropland, amounting to one-third of the country's total (UN-WWAP 2003).

Aquatic and terrestrial ecosystems vary in their degree of dependency on groundwater to maintain composition and function (Hatton and Evans 1998; Humphreys 2006), and therefore they have different vulnerabilities to changes in surface water and groundwater hydrology. Quantifying the ecological responses of surface and subsurface groundwater-dependent ecosystems to groundwater alterations is made difficult by the variety of systems likely to be affected. The conceptual framework of Tomlinson and Boulton (2010) provides insight into the different types of SGDEs and their potential connectivities to each other and to surface aquatic ecosystems (springs, rivers, wetlands), terrestrial ecosystems (riparian and terrestrial vegetation), and estuarine and marine ecosystems.

Human activities contributing to water-table decline include groundwater abstraction for irrigation and domestic water use and purging of mines that penetrate below the water table (Hancock 2002), whereas the recharge characteristics of groundwater systems can be altered by various land uses (deforestation, afforestation, cropping, urbanization). Dam construction, water impoundment, river flow regulation, channelization, and the construction of drainage ditches further affect groundwater tables.

In extreme cases, declines in the groundwater table completely sever the river baseflow system from its underlying aquifer (Hancock 2002; Fleckenstein et al. 2004). Uncoupling a river baseflow system from its underlying aquifer can also result from physical changes in the streambed and stream banks. Blocking of interstitial spaces of the hyporheic zone with silt or bacterial biofilms (Stubbington et al. 2009) can reduce the exchange processes between groundwater and surface water. Maintaining permeable parafluvial and hyporheic zones in the river baseflow system is essential to sustain normal surface and groundwater exchanges and ecological processes (Boulton and Hancock 2006).

Periodic drying occurs naturally in many streams in regions of low precipitation (Larned et al. 2010; Stubbington et al. 2010) and in general occurs far more frequently in arid and semiarid ecosystems. Their dry and highly variable climates place huge demands on water for human use, especially irrigated agriculture, and many dryland rivers are subject to extensive diversion directly onto crops or into storage sites as well as to direct usage of groundwater. Water abstraction for irrigation has led to water scarcity and significant hydrologic changes in dryland rivers worldwide, including waterways and wetlands in the United States, Australia, Spain, and Africa (Kingsford et al. 2006).

Human interception or extraction of groundwater can prolong the natural periods of zero flow characteristic of dryland rivers or can change the timing of their onset or conclusion. As an example, increasing irrigation abstractions from groundwater threaten the Lower Selwyn (Waikirikiri) River on the Canterbury Plains of New Zealand's South Island. The mean annual length of dry river channel has increased by 0.6 kilometer per annum over the past two decades. These dry reaches present a significant barrier for fish migrating between Lake Ellesmere and the Selwyn River headwaters (Kelly et al. 2006). Stream biota possess adaptations to cope with the variability of the natural flow regime in each catchment or region (Poff et al. 1997; Lytle and Poff 2004); however, extended low-flow periods or changes in timing of dry periods through the extraction of groundwater potentially lead to localized extinctions of vulnerable species (Arthington and Balcombe 2011; Larned et al. 2010). This can mean the elimination of all obligate aquatic species (fish, mollusks, many invertebrates), while those with resting stages may survive for some time.

Ecosystem processes of leaf-litter breakdown (both coarse and fine particulate organic matter), nutrient transformations, and in-stream primary production are linked to water availability (Pinay et al. 2002); thus, extended dry periods can disrupt ecosystem processes and, ultimately, food web structure in fragmented habitats (Bunn et al. 2006). Alterations of linkages to groundwater can also affect the resilience of a surface-river baseflow system to physical disturbances such as flooding, which is when invertebrates take refuge in the parafluvial and hyporheic zones of rivers and streams.

In North America, dryland rivers occur not only in desert regions but also in the Great Plains, which span the entire midcontinent and constitute the third-largest ecoregion in North America. The Great Plains is one of the most productive and economically important agricultural areas in the world, producing approximately 25% of the world's grains (CGC 2009). Groundwater makes a major contribution to flows in Great Plains streams, especially in their headwaters, and maintains baseflows and connectivity among habitats important for the persistence of aquatic biota. Widespread groundwater mining for irrigated crop production has caused significant declines in groundwater levels and stream habitat fragmentation and loss across the western Great Plains (Falke et al. 2010). Native fish in the western Great Plains are in serious decline; for example, of 37 species native to the Platte, Arkansas, and Republican River basins in eastern Colorado, 20 have become either extirpated, endangered, or threatened or are listed as species of concern in Colorado (Hubert and Gordon 2007).

Salmonids appear to be particularly sensitive to the groundwater dependencies of their spawning habitats. In a Danish stream, groundwater abstraction affected habitat conditions for brown trout *(Salmo trutta)* (Olsen et al. 2009). For rainbow trout *(Salmo gairdneri,* now known as *Oncorhynchus mykiss),* the survival of preemergent embryos was not related to the substrate particle size composition but to the velocity and dissolved oxygen concentration of groundwater in redds (Sowden and Power 1985). In a Scottish river, Soulsby et al. (2009) examined connectivity of the groundwater and surface water in the hyporheic zone and found that low oxygen levels recorded during wetter periods when groundwater input increased had implications for egg survival of Atlantic salmon *(Salmo salar)*.

When groundwater-production bores are placed too close to a river, they often accelerate the flux of surface water through the hyporheic zone. This can raise water temperature, dissolved oxygen, and conductivity levels in the parafluvial zone (Mauclaire and Gibert 1998). An influx of oxygen-rich water could change the sediment microbial community from predominantly anaerobic to aerobic, and, as denitrification is essentially an anaerobic process, could result in an increase in nitrate entering the stream, with major implications for river water quality and productivity (Boulton and Hancock 2006).

Other water-quality changes associated with groundwater processes involve rising salinity levels when salts stored in the soil are mobilized and concentrated in irrigation water (Halse et al. 2003). Excessive use of irrigation water and the removal of deep-rooted plants can cause soil salinization and also can increase nearby stream and river salinity levels. High salinity affects hyporheic and surface aquatic biota that are not adapted to high levels of salts (Nielsen et al. 2003). Where the groundwater in agricultural areas is also high in nutrients, which is not unusual, this increased baseflow may lead to eutrophication and other water-quality problems.

While the lowering of groundwater tables is a major concern for groundwater-dependent ecosystems, increases in groundwater tables that change the flow regime of the receiving river's baseflow system can have ecological effects. It is possible for an intermittent stream to become a permanently flowing stream, with many ecological consequences (Bond et al. 2010). Some of these have been discussed in earlier chapters in the context of reservoir management to provide irrigation water. One possible outcome is that species adapted to living in an intermittent and variable environment may be replaced by species adapted to the permanent availability of water and habitat. Often these successful species are alien to the catchment or bioregion (Bunn and Arthington 2002).

In some coastal areas, overpumping through groundwater wells has led to saltwater intrusion into precious freshwater aquifers. One-third of the water supply for coastal areas of Greater Los Angeles comes from local groundwater sources that are now at risk from saltwater intrusion (Edwards and Evans 2002; Barlow and Reichard 2010). In the Mekong Delta, about 2 million ha of coastal cropland are affected by saltwater infiltration into aquifers as a result of groundwater withdrawals through deep wells.

16

SUSTAINING GROUNDWATER-DEPENDENT ECOSYSTEMS

INTRODUCTION TO METHODS

Providing water for the environment is more than just allocating water for the maintenance of surface water flows in rivers. It must also consider the water regimes that maintain terrestrial, riparian, wetland, and stygian (groundwater-inhabiting organisms) systems that require groundwater for their survival (Murray et al. 2003). The global literature on environmental flow methods for rivers has little to offer in relation to the integration of groundwater-dependent ecosystems into riverine assessments (Tharme 2003), even though many countries have committed to protecting the ecological integrity of both surface water and groundwater ecosystems. Although international literature on stream and river ecology has long recognized the three-dimensional nature of running-water systems (see Chapter 4), and the concept of a hyporheic corridor that parallels the surface water ecological continuum is not new (Stanford and Ward 1993), the general opinion is that environmental flows for rivers and water regimes to protect or restore groundwater-dependent ecosystems have largely been evaluated separately.

Consequently there have been many calls for the development of interdisciplinary, multiscale conceptual frameworks and cross-system

TABLE 32   *Tools to identify groundwater-dependent ecosystems*

Category	Definition
Mapping tools	Mapping of geology and geological structures, water-table depth or aquifer pressure, and the distribution, composition, and/or condition of vegetation as a means of identifying ecosystems that are likely to have access to and use groundwater
Water-balance techniques	Identification and quantification of groundwater use by measuring or estimating various components of an ecosystem's water cycle and water balance
Predawn leaf water potential	Predawn leaf water potential measurements to identify groundwater use and depth of water uptake
Stable isotope analysis of vegetation	Comparison of the fractionation of isotopes in plant xylem water with potential source waters to identify groundwater uptake
System response to change	Long-term monitoring of ecosystem composition and ecological function in response to management intervention, climate, and soil water, surface water, and groundwater conditions
Groundwater–surface water hydraulics	Application of hydraulic principles and statistical analyses of stream hydrographs and site measurements to derive the degree of interaction between groundwater and surface water features
Physical properties of water	Measurement of water electrical conductivity and temperature change along the length of a river/wetland, or over time, to identify a groundwater contribution
Analysis of water chemistry	Chemical analysis of surface water and groundwater for isotopes, major anions and cations, and trace elements; mixing relationships identify groundwater contribution

(continued)

comparisons as well as integrated multidisciplinary evaluation of surface water and groundwater relationships, such that the water requirements of both can be satisfied and accommodated within various climatic and socioeconomic settings (e.g., White 1993; Krause et al. 2010; Tomlinson and Boulton 2010). The challenge is enormous, given increasing demands on groundwater resources for human use (see Chapter 15) and the difficulties of assessing the groundwater regime on which the ecological processes, biodiversity, and ecosystem services of each system depend.

TABLE 32 *(continued)*

Category	Definition
Introduced tracers	Use of introduced chemical tracers to observe mixing and dilution relationships and assess the contribution of groundwater to a stream
Plant water-use modeling	Mathematical representations (or models) of plant water balance to estimate plant water requirements, and/or groundwater uptake, and/or response to water-table drawdown
Groundwater modeling	Two- or three-dimensional mathematical representations (or models) of water movement in the saturated and unsaturated zones to assess the potential level of interaction between groundwater and surface water bodies and between groundwater and terrestrial ecosystems
Conceptual modeling	Use of expert knowledge of similar ecosystems, biophysical environments, and relevant data to develop a conceptual model of the ecosystem and its interaction with groundwater
Root depth and morphology	Assessment of the depth and morphology of plant root systems and comparison with measured or estimated water-table depth to assess potential for groundwater uptake
Analysis of aquatic ecology	Use of ecological survey techniques to identify aquatic species with reproductive behavior or habitat requirements that indicate groundwater dependency

SOURCE: After Clifton et al. 2007 and references therein

For groundwater-dependent ecosystems (GDEs) in general, several formal procedures have been outlined. For example, Colvin et al. (2003) and Clifton et al. (2007) produced "toolboxes" of the various techniques available to indicate groundwater use, considering each method in terms of its technical basis, costs, constraints, suitability, time requirements, resolution of results, format of outputs, and previous use (Table 32).

From a broader perspective, Eamus and Froend (2006) listed the following issues as necessary to consider during GDE assessments:

1. Consider the environmental water requirements (EWRs) for as many components of a GDE as possible given available data (e.g., aim for integration of physicochemical water requirements of vegetation, macroinvertebrates, and vertebrates). "Single components may dominate the EWR assessment of particular GDEs if insufficient data exist to incorporate the other components of the ecology, or if the requirements of one component (e.g., 'umbrella' species) can be demonstrated to cater for the needs of all other key components."

2. Acknowledge variability in the groundwater requirements of each ecological component of a GDE; for example, not all phreatophytic vegetation has the same degree of dependence on groundwater and therefore the same response to drawdown. This variability in dependence and response may have a significant effect on the risk of impact from groundwater drawdown. The description of EWRs should therefore incorporate the range in water requirements (not absolute threshold values only) and/or categories of differing requirements and dependency.

3. Recognize other groundwater regime variables important to the ecology of the GDE (e.g., timing, duration, and rate of seasonal flooding/drying and the episodicity or predictability of extreme flooding and drying events).

4. Consider the cumulative effects of reduced groundwater availability by assessing historical changes in groundwater over key periods of time. This history of change should then be considered in addition to any proposed impacts from future developments or increased allocations. A lag-response in a GDE may be evident after initial alteration to groundwater availability; therefore assessment of EWRs should consider the rate at which GDEs are likely to respond to changes in groundwater availability.

5. Acknowledge the resilience of GDEs to altered groundwater availability, and work around the possibility that ecological values can be restored or maintained if remedial or mitigation practices are put in place. Taking a longer-term perspective on the water requirements necessary to maintain ecological values should be the normal practice.

6. "Consider system/catchment-level groundwater requirements as well as single GDE requirements"; for example, important landscape-level ecological processes should be considered, such as acid sulfate soils.

7. Define the uncertainty surrounding the water requirements of GDEs and the uncertainty of groundwater models used to predict hydrological changes (e.g., those caused by future borefields, catchment land use, and climate).

Eamus and Froend (2006) stressed that "there is no level of groundwater extraction that will not, in the long run, result in declines of natural discharges, with consequent environmental impacts." The task of groundwater managers is therefore to determine what level of environmental impact is acceptable and then to manage extraction to maintain the impacts within these "acceptable limits." The remainder of this chapter focuses on the groundwater dependencies of riverine corridors and the methods available to assess those dependencies and to protect and manage groundwater resources as part of frameworks for managing surface stream flows and catchment water resources.

GROUNDWATER DEPENDENCIES OF RIVERINE CORRIDORS

HYPORHEIC FLOW PATHS IN STREAMS

If river ecosystems are to be protected and/or rehabilitated, it is clearly necessary to understand and quantify the landscape-level significance and connectivity of processes along the hyporheic corridor from source to sea or inland water body (Stanford and Ward 1993; Boulton and Hancock 2006). River corridors can be viewed as mosaics of surface-subsurface exchange patches through which surface water downwells into the sediment, travels for some distance beneath or along the stream, eventually mixes with groundwater, and then returns to the stream (Bencala 2000; Malard et al. 2002). Hyporheic flow paths are usually embedded within a larger hillslope groundwater system, and the pathways of groundwater flow toward a stream are also spatially segregated.

Several methods can be used to identify hyporheic flow paths in streams, including the use of natural tracers such as temperature and chloride, the injection of conservative tracers, and the modeling of subsurface flow based on the distribution of hydraulic heads and aquifer properties (Malard et al. 2002). Stream water typically infiltrates in areas of high surface pressure (e.g., the upstream end of a riffle) and upwells in areas of low surface pressure (e.g., the downstream end of a riffle). Therefore, well-defined geomorphic units such as riffles and bars may be considered as patches within which hydrological exchange with the surface stream flow is likely to be high relative to the surrounding sediment matrix.

CLASSIFICATION SCHEMES

Tomlinson and Boulton (2010) discuss the merits of classification schemes and criteria to capture different types of groundwater–surface water interactions and how they might assist groundwater ecosystem studies and management of subsurface groundwater-dependent ecosystems (SGDEs). For example, Dahl et al. (2007) propose a multiscale typology based on geomorphic, geological, and hydrological concepts reflecting functional linkages and controlling flow processes at progressively smaller scales. Their classification embodies the following: Landscape Type (catchment scale >5 km), Riparian Hydrogeological Type (intermediate or reach scale of 1–5 km), and Riparian Flow Path Type (local scale of 10–1000 m).:

Although recognizing the value of SGDE typologies (for example, to predict stygofaunal characteristics and to support vulnerability assessments), Tomlinson and Boulton (2010) argue that the most effective typology will be based on "ecohydrogeological principles." They call for deeper understanding of relationships between broad-scale "filters" (sensu Poff 1997) of climate, surface drainage and recharge, geology, and topography, and finer-scale aspects such as porosity and permeability, groundwater regime, and connectivity across aquifers and to adjacent ecosystems. From this ecohydrogeological perspective, these broad-scale filters and fine-scale aspects determine ecological processes and habitat availability, influence productivity and stygobite diversity, and control the provision of groundwater ecosystem goods and services.

An essential step in any groundwater-management protocol is to document the characteristics and diversity of faunal assemblages and their environmental dependencies. Gibert and Culver (2009) summarize the outcome of a large-scale European survey, the PASCALIS project (Protocol for the Assessment and Conservation of Aquatic Life in the Subsurface), with emphasis on methods for the assessment of groundwater diversity based on a rigorously standardized sampling protocol. This protocol involved assessment at four spatial scales: region, basin, aquifer type (e.g., karst versus alluvial aquifers), and zone in each aquifer (e.g., unsaturated versus saturated zones in karst aquifers and hyporheic versus phreatic zones in alluvial aquifers) (Malard et al. 2002).

One relevant finding is that groundwater communities display much larger differences in species composition among sampling sites than is found for surface-dwelling freshwater fauna in comparable spatial units. Hancock and Boulton (2008) stress the need to employ a combination of sampling methods for a comprehensive assessment of groundwater biodiversity, while Eberhard et al. (2009) suggest that sample periods of greater than 1 year are needed for complete assessments of biodiversity. Summing up sampling issues, Gibert et al. (2009) recommend that the PASCALIS scheme could be further improved by "(i) identifying the spatial level (basin, aquifer type, or habitat type) where environmental heterogeneity is highest, (ii) sampling during optimal hydrological periods, such as times of rising water, and (iii) capturing specific sources of environmental heterogeneity, such as historical factors (e.g., marine embayments, glaciation), pollution or natural or anthropogenic disturbance."

To avoid the challenges of comprehensive biodiversity assessment, Stoch et al. (2009) used three indicator groups (Gastropoda, Harpacticoida, and Amphipoda) as surrogates to predict overall species richness in karstic and porous aquifers in Europe; the proposed model explained more than 80% of the variance in total richness. Applications to regions beyond the test locations would require calibration to area-specific groundwater assemblages. Another line of inquiry has considered functional classification of groundwater species based on traits (e.g., feeding groups). However, subterranean food webs are largely composed of detritivores and omnivores; therefore, Claret et al. (1999) applied a combined classification based on many species traits (diet, locomotion, body size, reproduction type, and parental care) and habitat affinities (stygoxenes, stygophiles, and stygobionts) to a hyporheic assemblage. This proved useful in detecting responses of invertebrates to natural and human disturbances.

Understanding how various factors govern the heterogeneity and distribution of groundwater fauna represents an important step in protecting SGDEs. The composition and density of interstitial fauna generally exhibit differences between patches of contrasting hydrological exchange with the surface stream in relation to sediment particle size distribution, water chemistry (ions and dissolved oxygen), and organic-matter content. Multiple regression models of these relationships demonstrate the importance of measuring spatially explicit habitat variables (e.g., distance between leaf patches and contagion) as well as hydrological variables.

Temporal patterns in surface water–groundwater interactions must be understood as part of any protocol for assessment of groundwater dependencies. Changes in the flow regime, groundwater recharge, flood patterns, and geomorphic structures repeatedly modify the spatial extent and distribution of surface-subsurface exchange patches in streams. Morrice et al. (1997) used sodium bromide injections to demonstrate that the standardized storage zone area (a surrogate for the relative extent of the hyporheic zone) decreased with increasing stream discharge in a New Mexico stream. There are significant difficulties associated with measuring the responses of biota to these spatial and temporal patterns of hyporheic flow paths. Malard et al. (2002) suggested that river restoration projects could be used as large-scale manipulation experiments for testing the influence of the shape of islands and meander bends on hyporheic processes, for example. This contribution also promoted the need to integrate information on the life span, hydrological connection with neighboring patches, and movement patterns of organisms into investigations of the spatial and temporal patchiness of hyporheic assemblages.

GROUNDWATER ECOSYSTEM HEALTH

The definition and assessment of groundwater ecosystem health is emerging as a dynamic field that parallels river health assessment using surface water biota and other indicators. Steube et al. (2009) describe four steps toward an integrated ecological assessment of groundwater ecosystems: (1) the identification of the typology of groundwater ecosystems, (2) the derivation of natural background values, (3) the identification of potential bioindicators, and (4) the development of an assessment model. Such an approach requires the collaboration of ecologists, hydrogeologists, and geochemists as well as the application of quantitative approaches such as multivariate statistics.

Korbel and Hose (2010) propose a tiered framework for assessing groundwater ecosystem health, wherein tier 1 presents primary indicators of health and benchmarks that, if exceeded, indicate that more detailed assessment is required (tier 2) based on indicators that may together generate a multimetric index of groundwater health. A case study on an alluvial aquifer in northwestern New South Wales, Australia, demonstrates how the approach can be used to separate disturbed and undisturbed groundwater sites. The framework is flexible enough to be applied and adapted to other site-specific contexts. Tomlinson and Boulton (2010) regard standard methods and protocols for monitoring and assessing indicators of SGDE health as a high priority for further development to identify high-conservation-value ecosystems and guide SGDE-specific management actions that will maintain biodiversity, ecosystem function, and water quality.

MANAGEMENT OF GROUNDWATER SYSTEMS

Questions that arise from a management perspective include the following: Which GDEs are important and how can their level of importance be assessed? How can systems at risk be identified? Are there definable indicators of environmental stress for GDEs? How can GDEs be valued? How can system behavior and processes be described qualitatively and represented quantitatively? Can representative systems be investigated to answer the above, to facilitate transferability of site-specific results to a range of similar situations? What innovative tools can be developed and used to manage ecosystems in a way that allows maximum consumptive use of the resource while meeting agreed-upon environmental needs?

One group of tools to assess "maximum consumptive use" revolves around the concept of "sustainable groundwater yield," defined as "the groundwater extraction regime, measured over a specified planning timeframe, that allows acceptable levels of stress and protects dependent economic, social, and environmental values" (Land and Water Australia 2009). This definition recognizes that sustainable groundwater yield should be expressed in the form of an "extraction regime," not just an extraction volume, where a regime is "a set of management practices that are defined within a specified time (or planning period) and space."

Although this definition is essentially utilitarian, it requires attention to the pattern of water take in terms of sustaining four key groundwater attributes: flow or flux (the rate and volume of supply of groundwater); level (for an unconfined aquifer, the depth below the surface of the water table); pressure (for confined aquifers, the potentiometric head of the aquifer and its expression in groundwater discharge areas); and quality (the physicochemical properties of groundwater, including oxygen, temperature, pH, salinity, nutrients, contaminants) (Clifton and Evans 2001). Extraction limits may be expressed in terms of volumetric quantity but should further specify "the extraction or withdrawal regime in terms of accounting rules and/or rates of extraction over a given period and/or impact, water level or pressure and water quality trigger rules," and the limits may be probabilistic and/or conditional (Land and Water Australia 2009). Often the method for defining the extraction regime has been to state a maximum volume that may be taken in any single year; but in some cases, where drawdown beyond the rate of recharge may be acceptable, this may be permitted only for a specified period, after which time the rate may be less than the rate of recharge to compensate. Sometimes there may be specific circumstances (e.g., high- or low-rainfall years) when the amount of water that may be taken may be greater or less than the longer-term value, and the conditions for this should be specified.

The proposed sustainable yield approach recognizes that any extraction of groundwater will result in some level of stress or impact on the total system, including GDEs. To accommodate ecological stress on GDEs, the concept of "acceptable levels of stress" has been proposed (Land and Water Australia 2009; Krause et al. 2010). In essence this concept duplicates the definition of surface water environmental flows, because it incorporates the need for trade-offs to determine what is acceptable and what is not, and for whom. Typically making trade-offs will involve balancing environmental, social, and economic needs. In some cases, the environmental and ecological stress of groundwater removal may be temporary as the system adjusts to a new equilibrium. However, the inherent time lags associated with GDE management need to be taken into account before assuming that any observable ecological stress is minimal and therefore acceptable. The first of these is the hydraulic time lag between the actual commencement of groundwater pumping and reduction in water availability to a GDE, because groundwater development always results in declines in natural discharge with consequent environmental impacts. The second time lag is the time that it takes for an ecosystem to respond by deteriorating or perishing (see Petts et al. 1999).

The concept of acceptable stress further recognizes that the entire "groundwater system" must be considered, by taking into account interactions between aquifers and between surface water and groundwater systems and associated water-dependent ecosystems. This systems approach implies that integrated management decisions must be implemented to fully satisfy the intent of acceptable levels of stress for groundwater and surface water ecosystems (e.g., Krause et al. 2010). The precautionary approach provides a further guiding principle, with estimates of sustainable yield being lower where there is limited knowledge of the ecological and other consequences of water extraction. Finally, the calculated sustainable yield as a limit on groundwater extractions must be applied through a process of adaptive management that involves monitoring the subsequent impacts of extraction. Sustainable yields should be regularly reassessed and adjusted in accordance with a specified planning framework to take account of any new information, including improved ecological understanding and better valuations of groundwater-dependent ecosystems (Land and Water Australia 2009).

VALUING AND PRIORITIZING GROUNDWATER-DEPENDENT ECOSYSTEMS

When faced with threats to diverse GDEs, resource managers must allocate scarce resources (money, time, expertise) to the most valuable

GDEs. Murray et al. (2006) propose an eight-step method for a valuation and prioritization process that employs both economic and ecological values:

1. Identify the ecosystem services (ES) relevant to each GDE.

2. Determine whether the ES of the GDEs are likely to be affected directly or indirectly by alterations to the natural groundwater regime.

3. Provide an economic value for the ES (that will be directly or indirectly affected) of the GDEs in their original condition. Valuation methods include willingness to pay; valuation of ES that already have a known market value (e.g., timber); the cost of a human-made substitutable goods and services (e.g., production of clean water through desalination or sewage treatment; or concrete flood drains and water-storage facilities and sediment traps in place of forested catchments that naturally trap water and silt); willingness to accept compensation for loss of an ES; and finally, valuation of the loss of economic activity directly arising from the loss of an ES (e.g., the lost value of agricultural productivity in saline landscapes). As an interim method, values of Costanza et al. (1997) may be used to provide a relative value for each ES.

4. Add the values of the ES determined for each GDE, and multiply by the area of the GDE to provide a total value of ES provided by each GDE

5. Rank all *n* GDEs from 1 to *n,* on the basis of the total value of ES for each GDE.

6. To account for ecological values, such as the presence of rare and threatened species, communities, or biodiversity hot spots, GDEs may be ranked in terms of their conservation value.

7. Each GDE should then be ranked on the basis of its areal cover (i.e., landscape abundance) so as to increase the weighting of uncommon or small GDEs, which will have low ES values because of their small areal extent; this process will indirectly increase the weighting given to GDEs that are threatened because of their limited range.

8. Add the ranks for (1) economic values of ES, (2) ecological values of GDEs, and (3) landscape abundance of GDEs. This additive process provides an overall prioritized list of GDEs.

Step 6 of the protocol pays attention to the conservation value of GDEs; but to value conservation importance, more detailed assessment is required beyond just ranking based on biodiversity and the presence of rare and endangered species. Dole-Olivier et al. (2009) suggest that recognizing SGDE diversity, at least on the basis of aquifer type, can aid identification of conservation priorities by locating probable biodiversity hot spots. Tomlinson and Boulton (2010), on the other hand, propose that an understanding of the ecohydrogeological characteristics of connectivity to other ecosystems and aquifer permeability "explicitly recognises the features that deserve protection, both in 'open' systems when connectivity is high and the integrity of adjacent surface ecosystems is also worthy of conservation, and in discrete habitats with low connectivity, such as calcretes, where endemism is potentially high."

In summing up the state of the science-management-policy interface of GDEs, MacKay (2006) concluded, "There is no single right way to solve the problem of protecting groundwater-dependent ecosystems, while still allowing the use of groundwater to support social and economic development, poverty alleviation and improved food and water security." King and Caylor (2011) concluded that there remains "great opportunity to leverage the strengths of ecological and hydrological traditions to more aggressively build our understanding of coupled ecological and hydrological system functions." Perhaps this is nowhere more needed than in the merging of surface water and groundwater hydrology with equivalent ecological understanding of groundwater-dependent ecosystem processes and biota. While the Riverine Ecosystem Synthesis (Thorp et al. 2008) may offer a suitable construct for framing these essential inquiries in running-water systems, the ecohydrogeological framework of Tomlinson and Boulton (2010) presents a broader vision of groundwater dependencies and challenging opportunities for management (see Fig. 40, Chapter 15).

17

WETLANDS, THREATS, AND
WATER REQUIREMENTS

WETLAND ECOLOGY AND WATER REGIMES

Wetlands are areas where standing water covers the soil or is present at or near the surface of the soil for some part of the year (Mitsch and Gosselink 2007). Many different types have been recognized, their character depending on climatic and hydrogeomorphic setting, inundation regime, groundwater, water chemistry, and associated factors. The wetland classification scheme proposed by Cowardin et al. (1979) includes riverine, lacustrine, palustrine, and estuarine systems (Table 33). This classification recognizes a small number of essential criteria, namely shallow water, hydric soils, and specialized plant communities. Semeniuk and Semeniuk (1995) extended earlier work to provide a hydrogeomorphic scheme for global wetlands that incorporated hydrology, landforms, and geomorphology, linked to vegetation patterns.

Wetlands receive their water from precipitation, groundwater, water flowing over the land surface, or tidal hydrological processes, so their waters may be fresh or saline or somewhere in between. Freshwater wetlands include pools and high tarns, high-altitude sponges, peat bogs and other boggy habitats, fens, swamp forests, marshes, pans, playas, and oxbow lakes (cutoff river meanders). Some contain permanent water and aquatic or water-loving (hydric) plants, while others transition between wet, vegetated aquatic phases and dry terrestrial phases

TABLE 33   *Wetland classification scheme*

Category	Definition
Riverine	Riverine systems include all wetlands and deepwater habitats contained within a channel, with two exceptions: wetlands dominated by trees, shrubs, persistent emergent vegetation, emergent mosses, or lichens; and habitats with water containing ocean-derived salts in excess of 0.5%. A channel is an open conduit either naturally or artificially created which periodically or continuously contains moving water or which forms a connecting link between two bodies of standing water.
Lacustrine	Lacustrine systems include wetlands and deepwater habitats with the following characteristics: situated in a topographic depression or a dammed river channel; lacking trees, shrubs, persistent emergents, emergent mosses or lichens with greater than 30% areal coverage; and total area exceeds 8 ha. Similar wetlands and deepwater habitats totaling less than 8 ha are also a lacustrine system if an active wave-formed or bedrock shoreline feature makes up all or part of the boundary, or if the water depth in the deepest part of the basin exceeds 2 m at low water. Includes coastal dune lakes, inland saline and freshwater lakes, billabongs, lagoons, and pools.
Palustrine	Palustrine systems include all nontidal wetlands dominated by trees, shrubs, persistent emergent vegetation, emergent mosses or lichens. They also include wetlands lacking such vegetation that have the following three characteristics: (1) where active waves are formed or bedrock features are lacking; (2) where water depth in the deepest part of the basin is less than 2 m at low water; and (3) where salinity due to ocean-derived salts is still less than 0.5%. Includes forest and woodland swamps; swamps dominated by shrubs; wet heath and fens; swamps dominated by grass, sedge, reed, or rushes; pans; and spring wetlands.
Estuarine	Estuarine systems include wetlands with oceanic water that are occasionally diluted with freshwater runoff from the land. Includes mangroves, salt marshes, and salt flats.

SOURCES: Cowardin et al. 1979; Dyson et al. 2003

(Mitsch and Gosselink 2007). This chapter briefly introduces freshwater wetlands and their water requirements; the water requirements of estuaries are the subject of Chapter 18.

The Ramsar Convention on Wetlands of International Importance (signed in 1971 at the small Iranian town of Ramsar) aims to halt the worldwide loss of wetlands and to conserve those that remain (Carp 1972). The convention recognizes three main categories of wetlands, each with a number of well-defined types: marine/coastal (12 types), inland (20 types), and human-made (10 types). According to the convention, "Wetlands are areas of marsh, fen, peatland or water, whether natural or artificial, permanent or temporary, with water that is static or flowing, fresh, brackish or salt, including areas of marine water the depth of which at low tide does not exceed six metres" (Carp 1972). Underground (groundwater-dependent) wetlands are also recognized and protected by the convention.

Under the Ramsar Convention, each wetland designated as a "wetland of international importance" must be described in terms of its "ecological character," and that ecological character must be protected through wise use and management. An ecological character description sets out the wetland's water dependencies and describes how the water regime determines the habitats, vegetation and other ecological communities and species that are found in that wetland, which in turn influence the benefits and ecosystem services provided. The physical, chemical, and biological functions that give wetlands their unique ecological character and conservation value are driven to a large extent by water availability and overall water regime (Gippel 1992). Daily, seasonal, interannual, and decadal variations in rainfall and runoff produce natural cycles of water-level fluctuation in wetlands. These fluctuations in water level, including the complete wetting or the complete drying of the bed, provide variable conditions for the germination, establishment, growth, and reproduction of wetland vegetation.

Brock and Casanova (1997) showed that groupings of "terrestrial" species (unable to tolerate flooding) and "submerged" plants (unable to tolerate drying) occupy the upper and lower sections of a wetland together with a large group of "amphibious" species that tolerate or respond to fluctuations of flooding and drying in the wet-dry ecotone. Life-history strategies further distinguish plant adaptations to variable water regimes. For example, amphibious species can be divided into "amphibious fluctuation-tolerant" species (e.g., emergents such as *Eleocharis* and *Juncus* spp. and low-growing plants such as *Utricularia* and *Hydrocotyle*) able to endure variations in flooding patterns without changing their morphology or growth; whereas "amphibious fluctuation-responding" plants (e.g., *Myriophyllum, Potamogeton*) change their morphology or growth form in response to the presence or absence of water (Brock and Casanova 1997). Different leaf forms (heterophylly) for underwater and above-water photosynthesis is one mechanism of adaptation (Sculthorpe 1967). One example is the creeping growth form of species that put down roots at nodes when stranded out of water and that then extend those nodes and leaves vertically when flooded.

Changing the water regimes of wetlands can be expected to alter the composition of wetland plant communities by shifting the proportions of functional (or trait) vegetation groups. Brock and Casanova (1997) provided a useful tabulation of the predicted plant community and functional group responses to changes in water regime in the wet-dry ecotone of wetlands. More permanently wet systems can be expected to encourage competitive submerged and amphibious species and declining native species richness, and plant survival depends on the longevity of seed banks. In more permanently dry wetlands, woody terrestrial species may be encouraged, amphibious and submerged species may decline, species richness may decline, and survival of the natural flora depends on the longevity of seed banks.

HYDROLOGIC ALTERATIONS AND THREATS TO WETLANDS

Freshwater wetland ecosystems are listed among the most impacted and degraded of all ecological systems (Davis and Froend 1998), and by some accounts over 60% of the world's wetlands have been lost already. In part due to the US Swamp Lands Act of the mid-1800s, more than 50% of the original wetlands in 43 states of the continental United States have been drained. In 1906 the US Department of Agriculture offered technical assistance to landowners to convert wetland "waste-land" to cropland. Wetlands the world over continue to be drained, diked and dammed, leveed, dredged and canalized, logged and mined, grazed, converted to shrimp and prawn farms and rice paddies, filled with solid wastes, and even concreted over (Pearce 2007; Cech 2010).

Activities in the catchments of wetlands can deliver pollutants, bring about eutrophication and salinization, and alter runoff and inflow of water to wetlands. The water regimes of many wetlands have been altered by river regulation; extraction of water for agricultural, domestic, and industrial uses; and the use of wetlands as areas for enhanced water storage. Groundwater extraction also poses a threat to some wetlands, typically in the form of lower water levels and prolonged dry phases. Reducing the availability of groundwater may lead to a gradual decline in the spatial extent of the wetland ecosystem or in the health and species composition of vegetation. In extreme cases, a threshold is reached and the entire wetland ecosystem is destroyed (Hatton and Evans 1998).

Human impacts on wetland water regimes can result in both increased and decreased inundation as well as altered variability in inundation and seasonality. Land drainage into wetlands and inundation as a result of rising water tables can affect wetlands, that is, they can have too much water as well as too little water (Davis et al. 2001). Many of these threats and stressors reduce the capacity of wetlands to function as "hydrologic sponges" (Leigh et al. 2010) that attenuate high flows and floods, store water, and sequester excess waterborne nutrients and chemicals that would otherwise contaminate downstream environments.

Wetlands closely associated with rivers, and therefore likely to be affected by river flow regulation, have been divided into two broad categories: floodplain wetlands and terminal wetlands. Dams can affect floodplain wetlands by capturing flood pulses that would otherwise have led to overbank flows into meanders, backwater habitats, oxbow lakes, and higher elevations of the floodplain itself (Kingsford 2000). When stored water is later released to the river channel for diversion to irrigation schemes and other consumptive uses, the flow volume is often larger than natural, so increased flows may bring about increased permanence of the water regimes of some backwater and floodplain wetlands (Davis et al. 2001). The water regimes of floodplain wetlands can also be altered by conversion into off-river storages or can be flooded by dams (Kingsford 2000). Other water-regime issues for wetlands resulting from river regulation include loss of connectivity pathways, alteration of hydrologic processes due to levee banks, and loss of variability in water regimes, including reduced flood pulses and the loss of normal seasonal patterns (Davis et al. 2001). Infrastructure such as irrigation regulators and water-supply channels may also impact wetlands because they modify water levels and connectivity pathways.

Terminal wetlands fed by streams and rivers are extremely vulnerable to the impacts of dams and diversions of their inflowing water regime, with overall reduction in the quantity of water a frequent outcome of river regulation upstream. The destruction of the ecosystems and fisheries of the Aral Sea in Uzbekistan and Kazakhstan stands out as one of the worst environmental and human disasters caused by diverting large rivers for irrigation purposes. The Aral Sea is supplied by the Amu Dar'ya and Syr Dar'ya Rivers and in 1960 formed a terminal lake system of 68,000 km². By 1987 it was reduced to 41,000 km², and by 1990 it was only 33,500 km². Its volume fell from 1,090 km³ in 1960 to 310 km³ in 1990 (Micklin 1988; Aladin and Williams 1993). Water diverted from the inflowing rivers supplies an irrigation industry, mainly cotton and rice, estimated to be 7 million ha (Kotlyakov 1991). The shrinking ecosystem of the Aral Sea suffered devastating impacts: 20 of 24 species of fish became extinct; 550,000 ha of reedbeds declined to 20,000 ha; of some 200 species of free-living macroinvertebrates, only 8 species survive (almost all introduced); only 168 of 319 bird species still nest; and only 30 of an original 70 mammal species remain (Micklin 1988; Kotlyakov 1991). Loss of inflowing water and high evaporation rates caused the lake's salinity to rise threefold to nearly 30 grams per liter virtually destroying a commercial fishing industry that once supported 60,000 workers. With ecological damage have come significant losses of fishing income, other economic costs, and human health problems (e.g., respiratory diseases associated with inhalation of dust and pesticides). A restoration program is in progress.

In another example, escalating demands for off-stream water use have depleted inflows of freshwater to the Coorong, Lower Lakes, and Murray Mouth (CLLMM)—a 140,500 ha complex of shallow lakes, streams, lagoons, and wetlands at the terminus of the Murray-Darling river system in southern Australia. The Murray Mouth now receives less than 30% of its original annual flows, largely due to irrigation demands in the river's upstream catchments. The CLLMM was recognized as a Ramsar site in 1985 for its physical and biological diversity and spectacular populations of migratory shorebirds (Paton et al. 2009). As a result of insufficient freshwater inflows, salinities in the north and south lagoons of the Coorong have increased, and falling water levels have exposed acid sulfate soils around the margins of Lake

Alexandrina, Lake Albert, and tributary streams. Many species, including shorebirds and other waterbirds, have declined sharply over the past two decades (Paton et al. 2009), and in the lakes affected by water deficits and rising salinity, the biota is changing to salt-tolerant estuarine and marine species (Phillips and Muller 2006; Wedderburn and Barnes 2009). The Yarra pygmy perch *(Nannoperca obscura)* is now considered extinct in the wild in the Murray-Darling Basin, the southern pygmy perch *(N. australis)* hangs on in remnant pockets, and the Murray hardyhead *(Craterocephalus fluviatilis),* faces imminent extinction (Wedderburn and Barnes 2009). Diadromous fish, including common galaxias *(Galaxias maculatus)* and congolli *(Pseudaphritis urvillii)* can no longer migrate between marine and freshwater environments. Kingsford et al. (2009) stress that "without addressing the underlying cause of lack of water, the likelihood of Australia meeting its obligations for this Ramsar site are remote."

The Pantanal—another wetland of international importance, and the world's largest wetland of any kind—forms a vast complex of savanna wetlands and internal deltas within the Brazilian state of Mato Grosso do Sul and portions of Bolivia and Paraguay. The Pantanal is under threat from many human activities (Harris et al. 2005). Agricultural development and cattle ranching cause erosion and sedimentation (approximately 99% of land in the Pantanal is privately owned for the purpose of agriculture and ranching); deforestation is causing silt runoff from deforested highlands; pollution from agroindustrial plants, sewage wastes, and mercury tailing from old gold mines have caused fish kills; hunting and smuggling of endangered species and commercial and sport fishing and tourism enterprises threaten aquatic diversity and wildlife.

Wetlands of the Pantanal depend on periodic flooding, when 80% of the floodplains are submerged. The entire ecosystem responds dramatically to the flood pulse, and this dynamic wetland system is threatened by the construction of the Paraguay-Paraná waterway (or *hidrovía*). This project, supported by the Inter-American Development Bank, aims to dredge and change the course of the Rio Paraguai to allow for fluvial transport of mainly agricultural produce from inland areas to the sea (Harris et al. 2005). Modeling has already indicated that the proposed changes would alter the flow of the Rio Paraguai and cause the loss of large areas of wetland in the Pantanal (Hamilton 1999), with subsequent large-scale disruption of the ecological processes that determine the spatial and temporal variability of habitats vital for maintenance of biodiversity. Furthermore, the Brazil-Bolivia natural-gas pipeline will intensify the mining of iron and manganese in the Urucum Mountains in the state of Mato Grosso do Sul, and the installation of large steelworks and petrochemical plants will be significant sources of pollution (Harris et al. 2005).

Coastal wetlands, shoreline habitats, and their biota face different threats. After the *Deepwater Horizon* oil rig burned and sank in the Gulf of Mexico in April 2010, oil began to threaten wetlands and beaches from Texas to Florida, with Louisiana's coastal wetlands and the Mississippi Delta most at risk. Delta wetlands act as nursery grounds for shrimp, crabs, and oysters, and thousands of migratory birds nest in the wetlands' inner reaches, a complex network of bayous, bays, and canals. The US Fish and Wildlife Service believes the spill potentially threatens 32 national wildlife refuges and dozens of threatened and endangered species, including the West Indian manatee *(Trichechus manatus),* whooping cranes, Mississippi sandhill cranes, wood storks, and four species of sea turtles reliant on the Mississippi Delta. As the delta is the meeting point of the Central and Mississippi Flyways, damage to delta wetlands has conservation consequences for many species of migratory birds.

WATER REQUIREMENTS OF WETLANDS

Despite an enormous literature on the ecology and threats to wetlands, there is limited material focused specifically on methods for estimating the water requirements of wetlands to parallel the decades of development in running waters. In her review of environmental flow methods for rivers, Tharme (2003) commented that "the vast majority of methodologies available globally have focused exclusively on rivers, with the considerable scope for adaptation of such approaches for other aquatic ecosystems (e.g., groundwater-dependent wetlands and estuaries) being as yet, largely unexploited." Since that review, the Ramsar Convention has published a 21-volume "tool kit" for the conservation and wise use of wetlands (Ramsar Convention Secretariat 2010). Each handbook provides convention resolutions, technical advice, case studies, and background documents. Relevant volumes include *Handbook 9: River*

Basin Management, Handbook 10: Water Allocation and Management, Handbook 11: Managing Groundwater, and *Handbook 12: Coastal Management.*

Several reviews of water-allocation methods for wetlands describe the main approaches. For example, McCosker (1998) recognized two broad types of freshwater wetlands: riverine floodplain wetlands (depressions within the floodplain that are fed by the adjacent river, e.g., oxbow lakes) and terminal wetlands situated at the lowest point in a catchment and receiving water that drains from that catchment. This distinction leads to two main categories of methods: those based on developing a water budget and those dependent on estimating the river and floodplain flows required to inundate wetlands associated with the river channel, the floodplain, or terminal water bodies.

A water budget is a simple model of the inputs and outputs of water to a wetland expressed by the following equation: $\Delta S(t) = P + Qi + Gi - E - Qo - Go$, such that over a specified time interval (t), ΔS = change in water quantity stored in the wetland, P = precipitation falling on the wetland, Qi = surface water flowing into the wetland, Gi = groundwater flowing into the wetland, E = evapotranspiration volume, Qo = surface water flowing out of the wetland, and Go = groundwater flowing out of the wetland (McCosker 1998). Seasonal variations in water inputs and outputs give rise to seasonal variations in water depth and area of wetland inundated. In the longer term, the water level may be low or high for unusually long periods, or at unseasonal times, in response to erratic weather patterns or extended wet or drought years.

Water-level variations over time can be characterized statistically in terms of the frequency of wet and dry periods, the average and extreme duration of wet and dry periods, and the seasonality of wet and dry periods (Gippel 1992); or they can be described in more detail according to variables that parallel those of the Range of Variability Approach (RVA) used to characterize river flows (Richter et al. 2006). Characteristics of the desired water regime of wetlands may include extent (area inundated), depth (minimum and maximum), seasonality (whether inundation is permanent, seasonal, or ephemeral), season of maximum inundation, rate of rise and fall, size and frequency of floods, size and frequency of dry periods, duration of floods, duration of dry periods, and variability (adapted by Davis et al. 2001 from Roberts et al. 2000).

Water budgets have been used to estimate volumes of water required to inundate terminal wetlands in river systems that have been subjected to hydrological changes as a result of upstream impoundment and flow regulation (e.g., McCosker and Duggin 1993; Keyte 1994). Estimates of the water requirements of terminal wetlands based on water budgets can be verified with the aid of historical discharge data and remote-sensing images. For example, Bennett and Green (1993) used Landsat multispectoral scanner images to establish a relationship between the area of wetland inundated and discharge volume during a particular flow event in the Gwydir Wetlands, Murray-Darling Basin, Australia.

Remote-sensing techniques have been used as a practical means of observing a number of actual watering events in riverine wetlands and are especially useful when wetlands are hydraulically complex, have no gauging records, or are inaccessible and expensive to survey topographically (Shaikh et al. 2001). Studies to determine the aerial extent of flooding have commonly involved optical satellite image analysis (e.g., Sheng et al. 2001; Frazier et al. 2003), radar remote sensing (Townsend and Walsh 1998), or integration of remote sensing and geographical information systems (GIS) (Brivio et al. 2002).

Overton (2005) developed a floodplain inundation model for the 600 km long and 1–5 km wide portion of the Murray River in southern Australia integrating GIS, remote sensing, and hydrological modeling. Flood inundation extents were monitored from Landsat satellite imagery for a range of flows, interpolated to model flood growth patterns and linked to a hydrological model of the river. The GIS model allowed prediction of flooding extent for flows ranging from minimum flow to a 1-in-13-year flood event, enabling prediction of the effects of flooding on wetlands and floodplain vegetation. This contribution provides a flow diagram of the process of building the flood inundation model and full details of the steps involved.

These observational methods for determining the relationships between flood magnitude and the area of floodplain inundated have proved useful and economical for large-area flood analysis, whereas more detailed studies have used digital elevation models to create a floodplain surface that can be inundated at certain river heights (e.g., Townsend and Walsh 1998). Elevation methods can be used to predict changing flow paths through a floodplain by manipulating flood levels and barriers to flow (Overton 2005). They can also be applied to studies of the timing and frequency of inundation and the extent to which isolated floodplain water bodies are connected to main river channels.

For example, Karim et al. (2011) developed a method of quantifying flood-induced overbank connectivity using a hydrodynamic model to calculate the timing, duration, and spatial extent of the connections between a number of wetlands and the main rivers in the Tully-Murray floodplain, north Queensland, Australia. The wetlands on the floodplain were identified using high-resolution laser altimetry (LiDAR) data that was incorporated with areal photogrammetry data to form a digital elevation model (DEM) of the floodplain. Propagation of flood waves and associated floodplain inundation were simulated using a two-dimensional hydrodynamic model (MIKE 21) that computed water depth and flow velocity on a 30 m grid. This model found that the duration of connection of individual wetlands varied from 1 to 12 days, depending on flood magnitude (1-, 20-, and 50-year recurrence intervals) and location in the floodplain, with some of the more isolated wetlands only connected during large floods. Dynamic models of this type can be used to evaluate the effects of water availability and water management scenarios and their implications for floodplain biota and processes.

Water budgets and flood inundation and connectivity models are founded on hydrological processes and their relationship with areas and depths of wetland inundated, providing a surrogate for the likely ecological responses and benefits of water availability, timing, seasonality, and so on. Methods founded on the water requirements of wetland vegetation and other biota, especially fish and waterbirds, form a more advanced category (Davis et al. 2001; Welcomme et al. 2006). For example, Roberts et al. (2000) developed a methodology for determining environmental water allocations for floodplain wetlands based on plant water regimes, defined as "the pattern of water level changes required for the maintenance and regeneration of plant species." McCosker and Duggin (1993) examined water requirements for four vegetation communities dependent on different flood frequencies using a water budget to determine the quantity of water required to inundate these vegetation formations. Briggs and Thornton (1999) developed guidelines for the management of river red gum *(Eucalyptus camaldulensis)* wetlands for waterbird breeding, defining a minimum inundation period of 5 to 10 months for various waterbirds to complete breeding.

Peake et al. (2011) developed a methodology to prioritize wetland water allocations to meet the flooding requirements for flood-dependent "ecological vegetation classes" (EVCs), based on the life-history traits, tolerances, and competitive advantages of dominant and characteristic plant taxa. The "critical interval" (the estimated maximum period that an EVC can persist without flooding and remain capable of returning to its reference or benchmark condition) was estimated on the basis of "familiarity of the assessors with field indications of decline, combined with a knowledge of past flood intervals" (Peake et al. 2011). In addition, the minimum flood duration required to maintain each EVC in a condition comparable to its reference state was estimated based on the requirements of characteristic species and physical conditions at sites of occurrence. This method also included assessment of the flood dependencies of threatened fauna (birds, mammals, reptiles, and amphibians) through literature reviews and discussions with experts. From a combined georeferenced database for floodplain vegetation and fauna linked to hydrological modeling, it was possible to investigate the benefits of environmental watering and to estimate the risk of insufficient watering of individual wetland and vegetation complexes. The methodology is flexible and sufficiently adaptable to take in new data and better knowledge of the flooding requirements of flora and fauna over time.

Water regime recommendations for wetlands can be defined more precisely based on an appreciation of their ecological character. Davis and Brock (2008) provide a framework for ecological character description using a shallow Australian coastal sandplain wetland sustained by groundwater and local rainfall as an example. In their pro forma wetland character description, they propose three main steps: (1) describe the landscape context and identify relevant spatial scales using a hierarchy of maps and aerial photographs; (2) develop a driver/stressor conceptual ecological model with an accompanying synthesis of relevant biophysical data; and (3) use these as the basis for recognizing a unique set of wetland identifiers that, together with critical processes, sustain the ecological character of the wetland. Unacceptable changes in ecological character are those that result in "a loss of identifiers, disrupt critical processes and reduce services or benefits" (Davis and Brock

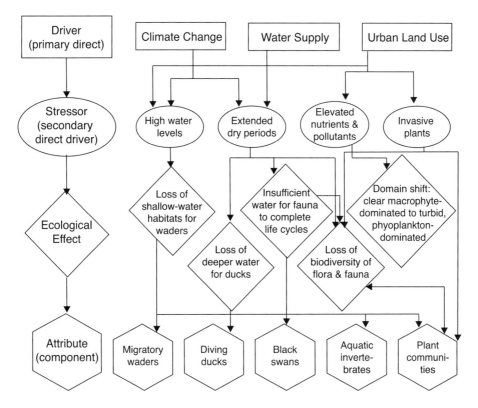

FIGURE 41. Driver/stressor model for Thomsons Lake, western Australia, show-ing drivers, stressors, ecological effects, and attributes (components). (Redrawn from Figure 5 in Davis and Brock 2008, with permission from Blackwell Science Pty Ltd)

2008). The driver/stressor conceptual ecological model (Fig. 41) can be accompanied by a diagrammatic model of wetland processes, for example, during the wetland's wet and dry phases.

In this framework, descriptions and representations of wetland eco-logical character serve as the "benchmark" for recognizing unaccept-able changes, defined as those that result in "a loss of identifiers, disrupt critical processes and reduce services or benefits. Less dramatic change towards such a loss, if it is outside the limits of acceptable change in character as established through management planning processes, would also be regarded as 'unacceptable.'" (Davis and Brock 2008). Using the Thomsons Lake case study, Davis and Brock (2008) suggest

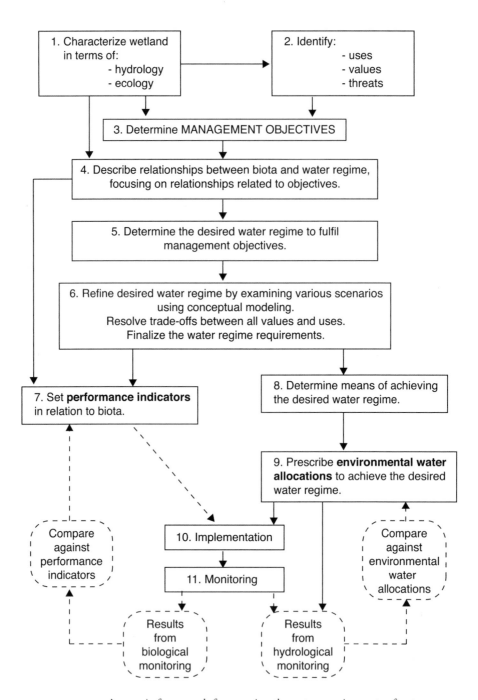

FIGURE 42. A generic framework for assessing the water requirements of wetlands. (Redrawn from Figure 11 in Davis et al. 2001)

that unacceptable adverse ecological changes would include changes to the unique set of identifiers, for example, the wetland becoming permanently wet, permanently dry, deep (>3 m), saline or hypersaline, acidic, eutrophic or hypertrophic, dominated by invasive plants, or unsuitable as a habitat for aquatic biota (especially waterbirds) or undergoing an ecological regime shift (e.g., from clear, aquatic plant–dominated to turbid, phytoplankton-dominated, turbid, sediment-dominated, or clear, benthic microbial mat–dominated). These changes would be identified using preexisting quantitative thresholds (e.g., for eutrophic and hypertrophic systems in the region) or expert knowledge, which is the accepted practice in many wetland studies (e.g., the Everglades restoration program) and in ecological flow assessment methods for rivers (e.g., DRIFT).

The individual methods outlined above are all amenable to incorporation into generic frameworks for wetland water allocation. Davis et al. (2001) proposed an 11-step framework for assessing the water requirements of wetlands reminiscent of several ecological flow assessment frameworks for rivers (Fig. 42).

18

ESTUARIES, THREATS, AND FLOW REQUIREMENTS

ESTUARINE ECOLOGY AND
HYDROECOLOGICAL PRINCIPLES

An estuary is a wide lower course of a river where the freshwater flow meets and is influenced by ocean tides, or it can be visualized as an arm of the sea extending inland to meet the mouth of a river (Maser and Sedell 1994). There are many definitions of estuaries. Fairbridge (1980) defines an estuary as "an inlet of the sea reaching into a river valley as far as the upper limit of tidal rise, usually being divisible into three sectors: (a) a marine or lower estuary, in free connection with the open ocean; (b) a middle estuary, subject to strong salt and fresh water mixing; and (c) an upper or fluvial estuary, characterised by fresh water but subject to daily tidal action." Day (1981) includes hypersaline lakes and other temporarily closed or "blind" estuaries in another definition: "An estuary is a partially enclosed coastal body of water which is either permanently or periodically open to the sea and within which there is a measurable variation of salinity due to the mixture of sea water with fresh water derived from land drainage."

The physical configuration of estuaries reflects inherited factors—the antecedent morphology of the coast, lithology, and sediment supply— while the present-day morphology is controlled by climate, the flow regime of the river, sediment supply, and the oceanographic regime of waves and tides. Estuaries can be classed as embayments and drowned river valleys, wave-dominated estuaries, wave-dominated deltas, intermittently closed and open coastal lakes and lagoons (ICOLLS), tide-dominated estuaries, tide-dominated deltas, and tidal creeks. All types of estuarine environments in the broadest sense reflect the interplay between fresh and saline water operating along gradients of salinity, with the upper reaches of estuaries where freshwater flows enter being the least saline. This inflowing freshwater forms a shallow layer over the deeper, denser seawater, which penetrates inland as a wedge of saline water. The extent of mixing of the two layers depends on the forces of flowing freshwater and tidal energy, and usually neither is sufficiently powerful to mix the layers, hence a salt wedge persists for some distance upstream. Salinity variations contribute to diverse habitat types in many estuaries, such as salt marshes, mangrove forests, mudflats, open waters, rocky intertidal shores, reefs, and barrier beaches.

Estuaries form the lower end of the "river continuum" in that they are connected to their parent rivers by inflowing freshwater, and their ecological character (to use Ramsar terminology) is deeply dependent on the incoming freshwater flow regime. Hence river discharge and the inflowing regime of freshwater can be described in terms similar to river flows, that is, in terms of magnitude (discharge volume), seasonal timing, frequency and duration of floods and low flows, spell characteristics, and flow variability and predictability. To these must be added the sedimentary and water-quality characteristics of the inflowing fresh water: temperature, salinity, nutrient and organic-matter levels, and contaminants (Wolanski 2007). How vitally important freshwater inflow is to the ecological status and resilience of an estuary is revealed by many examples of the adverse effects of artificially altered inflow regimes.

ALTERATIONS AND THREATS TO ESTUARINE ECOSYSTEMS

Estuaries were among the first places settled by humans and a great many have experienced a long history of changing human activities, from minimal habitation and fishing impacts through periods of increasing land cultivation and water-resource development, to the establishment and expansion of some of the world's greatest cities and ports (Lotze 2010). About 60% of the world's population lives along estuaries, and coastal waters supply about 90% of the global fish catch (Wolanski 2007). Recent and intense land-use changes along many coastlines in the immediate vicinity of estuaries, and in catchments that drain into estuaries, have transported the by-products of agricultural, urban, and industrial development directly into estuarine waterways and surrounding ecosystems. Most of the threats discussed for upstream catchments and freshwater systems, especially rivers, can be transmitted downstream into estuaries and coastal wetlands (Alber 2002).

Processes listed as degrading estuaries include the following: increased siltation resulting from land clearance and urban and rural runoff; modification to water flow through dams and weirs; increased nutrient loads resulting from sewage and agricultural use of fertilizers; urban and industrial effluents; acidification of rivers and heavy-metal pollution from mines, oil spills, foreshore development, and dredging; tourism developments and activities; marine aquaculture farms; the spread of introduced pest species; and overfishing (Edgar et al. 2000; Kennish 2002). In addition, estuarine waterways are affected by construction of port facilities, tidal barrages, and training walls and by shifts to the orientation of openings to the sea and artificial opening of closed estuary and ICOLL mouths (Pierson et al. 2002).

LAND-BASED THREATS

Land-based runoff generated largely by human activities in coastal catchments threatens the water quality of coastal ecosystems around the globe. Decline in water quality is related to land clearing, agricultural and urban development, and industrial and sewage discharge, aggravated by loss of the filtering and buffering capacity of vegetated catchments and riparian zones (Smith and Schindler 2009). The effects of declines in water quality range from sedimentation, eutrophication, harmful algal blooms, and large-scale hypoxia to fish kills, reductions in marine biodiversity, and impacts on fisheries catches (Rabalais et al. 2009; Waycott et al. 2009). Diffuse and point anthropogenic sources dominate the export of dissolved inorganic nitrogen and dissolved inorganic phosphorus from coastal catchments at the global scale, but there are hot spots: some regions also export high levels of organic nitrogen and phosphorus, for example, Indonesia, Japan, southern Asia, and Central America. Rapid cultural (human-induced) eutrophication occurs in the Baltic and Black Seas in Europe, in Chesapeake and San Francisco Bays in the United States, and in various water bodies around Japan, Hong Kong, Australia, and New Zealand (Cloern 1996).

Sedimentation is a natural process within estuaries and provides a range of important functions by supplying nutrients, burying contaminated sediments, building habitat structure, and buffering coastal erosion. Environmental problems arise when the rate at which sediment is transferred to and deposited within estuarine and coastal regions increases above natural levels; furthermore, depending on geology and land use, sediments may also contribute contaminants such as hydrocarbons, heavy metals, and nutrients (Thrush et al. 2004). Although sediment delivery rates have been reduced in many coastal areas by water storage and sediment trapping by dams (Vörösmarty et al. 2003), increased sedimentation is a growing issue in other areas. For example, average sedimentation rates in Chesapeake Bay have increased by an order of magnitude since 1760, when land-clearing activities commenced, while hydraulic mining and extensive forestry during California's gold rush resulted in massive sediment inputs into San Francisco Bay (Nichols et al. 1986).

Most terrestrial sediment enters estuaries during storm events, resulting in sediment loads that are orders of magnitude higher than average for short periods of time. Fine silts and clays flocculate on contact with seawater and are rapidly deposited, either smothering estuarine and marine sediments and associated biota or forming thinner layers that may have chronic rather than mortality effects on macrofauna. Fine sediments delivered from estuarine catchments can also impact estuarine communities by increasing the concentration of suspended solids. Highly turbid water can restrict light transmission and influence the relative importance of primary production by phytoplankton versus production by seaweeds and seagrasses, which typically require more sunlight for photosynthesis than phytoplankton (Thrush et al. 2004).

Low levels of nutrient enrichment can increase productivity and growth of seagrass beds, but a decline in area and density of seagrass beds generally follows eutrophication in low-nutrient coastal environments (Brodie 1995). Nutrient enrichment enhances growth of phytoplankton and epiphytic algae, so much so that increased epiphyte load can result in shading of seagrass beds, reducing photosynthesis and seagrass density. Increased levels of suspended sediments and the settlement of fine sediments on seagrass leaf blades also reduce light penetration and photosynthesis (Orth et al. 2006).

Seagrasses often form extensive meadows in shallow coastal waters and estuaries where their high productivity and complex structural forms influence the habitats of so many other species that they can be regarded as ecological engineers—modifiers or creators of habitat (sensu Wright and Jones 2006). Seagrasses also provide numerous important ecological services to the marine environment (Costanza et al. 1997). They stabilize sediments, alter water-flow patterns, produce large quantities of organic carbon, and influence nutrient cycling and food web structure (Hemminga and Duarte 2000). For many large herbivores, such as green sea turtles, dugongs, and manatees, seagrasses provide the main food resource; and with their structural complexity and variety seagrasses provide critical habitat for many animals, including commercially and recreationally important fishery species (Orth et al. 2006). Eleven of 28 fish species vulnerable to extinction in the United States use seagrass habitat during at least part of their life cycle.

ALTERED FLOW REGIMES

Much of the high temporal and spatial variability in physical, chemical, and biological conditions in estuaries occurs through seasonal and interannual variability in freshwater inflows. Reviewing the management of freshwater flow into estuaries, Estevez (2002) commented that "changes to inflows have harmed many estuaries in the world, and have the potential to harm more." Land-use changes, urbanization, and water engineering in river corridors; large water-supply dams, farm dams, and flow diversion; and water extraction from rivers and groundwater pumping can all alter the amount, the quality, and the timing of freshwater flows into estuaries (Gillanders and Kingsford 2002; Alber 2002).

Altered freshwater inflows have a wide range of ecological consequences for estuarine systems and coastal lakes/lagoons. By interrupting the downstream transport of sediments and nutrients, impoundments may drastically affect the amount and timing of nutrients and organic resources delivered downstream, and these changes can restructure biotic communities and affect the productivity of fisheries. Sediment trapping by dams and the inhibition of sediment transport by river water has contributed to extensive losses of wetlands and deltas. At a global scale, Vörösmarty et al. (1997) estimated that 16% of sediments are already trapped by the world's large dams. Reductions in nutrients due to retention by dams on the Danube, Dnieper, Dniester, and Don Rivers in Europe have been associated with reductions in fisheries in the Black, Azov, and Caspian Seas. The most valuable commercial fisheries in these seas have been reduced by 90% to 98%, while sturgeon catches in the Caspian Sea are only 1–2% of historical levels and have been totally eradicated in the northwestern Black Sea and Sea of Azov (McCully 2001). A similar decline occurred in fishery production in the entire eastern Mediterranean Sea following nutrient trapping behind the Aswan High Dam on the Nile River (Nixon 2003).

Irrespective of the load of sediments and nutrients carried by freshwater, changing the amount of freshwater input to an estuary by any of the perturbations described above will have profound effects on estuarine conditions. One of the most obvious consequences of decreased freshwater input is that saline water may intrude farther upstream, resulting in increased salinity along the estuarine gradient (Alber 2002). In extreme cases of high evaporation coupled with low rainfall and runoff, an estuary can become hypersaline. In addition to an upstream shift in salinity, decreased outflow can also lead to expansion of the zone of transition from very low salinity (i.e., the freshwater inflow zone) to full seawater, thereby lengthening the estuarine environment, with many consequences for habitat and organismal distribution patterns.

Decreases in river discharge that serve to increase the influence of the tide on water-circulation patterns can alter the entire hydrodynamic regime of an estuary. A stratified system with well-developed gravitational circulation can shift to a well-mixed system where tidal exchange increases in importance (Alber 2002). A change in stratification as the result of changes in inflow can in turn affect bottom-water oxygen levels and can lead to hypoxia, as has been observed in Chesapeake Bay.

Another hydrodynamic effect of freshwater discharge is the creation of the estuarine turbidity maximum (ETM), where suspended solids and other surface materials accumulate to form a front along the longitudinal axis of the estuary. The position of the ETM in the northern San Francisco Bay estuary is controlled by river discharge (Cloern et al. 1983). When river discharge falls within a critical range (100–350 m^3 per second), it positions the ETM adjacent to productive shallow embayments where light limitation is less severe than in the open estuary, enabling populations of neritic diatoms to increase.

Decreased freshwater inflow can also result in an increase in the flushing or freshwater transit time of estuaries, with consequences for the ability of an estuary to flush out materials; as transit times increase, the concentrations of pollutants and pathogens can increase as well. Reductions in freshwater inflow tend to promote phytoplankton blooms because the residence times of nutrients and cells are increased and populations can accumulate to bloom proportions. Algal blooms can be short-term episodic events, recurrent seasonal phenomena, or rare events associated with exceptional climatic or hydrologic conditions, depending on the relative influence of tides, wind, and freshwater inflows (Cloern 1996).

Estuarine responses to altered freshwater flows often show a lag effect, taking months to develop and persisting for months after an alteration to the inflowing regime. Livingston et al. (1997) recorded a strongly lagged response to a natural drought and a shift in carbon sources in Apalachicola Bay, Florida; this transformed the trophic structure of the bay as light penetrated to the bottom and stimulated the growth of phytoplankton, benthic algae, and other plants. Time-lagged effects often show up in the response of fishery stocks to altered inflows of freshwater; they have been reported in the Caspian Sea, in various European fish stocks, in the estuaries of Texas and Florida, and in several Australian studies (Estevez 2002; Loneragan and Bunn 1999).

The river inflow–fisheries response relationship in estuaries has been long recognized by commercial fishermen, and several mechanisms are thought to underlie strong correlations between estuarine fish and crustacean catches and freshwater inflow (Loneragan and Bunn 1999; Robins et al. 2005). Freshwater flows may enhance the biological productivity of estuaries through the input of organic and inorganic matter (including nutrients) that stimulate the lower end of the food chain (e.g., phytoplankton and bacteria), with flow-on effects for the growth and survival of species at higher trophic levels (Robins et al. 2006).

Alterations to flow volumes into an estuary can alter the accessibility and availability of important nursery habitats such as seagrass beds, coastal lagoons, and floodplains, thereby influencing recruitment and subsequent abundance of estuarine species (Staunton-Smith et al. 2004; Halliday and Robins 2007). Flow pulses may reduce salinity regimes and affect the environmental envelopes that stimulate and maintain movement behavior and the distributions of estuarine species. Pulses of flow can stimulate aggregation behavior (e.g., prawn "boils") that facilitate enhanced catch rates in estuarine and coastal fisheries (Loneragan and Bunn 1999), giving an impression of more fish rather than just redistribution and more effective capture of available biomass.

The work of Kimmerer (2002) on the effects of freshwater flow on the food web of the northern San Francisco Estuary reinforces the possible individuality of estuaries. Taxa at lower trophic levels either did not respond to flow, or they responded inconsistently by season; there was no evidence that seasonally averaged phytoplankton biomass responded to flow through either increased nutrient loading or increased salinity stratification brought about by freshwater inflow. There was evidence of bottom-up effects in the pelagic food web, propagating from the decline in phytoplankton through rotifers, copepods, and mysids and into starry flounder and longfin smelt, but other fish and shrimp remained unaffected. Kimmerer's conclusion was that the mechanisms underlying flow effects on each fish and crustacean species were apparently different and arose through specific features of the San Francisco Estuary that may not exist in other estuaries. Livingston et al. (1997) found that lower trophic levels in Apalachicola Bay were affected directly by river flow, while higher trophic levels were affected mainly by biological interactions.

All of the mechanisms described above may be involved and interact but in different ways and to different degrees from one estuary to another, with direct effects of flow on physical parameters (e.g., water velocity, salinity, water temperature, turbidity, nutrients) impacting estuarine fishery species through several intervening processes. An understanding of which mechanism is most important, and/or how various mechanisms interact with one another and with other stressors in the estuarine environment, is central to the development of environmental flow regimes for estuaries (Alber 2002; Estevez 2002).

FLOW REQUIREMENTS OF ESTUARIES

Estevez (2002) introduced his review of estuarine inflow studies by putting two basic questions to estuarine scientists and resource managers: By how much can natural flows be changed without causing harm? By how much or little must damaging flow regimes be moderated? He concluded with the following summary: "The most successful estuarine inflow tools will most likely be those traceable to flow and salinity, workable at several spatial and temporal scales, operated at different levels of biological and ecosystem organization, advantaged by the discovery of non-linear functions, and transferable to other systems." Several approaches and methods are used for estuarine inflow studies, many offering parallels to the main groups of methods employed by river scientists. Methods vary from hydrological variability techniques, habitat approaches, indicator species techniques, valued ecosystem component approaches, food web techniques, community index approaches, and landscape and adaptive management approaches (Estevez 2002). According to Alber (2002), environmental flow methods for estuaries can be divided into three types based on achieving inflows (e.g., a percentage relative to natural inflows), a specified estuarine condition, or the needs of particular estuarine resources. The following section presents selected examples of these methods, ending with a proposed framework for holistic (ecosystem) assessment of estuarine inflow requirements.

HYDROLOGICAL VARIABILITY OR INFLOW TECHNIQUES

In 1970 the US Congress passed legislation that established minimum flows to the Everglades National Park (Alber 2002). Following this, the Water Resources Act of 2000 addressed the issue of freshwater inflow by requiring that water management districts establish minimum flows and levels (MFLs) for surface waters and aquifers within their jurisdiction. Minimum flow was defined as "the limit at which further withdrawals would be significantly harmful to the water resources or ecology of the area" (Florida Statute Ann. § 373.042 [2000]). Water management districts have taken a variety of approaches to implement MFL directives. The South Florida Water Management District established the 10% daily flow rule in relation to water withdrawal permits, based on studies (e.g., Browder and Moore 1981) showing that reducing inflow by 10% or less had a minimal impact on estuarine conditions. Although the 10% presumption is no longer in effect, this water management district still limits withdrawals to a percentage of freshwater inflow.

CONDITION-BASED METHODS

In this type of approach, the inflow standard is based on the location of water of a given salinity deemed beneficial for aquatic biota and the maintenance of salinity at that location. The San Francisco Estuary Project developed an inflow standard such that location X_2—the distance from the Golden Gate Bridge to the 2 psu (practical salinity unit) isohaline—is positioned where it may be beneficial to aquatic life (Ritche 2003). Significant statistical relationships between X_2 and the supply of phytoplankton and detritus, the abundance of mysids and shrimp, the survival of salmon smolts, and the abundance of planktivorous, piscivorous, and bottom-foraging fish support this standard (e.g., Jassby et al. 1995). This X_2 location moves in relation to the freshwater inflow into the estuary.

HABITAT METHODS

A method to assess the freshwater requirements of the Suwannee River estuary, Florida, involved the identification of "target habitats" to be protected within the estuary and the salinities needed to sustain these target habitats (Mattson 2002). Five target habitats were identified (tidal freshwater swamps, tidal marshes, low-salinity submerged aquatic vegetation, oyster reefs and bars, and tidal creeks), and recommendations were made in terms of the freshwater inflow needs to maintain the salinity regime suitable for each habitat. Recommended salinities ranged from less than or equal to 2 parts per thousand for tidal freshwater swamps to less than 35 parts per thousand for oyster habitat requirements.

VALUED ECOSYSTEM COMPONENT METHOD

The South Florida Water Management District takes a resource-based approach for setting inflow requirements known at the Valued Ecosystem Component Method. An important resource (or sets of resources) is identified and suitable environmental conditions are provided to maintain that resource (Alber 2002). In the Caloosahatchee Estuary, three species of seagrasses (*Vallisneria americana, Halodule wrightii,* and *Thalassia testudinum*) were identified as key species that provide important benthic habitat for juvenile estuarine and marine species (Doering et al. 2002). These seagrasses have different salinity requirements, and therefore maintaining their distribution patterns along the longitudinal axis of the estuary was proposed as an overall indicator of estuarine health (Alber 2002). Hydrologic analysis and modeling determined the flows needed to maintain target salinities within the estuary.

RESOURCE-BASED METHODS

This type of method uses a series of relationships between historical monthly (or other) inflows and the catch of various estuarine fish, crustaceans, or mollusks (Alber 2002). For seven major Texas bays and estuaries, the Texas estuarine mathematical programming model (TxEMP) provides a nonlinear, stochastic, multiobjective optimization model of salinity-inflow and inflow–fishery harvest relationships. Variability in the inflow-salinity relationship is used to set statistical bounds on salinity levels. TxEMP can be run in a GIS in conjunction with a two-dimensional hydrodynamic circulation model (TxBLEND) to produce maps of wetlands and oyster reefs under salinity conditions related to differing inflows (see Estevez 2002). This modeling approach provides an estuary performance curve that allows both scientists and water managers to examine the various solutions offered as well as to evaluate these results in terms of water planning and permitting (Powell et al. 2002).

Similar resource-based modeling frameworks are becoming common practice in Australian studies of freshwater flows to estuaries. Early insights were provided in a study of fisheries production in the Logan River estuary, southeast Queensland, during a trial of the Building Block Methodology for rivers (Loneragan and Bunn 1999). This study was followed by several applications of inflow–fish catch relationships during the development of catchmentwide water resource plans for Queensland's coastal rivers. Subsequent research developed an understanding of the importance of freshwater flows in maintaining growth rates and age structure of barramundi *(Lates calcarifer)* populations (Halliday et al. 2007; Robins et al. 2006). A review of the freshwater

TABLE 34   *Two-phase holistic methodology for evaluating
the environmental water requirements to maintain estuarine processes*

Phase	Definition
Preliminary evaluation	Step 1: Define the environmental flow issue to be investigated
	Step 2: Assess the value of the estuary (e.g., fishing, recreation)
	Step 3: Assess changes to inflow hydrology
	Step 4: Assess the vulnerability of the estuary to altered hydrology
Detailed investigation	Step 1: Examine the likely impact of current water use on transport, mixing, water quality, and geomorphology using catchment runoff and estuarine flow models
	Step 2: Define environmental flow scenarios for the estuary (e.g., to protect particular resources)
	Step 3: Use the established models to assess the impact of proposed scenarios of modified freshwater inflow
	Step 4: Assess the risk to estuarine biota from each scenario
	Step 5: Licensing and development approval
	Step 6: Adaptive management

SOURCE: Adapted from Pierson et al. 2002

flow requirements of estuarine fisheries in tropical Australia and application of a suggested approach is provided by Robins et al. (2005).

HOLISTIC APPROACH

Pierson et al. (2002) proposed a two-phase methodology to evaluate the environmental water requirements to maintain estuarine processes: preliminary evaluation and detailed investigation (Table 34). To underpin the methodology, this contribution also sets out details of how various inflow volumes influence estuarine characteristics and ecosystem processes.

In a final synthesis of developments toward methods for the determination of flow regimes into estuaries, Estevez (2002) forecast a search for relationships that are robust and transferable across river and estuarine systems of similar hydrological and ecological character. Or must each estuarine system be treated as unique? This issue remains to be resolved in both rivers and estuaries. Wolanski (2007) recommends "ecohydrology" as the principle to guide the management of the entire river basin from the headwaters down to the coastal zone, by "manipulating estuaries using a combination of physical and biological interventions to increase the system robustness and its ability to cope with human stresses, while regulating human activities on land when necessary."

19

SETTING LIMITS TO HYDROLOGIC ALTERATION

THE FRESHWATER CRISIS

If indeed the world has now entered the Anthropocene—a new epoch where humans dominate the biosphere and largely determine environmental conditions (Zalasiewicz et al. 2008)—then humans hold the keys to future environmental quality and global prosperity. There is growing agreement that because the risks to freshwater resources and ecosystems are so enormous, a new vision and action agenda for freshwater management should rank foremost among global environmental priorities (Alcamo et al. 2008; Dudgeon 2010; Vörösmarty et al. 2010). Climate change intensifies the urgency of resolving the freshwater crisis because water is the key medium though which the consequences of global warming and climate change will become evident (Naiman and Dudgeon 2010). The concept of a dynamic flow regime sculpting landscapes and driving the ecology of rivers, wetlands, and estuaries is now universally accepted.

Environmental flow regimes are widely recognized as a central tool for helping countries to protect freshwater biodiversity, resiliency, and the ecological goods and services provided by healthy aquatic ecosystems. Freshwater issues are embedded in nearly all of the Millennium Development Goals, and good water stewardship, involving strategies such as environmental flows, are fundamental to their success. A number of prominent international programs with a strong focus on resolving water conflicts have embraced the concept of environmental flows (e.g., the Global Water System Project, UNESCO-IHP, the IUCN, the DIVERSITAS freshwaterBIODIVERSITY Cross-cutting Network, Conservation International, the World Wide Fund for Nature, the Ramsar Convention, and the European Water Framework Directive). Flow regimes for ecosystem protection are being assessed and implemented in many countries through international river-basin partnerships and projects. Examples include the Freshwater Sustainability Project of The Nature Conservancy (TNC) and the work of the International Water Management Institute, the World Bank (Hirji and Davis 2009), the Swedish Water House, the USAID Global Water for Sustainability Program (GLOWS), and the Brisbane International RiverFoundation. The World Water Forums, Stockholm's World Water Weeks, three recent international conferences (Cape Town in 2002, Brisbane in 2007, and Port Elizabeth in 2009) and numerous scientific meetings have given prominence to the science and implementation of environmental flows.

In spite of tremendous advances, setting limits to hydrologic alteration of rivers, groundwater, and wetlands remains the core challenge of environmental flow science and management. Where should those responsible draw the boundaries of acceptable change in a river's or estuary's flow regime, or in a wetland's water regime? In the DRIFT and ELOHA frameworks, and several restoration protocols (e.g., Poff et al. 2003; Richter et al. 2006), scientists, stakeholders, and managers consider a suite of flow alteration–ecological response relationships and expert judgments across a range of hydrologic metrics describing the system's flow regime. Where there are clear threshold responses (e.g., overbank flows needed to support riparian vegetation or to provide fish access to backwater and floodplain habitat), a "low-risk" environmental flow would be one that does not cross the threshold of hydrological alteration for overbank flows. For a linear response where there is no clear threshold demarcating low from high risk, a consensus stakeholder process is needed to determine "acceptable risk" to a valued ecological asset, such as an estuarine fishery dependent on freshwater inflows (e.g., Loneragan and Bunn 1999).

It is important to differentiate the scientific assessment of ecological limits to hydrologic alteration from the process of finally deciding on the recommended flow regime. The second step is fundamentally a societal, value-laden activity informed by science but not decided by scientists. The scientist's role is to support the societally driven risk assessment, to respond to concerns about the likely ecological risk if the ecological limits to hydrologic alteration are exceeded, and to give advice on follow-up monitoring or research to fill knowledge gaps. From this it follows that there is no single "correct" environmental flow regime for any river or stream (unless absolute conservation/restoration of the natural regime and the ecosystem is the goal). Instead, governments, managers, and stakeholders must consider the implications of a series of scenarios or options ranging from very low to very high risk of damage to ecological systems and the people who depend on them.

There are many possible outcomes. A stakeholder-driven process may decide to settle for high risk to certain ecological assets in favor of drawing more water out of the system for some other purpose, or stakeholders may opt for a certain temporal shift to allow for controlled off-stream water use. What ELOHA and DRIFT aim to achieve is a consensus around defining risks that are acceptable and those that are not in the judgment of the participating stakeholders, who are informed by the "best available" science. It is the stakeholders who should decide the "desired future state" of the river or wetland system within the context of a shared vision for other uses of the water resource and the desired long-term character of the aquatic ecosystem and its landscape setting.

Postel and Richter (2003) proposed the concept of a "sustainability boundary" (Fig. 43) to set limits on the extent to which water withdrawals and discharges, water infrastructure operations, and land use can alter natural variability in water flows and water chemistry. This approach employs a scientific process to develop environmental flow recommendations in the form of water volumes required for ecosystem protection throughout the entire calendar year, around which the sustainability boundaries are set by water managers in collaboration with stakeholders "to achieve mutual benefits through a negotiated balance between benefits derived from water extractions with benefits derived from keeping water in the freshwater ecosystem" (Richter 2010). In addition to protecting the natural dynamism of river regimes, the boundaries themselves are seen as dynamic, "to allow for changing

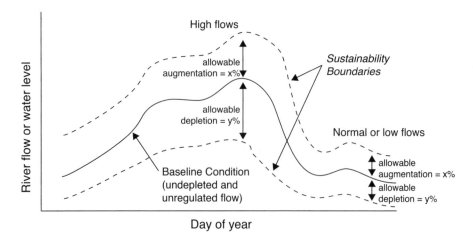

FIGURE 43. Illustration of the Sustainability Boundary Approach (SBA) to set-ting goals for sustainable water management. Uses of water and land are managed such that hydrologic regimes are not altered beyond agreed-upon sustainability boundaries. (Redrawn from Figure 1 in Richter 2010, with permission from John Wiley and Sons)

societal needs and values over time as well as new scientific understand-ing of flow-ecology relationships" (Richter 2010).

King and Brown (2010) proposed a similar concept with their term "development space," defined as the difference between current condi-tions in a river basin and the furthest level of water-resource develop-ment found to be acceptable to stakeholders through consideration of scenarios of flow regime alteration related to ecosystem degradation (as developed using DRIFT). Beyond this level, costs would be perceived to outweigh the benefits of development. In overdeveloped basins, with unacceptable degradation of the natural resources of the river already present, development space is perceived to be "negative" and to indicate the need for rehabilitation of the flow regime and river.

Implicit in these approaches is the perception that compromises are possible along the spectrum from protection of the ecological integrity and resiliency of aquatic ecosystems, to extensive development of basin water resources for human benefit. How can these compromises be achieved when different interest groups may have different, and often irreconcilable, objectives for water use versus ecosystem protection?

STAKEHOLDER ENGAGEMENT

A degree of consensus appears to be emerging around the notion of actively engaging all stakeholders from the outset of an environmental flow assessment or river restoration program (Bunn et al. 2010; Ryder et al. 2010). The stakeholder concept involves all potentially affected parties and groups with an interest (stake) in the outcomes: water-management agencies, native title and home/landowners, farmers, businesses, periurban interests, and so on. Arguably, the stakeholder group will also include representatives of jurisdictions with responsibilities that transcend local and catchment boundaries, who can therefore inject concerns about broader conservation/management issues, such as biodiversity protection, regional and national Ramsar obligations, and international treaties as well as broader socioeconomic issues.

Reed (2008) observed that stakeholder participation needs to be underpinned by a philosophy that gives emphasis to empowerment, equity, trust, and learning. Furthermore, stakeholder participation must be institutionalized, creating organizational cultures and structures that can facilitate the negotiation of goals and clear objectives from the outset. Effective facilitation of knowledge exchange is also essential and a successful facilitator "needs to be perceived as impartial, open to multiple perspective and approachable . . . capable of maintaining positive group dynamics, handling dominating or offensive individuals, encourage participants to question assumptions and re-evaluate entrenched positions, and get the most out of reticent individuals" (Reed 2008).

If stakeholder engagement is to become the normal or "best" practice, how can seemingly irreconcilable differences of perspective be accommodated and brought into some form of alignment for the common good of the aquatic systems to be managed and the people who depend on them? Conflicts abound in the history of water management in all types of regulated systems, from agricultural and rural catchments to rivers and streams flowing through urban areas (Postel and Richter 2003; Pearce 2007). Each can present seemingly irreconcilable areas of divergence between the river's need for a dynamic, naturally variable flow regime and the human demand for stability and reliability of freshwater supplies to serve societal water demands. In the case of hydropower systems, the human demand for regular and peak electricity generation brings about extreme daily variability of flows far beyond the bounds of natural water-level fluctuations. By what common currency can the benefits and losses associated with altered flow regimes be accounted, and the risks defined in a manner transparent to everyone? One of the most useful concepts in this context is that natural aquatic ecosystems and water flows provide ecosystem goods and services of immense value to all humans (see Chapter 1).

IDENTIFYING ECOSYSTEM GOODS, SERVICES, AND ASSETS

In undertaking an environmental flow assessment, it is necessary to be specific about which ecosystem goods and services should be protected or restored in a particular river, wetland, or estuary. A broadly based stakeholder group should make this initial assessment of what is important and worthy of protection/restoration and to what degree. This process can be achieved by applying the framework established by the Millennium Ecosystem Assessment (MEA 2005) to identify ecosystem goods and services in three main categories: provisioning, regulating, and cultural services (see Chapter 1; see also Richter 2010). Increasingly, environmental flow assessments include conservation values: species, ecological communities, habitats, and ecosystems of conservation importance. In several frameworks, these goods and services are termed "assets," which may include any attribute of the natural ecosystem of value to society. River assets can include in-stream, off-stream (e.g., floodplains and wetlands), groundwater, and estuarine ecosystems and marine receiving waters. In some rivers, the focus may be on maintaining a single critical asset (e.g., a fishery), while in most rivers the objectives include a number of different environmental assets.

The identification of ecosystem services or assets serves four main purposes. First, it provides the common currency by which all stakeholders, no matter what their background, can gain a clear understanding of the goods and values supported by the aquatic system, the societal benefits of providing flows to maintain those "assets," and what will be put at risk, or lost entirely, if environmental flows are not provided. Second, the specificity of asset identification allows the scientific assessment to focus on the particular flow requirements of priority assets—

and to decide which aspects of the flow regime (low flows, channel pulses, occasional floods, daily flow variability) are most important for maintaining these assets (water quality, fish, floodplain productivity, endangered species). Third, this process can help to form a shared perception of what is known about a particular aquatic system and to identify any prominent knowledge gaps. This may in turn stimulate further monitoring or research to add new information to the existing database. Finally, inviting a broadly based group of stakeholders to work together in this fashion can strengthen their sense of engagement, of being heard regardless of background and personal views, and of collaboration for the good of a higher cause rather than a "them and us" attitude that often bedevils water planning and allocation.

Assets may be identified through a combination of any of the following information sources and approaches: field surveys, data from existing monitoring programs and research projects, existing species and habitat databases (e.g., museum and herbarium records), literature reviews and consultation with management and conservation agencies, research groups, and people dependent on the aquatic ecosystem and its values. Where there are multiple river assets, they may need to be prioritized based on a hierarchy of factors: these might include national or international recognition of importance (e.g., Ramsar listing, CAMBA and JAMBA migratory bird agreements), decreed uniqueness (threatened, rare, or endemic species or communities present), legislative obligations, and the importance of the asset for other river values (e.g., tourism, fishing, recreation). Knowing the ecological condition of the asset is also important—that is, can the health of the asset be improved or would environmental flows be better directed toward protecting other assets? In addition to hard data inputs, the process must also take account of all stakeholder perspectives on assets of importance, and the stakeholder group as a whole must endorse the final priority list.

Once priority assets and their desired future characteristics and condition have been decided by stakeholders, it becomes feasible to develop scenarios of flow requirements for the river system. In some jurisdictions, rivers are classified according to acceptable levels of protection versus development, such that environmental flow assessments can focus on meeting these broader condition targets. For example, in South Africa, an environmental flow regime is designed to achieve a specific predefined river condition, which may vary between class A (negligible modification from natural conditions and negligible risk to sensitive species) to class D (with a high degree of modification from natural conditions and the expectation that intolerant biota are unlikely to be present) (Dollar et al. 2010). A somewhat similar process is employed in the UK water-allocation method known as CAMS (Catchment Abstraction Management Strategies).

Presentation of alternative environmental flow scenarios remains essential to these procedures (King and Brown 2010). Even if the stakeholder group has identified a particular asset and its acceptable condition, the extent to which a particular component or feature of the flow regime must be maintained to achieve that condition has to be demonstrated by presenting the risks of *not* providing the required amount or quality or timing of flows (as in DRIFT and ELOHA). Although the science of environmental flows is not (and will never be) absolute, several methods are available to identify different levels of certainty of achieving the desired ecological outcomes (see Chapters 11–13). The scientific process should be able to estimate the risk of certain outcomes (e.g., critical loss of refuge habitat, loss of floodplain or estuarine productivity) by using one or several of the available quantitative or Bayesian methods (e.g., Chan et al. 2010; Webb et al. 2010). Once the risks are identified and quantified as accurately as possible, it is a matter for stakeholders, supported by enabling policies and governance systems, to determine the acceptable level of risk to each important asset.

WATER-ALLOCATION TRADE-OFFS

An environmental flow assessment and its related socioeconomic assessments should be designed to allow government to make informed decisions about how to balance conflicting and/or competing water requirements. Through the stakeholder-driven processes described above, it will usually become apparent that not all desirable in-stream and off-stream uses of water are compatible. The flows required to support one asset may compromise the needs of another, or, frequently, the amount of water needed for ecosystem protection will reduce the amount available for off-stream use. Conflicts of timing may also arise; for example, irrigation systems typically demand steady supplies during naturally dry periods, and this regular water supply must be sourced from the nearby river or groundwater systems. To provide it, the river system is often impounded and the high river flows are stored, to be released downstream later, when normally the river would experience much lower and more variable flows (Richter and Thomas 2007). This seasonal reversal of low- and high-flow periods can have catastrophic impacts on the native riverine ecosystem and can facilitate the establishment of exotic species (see Chapter 8). In such circumstances, trading off between these competing needs for water volumes of the right quality at the right time becomes a central task of the water-allocation process.

In some instances, governments may decide to allocate water primarily to meet the formal requirements of prevailing environmental legislation or international conservation agreements (e.g., the Ramsar Convention). Decisions dependent on legislated principles may range across the full spectrum from water allocations of various scope and intent in developed rivers to halting the development of new water infrastructure in less developed or pristine basins. As an example, the proposal to construct a new water-storage impoundment (Traveston Dam) on the Mary River in Queensland was overturned by commonwealth legislation that protects threatened species, in this case the Australian lungfish *(Neoceratodus forsteri)* and other endangered fish and turtles (Arthington 2009). Local, national, and international stakeholder support for the no-dam option also played a prominent role through formal submissions to government calling for protection of catchment landscapes, riverine biodiversity, and Ramsar wetlands.

Strong conservation legislation may offer the means to ensure adequate environmental flows in many jurisdictions but is by no means universal. Thousands of streams and rivers have no recourse to the appeal for environmental flows to conserve threatened species and valued aquatic ecosystems, and, accordingly, freshwater biodiversity is declining rapidly (Dudgeon et al. 2006). In developing countries there is typically a weaker political and governance system for the conservation of environmental resources, and water is often seen as an exploitable resource to generate funds for relieving poverty and improving standards of living. In Africa for instance, at least 114 new major dam developments, mostly for hydropower generation, are either under construction or review (McCartney 2007). For new dams and developments such as these, King and Brown (2010) identify a major challenge: "to develop the targeted rivers within the ethos of sustainable development, ensuring that the full suite of environmental and social costs is considered as seriously as are traditional economic and social benefits before development decisions are made." It is well accepted that poor rural populations with close livelihood links to rivers and floodplain systems are likely to be impacted most and benefit least from river development (WCD 2000; Richter et al. 2010). To change this situation requires decision makers to consider the full suite of implications of development instead of only those illustrating a narrow range of human benefits.

An important principle for every country/region is that water-allocation decisions should be made strategically, with a long-term vision for the river or entire basin, rather than on an incremental basis that may lead to none of the streams or rivers of a basin receiving an adequate environmental flow. Adopting a strategic, integrated approach to this decision-making process allows consideration of a range of future scenarios for a river basin in a process of "integrated river basin assessment," or IBFA (King and Brown 2010). A matrix of water-allocation scenarios can be identified, with each scenario ranking the "man-made benefits" derived from utilitarian uses of water versus the ecosystem attributes and values that could be protected by environmental flows (Table 35).

A matrix of this type must be backed up by quantitative estimates of the water required to meet each option, and this is where the science of environmental flows makes its greatest contribution. Trade-off curves can be plotted for each environmental flow scenario, showing losses to the river ecosystem associated with various human-demand scenarios. Sometimes these trade-off procedures clearly reveal the possibility of making relatively minor adjustments to dam release schedules for major environmental gain, for example, a small fresh to stimulate fish spawning, or a large water release added to seasonal tributary inflows such that together the flows inundate an important floodplain wetland (e.g., King et al. 2010).

In many instances the complexity of a basin-scale approach presents enormous challenges because the options are so varied and the

TABLE 35 *Hypothetical matrix of water-allocation scenarios showing their relative costs and benefits for an entire river basin*

Many scenarios can be developed and will differ from one basin to another

Basin resources (man-made benefits)	Scenarios of increasing levels of water-resource development			
	PD	B	C	D
Hydropower generation	x	x	x	xx
Crop production	x	x	xx	xxx
Water security	x	xx	xxx	xxx
Aquaculture	x	xx	xx	xxx
Regional economy	x	xx	xxx	xxxx

SOURCE: Adapted from King and Brown 2010

NOTES: Xs indicate the level of benefit with increasing water-resource development and would normally be replaced with quantitative or qualitative values derived from research; PD = present-day, not necessarily pristine.

stakes so high for everyone concerned. The Murray-Darling Basin Plan (see Murray-Darling Basin Authority 2011) offers an example of integrated basin flow planning where the gains for environmental recovery of overallocated and degraded subregions may be considerable. The key outcome of the plan will be setting "sustainable diversion limits" and, therefore, significant reductions in water abstraction for off-stream use within the entire basin. Key "ecosystem functions" (provision of habitat; transportation and dilution of nutrients, organic matter, and sediment; and provision of lateral and longitudinal connectivity) and numerous "environmental assets" (rivers, wetlands, floodplains, and the river mouth) are the nominated targets for environmental flows. Based on estimates of the water required to maintain priority assets in good ecological health, the draft Murray-Darling Basin Plan initially (i.e., in 2010) determined that an additional average of 3,000–4,000 GL per annum should be returned to the river system for environmental purposes. However, the perception that there will be high socioeconomic impacts associated with reallocating water to the riverine environment led in 2011 to a lower recommended figure (2,750 GL per annum). Scientists question whether this average annual inflow will be sufficient to restore the health of the river's fish populations, its extensive river red gum forests, the sand-clogged river mouth, and highly salinized coastal wetlands (e.g., Connell and Grafton 2011). Working out the details of how and where environmental flows will be provided to particular wetlands constitutes the next phase of the basin plan.

INTEGRATING ENVIRONMENTAL FLOWS AND CONSERVATION PLANNING

The Murray-Darling Basin Plan highlights the need for discussion of priority setting when such a large-scale environmental flow assessment is undertaken. How best to provide environmental water allocations to restore the ecological functions and resiliency of this enormous catchment (1.073×10^6 km^2, or about 14% of the total area of Australia)? Addressing these issues seems to demand a strong alignment between environmental flow assessments and conservation planning, and in particular, the process known as "systematic conservation planning." Most systematic conservation plans address four key principles: comprehensiveness, adequacy, representativeness, and efficiency (CARE). "Comprehensiveness" refers to the inclusion of the full range of species, processes, and ecosystems (i.e., biodiversity attributes) in a study region and thereby avoids bias toward certain areas or bioregions. "Representativeness" ensures that the full range of biodiversity is represented within the regions chosen for comprehensiveness; usually this involves choosing surrogates (proxy measures) for all desirable biodiversity attributes. "Adequacy" is concerned with how a conservation area network should be designed to ensure persistence of all desirable biodiversity attributes. "Efficiency" recognizes that social factors (e.g., land tenure) may affect conservation objectives and choices, while financial constraints will limit expenditure on conservation measures and strategies; an efficient conservation plan will maximize conservation gains, minimize costs, and limit impacts on stakeholders (Linke et al. 2011).

The CARE principles have been encapsulated in many terrestrial, marine, and freshwater conservation planning frameworks worldwide (Margules and Pressey 2000), and most use complementarity algorithms and software packages such as MARXAN to guide decisions about the selection and placement of conservation areas (Possingham et al. 2000). To date most complementarity-based approaches in freshwater planning focus on river ecosystems, more or less completely ignoring connected wetlands, lakes, and groundwater ecosystems. It is recognized that this simplification must be resolved to fully realize the benefits of systematic conservation planning. A further emerging theme involves how best to select conservation areas or zones in highly developed landscapes where many stressors originating on land have impacts in aquatic ecosystems, yet where it is not feasible to suggest total protection of upstream or even adjacent parts of subcatchments. Despite these unresolved issues, systematic conservation planning appears to offer a robust package of concepts and software for evaluating the best conservation options in complex, mixed land- and water-use catchments.

The integration of a systematic "biodiversity attribute" conservation plan, which sets out the CARE priorities, with a scenario-based holistic environmental flow assessment, which identifies the flow regimes needed to protect the chosen biodiversity attributes at the basin scale, would appear to offer huge advantages over present frameworks. Such integration could maximize aquatic conservation objectives at the basin scale while minimizing the impacts and costs of environmental water-allocation scenarios for other stakeholders. A useful discussion of these possibilities can be found in Nel et al. (2011).

Systematic conservation planning integrated with scenario-based environmental flow assessment could be applied to aquatic systems at any geographic scale, from large river basins to bioregions with many streams, rivers, and other aquatic resources. The classification principles of the ELOHA framework seem applicable as a means to ensure comprehensiveness and representativeness based on different hydrologic and geomorphic classes of rivers and their associated biodiversity attributes at user-defined regional scales.

20

IMPLEMENTING AND MONITORING ENVIRONMENTAL FLOWS

IMPLEMENTATION

Converting the recommendations from environmental flow assessments into management actions that produce the desired river flow regime has lagged behind the actual assessment process in most countries (Le Quesne et al. 2010). Two major forms of regulatory process may be involved in the provision of an environmental flow regime: restrictive and active (Acreman and Ferguson 2010). Restrictive methods involve setting water-abstraction limits (e.g., sustainable diversion limits, "caps" on further abstraction) that maintain a healthy river ecosystem, while active measures involve ecologically appropriate flow releases from reservoirs; there will often be some combination of the two. Both regulatory processes involve rules to govern the total volume of water allowed to be abstracted from a river or released from a dam and also the seasonal and daily timing and variability of regulated flows. All of these flow conditions influence the desired ecological outcomes and resiliency of the river ecosystem.

DAM RELEASE STRATEGIES

OPPORTUNITIES

The global potential for implementation of environmental flows by modifying dam operations is enormous. One recent analysis suggests that opportunities for environmental flow restoration exist at virtually all of the world's 45,000+ large dams (>15 m height or capacity >3 × 10 m³) and at hundreds of thousands of smaller dams and weirs (Richter and Thomas 2007). Appropriate mechanisms for modification of dam release rules depend upon the purposes of water storage (from flood mitigation, urban water supply, individual hydropower dams, cascades of hydropower or water supply dams along a river, to regional water grids involving surface and groundwater harvesting, storage and inter-basin transfers).

DAM RELEASE CAPACITIES

The volumetric operational release capacities of a dam (e.g., spillway, adjustable reservoir gates, multiple off-take towers, power tunnels and turbines, diversion tunnels located on dam abutments, low-pressure outlets, pipes and valves, and fish ladders) are critically important issues when designing a reservoir release strategy. Redesign of new dams or retrofitting of existing ones may be required if the existing structures cannot accommodate the volumetric and timing requirements of the environmental flow regime (Dyson et al. 2003).

The Lesotho Highlands Water Project (LHWP), a multibillion-dollar water transfer and hydropower project implemented by the governments of Lesotho and South Africa, provides a good example of infrastructure redesign to accommodate environmental flow releases. By completion of the first dam, Katse, on the Malibamatso River in 1998, global concerns over environmental degradation forced consideration of the downstream impacts of the proposed LHWP dams. Using the DRIFT framework, the biophysical consequences of various development scenarios were assessed, and the losses of river resources (e.g., food fishes; see Arthington et al. 2003) and health benefits were converted to compensation estimates for riparian peoples (JM King et al. 2003; King and Brown 2010). These scenarios formed the basis for negotiations between the Lesotho Highlands Development Authority, the World Bank, and the governments of Lesotho and South Africa over environmental flows and water releases from dams. To accommodate flood releases for river maintenance, it became necessary to change the design of the dam outlet valves and operating rules for Mohale Dam (King and Brown 2010). Downstream releases increased by 300% to

400% compared to those that were originally specified for Katse and Mohale Dams before the environmental flow assessment.

HYDROPOWER DAMS

Dams built for hydropower generation present particular challenges because the volumetric alterations, water-level fluctuations, and seasonal flow changes involved in power generation bring about severe ecological changes to downstream ecosystems (see Chapter 8). Krchnak et al. (2009) and Renöfält et al. (2010) highlight a number of structural and operational considerations in hydropower dam development that can facilitate integration of environmental flow objectives. They include variable outlet and turbine-generator capacities; multilevel, selective withdrawal outlet structures; reregulation reservoirs; coordinated operations of cascades of dams, sediment bypass structures, and sediment sluice gates; fish passage structures; and dam decommissioning. As an example, in British Columbia, the Coquitlam-Buntzen Water Use Plan—prepared by BC Hydro and approved by the Comptroller of Water Rights—prescribes an in-stream flow release target (in m³ per second) for each month of the year, as well as setting "ramping rates" that define the maximum rate of increase or decrease in water releases from the reservoir and a series of rules for prioritizing between these environmental flow targets, hydropower production, and town water supply.

FLOOD-CONTROL DAMS

Flood-control dams are designed to capture a portion of inflowing floodwaters and to release some of that water as lower-volume controlled pulses that generate artificially attenuated high-flow pulses following flood peaks. Small floods of 2- to 10-year recurrence interval are typically fully captured, and only extreme large floods (>50- to 100-year recurrence interval) escape the storage system via a spillway or by overtopping. In these situations, one environmental flow objective should be to release some small to medium-sized floods in a controlled fashion, to complete the full range of flow volumes normally experienced by the river system. Ecological benefits flowing from such a strategy are well-established (e.g., fisheries; wildlife habitat; bird breeding; wetland, riparian, and floodplain forest diversity; and ecosystem productivity). Flooding can also benefit flood-recession agriculture and grazing on floodplains through the regular deposition of nutrients, flushing of soil salinity, and the recharge of groundwater aquifers.

Many flood-control dams include an outlet pipe or small channel and a large spillway, giving the system's operators limited flexibility in achieving desirable flow releases. Moreover, it is typical for the capacity of the outlet pipe to be too small to pass flows of even moderate magnitude, and dam managers may be reluctant to allow water to overtop the spillway due to structural, safety, or other concerns. Structural modification (e.g., a gated spillway system) is required in these situations to allow more flexibility in releasing higher-magnitude events in a controlled fashion (Richter and Thomas 2007). Even then, managers may baulk at releasing flows that achieve some level of downstream flooding because of developments on the floodplain that would be threatened by high flows. Yet with a controlled flow release strategy in place and adequate forewarning that certain roads, bridges, and parklands will be inundated for a day or so, it is possible to achieve some ecological floodplain benefits. Controlled releases are often instigated to open up storage space in flood-mitigation reservoirs, and the practice of announcing them and warning affected populations is not unusual when dam safety and future flood mitigation are priorities. These managed releases could readily be designed to meet ecological as well as utilitarian objectives.

Infrastructure for flood control does not necessarily involve large dams. Small "check or dry dams" located throughout an upper catchment can be used to create storage through a system of strategically placed impoundments or diversions of water into natural storage areas (side channels, abandoned channels, oxbows, wetlands, floodplain forests, or groundwater recharge areas). The dam reservoirs themselves may seldom fill, reducing the ecological impact on upland ecosystems. A system of dry dams in the catchment of the Great Miami River (Miami Valley Conservation District, upstream of Dayton, Ohio) have slots that allow normal flow of water and fish passage under low-flow conditions (Freitag et al. 2009). The land behind such dams remains in agricultural use or as forest for most of the time until peak flood events, when the dams close and water is stored temporarily behind their walls or is diverted onto neighboring fields. Dayton experienced a severe flood in 1913 but has been protected from flooding ever since by this dry dam system.

The major hydrologic function of floodplains is to receive, utilize, store, and slowly release excess river water. Reinstatement of certain former floodplain areas as parkland, wetlands, and riparian forests can help to soak up excess floodwater during severe and uncontrollable flood events. Construction of embankments to prevent inundation of high-value areas, and resettlement of critical infrastructure and housing to higher ground, can allow moderate levels of floodplain inundation for ecological benefit. Through strategic land-use planning, floodplains can be managed, with setbacks to reduce the threat to human life, health, and property in ways that are sensitive to ecological and environmental benefits. Changing land uses on floodplains to accommodate modest flood events might sound expensive but could save the millions of dollars so often associated with disaster relief for homeowners and business who were encouraged to build in a floodplain zone, or who were not restricted from doing so by urban and municipal planning policies. Given the increasing incidence of extreme floods around the globe, it is necessary to rethink how floodplains can be used safely and profitably for human purposes while also protecting the ecological goods and services delivered by rivers with intact floodplains.

IRRIGATION DAMS

Water-supply reservoirs for irrigation constitute half of the 50,000 large dams constructed globally since the 1950s, with the largest number in China, India, Pakistan, and the United States (WCD 2000). These dams generally provide both seasonal and interannual storage of water to buffer natural variations in rainfall and runoff, and to provide a reliable supply of water for irrigation. When water is stored and released largely for irrigation purposes, a common outcome is disruption of the seasonal patterns of the natural river flow regime, such that in extreme cases, almost all high flows and potential floods are captured during the high-flow season and released downstream during the low-flow season, when there is little precipitation and crops need water. This artificial enhancement of the natural low flows in the river is frequently detrimental to native species adapted to low-flow conditions for various biological functions, whereas exotic species will often proliferate and may outcompete valued native species (see Chapter 8).

A range of techniques is available to modify the operation of irrigation-supply reservoirs, but Richter and Thomas (2007) emphasize that "the best way to open up flexibility in infrastructure operations in agricultural settings is to reduce the overall demand for water in the first place" while maintaining productivity. Irrigation water use can be reduced through a range of technical and management practices, such as drip and sprinkler irrigation; more precise application practices; canal lining or delivery through pipes; reusing return flows by controlling, diverting, and storing drainage flows; reduced allocations of water to farmers; or pricing to influence water demand. However, Molden et al. (2010) urge caution about the expectations of overall water saving, because reduced water deliveries typically also reduce drainage outflows that farmers would commonly reuse by pumping water from groundwater or by withdrawing water from open drains. Also, the water saved by farmer conservation practices may be seen as an opportunity to expand irrigation rather than to redistribute water for environmental and other benefits. On the positive side, reducing water deliveries to crops and reducing drainage can be beneficial in situations where return flows would otherwise cause damage or water pollution (nutrients, agricultural chemicals) or go to a saline sink.

SURFACE AND GROUNDWATER MANAGEMENT

Many major agricultural areas overlie groundwater basins and draw significant amounts of water from aquifers. Across much of Australia, North Africa, the Middle East, South and Central Asia, Europe, and North America, excessive groundwater extraction has reduced surface-stream discharge, dried up groundwater-fed springs, and altered river flow regimes (Konikow and Kendy 2005). Some of this massive loss to aquifers may be replenished by return flows from agriculture, and conveyance losses may also provide significant recharge. Conjunctive management of surface water and groundwater supplies can increase opportunities for environmental flow restoration in agricultural systems supplied by irrigation dams. Dam management in this instance is designed to expand the amount of storage available for irrigation supply by enhancing groundwater recharge using surface water from the water-supply reservoir (see details in Richter and Thomas 2007). By using enhanced groundwater storage during the irrigation season instead of water released from an upstream reservoir, the problem of artificially elevated low flows can be ameliorated. In addition, the water supply held in a reservoir for irrigation purposes may become available for controlled releases of low flows, high-flow pulses, or even small floods for ecological purposes.

MANAGING WATER ABSTRACTIONS

There are numerous opportunities to modify water-abstraction procedures in ways that accommodate environmental flow requirements and minimize environmental damage. Infrastructure issues need to be considered when an environmental flow regime is to be managed by means of restrictions on water abstractions. The type of pumping or diversion system and the location of this in-stream infrastructure can be designed to minimize disturbance to key ecological assets, loss of connectivity, and adverse impacts on the extant flow regime of the system being managed. Insensitively placed water pumps in a stream can suck up hundreds of small organisms and dump them into hostile environments. Pumped water used to flood-irrigate alfalfa fields along the Groot River in South Africa entrained 131 individuals of the endangered redfin minnow *(Pseudobarbus asper)* every five minutes at a single small water withdrawal site, resulting in fish stranding and eventual mortality (Cambray 1990). The use of suitable screens at pump intakes has potential to reduce the number of fish removed from streams during irrigation periods.

Very large pumping systems, such as those being developed in Australia to raise water from the depleted Murray-Darling main channels to elevated floodplain wetlands, may present special challenges. In effect, this new water infrastructure represents an "environmental irrigation system" with the explicit purpose of providing localized beneficial flooding to support wetland biota. In those instances where floodplain levee banks and regulators control the passage of water into wetlands, it may be necessary to allow for natural movements of fish into floodplain rearing habitats and for the return of fish from floodplains to main river channels.

USE OF WATER "CAPS"

Placing a "cap" on water abstractions directly from streams can be a critical first step in protecting flows for the environment, either as a precautionary measure or to recover water from existing users and keep it within the river system for environmental purposes. This approach can be effective in reserving water for the environment, but it may be risky if an allocation plan overestimates the amount of water available or where interannual rainfall patterns or climate change reduce the amount in the system. Often it is the aquatic environment that is sacrificed first in times of water shortage or drought (Bond et al. 2008). Water reserves can be established to provide priority for environmental flow purposes; for example, South Africa's National Water Act of 1998 requires an "ecological reserve" for every catchment based on a predetermined ecological class. Australia's Murray-Darling Basin Agreement (negotiated by the federal and relevant state governments in October 1985) placed an interim basin-wide cap on further water diversions in 1995, based on the level of development in 1993–94. The 2011 Murray-Darling Basin Plan replaces this cap with specific "sustainable diversion limits" that define the long-term maximum level of abstraction permitted from each valley, to be implemented through state/regional water-allocation plans and water-licensing systems. The UK Catchment Abstraction Management Strategies (CAMS) divide the country's surface water and groundwater catchments into regional groups and each catchment into one of four categories (water available, no water available, overlicensed, and overabstracted) to guide the adjudication of new license applications and conditions.

WATER RIGHTS AND TRADING

Getting water back from existing users when new limits are placed on water rights is a major challenge in most jurisdictions. Users who have previously been licensed to take water for legitimate purposes (irrigation, stock, and domestic) may vigorously object and challenge new arrangements under new systems of legislation and governance. How should they be treated, compensated, or punished? This challenging topic cannot be covered adequately here; suffice it to mention a few major options. Water markets provide one mechanism, wherein a licensed water user may elect to sell that license to an environmental buyer (e.g., a conservation group) on an open market or through a process driven and funded by the government acting as an environmental water manager. In Australia, the Commonwealth Environmental

Water Holder (CEWH) is a statutory position created under the Water Act of 2007 to enable the federal government to purchase water entitlements from willing sellers in the Murray-Darling Basin, using an A\$3.1 billion river rescue fund. The Murray-Darling Basin Plan includes an environmental watering plan to guide future environmental water decisions, purchases, and trades (see Murray-Darling Basin Authority 2011).

MONITORING ENVIRONMENTAL FLOWS

The design and establishment of appropriate monitoring arrangements is a critical final step in the assessment and implementation of environmental flows. Monitoring is needed for two main purposes. Compliance monitoring assesses whether the recommended environmental flow rules have been met, for example, whether a dam operator has made releases of appropriate volume and timing or whether water abstraction has been curtailed in accordance with any prescribed limitations, such as the taking of water only when flows exceed a specified discharge level or only at certain times of year. Effectiveness monitoring is far more demanding. This type of monitoring assesses whether the water-management arrangements and environmental flow rules are achieving the desired biogeochemical and ecological outcomes. Many scientists have called for environmental flow restoration projects to be viewed as experiments that can generate sound understanding of hydroecological relationships in rivers and other aquatic ecosystems through monitoring within an adaptive management framework (Walters 1986; Poff et al. 2003). Furthermore, monitoring to track the ecological consequences of climate variability and change is essential as flow regimes, species, and ecosystems adjust to new climatic envelopes and management arrangements.

Palmer et al. (2005) advocate building an initial "guiding image" based on a mechanistic understanding of how an ecosystem functions, how it has been impaired, and how on-ground strategies can be expected to move it along a restoration trajectory. A conceptual model (or several models) of drivers, interactions, and ecosystem responses helps to engage stakeholders, managers, and scientists and to focus on the dimensions of the flow regime that need to be reinstated to achieve each objective of the common vision.

Deciding which ecological variables should be monitored is a vital step. The ELOHA framework proposes a range of variables at genetic, species, community, and ecosystem levels (Table 29, Chapter 13) that can be expected to respond to flow regime alterations by dams and abstraction and also to flow regime restoration and climate change. Systematic monitoring of these variables (indicators) against known gradients of hydrologic alteration would help to identify those that respond sensitively and consistently to particular flow regime components (Poff et al. 2010).

Although not designed to identify flow response indicators, the freshwater Ecosystem Health Monitoring Program (EHMP) designed for streams in southeast Queensland, Australia, provides a comprehensive model for testing and calibrating freshwater indicators in a stakeholder-driven adaptive framework (Fryirs et al. 2009; Bunn et al. 2010). One of the most important outcomes of the EHMP has been its successful communication strategy, culminating in public presentation to local mayors of annual "report cards" on the health of waterways in the region. Although the report card is a simple communication tool, each report card is underpinned by a robust dataset, and the underlying science is continually improving through research and, ultimately, through applying and testing the chosen indicators in restoration programs (Bunn et al. 2010).

Monitoring for compliance and to assess ecosystem response to environmental flows is most effective when accompanied by monitoring of social responses to ecosystem change, to identify stakeholder satisfaction with the ecological outcomes of flow management (Dyson et al. 2003). Stakeholders are likely to value ecological outcomes in the form of goods and services they wish to sustain or improve (as expressed in a vision statement), so their reactions to alterations in these services provide another barometer of success. Social monitoring should be designed to capture instances where the outcomes do and do not meet stakeholder expectations and also to track any changes in the perceptions and values of stakeholders over time.

In the case of stream and river ecosystems, these values are likely to include familiar goods and services such as clean drinking water and fisheries production, overlain by health issues for people and livestock, aesthetics, and cultural values sustained by water, biodiversity, and landscape functions (MEA 2005). In the absence of a commitment to understand and monitor how people benefit from ecosystems, it is "difficult to justify public investment in monitoring and even harder to argue for management interventions to protect or restore when issues are identified" (Bunn et al. 2010). The DRIFT framework is one of the few methods to explicitly translate environmental flow scenarios and biophysical outcomes into social issues and associated resource losses and costs for the "people at risk" (JM King et al. 2003; King and Brown 2010).

Adaptive environmental flow monitoring has recorded some outstanding examples of success, even though it is said to be undertaken too infrequently (Richter et al. 2006). In Australia, a major river restoration program ("The Living Murray" initiative) was established in 2004 and set out to return the highly regulated River Murray to the status of a "healthy working river" by recovering a long-term average of up to 500 GL per year of water over a five-year period). This environmental water is expected to achieve defined ecological objectives at six iconic wetland sites along the river and in the channel itself. King et al. (2010) describe the history of flow regulation by dams and water abstraction, the institutional context, and the monitoring program and its ecological outcomes following delivery in 2005 of the largest environmental flow in Australia's history (513 GL) to river red gum *(Eucalyptus camaldulensis)* forests at Barmah-Millewa on the River Murray. This Ramsar wetland supports native fishes, frogs, and waterbirds protected under JAMBA and CAMBA agreements. The 2005 managed flood event resulted in enhanced growth and health of significant native vegetation species and the largest bird breeding event ever recorded at the Barmah-Millewa Forest, with more than 52,000 colonial waterbirds from a number of different species breeding successfully after years of recruitment failure. Monitoring also recorded successful breeding of a number of frog and fish species and a significant exchange of organic material (including particulates, soluble nutrients, and carbon) between the floodplain and main channel that stimulated secondary production in both environments.

Long-term flow restoration experiments integrated with a wider range of river restoration options obviously require a strong commitment from management agencies to secure funding and resources and to integrate monitoring into restoration research over years to decades. Poff et al. (2003) discuss fund-raising strategies (see Chapter 12). Monitoring and adaptive management programs also require strong institutional commitment supported by legislation, policy, and regulatory structures. These issues are discussed in Chapter 21.

21

LEGISLATION AND POLICY

CONVENTIONS, AGREEMENTS, AND SOFT LAW

Intense interest in the concept and practice of environmental flows at national and international levels has generated significant debate about how to embed environmental water allocations into legislation, policy, and governance (Naiman et al. 2002; Dyson et al. 2003). The Brisbane Declaration (2007; see this book's appendix) envisions that environmental flow assessment and management should be a basic requirement not only of integrated water resource management (IWRM) but also of environmental impact assessment (EIA); strategic environmental assessment (SEA); infrastructure and industrial development and certification; and land-use, water-use, and energy-production strategies. Consistent integration of environmental flows into land, water, and energy management requires legislation, policies, and regulations at local, regional, and national scales and across political boundaries.

Various legally binding and "soft law" instruments as well as national constitutions, conventions, treaties, and agreements have a bearing on natural resource management and ecosystem protection. Although not necessarily directly concerned with rivers and wetlands, or actively endorsing the concept of environmental flows and water regimes as part of national policy, conventions and agreements are relevant and powerful. Examples include the Convention on Biological Diversity, the

Ramsar Convention on wetlands, and conventions to protect Japanese, Chinese, and Korean migratory waterbirds (Dyson et al. 2003). As a signatory to these conventions, Australia invoked migratory bird agreements to support its earliest water-management decisions to protect the Ramsar-listed Barmah-Millewa river red gum forest on the River Murray. In 2000–2001, the first effective natural flood since 1993 was enhanced by the largest environmental water release in Australia (a total of 341 GL, released in three parcels of water). These environmental water releases enabled at least 15,000 pairs of 20 species of birds to breed successfully in the Barmah-Millewa Forest, and one endangered egret species bred for the first time since 1975 (Leslie and Ward 2002).

International and national recognition of the conservation status of endangered aquatic species also places a legal obligation on jurisdictions to protect the resources and river or wetland water regimes essential to their long-term viability in nature. Protection is often achieved by means of species recovery plans that take a broad view of the threats and mitigation options throughout the range of the threatened taxon (e.g., Knight et al. 2011). For fully aquatic species (fish) and waterbirds, maintenance of a suitable water regime is often central to recovery plans, and the needs of threatened fish have saved several rivers from construction of new impoundments and further flow regulation.

As an example, protected fish species and a turtle listed under Australia's Environment Protection and Biodiversity Conservation Act of 1999 became the focus of the decision to reject Traveston Dam, which was proposed for construction on Queensland's Mary River (Arthington 2009). In making his final decision on the dam proposal, the federal Minister for Environment, Heritage and the Arts declared that "the science is very clear about the adverse impacts this project would have on the nationally protected Australian lungfish, Mary River turtle and Mary River cod. . . . For the Traveston Dam proposal, however, the species' breeding and their ability to maintain their population numbers would be seriously affected by the flooding of their habitat and by the fragmentation of significant populations, and I was not satisfied that adequate measures were proposed to mitigate these impacts" (Garrett 2009). In another example, environmental flow recommendations for the regulated Júcar River basin, Spain, concentrated on watering the habitats critical for survival, spawning, and larval recruitment of the endangered cyprinid fish *Chondrostoma arrigonis* (Navarro et al. 2007). Case studies such as these provide international precedents for assessing the water requirements of species and ecosystems and staking a claim on water to provide an environmental flow regime for biodiversity protection.

INTERNATIONAL RIVERS

Rivers that cross international borders have received special attention in conventions and agreements: the UN Convention on the Law of the Non-navigational Uses of International Watercourses (1997); the Convention Relating to the Development of Hydraulic Power Affecting More Than One State and Protocol of Signature (1923); and the Barcelona Convention and Statute on the Regime of Navigable Waterways of International Concern (1921). The UN Convention on the Law of the Non-navigational Uses of International Watercourses requires states (contracting parties) that share a watercourse to protect ecosystems, manage the flow regime, control pollution, take preventative action on exotic species, and preserve estuaries and the marine environment. The Convention Relating to the Development of Hydraulic Power obligates countries to negotiate with riparian states when planning for a hydropower project. The Helsinki Convention: Trans-boundary Watercourses and International Lakes was signed on behalf of the European Community in Helsinki in 1992. The Helsinki Convention requires that transboundary waters are used with due regard to conservation of water resources, environmental protection, and ecologically sound and rational water management. Water pollution must be prevented, reduced, or controlled, and waterway ecosystems must be conserved and, when necessary, restored. Parties are encouraged to negotiate common approaches to management and to adjust existing agreements to meet the provisions of the convention. As an umbrella framework, the Helsinki Convention has facilitated agreements for the protection and sustainable management of the Danube and Rhine Rivers.

THE MEKONG RIVER AGREEMENT

The Mekong River Agreement has a special place in the category of international river treaties. The Mekong is one of the least developed and least degraded of the world's great rivers, and with an essentially natural flow regime supporting millions of people dependent on river and delta fisheries, a comprehensive program of basin-wide management is imperative. Fourteen large dams already exist in the Mekong River system, and 30 more are planned, mostly for hydropower generation, including a cascade of 8 dams within China. There can be no doubt that dam construction on this scale will impact the river's flow and sediment regimes (Xue et al. 2011) and human economies (Lamberts 2006, 2008).

The 1995 'Agreement on the Cooperation for the Sustainable Development of the Mekong River Basin' (1995 Mekong Agreement) came about as four riparian countries—Cambodia, Lao People's Democratic Republic (PDR), Thailand, and Vietnam—recognized their common interest in jointly managing shared water resources and developing the economic potential of the river basin. The Mekong River Agreement established a new governance structure—the Mekong River Commission (MRC)—to "cooperate in all fields of sustainable development, utilization, management and conservation of the water and related resources of the Mekong River Basin including, but not limited to irrigation, hydro-power, navigation, flood control, fisheries, timber floating, recreation and tourism, in a manner to optimize the multiple-use and mutual benefits of all riparians and to minimize the harmful effects that might result from natural occurrences and man-made activities" (MRC 1995). The two upper states of the Mekong River basin, China and the Myanmar, are dialogue partners in the Mekong River Commission.

Articles of the Mekong River Agreement commit the parties to protection of "the environment, natural resources, aquatic life and conditions, and ecological balance of the Mekong River Basin from pollution or other harmful effects resulting from any development plans and uses of water and related resources in the Basin." Specific guidelines for the management of environmental flows include "maintenance of the flows on the mainstream from diversions, storage releases, or other actions of a permanent nature; except in the cases of historically severe droughts and/or floods"; acceptable minimum monthly natural flows during each month of the dry season; maintenance of the natural reversal of flow into the Tonle Sap during the wet season; and "prevention of average daily peak flows greater than what would naturally occur on average during the flood season."

As part of the MRC's Integrated Basin Flow Management (IBFM) activities, the positive and negative impacts of several development scenarios have been assessed for representative reaches of the Mekong from the China border to the Mekong Delta. These IBFM studies estimate the present and predicted total value of all beneficial uses of the river system, by country, including biodiversity, fisheries and livelihoods, and regulatory and cultural services, using techniques pioneered during the development of DRIFT (see King and Brown 2010). The new Basin Development Plan, which started in 2008, is based on the results of the IBFM (see Hirji and Davis 2009).

MILLENNIUM DEVELOPMENT GOALS

In addition to these examples of river agreements, various non-binding "soft law" instruments that are not legislation in the strict sense offer opportunities for river protection and guidance on river management, dam design and management, and environmental flows. They include principles, codes of conduct, guidelines, recommendations, resolutions, and standards adopted by organizations such as the UN Environment Programme, the International Maritime Organisation, and the International Atomic Energy Agency (Dyson et al. 2003). In September 2000, world leaders adopted the UN Millennium Declaration (UN General Assembly 2000) and eight global Millennium Development Goals (MDG) for cutting world poverty in half by 2015. The seventh of the eight Millennium Development Goals commits nations to "ensure environmental sustainability" and reverse the loss of environmental resources.

At the World Summit on Sustainable Development held in Johannesburg in 2002, the international community established additional targets related to environmental sustainability and water, known as MDG Plus (United Nations 2002). Paragraph 26 (to "develop and implement national/regional strategies, plans and programmes with regard to integrated river basin, watershed and groundwater management and introduce measures to improve the efficiency of water infrastructure to reduce losses and increase recycling of water" by 2005) and paragraph 31 (to "maintain or restore stocks to levels that can produce the maximum sustainable yield with the aim of achieving these goals for depleted stocks on an urgent basis and where possible not later than 2015") are of most relevance to environmental flow management. The Millennium Ecosystem Assessment (MEA 2005) has contributed substantially to bringing forward the concept of ecosystem services as a policy tool to achieve the sustainable use of natural resources.

THE EUROPEAN WATER FRAMEWORK DIRECTIVE

At a regional level, the European Water Framework Directive (WFD) is a groundbreaking regional environmental policy that integrates water management and ecosystem conservation. Its intent is to resolve the piecemeal and divisive approach to European water legislation and managerial responsibility that has developed since 1975. The WFD has several key aims: expanding the scope of water protection to all waters, surface waters, and groundwater; achieving "good status" for all waters by a set deadline; implementing water management based on river basins; using a "combined approach" of emission limit values and quality standards; getting the prices right, achieving close citizen involvement; and streamlining legislation (EP and EU 2000).

Under the WFD, all EU member states are required by 2015 to achieve at least "good ecological status" (GES), in which biology and water quality deviate only slightly from natural conditions, in all surface water and groundwater bodies (rivers, floodplain wetlands, lakes, canals, reservoirs, groundwater, and transitional waters such as estuaries and deltas) and to prevent deterioration in the status of those water bodies. National legislation must be put in place to achieve the directive and competent agencies selected to implement it by developing river basin management plans that lay out the measures required to achieve at least GES by 2015.

The WFD allows limited exceptions to achieving GES; for instance, water bodies that have physical modifications, such as dams, weirs, and embankments, or that have been straightened or deepened, can be designated as Heavily Modified Water Bodies (HMWB) or Artificial, in the case of man-made lakes or canals. The goal for these water bodies is to achieve at least "good ecological potential" (GEP), taking account of the constraints imposed by existing physical modifications. GEP is defined as the best example of biological conditions in a similar water body with the same modifications, that is, where reasonable mitigation measures have been implemented and best practice management has been applied. In the case of a water body containing a dam, for example, best practice could mean provision of appropriate environmental flows (Acreman and Ferguson 2010). Although no specific project has been undertaken to develop consistent environmental flow guidance and procedures across Europe, significant progress has been made to document methods, to classify rivers into hydrological categories and regions, and to recommend approaches for recovering water in overabstracted river basins (Acreman and Ferguson 2010).

NATIONAL LEGISLATION AND POLICY

Implementing global and regional environmental agreements is the responsibility of individual national, state (provincial), and local governments. There is significant diversity of approaches (Dellapenna and Gupta 2009). Several countries have adopted legislation to nominate and protect rivers in their free-flowing state and to ensure long-term management and conservation of their natural, cultural, and recreational values for the enjoyment of present and future generations. Examples include the United States' Wild and Scenic Rivers Act, the Canadian Heritage Rivers System (CHRS n.d.), Swedish legislation to protect four unspoiled rivers of national importance (the Kalix, Torne, Pite, and Vindel Rivers), and Australian legislation to protect "wild rivers" (Wild Rivers Act 2005). Some of these articles of law recognize the potential for appropriate use and development of rivers and encourage river management that crosses political boundaries and promotes public participation.

As of 2011, the 43rd anniversary of the US Wild and Scenic Rivers Act, the national system protects more than 19,300 km of more than 252 rivers in 39 states, representing more than one-quarter of 1% of the nation's rivers. By comparison, more than 75,000 large dams across the country have modified at least 965,600 km, or about 17%, of American rivers. In Canada, 41 rivers have been nominated to the Canadian Heritage Rivers System, totaling almost 11,000 km; 37 of these have been designated, meaning that management plans detailing how their heritage values will be protected have been lodged with the Canadian Heritage Rivers Board (CHRS n.d.).

In Queensland, Australia, 10 wild rivers have been declared, mostly in the north of the state. A Queensland wild river declaration ensures extra protection for the river system and its catchment but in practice means no change for most people who live or work around the river system or who use the river. Therefore, activities including grazing, fishing, tourism, camping, hunting, and gathering continue unaffected. Indigenous cultural activities, ceremonies, and harvesting of bush food and medicines are also permitted; native title is unaffected; outstation development, mining, grazing, and irrigation can continue; and recreational boat users retain their rights to use rivers and creeks. Furthermore, new developments that do not impact the health of the river can still occur.

As well as wild and scenic river declarations, the ecosystems and surrounding landscapes of river and wetland complexes may be protected by conservation statues such as World Heritage listings (UNESCO 1972), national and conservation parks, and other national designations. The UN Educational, Scientific, and Cultural Organization (UNESCO) mandates the identification, protection, and preservation of outstanding examples of cultural and natural heritage around the world, through an international treaty called the Convention Concerning the Protection of the World Cultural and Natural Heritage, adopted in 1972. Rivers figure prominently in some listings and have been saved from development by their heritage status.

The World Heritage–listed Royal Chitwan National Park in southern central Nepal, on the border with India, protects the basins of the Rapti, Reu, and Narayani Rivers that originate in the Himalaya and drain to the Bay of Bengal. In the early 1990s the proposed Rapti River Diversion Project threatened riparian habitats critical to the last Nepalese population (estimated at 400) of the endangered great one-horned Asian rhinoceros *(Rhinoceros unicornis)* and other threatened vertebrates. The river diversion project was abandoned and this World Heritage area now protects aquatic species such as the gangetic dolphin *(Platanista gangetica),* the mugger crocodile *(Crocodylus palustris),* and the endangered gharial crocodile *(Gavialis gangeticus).*

UNESCO also designates Biosphere Reserves and conservation complexes—areas of terrestrial, wetland, and coastal ecosystems recognized within the framework of UNESCO's Man and the Biosphere (MAB) Programme. Everglades National Park in Florida protects the southern 25% of the original Everglades wetlands. It has been declared an International Biosphere Reserve, a World Heritage Site, and a Wetland of International Importance, one of only three locations in the world to appear on all three lists. The Pantanal Conservation Complex located in western central Brazil in Mato Grosso do Sul represents 1.3% of Brazil's Pantanal region, one of the world's largest freshwater wetland ecosystems. It was declared a World Heritage Site in 2000.

In the United States, the historical legal doctrine of the "public trust" (Dunning 1989) has helped to redefine water rights and preserve environmental flows and water regimes for lakes and wetlands, for example, Mono Lake, the second-largest freshwater lake (after Lake Tahoe) in California. Situated east of Yosemite National Park, Mono Lake is sustained by the flows of five Sierra Nevada snowmelt streams. In 1940, the California Water Board granted a permit to appropriate virtually all of these freshwater inflows to the City of Los Angeles, depleting the lake by one-third of its area and degrading its environmental values.

A landmark case in the Supreme Court of California in 1983 imposed a duty on the City of Los Angeles Department of Water and Power, as public trustee, to act in a way protective of the public-trust uses of water and to reallocate water, if deemed necessary, to protect the Mono Lake ecosystem. The whole story is recounted by Koehler (1995), who served as cocounsel to California Trout Inc. in the State Water Resources Control Board Mono Lake Proceedings. Although invoked in individual cases (e.g., the Sacramento–San Joaquin Delta dispute over saline intrusions upstream), the public-trust doctrine has not "been transformed into a broadly applied judicial ecosystem protection program in any state." However, by framing the uses of public-trust lands and waterways in terms of ecosystem services, the public-trust doctrine could be invoked to protect natural capital without challenging its original utilitarian core—commerce, navigation, and fishing (Ruhl and Salzman 2006).

Legislation and policies that explicitly enshrine and regulate environmental flow provisions vary from country to country. Many countries and jurisdictions require statutory management plans that set aside environmental flow provisions under legislative instruments that define and protect features of water resources and river flow regimes for ecological and other purposes. Several authorities (the IUCN, Dyson et al. 2003; the World Bank, Hirji and Davis 2009) suggest that the best recent examples of good legislation to provide water for environmental purposes are those promulgated in South Africa and Australia.

In South Africa, the National Water Act of 1998 requires the water minister to establish a reserve consisting of two parts: the basic human needs reserve (which provides for the essential needs of individuals served by the water resource in question and includes water for drinking, food preparation, and personal hygiene) and the ecological reserve (the water required to protect the aquatic ecosystems of the water resource). Both the quantity and quality of the water are protected in each reserve (National Water Act 1998). The South African Water Resource Classification System provides for the development of environmental objectives for different stretches of river, ranging from class A to class D (Dollar et al. 2010). Rivers of class A receive the highest levels of environmental flow protection, while significant alterations to the natural flow regime are permitted in class D reaches. Two further classes, E (seriously modified) and F (critically modified, impacts may be irreversible), are not considered acceptable outcomes for any reaches or tributaries. King and Pienaar (2011) review progress with implementation of the Ecological and Basic Human Reserves in South Africa, and canvass ideas to resolve the challenges for sustainable use of South Africa's inland waters.

Australia committed to a process of national water reform in 1994, when the Council of Australian Governments (COAG) agreed to "implement comprehensive systems of water allocations and entitlements backed by separation of water property rights from land title and clear specification of entitlements in terms of ownership, volume, reliability, transferability and, if appropriate, quality" (COAG 1994). To give policy guidance to jurisdictions and water managers responsible for implementing the reforms, 12 National Principles for the Provision of Water for Ecosystems (ARMCANZ and ANZECC 1996) were formulated. The basic premise of these principles is that rivers and wetlands are legitimate "users" of water and that the provision of water allocations is critically important to ecological sustainability. While many of these principles may now seem self-evident, when they were first implemented they were hard won and a milestone in developing consensus on how the issue of environmental flows should be addressed in Australia (Arthington and Pusey 2003; McKay 2005). Many are now reflected in state and national water legislation as well as in the key national water-policy blueprint, the National Water Initiative, or NWI (COAG 2004). Under this initiative, each state and territory government is required to prepare a NWI implementation plan for managing surface water and groundwater resources for rural and urban use that optimizes economic, social, and environmental outcomes, and to recover water from overstressed rivers.

The NWI is managed by the National Water Commission (NWC). The NWC reports to the Council of Australian Governments on progress toward national water reform and implementation of the NWI through biennial assessments. In its third biennial assessment, the NWC made 12 recommendations to COAG to reinvigorate the water-reform agenda and fully deliver its economic, environmental, and social benefits (NWC 2011). In terms of sustainable water management, the 2011 biennial report concludes that "the water plans and environmental management arrangements established under the NWI are improving Australia's capacity to maintain important environmental assets and ecosystem functions and to support economic activity. [However] they have not yet had time to deliver fully their intended outcomes or to demonstrate their efficacy over the long term, including during periods of climatic extremes" (NWC 2011).

For those seeking to establish a legislative and policy framework for the protection and management of environmental flows, a series of steps is recommended in the IUCN publication *Flow: The Essentials of Environmental Flows* (Dyson et al. 2003). It includes consideration of multilateral environmental and global river agreements, regional river agreements, binding provisions in treaties and customary law, recent international water-policy documents, constitutional provisions for the environment and water, and national and subnational laws and agreements on water and natural resources. The power of legal precedent should not be overlooked in efforts to establish effective legislative and regulatory instruments for environmental purposes and to negotiate for environmental water in individual situations. Dellapenna and Gupta (2009) provide a useful global review of international water law and its intricacies, ending with a call upon the UN General Assembly to set up an Intergovernmental Negotiating Committee to deal with global water challenges, supported by the legal expertise of the UN International Law Commission.

22

ADAPTING TO CLIMATE CHANGE

CLIMATE CHANGE

The decadal drought, floods, cyclones, and firestorms in Australia, flooding and mudslides in Brazil, volcanic activity in Indonesia, earthquakes in New Zealand and Japan, extensive intense snowfalls in North America—the list of catastrophic events goes on, bringing into sharp focus the dynamic nature of planet Earth. People are seeking explanations for what appears to be an increase in the incidence and violence of extreme weather events and their dreadful human and environmental consequences. What is driving them and what is the role of human activities? Opinions vary as to the relationship between such events and climate change and even whether Earth's climate is changing at all.

Global scientific consensus presents the following understanding of the world's changing environment. Global climate change is linked to, and induced by, increases in greenhouse gases (CO_2, CH_4, N_2O, and halocarbons) in the world's atmosphere. Levels of these gases have been steadily rising since advent of the industrial age (i.e., 1750) and are predicted to reach double preindustrial concentrations by 2065. The greatest rates of change have occurred within recent decades. The *Fourth Assessment Report* of the Intergovernmental Panel on Climate Change (IPCC 2007) concludes that "warming of the climate system is unequivocal, as is now evident from observations of increases in global average air and ocean temperatures, widespread melting of snow and ice and rising global average sea level. Changes in the ocean and on land, including observed decreases in snow cover and Northern Hemisphere sea ice extent, thinner sea ice, shorter freezing seasons of lake and river ice, glacier melt, decreases in permafrost extent, increases in soil temperatures and borehole temperature profiles, and sea level rise, provide additional evidence that the world is warming."

It is undoubtedly a fact that carbon dioxide and other greenhouse gasses are accumulating in the atmosphere. With CO_2 residence times and effects lasting for centuries to millennia, some scientists suggest that it may not be possible to stabilize Earth's climate through small incremental reductions in CO_2 emissions. Schellnhuber (2009) suggests that at certain "tipping points" higher temperatures could cause areas of the ocean to become deoxygenated, resulting in "oxygen holes" between 600 and 2,400 feet deep that would severely disrupt oceanic food chains. Unabated warming would also lead to "disruption of the monsoon, collapse of the Amazon rain forest and the Greenland ice sheet will meltdown." The suggestion is that these thresholds of change, beyond which no amount of effort can forestall ongoing climatic alterations, will have severe consequences for ecosystems and people.

An optimistic perspective on climate change is that it presents opportunities for mitigation. One suggestion to "defuse the global warming time bomb" is to focus on developing technological solutions to combat emissions of methane, tropospheric ozone, black carbon particles and chlorofluorocarbons (CFCs); this could allow carbon dioxide levels to stabilize at a higher value before they tip the warming effect to alarming levels (Hansen et al. 2000). Methane emissions from ruminants are already being reduced through dietary adjustments, while reducing methane leakage from natural gas systems, landfill sites, coal mining, and oil drilling presents feasible options. Ozone and black carbon emission levels can also be addressed (Hansen et al. 2000). Yet even with significant reductions in these greenhouse gasses as well as carbon dioxide levels, middle-range scenarios of greenhouse gasses forecast by the IPCC (2007) suggest that the global atmosphere might resemble that of the Eocene by the end of the twenty-first century.

The Eocene was an exceptionally warm period in Earth history. At the Early Eocene Climatic Optimum (EECO) 51 million to 33 million years ago, the partial pressure of CO_2 was high, global temperatures reached a long-term maximum, and the poles had little or no ice (Zachos et al. 2008). Fossils of *Nypha* palms, crocodiles, alligators, turtles, and subtropical rainforest species reveal that southern England was far warmer than it is today, resembling the coastal lowlands of southeastern Asia. Similar fossils occur in sediments from the Canadian Arctic (Estes and Hutchison 1980). In the Antipodes, fossil fern fronds, seeds, and *Nypha* palms have been recorded from Tasmania at latitudes equivalent to those of southern England. Antarctica 50 million years ago was much warmer than it is today, supporting mammals and marsupials characteristic of the humid forests of Patagonia (Reguero et al. 2002).

This exceptionally warm period in Earth history has been invoked as an analogue for the forcing of modern climate warming (Zachos et al. 2008). Attempts to "breathalyze" the atmosphere 50 million years ago using various proxy measurements (e.g., boron and carbon isotope analysis of soils, fossil foraminifera and algae, the number of stomata in fossil leaves) have yielded Eocene estimates ranging from 4 to 10 times the amount of carbon dioxide in today's atmosphere (Beerling 2009). Yet when fed into Earth system climate models, these levels of carbon dioxide do not yield the known distribution of thermal regimes and fossils of the Eocene (Beerling and Valdes 2003). More realistic simulations can only be achieved when other greenhouse gasses (methane, nitrous oxide, water vapor, and ozone) and their positive feedbacks linked to CO_2 are incorporated into climate models. As Beerling (2009) concludes in *The Emerald Planet*, the climate and associated fossil distributions of the Eocene are "a stark warning as to what the future climatic consequences of that drastic alteration to the chemistry of our atmosphere might be."

CLIMATE CHANGE AND FRESHWATER ECOSYSTEMS

The 2007 IPCC synthesis report projects that by midcentury, annual average river runoff and water availability will increase by 10% to 40% at high latitudes and in some wet tropical areas, and decrease by 10% to 30% over some dry regions at midlatitudes and in the dry tropics, some of which are presently water-stressed areas. Drought-affected areas will likely increase in extent, and heavy precipitation events are very likely to increase in frequency and will augment flood risk. In the course of the century, water supplies stored in glaciers and snow cover are projected to decline, reducing water availability in regions supplied by meltwater from major mountain ranges, where more than one-sixth of the world population currently lives (IPCC 2007). Just how each aquatic ecosystem and species will respond depends on the new climatic envelope and its impacts on the variability of water and other environmental regimes on land and in water.

Aquatic ecosystems are particularly sensitive to climate change due to the high heat capacity of water, the probability of altered thermal regimes, and changes to coupled thermal–hydrological variability. Many freshwater organisms have precise thermal and hydrological tolerances; consequently, the characteristics and dimensions of both the thermal and hydrologic regime have specific ecological relevance for freshwater organisms throughout their life history (Olden and Naiman 2010; Poff et al. 2010). Freshwater fish can detect small differences in water temperature and typically seek to occupy a thermal band within +2 °C of a preferred temperature; occupation of thermal habitats above or below this thermal band typically reduces metabolic efficiency. Changes in water temperature may have several consequences, for example, distributional changes through abandonment of existing habitat, colonization of new areas, or both contractions and expansions at range edges as species seek habitats of suitable thermal range. However, fish are largely restricted to their resident watersheds, and because many major rivers flow east to west, movement to a cooler thermal latitude or altitude may be impossible. Physiological and behavioral constraints on dispersal capability and the disruption of dispersal corridors by barriers (waterfalls, degraded habitat, dams) will also limit how effectively stressed aquatic populations can cope with rising water temperatures by moving to more suitable conditions.

As the hydrology of the landscape is altered by new rainfall/runoff patterns, fish may experience several types of stress. Reduction in precipitation in the severely water-limited aquatic ecosystems of arid and semiarid areas may threaten species that are endemic, already rare, or endangered (e.g., Sheldon et al. 2010). More prolonged periods without flow will bring about increasing fragmentation of aquatic habitats and likely will reduce the number and quality of dry-season refugia essential for fish persistence in arid landscapes and intermittent rivers (Larned et al. 2010; Arthington and Balcombe 2011). Species that are susceptible to elevated temperatures (e.g., due to localized anoxia) may also be vulnerable to reduced flows and habitat fragmentation, resulting in a synergistic effect when both stressors operate simultaneously.

Additional synergies may develop as the quality of basal resources is altered in response to elevated CO_2, increased stoichiometric imbalances, and, ultimately, suppression of biomass production across entire food webs. Alterations in body-size distribution within food webs are already evident for taxa ranging from bacteria, phytoplankton, and zooplankton to fish (Daufresne et al. 2009), and there is a suggestion that shortening of food chains could compromise the supply of energy to higher-level consumers, impacting valuable commercial and artisanal fisheries. In drought-stricken areas, human activities, such as water abstraction, could intensify these perturbations. Xenopoulos et al. (2005) predict that by 2070, discharge will decrease by up to 80% in 133 rivers globally, and of these 25% are projected to lose more than 22% of their fish species.

At the opposite end of the hydrologic spectrum, some regions are predicted to receive increased rainfall, more frequent and severe flooding, and associated disturbances. High flows could exceed the ability of many organisms to persist, especially those that lack traits to resist turbulence and drag (e.g., extreme streamlining of fish; hooks, grapples, and suckers in invertebrates) or if the system has few options for biota to move into refugia from high flows. Habitat refugia can be completely wiped out during extreme flow events, such as the loss of whole riffle habitats, the undercutting of banks and root masses, or the loss of aquatic plant beds.

Higher stream flows may disrupt the spawning of many aquatic species that require shallow stream reaches and backwaters as nurseries. Coupled thermal and flow regimes in tropical floodplain rivers (the Flood Pulse Concept) have enormous implications for fish recruitment and fisheries productivity. Climate-induced changes in the temporal characteristics of temperature and flow in rivers may disrupt delicate relationships; for example, warmer temperatures and earlier spawning may place eggs and larval stages into wetter or drier or more variable

TABLE 36   *Categories of climate change effect, examples of ecosystem impacts, likely complicating stressors, and US regions likely to be affected*

Invasive exotic species may be a complicating stressor in many situations

Effects of climate change	Examples of impacts	Common complicating stressors	US examples
Early snowmelt	Species life histories out of synchrony with flow regime, reproductive or recruitment failure, decreased population viability	Dams, flow diversions, or changes in reservoir releases	Pacific Northwest
More flooding	Flood mortality, channel erosion, poor water quality, reduced survivorship and population viability, spread of invasive species	Development in watershed, levee banks	Northeast, upper Midwest
Droughts, intense heat, increased evapotranspiration	Drought mortality, shrinking habitat, loss of connectivity, habitat fragmentation, local species extinctions	Overextraction of surface water and ground water, invasive species	Southwest
Little change in rainfall, moderately warmer	Ecological impacts modest unless complexes of stressors are present	Development in watershed	Northern Florida, Mississippi, parts of middle and western states

SOURCE: Adapted from Palmer et al. 2009

environments that lack suitable hydraulic habitat and food resources. Human responses to increased flooding such as the construction of dams, levee banks, and floodplain regulators may drastically disrupt fish movements to and from essential habitats on the floodplain (Jones and Stuart 2008).

A pervasive vulnerability of freshwater ecosystems is their present stressed condition brought about by the cumulative effects of catchment land use, riparian degradation, pollution, channel and habitat degradation, flow regulation, floodplain alienation, overfishing, and exotic species (Dudgeon et al. 2006; Palmer et al. 2009; Lake 2011). As well as ubiquitous alterations to habitat, human exploitation of fish stocks and the presence of exotic species further confound prediction of the effects of climate change on fish and other taxa. Climate change will likely induce potentially damaging synergies with these localized stressors (Xenopoulos et al. 2005). Predicting precisely what syndromes of stress are likely to occur in any given catchment or stream/wetland will be much more difficult than if climate change is the only threat. Categories of climate change and common complicating stressors of anthropogenic origin are given in Table 36 for major regions of the United States.

Palmer et al. (2009) note that a very large number and variety of combinations are expected around the world, and some complicating stressors may be present in all regions (e.g., invasive exotic species). It is particularly unclear how the impacts of climate change and stressors will be manifested across different levels of biological organization. Few studies have considered higher trophic levels, or the links between levels, thus "hindering current ability to predict system-level responses" (Woodward 2009).

ENVIRONMENTAL FLOWS AND CLIMATE CHANGE

Climate change implications challenge the science and practice of water management and environmental flows and make ecosystem protection and restoration even more urgent as well as more complex (Palmer et al. 2009). Climate change adaptation strategies often propose activities that can enhance ecological resilience: the amount of disturbance a system can withstand before changing its state (sometimes termed "resistance"); the rate at which a system recovers after disturbance; and the way in which a system responds to gradual changes (Scheffer et al. 2001). Free-flowing rivers in largely undeveloped catchments are expected to be resilient in the face of climate change because they retain their inherent capacities to respond to, and recover from, disturbances associated with historical regimes of flow variability, sediment, nutrient and energy inputs, and water quality (Poff et al. 1997; Baron et al. 2002). This inherent capacity to adjust to the variability of environmental regimes allows a river to absorb disturbances and buffer its biotic communities and ecosystem against the impacts of floods, droughts (Lake 2011), and other disturbances. Regulated and degraded rivers tend to lack this adaptive capacity (Kingsford 2011).

Many of the world's rivers and wetlands are increasingly threatened by catchment processes that affect overland flows, flow regime alterations by dams and diversions, and excessive groundwater pumping. Their flow regimes already require remediation to restore and sustain ecological resilience. Predicted climate change scenarios are likely to exacerbate the risks associated with existing flow regime alterations through altered rainfall, temperature, and runoff patterns; loss of connectivity; and cumulative disruptions to biogeochemistry, biological communities, and ecosystem processes. Furthermore, rising human populations and projected future climate change will place increasing pressure on water resources and infrastructure. The demand for more secure water supplies is predicted to lead to new dams and water transfer schemes, greater pressure on groundwater reserves, catchment development, and more severe downstream effects on floodplain wetlands and estuaries.

Attention to environmental flows and water regime management must sit at the heart of climate change adaptation because water is the main medium and vehicle for climate change impacts (Naiman and Dudgeon 2010).Strategies to protect or restore environmental flow regimes in free-flowing and highly regulated rivers and wetlands as the climate changes and demands on water resources increase need urgent attention in most countries. Much of the content of this book and recent climate change literature suggests the following suite of strategies, options, and processes (e.g., Palmer et al. 2008, 2009; Kingsford 2011; Mawdsley 2011):

Freshwater Protected Area Management   Identify and gazette freshwater protected areas as a key focus for management of rivers and wetlands throughout entire catchments and broader bioregions, using rigorous conservation planning. Apply systematic conservation planning approaches (principles of comprehensiveness, adequacy, representativeness, and efficiency), from catchment to broad jurisdictional or bioregional scales, to identify priority habitats and water bodies (e.g., drought refugia) for designation and management as protected areas, or for mitigation of threats, or to establish priorities for environmental flow delivery (Nel et al. 2011). Protect flow regimes of rivers and tributaries that remain largely free-flowing. Build biological databases and predictive models that provide spatial and temporal information for conservation planning. Focus conservation attention on species where management actions can reduce vulnerability rather than focusing attention on the species that are most vulnerable per se. Ensure that legislative conservation obligations are met, and ecological values are protected or rehabilitated, by providing flow regimes to meet defined ecosystem targets.

Protection and Restoration of Flow Regimes   Ensure sound environmental flow and socioeconomic assessments of new and old dams and of plans for increasing diversions from rivers and groundwater pumping. Restore flow regimes or provide more suitable environmental flows to meet conservation obligations for endangered species, key habitats and processes, and internationally important wetlands listed under the Ramsar Convention and migratory bird agreements (JAMBA, CAMBA, ROKAMBA). Improve the science and modeling of hydroecological scenarios that demonstrate trade-offs between deleterious alterations to flow regimes and environmental costs versus benefits (Poff et al. 2010). Incorporate the potential effects of climate change in scenario modeling, to help forecast environmental flow requirements under changing thermal and flow regimes.

Alteration of Dam Operations and Floodplain Management   Introduce time-limited licensing for all dams through legislation, allowing for regular (e.g., 5–10 year) reviews of safety and risk of failure and socioeconomic and environmental impacts. Retrofit dam structures to improve environmental flow outcomes (e.g., release valves, pipes, channels, spillways). Establish multilevel offtakes to improve downstream water temperatures and water quality. Construct or improve the functionality of fishways to allow movement of organisms past dam and weir walls. Consider human-assisted movement of threatened species (Olden et al. 2011). Pulse flow releases to mimic natural flow variability wherever possible during delivery of water for human and environmental objectives. Recognize the ecological benefits of low-flow periods and flow intermittency in dryland rivers; avoid unnaturally elevated low flow levels in such systems. Maintain or enhance connectivity in fragmented landscapes to promote escape from uninhabitable conditions and enable colonization of new sites. Consider dam and weir removals to restore connectivity and ecological functions in freshwater systems. For cascades of dams, investigate opportunities to reregulate flows by capturing flows in the lowest dam of the cascade and then releasing flow to mimic natural flow patterns. Investigate opportunities for conjunctive groundwater storage/recharge and dam storage (Richter and Thomas 2007). Establish river operations that allow for environmental flow releases to enhance natural flood flows or releases for human use, thereby providing increased flow over banks and into floodplains and wetlands (Rolls and Wilson 2010). Implement structural modifications, including pumping of environmental water and adjustments to weir levels and regulators, to focus and enhance flooding of specific wetland areas and floodplains. Identify opportunities for rehabilitation of floodplains while mitigating flooding impacts on infrastructure and people (e.g., manage levee banks, acquire floodplain easements, establish floodplain hazard versus utility zones, restore floodplain vegetation and absorption capacities). Identify and address or remove multiple stressors on species and ecosystems, to give additional flexibility in adapting to climate change (Palmer et al. 2009).

Legislation, Policy, Governance, and Adaptive Management Identify governance responsibilities at the regional and catchment scale to ensure a coherent approach to legislation, policy, governance, and environmental flow management linked to monitoring. Review and implement conservation legislation that supports biodiversity and resilience of rivers and wetlands (e.g., wild rivers legislation, endangered species legislation, adequate environmental impact assessment for new water infrastructure, provisions for environmental flows, and other mechanisms to enhance ecosystem resilience, such as floodplain management). Establish and implement environmental flow monitoring integrated with river health monitoring in a framework for adaptive management involving all stakeholders (e.g., Poff et al. 2003).

Indigenous Engagement, Science, and Education Increase efforts to engage indigenous people/tribes and to incorporate indigenous value systems and beliefs into existing or novel environmental flow frameworks (Finn and Jackson 2011). Support the synthesis of scientific and indigenous knowledge generated from place-based studies into a wider body of knowledge, principles, and management "rules" for rivers of contrasting hydrologic and geomorphic character and socioeconomic setting. Encourage and support river ecosystem science, education, and knowledge dissemination. Enhance efforts to achieve ecologically sustainable development and resilience as the guiding integrative policy framework and higher-order social goal of all societies (Hirji and Davis 2009).

HUMAN AND ECOSYSTEM FUTURES

The Brisbane Declaration prepared by delegates at the 10th International River*symposium* and Environmental Flows Conference in 2007 (see this book's appendix) celebrated the remarkable fact that after only about 40 years of effort many countries and jurisdictions now recognize the importance of dynamic river flow regimes, to the extent that the water requirements of rivers and floodplains are protected through legislation and water rights. Similar progress in wetland, groundwater, and estuarine studies has enshrined the concepts of environmental flows and water regimes to protect these ecosystems. By placing groundwater systems at the core of their "ecohydrogeological approach" and conceptualization, Tomlinson and Boulton (2010) offer an overarching framework for novel developments around a more integrated concept of environmental water requirements.

Great progress has been made, and many new challenges and opportunities will undoubtedly arise as water becomes an increasingly valued but often disputed resource. In summing up their review of global alterations to freshwater systems and the resulting human consequences, Naiman and Dudgeon (2010) ask what the future will hold as the Anthropocene unfolds. They suggest that "visionary programs and dedicated individuals, in collaboration with governments and the earth's 6 billion human inhabitants, will help resolve the many serious and urgent issues that face us during the 'Water for Life' decade [2005–15]—and allow us to achieve the water-related Millennium Development Goals."

While there is still time to establish protective measures for the world's remaining free-flowing rivers, time is running out for the damaged remainder that will inevitably suffer further loss of resiliency with increasing human demands for water, exacerbated by climate change and other pressures. A vigorous global river and catchment restoration effort is needed if societies wish to enjoy the benefits of freshwater biodiversity and the ecological goods and services of healthy ecosystems. Rather than be known by a pejorative epithet—the Anthropocene—the third millennium could become the era of transformation and restoration of Earth's natural resiliency and healing power for the benefit of people, ecosystems and the "endless forms most beautiful and most wonderful" (Darwin 1859) that risk extinction unless humans learn to live with, and celebrate, variability, diversity, and change.

APPENDIX

THE BRISBANE DECLARATION
(2007)

Environmental Flows[1] Are Essential for Freshwater Ecosystem Health and Human Well-Being

This declaration presents summary findings and a global action agenda that address the urgent need to protect rivers globally, as proclaimed at the 10th International River*symposium* and International Environmental Flows Conference, held in Brisbane, Australia, on 3–6 September 2007. The conference was attended by more than 750 scientists, economists, engineers, resource managers and policy makers from more than 50 countries.

Key findings include:

Freshwater ecosystems are the foundation of our social, cultural, and economic well-being. Healthy freshwater ecosystems—rivers, lakes, floodplains, wetlands, and estuaries—provide clean water, food, fiber, energy and many other benefits that support economies and livelihoods around the world. They are essential to human health and well-being.

---

1. *Environmental flows* describe the quantity, timing, and quality of water flows required to sustain freshwater and estuarine ecosystems and the human livelihoods and well-being that depend on these ecosystems.

Freshwater ecosystems are seriously impaired and continue to degrade at alarming rates. Aquatic species are declining more rapidly than terrestrial and marine species. As freshwater ecosystems degrade, human communities lose important social, cultural, and economic benefits; estuaries lose productivity; invasive plants and animals flourish; and the natural resilience of rivers, lakes, wetlands, and estuaries weakens. The severe cumulative impact is global in scope.

Water flowing to the sea is not *wasted.* Fresh water that flows into the ocean nourishes estuaries, which provide abundant food supplies, buffer infrastructure against storms and tidal surges, and dilute and evacuate pollutants.

Flow alteration imperils freshwater and estuarine ecosystems. These ecosystems have evolved with, and depend upon, naturally variable flows of high-quality fresh water. Greater attention to environmental flow needs must be exercised when attempting to manage floods; supply water to cities, farms, and industries; generate power; and facilitate navigation, recreation, and drainage.

Environmental flow management provides the water flows needed to sustain freshwater and estuarine ecosystems in coexistence with agriculture, industry, and cities. The goal of environmental flow management is to restore and maintain the socially valued benefits of healthy, resilient freshwater ecosystems through participatory decision making informed by sound science. Ground-water and floodplain management are integral to environmental flow management.

Climate change intensifies the urgency. Sound environmental flow management hedges against potentially serious and irreversible damage to freshwater ecosystems from climate change impacts by maintaining and enhancing ecosystem resiliency.

Progress has been made, but much more attention is needed. Several governments have instituted innovative water policies that explicitly recognize environmental flow needs. Environmental flow needs are increasingly being considered in water infrastructure development and are being maintained or restored through releases of water from dams, limitations on ground-water and surface-water diversions, and management of land-use practices. Even so, the progress made to date falls far short of the global effort needed to sustain healthy freshwater ecosystems and the economies, livelihoods, and human well-being that depend upon them.

GLOBAL ACTION AGENDA

The delegates to the 10th International River*symposium* and Environmental Flows Conference call upon all governments, development banks, donors, river basin organizations, water and energy associations, multilateral and bilateral institutions, community-based organizations, research institutions, and the private sector across the globe to commit to the following actions for restoring and maintaining environmental flows:

1. *Estimate environmental flow needs everywhere immediately.* Environmental flow needs are currently unknown for the vast majority of freshwater and estuarine ecosystems. Scientifically credible methodologies quantify the variable—not just minimum—flows needed for each water body by *explicitly* linking environmental flows to specific ecological functions and social values. Recent advances enable rapid, region-wide, scientifically credible environmental flow assessments.

2. *Integrate environmental flow management into every aspect of land and water management.* Environmental flow assessment and management should be a basic requirement of Integrated Water Resource Management (IWRM); environmental impact assessment (EIA); strategic environmental assessment (SEA); infrastructure and industrial development and certification; and land-use, water-use, and energy-production strategies.

3. *Establish institutional frameworks.* Consistent integration of environmental flows into land and water management requires laws, regulations, policies and programs that: (1) recognize environmental flows as integral to sustainable water management, (2) establish precautionary limits on allowable depletions and alterations of natural flow, (3) treat ground water and surface water as a single hydrologic resource, and (4) maintain environmental flows across political boundaries.

4. *Integrate water quality management.* Minimizing and treating wastewater reduces the need to maintain un-naturally high streamflow for dilution purposes. Properly-treated wastewater discharges can be an important source of water for meeting environmental flow needs.

5. *Actively engage all stakeholders.* Effective environmental flow management involves all potentially affected parties and relevant stakeholders and considers the full range of human needs and values tied to freshwater ecosystems. Stakeholders suffering losses of ecosystem service benefits should be identified and properly compensated in development schemes.

6. *Implement and enforce environmental flow standards.* Expressly limit the depletion and alteration of natural water flows according to physical and legal availability, and accounting for environmental flow needs. Where these needs are uncertain, apply the precautionary principle and base flow standards on best available knowledge. Where flows are already highly altered, utilize management strategies, including water trading, conservation, floodplain restoration, and dam re-operation, to restore environmental flows to appropriate levels.

7. *Identify and conserve a global network of free-flowing rivers.* Dams and dry reaches of rivers prevent fish migration and sediment transport, physically limiting the benefits of environmental flows. Protecting high-value river systems from development ensures that environmental flows and hydrological connectivity are maintained from river headwaters to mouths. It is far less costly and more effective to protect ecosystems from degradation than to restore them.

8. *Build capacity.* Train experts to scientifically assess environmental flow needs. Empower local communities to participate effectively in water management and policy-making. Improve engineering expertise to incorporate environmental flow management in sustainable water supply, flood management, and hydropower generation.

9. *Learn by doing.* Routinely monitor relationships between flow alteration and ecological response before and during environmental flow management, and refine flow provisions accordingly. Present results to all stakeholders and to the global community of environmental flow practitioners.

LITERATURE CITED

Acreman MC, Dunbar MJ (2004). Defining environmental flow requirements: a review. *Hydrology and Earth System Sciences* 8: 861–876.

Acreman MC, Ferguson AJD (2010). Environmental flows and the European Water Framework Directive. *Freshwater Biology* 55: 32–48.

Aladin NV, Williams WD (1993). Recent changes in the biota of the Aral Sea, Central Asia. *Verhandlungen der Internationalen Vereinigung für theoretische und angewandte Limnologie* 25: 790–792.

Alber M (2002). A conceptual model of estuarine freshwater inflow management. *Estuaries* 25: 1246–1261.

Alcamo J, Vörösmarty C, Naiman RJ, Lettenmaier D, Pahl-Wostl C (2008). A grand challenge for freshwater research: understanding the global water system. *Environmental Research Letters* 3: 1–6.

Allan JD (2004). Landscape and riverscapes: the influence of land use on river ecosystems. *Annual Reviews of Ecology, Evolution and Systematics* 35: 257–284.

Allan JD, Castillo MM (2007). *Stream Ecology.* Dordrecht, Netherlands: Springer.

American Rivers (2007). *Dams Slated for Removal in 2007 and Dams Removed from 1999–2006.* Washington, DC: American Rivers. Available at: http://act .americanrivers.org/site/DocServer/Dam_Removal_Summary_2007.pdf ?docID=6861&JServSessionIda012=oivbf6c111.app12c

Andersen DC, Shafroth PB (2010). Beaver dams, hydrological thresholds, and controlled floods as a management tool in a desert riverine ecosystem, Bill Williams River, Arizona. *Ecohydrology* 3: 325–338.

Anderson K E, Paul AJ, McCauley E, Jackson LJ, Post JR, Nisbet RM (2006). Instream flow needs in streams and rivers: the importance of understanding ecological dynamics. *Frontiers in Ecology and Environment* 4: 309–318.

ARMCANZ, ANZECC (Agriculture and Resource Management Council of Australia and New Zealand, Australian and New Zealand Environment and Conservation Council) (1996). *National Principles for the Provision of Water for Ecosystems.* Occasional Paper SWR No. 3. Canberra, Australia: ARMCANZ and ANZECC.

Arthington AH (1998). *Comparative Evaluation of Environmental Flow Assessment Techniques: Review of Holistic Methodologies.* Occasional Paper 26/98. Canberra, Australia: Land and Water Resources Research and Development Corporation. Available at: http://lwa.gov.au/products/pr980307

Arthington AH (2009). Australian lungfish, *Neoceratodus forsteri,* threatened by a new dam. *Environmental Biology of Fishes* 84: 211–221.

Arthington AH, Balcombe SR (2011). Extreme hydrologic variability and the boom and bust ecology of fish in arid-zone floodplain rivers: a case study with implications for environmental flows, conservation and management. *Ecohydrology* 4: 708–720.

Arthington AH, Blühdorn DR (1994). Distribution, genetics, ecology and status of the introduced cichlid, *Oreochromis mossambicus,* in Australia. In *Inland Waters of Tropical Asia and Australia: Conservation and Management,* Dudgeon D, Lam P (Eds), 53–62. Mitteilungen (Communications) Societas Internationalis Limnologiae 24. Stuttgart, Germany: Schweizerbart Science Publishers.

Arthington AH, Pusey BJ (2003). Flow restoration and protection in Australian rivers. *River Research and Applications* 19: 377–395.

Arthington AH, Zalucki JM (Eds) (1998). *Comparative Evaluation of Environmental Flow Assessment Techniques: Review of Methods.* Occasional Paper 27/98. Canberra, Australia: Land and Water Resources Research and Development Corporation. Available at: http://lwa.gov.au/products/pr980303

Arthington AH, Milton DA, McKay RJ (1983). Effects of urban development and habitat alterations on the distribution and abundance of native and exotic freshwater fish in the Brisbane region, Queensland. *Australian Journal of Ecology* 8: 87–101.

Arthington AH, King JM, O'Keeffe JH, Bunn SE, Day JA, Pusey BJ, Blühdorn DR and Tharme R (1992). Development of an holistic approach for assessing environmental flow requirements of riverine ecosystems. In *Proceedings of an International Seminar and Workshop on Water Allocation for the*

Environment, Pigrim JJ, Hooper BP (Eds), 69–76. Armidale, Australia: Centre for Water Policy Research.

Arthington AH, Brizga SO, Kennard MJ (1998). *Comparative Evaluation of Environmental Flow Assessment Techniques: Best Practice Framework.* Occasional Paper 25/98. Canberra, Australia: Land and Water Resources Research and Development Corporation.

Arthington AH, Brizga S, Kennard M, Mackay S, McCosker R, Choy S, Ruffini J (1999). Development of a Flow Restoration Methodology (FLOW RESM) for determining environmental flow requirements in regulated rivers using the Brisbane River as a case study. In *Handbook and Proceedings of Water 99: Joint Congress, 25th Hydrology and Water Resources Symposium, 2nd International Conference on Water Resources and Environmental Research*, Boughton W (Ed), 449–454. Brisbane, Australia: Australian Institute of Engineers.

Arthington AH, Rall JL, Kennard MJ, Pusey BJ (2003). Environmental flow requirements of fish in Lesotho Rivers using the DRIFT methodology. *River Research and Applications* 19: 641–666.

Arthington AH, Bunn S, Poff NL, Naiman RJ (2006). The challenge of providing environmental flow rules to sustain river ecosystems. *Ecological Applications* 16: 1311–1318.

Arthington AH, Baran E, Brown CA, Dugan P, Halls AS, King JM, Minte-Vera CV, Tharme R, Welcomme RL (2007). *Water Requirements of Floodplain Rivers and Fisheries: Existing Decision Support Tools and Pathways for Development.* Comprehensive Assessment of Water Management in Agriculture Research Report 17. Colombo, Sri Lanka: International Water Management Institute.

Arthington AH, Naiman RJ, McClain ME, Nilsson C (2010a). Preserving the biodiversity and ecological services of rivers: new challenges and research opportunities. *Freshwater Biology* 55: 1–16.

Arthington AH, Olden JD, Balcombe SR, Thoms MC (2010b). Multi-scale environmental factors explain fish losses and refuge quality in drying waterholes of Cooper Creek, an Australian arid-zone river. *Marine and Freshwater Research* 61: 842–856.

Arthington AH, Mackay SJ, James CS, Rolls RJ, Sternberg D, Barnes A, Capon SJ (2012). Ecological limits of hydrologic alteration: a test of the ELOHA framework in south-east Queensland. Waterlines Report Series No. 75. Canberra, Australia: National Water Commission. Available at: www.nwc.gov.au/publications/waterlines/75

Balcombe SR, Bunn SE, Arthington AH, Fawcett JH, McKenzie-Smith FJ,

Wright A (2007). Fish larvae, growth and biomass relationships in an Australian arid zone river: links between floodplains and waterholes. *Freshwater Biology* 52: 2385–2398.

Barlow PM, Reichard EG (2010). Saltwater intrusion in coastal regions of North America. *Hydrogeology Journal* 18: 247–260.

Baron JS, Poff NL, Angermeier PL, Dahm CN, Gleick PH, Hairston NG, Jackson RB, Johnston CA, Richter BD, Steinman AD (2002). Meeting ecological and societal needs for freshwater. *Ecological Applications* 12: 1247–1260.

Bayly IAE (1999). Review of how indigenous people managed for water in desert regions of Australia. *Journal of the Royal Society of Western Australia* 82: 17–25.

Beatty SJ, Morgan DL, McAleer FJ, Ramsay AR (2010). Groundwater contribution to baseflow maintains habitat connectivity for *Tandanus bostocki* (Teleostei: Plotosidae) in a south-western Australian river. *Ecology of Freshwater Fish* 19: 595–608.

Beerling DJ (2009). *The Emerald Planet*. Oxford, UK: Oxford University Press.

Beerling DJ, Valdes PJ (2003). Global warming in the early Eocene: was it driven by carbon dioxide? Fall Meeting Suppl. PP22B-04, *EOS Transactions, American Geophysical Union* 84.

Bencala KE (2000). Hyporheic zone hydrological processes. *Hydrological Processes* 14: 2797–2798.

Benke AC, Cushing CE (2005). *Rivers of North America*. Burlington, MA: Elsevier Academic Press.

Bennett HH, Lowdermilk WC (1938). *General Aspects of the Soil Erosion Problem: Soils and Men*. Yearbook of Agriculture, USDA Soil Conservation Service. Washington, DC: US Department of Agriculture.

Bennett M, Green J (1993). Preliminary assessment of Gwydir Wetland water needs. Technical Services Division Report. Sydney, Australia: New South Wales Department of Water Resources.

Benson NG (1953). The importance of groundwater to trout populations in the Pigeon River, Michigan. *Transactions of the North American Wildlife Conference* 18: 260–281.

Berga L, Buil JM, Bofill E, De Cea JC, Garcia Perez JA, Manueco G, Polimon J, Soriano A, Yague J (2006). Dams and reservoirs, societies and environment in the 21st century. In *Proceedings of the International Symposium on Dams in Societies of the 21st Century,* Barcelona, Spain, 18 June 2006. London, UK: Taylor and Francis Group.

Bernez I, Daniel H, Hauryb C, Ferreira MT (2004). Combined effects of environmental factors and regulation on macrophyte vegetation along three rivers in western France. *River Research and Applications* 20: 43–59.

Beuster H, King JM, Brown CA, Greyling A (2008). Feasibility study: DSS software development for integrated flow management; conceptual design of the DSS and criteria for assessment. Report Project K5/1404. Pretoria, South Africa: Water Research Commission.

Beyene T, Lettenmaier DP, Kaba, P (2010). Hydrologic impacts of climate change on the Nile River basin: implications of the 2007 IPCC scenarios. *Climatic Change* 100: 433–461.

Biggs BJF (1996). Hydraulic habitat of plants in streams. *Regulated Rivers: Research and Management* 12: 131–144.

Biggs HC, Rogers KH (2003). An adaptive system to link science, monitoring and management in practice. In *The Kruger Experience. Ecology and Management of Savanna Heterogeneity,* Du Toit JT, Rogers, KH, Biggs HC (Eds), 59–80. Washington, DC: Island Press.

Blanch SJ, Ganf GG, Walker KF (1999). Tolerance of riverine plants to flooding and exposure indicated by water regime. *Regulated Rivers: Research and Management* 15: 43–62.

Bodie JR (2001). Stream and riparian management for freshwater turtles. *Journal of Environmental Management* 62: 443–455.

Bond NR, Lake PS (2003). Characterizing fish-habitat associations in streams as the first step in ecological restoration. *Austral Ecology* 28: 611–621.

Bond NR, Lake PS, Arthington AH (2008). The impacts of drought on freshwater ecosystems: an Australian perspective. *Hydrobiologia* 600: 3–16.

Bond N, McMaster D, Reich P, Thomson JR, Lake PS (2010). Modelling the impacts of flow regulation on fish distributions in naturally intermittent lowland streams: an approach for predicting restoration responses. *Freshwater Biology* 55: 1997–2010

Booker DJ, Acreman MC (2007). Generalisation of physical habitat–discharge relationships. *Hydrology and Earth System Sciences* 11: 141–157.

Boon PJ, Calow P, Petts GE (Eds) (1992). *River Conservation and Management.* Chichester, UK: John Wiley and Sons.

Boulton AJ (2000). River ecosystem health down under: assessing ecological condition in riverine groundwater zones in Australia. *Ecosystem Health* 6: 108–118.

Boulton AJ, Hancock PJ (2006). Rivers as groundwater-dependent ecosystems:

a review of degrees of dependency, riverine processes and management implications. *Australian Journal of Botany* 54: 133–144. Available at:www .publish.csiro.au/nid/65/paper/BT05074.htm

Boulton AJ, Findlay S, Marmonier P, Stanley EH, Valett HM (1998). The functional significance of the hyporheic zone in streams and rivers. *Annual Review of Ecology and Systematics* 29: 59–81

Bovee KD (1982). A guide to stream habitat analysis using the Instream Flow Incremental Methodology. Instream Flow Information Paper 12, FWS/ OBS-82/26. Washington, DC: US Department of the Interior, Fish and Wildlife Service.

Bovee KD, Milhous R (1978). Hydraulic simulation in instream flow studies: theory and techniques. Instream Flow Information Paper 5, FWS/OBS-78/33. Fort Collins, CO: US Fish and Wildlife Service, Office of Biological Services.

Bradford MJ, Taylor GC, Allan JA, Higgins PS (1995). An experimental study of stranding of juvenile coho salmon and rainbow trout during rapid flow decreases in winter conditions. *North American Journal of Fisheries Management* 15: 473–479.

Bravard JP, Amoros C, Pautou G, Bornette G, Bournaud M, des Chatelliers MC, Gibert J, Peiry JL, Perrin JF, Tachet H (1997). River incision in southeast France: morphological phenomena and ecological effects. *Regulated Rivers: Research and Management* 13: 75–90.

Brenkman SJ, Duda JJ, Torgersen CE, Welty E, Pess GR, Peters R, McHenry ML (2012) A riverscape perspective of Pacific salmonids and aquatic habitats prior to large-scale dam removal in the Elwha River, Washington, USA. *Fisheries Management and Ecology* 19: 36–53.

Briggs SV, Thornton SA (1999). Management of water regimes in River Red Gum *Eucalyptus camaldulensis* wetlands for waterbird breeding. *Australian Zoologist* 31: 187–197.

Brisbane Declaration (2007). The Brisbane Declaration: environmental flows are essential for freshwater ecosystem health and human well-being. Declaration of the 10th International River Symposium and International Environmental Flows Conference, 3–6 September 2007, Brisbane, Australia.

Brivio PA, Colombo R, Maggi M, Tomasoni R (2002). Integration of remote sensing data and GIS for accurate mapping of flooded areas. *International Journal of Remote Sensing* 23: 429–441.

Brizga SO, Arthington AH, Choy S, Duivenvoorden L, Kennard M, Maynard RW, Poplawski W (2000a). Burnett Basin Water Allocation and Management Plan: current environmental conditions and impacts of existing water resource development. Brisbane, Australia: Department of Natural Resources.

Brizga SO, Davis J, Hogan A, O'Connor R, Pearson RG, Pusey B, Werren G, Muller D (2000b). Environmental flow performance measures for the Barron River Basin, Queensland, Australia. In *Proceedings of the Hydrology and Water Resources Symposium.* Perth, Australia: Institution of Engineers.

Brizga SO, O'Connor R, Davis J, Hogan A, Pearson RG, Pusey BJ, Werren GL (2001). Barron Basin water resource plan: Environmental investigations report. Queensland, Australia: Department of Natural Resources and Mines.

Brizga SO, Arthington AH, Pusey BJ, Kennard MJ, Mackay SJ, Werren GL, Craigie NM, Choy SJ (2002). Benchmarking, a "top-down" methodology for assessing environmental flows in Australian rivers. In *Environmental Flows for River Systems: An International Working Conference on Assessment and Implementation, Incorporating the 4th International Ecohydraulics Symposium.* Conference Proceedings. Cape Town, South Africa: Southern Waters.

Brock MA, Casanova MT (1997). Plant life at the edge of wetlands: ecological responses to wetting and drying patterns. In *Frontiers in Ecology: Building the Links,* Klomp N, Lunt I (Eds), 181–192. Oxford, UK: Elsevier.

Brodie J (1995). The problem of nutrients and eutrophication in the Australian marine environment. In *State of the Marine Environment Report for Australia,* Zann L, Sutton D (Eds), 1–30. Canberra, Australia: Technical Annex 2, Pollution, Department of the Environment, Sport and Territories.

Brookes A (1988). *Channelized Rivers: Perspectives for Environmental Management.* New York, NY: John Wiley and Sons.

Brooks AP, Howell T, Abbe TB, Arthington AH (2006). Confronting hysteresis: wood based river rehabilitation in highly altered riverine landscapes of southeastern Australia. *Geomorphology* 79: 399–422.

Browder JA, Moore D (1981). A new approach to determining the quantitative relationship between fishery production and the flow of fresh water to estuaries. In *Proceedings of the National Symposium on Freshwater Inflow to Estuaries,* FWS/OBS-81/04, Cross R, Williams D (Eds), 403–430. Washington, DC: US Fish and Wildlife Service, Office of Biological Services.

Brown CA, Joubert A (2003). Using multicriteria analysis to develop environmental flow scenarios for rivers targeted for water resource development. *Water Science* 29: 365–374.

Brown CA, King JM (2012). Modifying dam operating rules to deliver environmental flows: experiences from southern Africa. *Journal of River Basin Management* 10: 13–28.

Brown CA, Watson P (2007). Decision support systems for environmental flows: lessons from Southern Africa. *International Journal of River Basin Management* 5: 169–178.

Brown CA, Pemberton C, Greyling A, King JM (2005). DRIFT user manual, vol. 1, Biophysical module for predicting overall river condition in small to medium sized rivers with relatively predictable flow regimes. Report No. 1404/1/05. Pretoria, South Africa: Water Research Commission.

Bruton MN (1985). Effects of suspensoids on fish. In *Perspectives in Southern Hemisphere Limnology,* Developments in Hydrobiology 28, Davies BR, Walmsley RD (Eds), 221–241. .Dordrecht, Netherlands: Dr W. Junk Publishers.

Bulkley RV, Berry CR, Pimentel R, Black T (1981). Tolerances and preferences of Colorado River endangered fishes to selected habitat parameters. Colorado River Fishery Project Final Report Part 3. Salt Lake City, UT: US Fish and Wildlife Service, Bureau of Reclamation (cited in Converse et al. 1998).

Bunn SE (1993). Riparian-stream linkages: research needs for the protection of in-stream values. *Australian Biologist* 6: 46–51.

Bunn SE (1999). The challenges of sustainable water use and wetland management. In *Water: Wet or Dry? Proceedings of the Water and Wetlands Management Conference,* 14–22. Sydney, Australia: Nature Conservation Council of NSW.

Bunn SE, Arthington AH (2002). Basic principles and ecological consequences of altered flow regimes for aquatic biodiversity. *Environmental Management* 30: 492–507.

Bunn SE, Davies PM, Kellaway DM (1997). Contributions of sugar cane and invasive pasture grass to the aquatic food web of a tropical lowland stream. *Marine and Freshwater Research* 48: 173–179.

Bunn SE, Davies PM, Winning M (2003). Sources of organic carbon supporting the food web of an arid zone floodplain river. *Freshwater Biology* 49: 619–635.

Bunn SE, Thoms MC, Hamilton SK, Capon SJ (2006). Flow variability in dryland rivers: boom, bust and the bits in between. *River Research and Applications* 22: 179–186.

Bunn SE, Abal EG, Smith MJ, Choy SC, Fellows CS, Harch BD, Kennard MJ, Sheldon H (2010). Integration of science and monitoring of river ecosystem health to guide investments in catchment protection and rehabilitation. *Freshwater Biology* 55 (Suppl. 1): 223–240.

Burnham KP, Anderson DR (2002). *Model Selection and Multimodel Inference: A Practical Information-Theoretic Approach.* New York, NY: Springer-Verlag (cited in Grossman and Sabo 2010).

Burt TP (1996). The hydrology of headwater catchments. In *River Flows and Channel Forms,* Petts G, Callow P (Eds), 6–31. Oxford, UK: Blackwell Science.

CALFED (2000). *Programmatic Record of Decision.* Sacramento, CA: CALFED Bay-Delta Program.

Cambray JA (1990). Fish collections taken from a small agricultural water withdrawal site on the Groot River, Gamtoos River system, South Africa. *Southern African Journal of Aquatic Sciences* 16: 78–89.

Cambray JA, Davies BR, Ashton PJ (1986). The Orange-Vaal River system. In *The Ecology of River Systems,* Davies BR, Walker KF (Eds), 89–122. Dordrecht, Netherlands: Dr W. Junk Publishers.

Campbell IC, Doeg TJ (1989). Impact of timber harvesting and production on streams: a review. *Australian Journal of Marine and Freshwater Research* 40: 519–539.

Camp Dresser and McKee Inc., Bledsoe BD, Miller WJ, Poff NL, Sanderson JS, Wilding TK (2009). Watershed Flow Evaluation Tool (WFET) Pilot Study for Roaring Fork and Fountain Creek watersheds and site-specific quantification pilot study for Roaring Fork watershed (draft). Denver, CO: Colorado Water Conservation Board. Available at: http://cwcb.state.co.us/IWMD/COsWaterSupplyFuture/

Canonico GC, Arthington AH, McCrary JK, Thieme ML (2005). The effects of introduced tilapias on native biodiversity. *Aquatic Conservation: Marine and Freshwater Ecosystems* 15: 463–483.

Capra H, Breil P, Souchon Y (1995). A new tool to interpret magnitude and duration of fish habitat variations. *Regulated Rivers: Research and Management* 10: 281–289.

Carolsfeld J, Harvey B, Ross C, Baer A (2004). *Migratory fishes of South America: Biology, Fisheries, and Conservation Status.* Washington, DC, and Ottawa, Canada: World Fisheries Trust/World Bank/International Development Research Centre (cited in Dudgeon et al. 2006).

Carp E (Ed) (1972). Final act of the International Conference on the Conservation of Wetlands and Waterfowl. In *Proceedings, International Conference on the Conservation of Wetlands and Waterfowl, Ramsar, Iran, 30 January–3 February 1971.* Slimbridge, UK: International Wildfowl Research Bureau.

Cech TV (2010). *Principles of Water Resources*. Hoboken, NJ: John Wiley and Sons.

CGC (Canadian Grains Council) (2009). *Online Statistical Handbook*. Winnipeg, Manitoba: Canadian Grains Council. Available at: www.canadagrains council.ca/html/handbook.html

Champion PD, Tanner CC (2000). Seasonality of macrophytes and interaction with flow in a New Zealand lowland stream. *Hydrobiologia* 441: 1–12.

Chan TU, Hart BT, Kennard MJ, Pusey BJ, Shenton W, Douglas MM, Valentinec E, Patel S (2010). Bayesian network models for environmental flow decision making in the Daly River, Northern Territory, Australia. *River Research and Applications*. doi: 10.1002/rra.1456

Chao BF (1995). Anthropogenic impact on global geodynamics due to reservoir water impoundment. *Geophysical Research Letters* 22: 3529–3532.

Chao BF, Wu YH, and Li YS (2008). Impact of artificial reservoir water impoundment on global sea level. *Science* 320: 212–214.

Charniak E (1991). Bayesian networks without tears. *Artificial Intelligence* 12: 50–63.

Chessman BC (2009). Climatic changes and 13-year trends in stream macro-invertebrate assemblages in New South Wales, Australia. *Global Change Biology* 15: 2791–2802.

CHRS (Canadian Heritage Rivers System) (n.d.). A Framework for the Natural Values of Canadian Heritage Rivers. Available at: www.chrs.ca/en/mandate.php

Church M (1996). Channel morphology and typology. In *River Flows and Channel Forms,* Petts G, Callow P (Eds), 185–202. Oxford, UK: Blackwell Science.

Claret C, Marmonier P, Dole-Olivier MJ, Creuzé des Châtelliers M, Boulton AJ, Castella E (1999). A functional classification of interstitial invertebrates: supplementing measures of biodiversity using species traits and habitat affinities. *Archiv für Hydrobiologie* 145: 385–403.

Clifton C, Evans R (2001). A framework to assess the environmental water requirements of groundwater dependent ecosystems. In *Proceedings of the 3rd Australian Stream Management Conference,* Rutherford I, Sheldon F, Brierley G, Kenyon C (Eds), 149–156. Brisbane, Australia: CSIRO Sustainable Ecosystems.

Clifton C, Cossens B, McAuley C (2007). A framework for assessing the environmental water requirements of groundwater dependent ecosystems. Report 1 Assessment Toolbox. Canberra, Australia: Land and Water Australia.

Cloern JE (1996). Phytoplankton bloom dynamics in coastal ecosystems: a review with some general lessons from sustained investigation of San Francisco Bay, California. *Reviews of Geophysics* 34: 127–168.

Cloern JE, Alpine A, Cole B, Wong R, Arthur J, Ball M (1983). River discharge controls phytoplankton dynamics in the northern San Francisco Bay estuary. *Estuarine, Coastal, and Shelf Science* 16: 415–429.

COAG (Council of Australian Governments) (1994). COAG communiqué, 25 February 1994, Attachment A: water resource policy, item 4a. Hobart, Tasmania: Council of Australian Governments, Department of the Prime Minister and Cabinet. Available at: http://ncp.ncc.gov.au/docs/Council%20of%20Australian%20Governments'%20Communique%20-%2025%20February%201994.pdf

COAG (Council of Australian Governments) (2004). COAG communiqué, 25 June 2004, intergovernmental agreement on a national water initiative. Canberra, Australia: Council of Australian Governments, Department of the Prime Minister and Cabinet. Available at: www.nwc.gov.au/__data/assets/pdf_file/0019/18208/Intergovernmental-Agreement-on-a-national-water-initiative2.pdf

Colvin C, le Maitre D, Saayman I (2003). An approach to the classification, protection and conservation of groundwater dependent ecosystems. Progress Report, Project No. K5/1330. Pretoria, South Africa: Water Research Commission.

Connell D, Grafton QR (Eds) (2011). *Basin Futures: Water Reform in the Murray-Darling Basin*. Canberra, Australia: Australian National University E Press.

Converse YK, Hawkins CP, Valdez RA (1998). Habitat relationships of sub-adult humpback chub in the Colorado River through the Grand Canyon: spatial variability and implications of flow regulation. *Regulated Rivers: Research and Management* 14: 267–284.

Costanza R, d'Arge R, de Groot R, Farber S, Grasso M, Hannon B, Limburg K, Naeem S, O'Neill R, Paruelo J, Raskin RG, Sutton P, van den Belt M (1997). The value of the world's ecosystem services and natural capital. *Nature* 387: 253–260.

Cottingham P, Thoms MC, Quinn GP (2002). Scientific panels and their use in environmental flow assessment in Australia. *Australian Journal of Water Resources* 5: 103–111.

Cowardin LM, Carter V, Golet FC, LaRoe ET (1979). *Classification of Wetlands and Deepwater Habitats of the United States*. Washington, DC: US Department of the Interior, Fish and Wildlife Service.

Craig JF, Kemper JB (Eds) (1987). *Regulated Streams: Advances in Ecology.* New York, NY: Plenum Press.

Craig JF, Halls AS, Barr JJ, Bean CW (2004). The Bangladesh floodplain fisheries. *Fisheries Research* 66: 272–286.

Crutzen PJ (2002). Geology of mankind: the Anthropocene. *Nature* 415: 23.

Cummins KW (1993). Riparian-stream linkages: in-stream issues. In *Ecology and Management of Riparian Zones,* Proceedings of a National Workshop, Bunn SE, Pusey BJ, Price P (Eds), 5–20. Canberra, Australia: Land and Water Resources Research and Development Corporation.

Cunnings KS, Watters GT (2005). Mussel/host database (cited in Strayer 2008).

Dahl M, Nilsson B, Langhoff JH, Refsgaard JC (2007). Review of classification systems and new multi-scale typology of groundwater–surface water interaction. *Journal of Hydrology (Amsterdam)* 344: 1–16.

Dahm CN, Grimm NB, Marmonier P, Valett HM, Vervier P (1998). Nutrient dynamics at the interface between surface waters and groundwaters. *Freshwater Biology* 40: 427–451.

Daigle NE, Colbeck G, Dodson JJ (2010). Spawning dynamics of American shad (*Alosa sapidissima*) in the St. Lawrence River, Canada-USA. *Ecology of Freshwater Fish* 19: 586–594.

Danielopol DL, Gibert J, Griebler C, Gunatilaka A, Hahn HJ, Messana G, Notenboom J, Sket B (2004). Incorporating ecological perspectives in European groundwater management policy. *Environmental Conservation* 31: 185–189.

Darwin C (1859). *On the Origin of Species by Means of Natural Selection.* London: John Murray.

Daufresne M, Lengfellner K, Sommer U (2009). Global warming benefits the small in aquatic ecosystems. *Proceedings of the National Academy of Sciences USA* 106: 12788–12793.

Davie P, Stock E, Low Choy D (Eds) (1990). *The Brisbane River. A Source Book for the Future.* Brisbane, Australia: Australian Littoral Society and Queensland Museum.

Davies B, Day J (1998). *Vanishing Waters.* Cape Town, South Africa: University of Cape Town Press.

Davies BR, Walker KF (1986). *The Ecology of River Systems.* Dordrecht, Netherlands: Dr W. Junk Publishers.

Davies BR, Thoms M, Meador MR (1992). An assessment of the ecological impacts of inter-basin water transfers, and their threats to river basin integrity and conservation. *Aquatic Conservation: Marine and Freshwater Ecosystems* 2: 325–349.

Davies PE, Humphries P, Mulcahy M (1995). Environmental flow requirements for the Meander, Macquarie and South Esk Rivers, Tasmania. Report to National Landcare Program. Canberra, Australia.

Davis J, Brock M (2008). Detecting unacceptable change in the ecological character of Ramsar wetlands. *Ecological Management and Restoration* 9: 26–31.

Davis JA, Froend RH (1998). *Regional Review of Wetland Management Issues: Western Australia (except Kimberley) and Central Australia*. Canberra, Australia: Land and Water Resources Research and Development Corporation.

Davis JA, Froend RH, Hamilton DP, Horwitz P, McComb AJ, Oldham CE (2001). Environmental water requirements to maintain wetlands of national and international importance. Environmental Flows Initiative Technical Report No. 1. Canberra, Australia: Commonwealth of Australia.

Day JH (Ed) (1981). *Estuarine Ecology with Particular Reference to Southern Africa*. Cape Town, South Africa: Balkema (cited in Pierson et al. 2002).

De Jalon DG, Sanchez P, Camargo JA (1994). Downstream effects of a new hydropower impoundment on macrophyte, macroinvertebrate and fish communities. *Regulated Rivers: Research and Management* 9: 253–261.

Dellapenna JW, Gupta J (Eds) (2009). *The Evolution of the Law and Politics of Water*. New York: Springer Science and Business Media BV.

De Moor FC (1986). Invertebrates of the Lower Vaal River, with emphasis on the Simuliidae. In *The Ecology of River Systems,* Davies, PR, Walker KF (Eds), 135–142. Dordrecht, Netherlands: Dr W. Junk Publishers.

Dent CL, Schade JJ, Grimm NB, Fisher SG (2000). Subsurface influences on surface biology. In *Streams and Ground Waters,* Jones J, Mulholland P (Eds), 377–404. New York, NY: Academic Press (cited in Boulton and Hancock 2006).

Di Stefano J (2001). River red gum *(Eucalyptus camaldulensis)*: a review of ecosystem processes, seedling regeneration and silvicultural practice. *Australian Forestry* 65: 14–22.

DNR (Department of Natural Resources) (2006). Great Artesian Basin Sustainability Initiative (GABSI) Cap and Pipe the Bores. State of New South Wales, Department of Natural Resources. Available at: www.water.nsw.gov .au/Water-management/Water-recovery/Cap-and-pipe-bores/default.aspx

Doering PH, Chamberlain RH, Haunert DE (2002). Using submerged aquatic vegetation to establish minimum and maximum freshwater inflows to the Caloosahatchee estuary, Florida. *Estuaries* 25: 1343–1354.

Dole-Olivier M-J, Castellarini F, Coineau N, Galassi DMP, Martin P, Mori N, Valdecasas A, Gibert J (2009). Towards an optimal sampling strategy to assess groundwater biodiversity: comparison across six European regions. *Freshwater Biology* 54: 777–796.

Dollar ESJ, Nicolson CR, Brown CA, Turpie JK, Joubert AR, Turton AR, Grobler DF, Pienaar HH, Ewart-Smith J, Manyaka SM (2010). Development of the South African Water Resource Classification System (WRCS): a tool towards the sustainable, equitable and efficient use of water resources in a developing country. *Water Resource Policy* 12: 479–499.

Douglas MM, Bunn SE, Davies PM (2005). River and wetland foodwebs in Australia's wet-dry tropics: general principles and implications for management. *Marine and Freshwater Research* 56: 329–342.

Downes BJ, Barmuta LA, Fairweather PG, Faith DP, Keough MJ, Lake PS, Mapstone BD, Quinn GP (2002). *Monitoring Ecological Impacts: Concepts and Practice in Flowing Waters*. Cambridge, UK: Cambridge University Press.

Dudgeon D (2010). Prospects for sustaining freshwater biodiversity in the 21st Century: linking ecosystem structure and function. *Current Opinion in Environmental Sustainability* 2: 422–430.

Dudgeon D, Arthington AH, Gessner MO, Kawabata ZI, Knowler DJ, Lévêque C, Naiman RJ, Prieur-Richard A-H, Soto D, Stiassny MLJ, Sullivan CA (2006). Freshwater biodiversity: importance, threats, status and conservation challenges. *Biological Reviews* 81: 163–182.

Dunbar MJ, Gustard A, Acreman M, Elliott CRN (1998). *Overseas Approaches to Setting River Flow Objectives*. R&D Technical Report W6B(96)4. Wallingford, UK: Institute of Hydrology.

Dunbar MJ, Pedersen M., Cadman D, Extence C, Waddingham J, Chadd R, Larsen SE (2010). River discharge and local-scale physical habitat influence macroinvertebrate LIFE scores. *Freshwater Biology* 55: 226–242.

Dunning HC (1989). The Public Trust: A fundamental doctrine of American property law. *Environmental Law* 19: 515–526.

DWAF (Department of Water Affairs and Forestry) (1999). *Resource Directed Measures for Protection of Water Resources*. Volume 4, *Wetland Ecosystems*. Version 1.0. Pretoria, South Africa: Institute for Water Quality Studies, Department of Water Affairs and Forestry.

Dynesius M, Nilsson C (1994). Fragmentation and flow regulation of river systems in the northern third of the world. *Science* 266: 753–762.

Dyson M, Bergkamp M, Scanlon J (2003). *Flow: The Essentials of Environmental Flows*. Gland, Switzerland, and Cambridge, UK: IUCN.

Eamus D, Froend F (2006). Groundwater-dependent ecosystems: the where, what and why of GDEs. *Australian Journal of Botany* 54: 91–96.

Eberhard SM, Halse SA, Williams MR, Scanlon MD, Cocking JS, Barron HJ (2009). Exploring the relationship between sampling efficiency and short range endemism for groundwater fauna in the Pilbara region, Western Australia. *Freshwater Biology* 54: 885–901.

Edgar GJ, Barrett NS, Graddon DJ, Last PR (2000). The conservation significance of estuaries: a classification of Tasmanian estuaries using ecological, physical and demographic attributes as a case study. *Biological Conservation* 92: 383–397.

Edwards BD, Evans KR (2002). Saltwater intrusion in Los Angeles area coastal aquifers: the marine connection. US Geological Survey Fact Sheet 030–02. Denver, CO: US Geological Survey, Information Services.

Elliott CRN, Dunbar MJ, Gowing I, Acreman MA (1999). A habitat assessment approach to the management of groundwater dominated rivers. *Hydrological Processes* 13: 459–475.

Ellis LM, Molles MC, Crawford CS (1999). Influence of experimental flooding on litter dynamics in a Rio Grande riparian forest, New Mexico. *Restoration Ecology* 7: 193–204.

Enders EC, Scruton DA, Clarke KD (2009). The "natural flow paradigm" and Atlantic salmon: moving from concept to practice. *River Research and Applications* 24: 2–15.

Environmental Protection Agency (1977). *Quality Criterion for Water*. Washington, DC: US Environmental Protection Agency, Office of Water and Hazardous Materials.

EP and EU (European Parliament and the Council of the European Union) (2000). Directive 2000/60/EC of the European Parliament and of the Council of 23 October 2000 establishing a framework for Community action in the field of water policy. *Official Journal of the European Communities* L 327/1.

Erskine DW, Webb AA (2003). Desnagging to resnagging: new directions in river rehabilitation in southeastern Australia. *River Research and Applications* 19: 233–249.

Escobar-Arias MI, Pasternack GB (2010). A hydrogeomorphic dynamics approach to assess in-stream ecological functionality using the functional flows model, part 1: model characteristics. *River Research and Applications* 26: 1103–1128.

Escobar-Arias MI, Pasternack GB (2011). Differences in river ecological functions due to rapid channel alteration processes in two California rivers using the functional flows model, part 2: model applications. *River Research and Applications* 27: 1–22.

Espegren GD (1998). Evaluation of the standards and methods used for quantifying instream flows in Colorado. Final Report. Denver, CO: Colorado Water Conservation Board (cited in Tharme 2003).

Estes R, Hutchison JH (1980). Eocene lower-vertebrates from Ellesmere Island, Canadian Arctic Archipelago. *Palaeogeography Palaeoclimatology Palaeoecology* 30: 325–347.

Estevez ED (2002). Review and assessment of biotic variables and analytical methods used in estuarine inflow studies. *Estuaries* 25: 1291–1303.

Extence CA, Balbi DM, Chadd RP (1999). River flow indexing using British benthic macroinvertebrates: a framework for setting hydroecological objectives. *Regulated Rivers: Research and Management* 15: 543–574.

Fairbridge RW (1980). The estuary: its definition and geodynamic cycle. In *Chemistry and Biogeochemistry of Estuaries,* Olausson E, Cato I (Eds). Chichester, UK: John Wiley (cited in Pierson et al. 2002).

Falke JA, Fausch KD, Magelky R, Aldred A, Durnford DS, Riley LK, Oad R (2010). The role of groundwater pumping and drought in shaping ecological futures for stream fishes in a dryland river basin of the western Great Plains, USA. *Ecohydrology* 4: 682–697.

Fausch KD, Torgersen CE, Baxter CV, Li HW (2002). Landscapes to riverscapes: bridging the gap between research and conservation of stream fishes. *Bioscience* 52: 483–498.

Fellows CS, Bunn SE, Sheldon F, Beard NJ (2009). Benthic metabolism in two turbid floodplain rivers. *Freshwater Biology* 54: 236–253.

Fenner P, Brady WW, Patten DR (1985). Effects of regulated water flows on regeneration of Fremont cottonwood. *Journal of Range Management* 38: 135–138.

Ferrar AA (Ed) (1989). *Ecological Flow Requirements of South African Rivers*. South African National Scientific Programmes Report 162. Pretoria, South Africa: Council for Scientific and Industrial Research.

Finlayson CM, Roberts J, Chick AJ, Sale PJM (1983). The biology of Australian weeds. II. *Typha domingensis* Pers. and *Typha orientalis* Presl. *Journal of the Australian Institute of Agricultural Science* 49: 3–10.

Finn M, Jackson S (2011). Protecting indigenous values in water management: a challenge to conventional environmental flow assessments. Ecosystems 14: 1232–1248.

Finston TL, Johnson MS, Humphreys WF, Eberhard SM, Halse SA (2007). Cryptic speciation in two widespread subterranean amphipod genera reflects historical drainage patterns in an ancient landscape. *Molecular Ecology* 16: 355–365.

Fleckenstein J, Anderson M, Fogg G, Mount J (2004). Managing surface water–groundwater to restore fall flows in the Cosumnes River. *Journal of Water Resources Planning and Management* 130: 301–310 (cited in Boulton and Hancock 2006).

Folke C, Carpenter S, Walker BH, Scheffer M, Elmqvist T, Gunderson LH, Holling CS (2004). Regime shifts, resilience and biodiversity in ecosystem management. *Annual Review in Ecology, Evolution and Systematics* 35: 557–581.

Forslund A, Renöfält BM, Barchiesi S, Cross K, Davidson S, Korsgaard L, Krchnak K, McClain M, Meijers K, Smith M (2009). *Securing Water for Ecosystems and Human Well-Being: The Importance of Environmental Flows.* Report 24. Stockholm, Sweden: Swedish Water House, SIWI.

Frazier PS, Page KJ, Louis J, Briggs S, Robertson A (2003). Relating wetland inundation to river flow using Landsat TM data. *International Journal of Remote Sensing* 24: 3755–3770.

Freitag B, Bolton S, Westerlund F, Clark JLS (2009). *Floodplain Management: A New Approach for a New Era.* Washington, DC: Island Press.

French TD, Chambers PA (1996). Habitat partitioning in riverine macrophyte communities. *Freshwater Biology* 36: 509–520.

Frissell CA, Liss WJ, Warren CE, Hurley MD (1986). A hierarchical framework for stream habitat classification: viewing streams in a watershed context. *Environmental Management* 10: 199–214.

Fryirs K, Arthington A, Grove J (2008). Principles of river condition assessment. In *River Futures: An Integrative Scientific Approach to River Repair,* Brierley GJ, Fryirs KA (Eds), 100–118. Washington, DC: Island Press.

Gan KC, McMahon TA (1990). *Comparison of Two Computer Models for Assessing Environmental Flow Requirements.* Centre for Environmental Applied Hydrology Report. Victoria, Australia: University of Melbourne.

Garrett P (2009). Traveston Dam gets final no. The Hon. Peter Garrett AM MP, Minister for the Environment, Heritage and the Arts, media release 2 December 2009, PG/384. Australian Government archived media releases and speeches. Available at: www.environment.gov.au/minister/archive/env/2009/mr20091202a.html

Gehrke PC, Brown P, Schiller CB, Moffatt DB, Bruce AM (1995). River regulation and fish communities in the Murray-Darling River system, Australia. *Regulated Rivers: Research and Management* 11: 363–375.

Ghassemi F, White I (2007). *Inter-Basin Water Transfer: Case Studies from Australia, United States, Canada, China and India.* Cambridge, UK: Cambridge University Press.

Gibert J, Culver DC (2009). Assessing and conserving groundwater biodiversity: an introduction. *Freshwater Biology* 54: 639–648.

Gibert J, Culver DC, Dole-Olivier M-J, Mallard F, Christman MC, Deharveng L (2009). Assessing and conserving groundwater biodiversity: synthesis and perspectives. *Freshwater Biology* 54: 930–941.

Gillanders BM, Kingsford MJ (2002). Impact of changes in flow of freshwater on estuarine and open coastal habitats and the associated organisms. *Oceanography and Marine Biology: an Annual Review* 40: 223–309.

Gillilan DM, Brown TC (1997). *Instream Flow Protection: Seeking a Balance in Western Water Use.* Washington, DC: Island Press.

Gippel CJ (1992). *Guidelines for Wetland Management.* Report for Victorian Department of Conservation and Environment Wetlands Unit. Victoria, Australia: University of Melbourne.

Gippel CJ (2001). Australia's environmental flow initiative: filling some knowledge gaps and exposing others. *Water Science and Technology* 43: 73–88.

Gippel CJ (2010). *ACEDP—River Health and Environmental Flow in China; Technical Report 3; A Holistic, Asset-Based Framework for Evaluating River Health, Environmental Flows and Water Re-allocation.* ACEDP Activity No. P0018. Brisbane, Australia: International WaterCentre.

Gippel CJ, Stewardson MJ (1998). Use of wetted perimeter in defining minimum environmental flows. *Regulated Rivers: Research and Management* 14: 53–67.

Gippel CJ, O'Neill IC, Finlayson BL, Schnatz I (1996). Hydraulic guidelines for the re-introduction and management of large woody debris in lowland rivers. *Regulated Rivers: Research and Management* 12: 223–236.

Gippel CJ, Bond NR, James C, Xiqin W (2009). An asset-based, holistic, environmental flows assessment approach. *International Journal of Water Resources Development* 25: 301–330.

Gladwell M (2000). *The Tipping Point: How Little Things Can Make a Big Difference.* Boston, MA: Little Brown and Company.

Global Water Partnership (2011). *GWP in Action 2010: Annual Report.* Stockholm, Sweden: Global Water Partnership.

Gordon N, McMahon TA, Finlayson BL (1992). *Stream Hydrology*. Chichester, UK: John Wiley and Sons.

Gore JA, Nestler JM (1988). Instream flow studies in perspective. *Regulated Rivers: Research and Management* 2: 93–101.

Gore JA, Petts GE (Eds) (1989). *Alternatives in Regulated River Management*. Boca Raton, FL: CRC Press.

Graf WL (2006). Downstream hydrological and geomorphic effects of large dams on American rivers. *Geomorphology* 79: 336–360.

Greer M, Ruffini J, Arthington A, Bartlett, Johansen C (1999). In *Handbook and Proceedings of the Water 99: Joint Congress, 25th Hydrology and Water Resources Symposium, 2nd International Conference on Water Resources and Environmental Research,* Boughton, W (Ed), 1129–1134. Brisbane, Australia: Australian Institute of Engineers.

Gregory KJ (2006). The human role in changing river channels. *Geomorphology* 79: 172–191.

Gregory SV, Swanson FJ, McKee WA, Cummins KW (1991). An ecosystem perspective of riparian zones. *BioScience* 41: 540–550.

Groffman PM, Tiedje JM (1988). Denitrification hysteresis during wetting and drying cycles in soil. *Soil Science Society of America Journal* 52: 1626–1629 (cited in Pinay et al. 2002).

Groffman PM, Boulware NJ, Zipperer WE, Pouyat RV, Band LE, Colosimo MF (2002). Soil nitrogen cycling processes in urban riparian zones. *Environmental Science and Technology* 36: 4547–4552.

Groffman PM, Bain DJ, Band LE, Belt KT, Brush GS, Grove JM, Pouyat RV, Yesilonis IC, Zipperer WC (2003). Down by the riverside: urban riparian ecology. *Frontiers in Ecology and the Environment* 1: 315–321.

Groom JD, Grubb TC (2002). Bird species associated with riparian woodland in fragmented, temperate deciduous forest. *Conservation Biology* 16: 832–836.

Grossman GD, Sabo JL (2010). Preface: structure and dynamics of stream fish assemblages. In *Community Ecology of Stream Fishes: Concepts, Approaches, and Techniques,* Symposium 73, Jackson DA, Gido KB (Eds), 401–405. Bethesda, MD: American Fisheries Society.

Gustavson K, Kennedy E (2010). Approaching wetland valuation in Canada. *Wetlands* 30: 1065–1076.

Gustard A (1996). Analysis of river regimes. In *River Flows and Channel Forms,* Petts G, Callow P (Eds), 32–50. Oxford, UK: Blackwood Scientific.

Gutreuter S, Bartels AD, Irons K, Sandheinrich MB (1999). Evaluation of the Flood-Pulse Concept based on statistical models of growth of selected fishes of the Upper Mississippi River system. *Canadian Journal of Fisheries and Aquatic Sciences* 56: 2202–2291.

Habermehl MA (1982). Springs in the Great Artesian Basin, Australia: their origin and nature. Report No. 235. Canberra, Australia: Bureau of Mineral Resources, Geology and Geophysics.

Haines AT, Finlayson BL, McMahon TA (1988). A global classification of river regimes. *Applied Geography* 8: 255–272.

Halleraker JH, Sundt H, Alfredsen KT, Dangelmaier D (2007). Application of multiscale environmental flow methodologies as tools for optimized management of a Norwegian regulated national salmon watercourse. *River Research and Applications* 23: 467–558.

Halliday IA, Robins JB (Eds) (2007). Environmental flows for sub-tropical estuaries: understanding the freshwater needs of estuaries for sustainable fisheries production and assessing the impacts of water regulation. Final Report Project No. 2001/022. Canberra, Australia: Fisheries Research and Development Corporation, Australian Government.

Halls AS, Hoggarth DD, Debnath K (1998). Impact of flood control schemes on river fish migrations and species assemblages in Bangladesh. *Journal of Fish Biology* 53 (Suppl. A): 358–380.

Halls AS, Hoggarth DD, Debnath K (1999). Impacts of hydraulic engineering on the dynamics and production potential of floodplain fish populations in Bangladesh. *Fisheries Management and Ecology* 6: 261–285.

Halls AS, Kirkwood GP, Payne AI (2001). A dynamic pool model for flood-plain-river fisheries. *Ecohydrology and Hydrobiology* 1: 323–339.

Halse SA, Ruprecht JK, Pinder AM (2003) Salinisation and prospects for bio-diversity in rivers and wetlands of south-west Western Australia. *Australian Journal of Botany* 51: 673–688.

Hamilton SK (1999). Potential effects of a major navigation project (Paraguay-Paraná Hidrovia) on inundation in the Pantanal floodplains. *Regulated Rivers: Research and Management* 15: 289–299.

Hancock PJ (2002). Human impacts on the stream-groundwater exchange zone. *Environmental Management* 29: 763–781.

Hancock PJ, Boulton, AJ (2008). Stygofauna biodiversity and endemism in four alluvial aquifers in eastern Australia. *Invertebrate Systematics* 22: 117–126.

Hansen J, Sato M, Ruedy R, Lacis A, Oinas V (2000). Global warming in the twenty-first century: an alternative scenario. *Proceedings of the National Academy of Sciences* 97: 9875–9880.

Harby A (2007). European aquatic modelling network. *River Research and Applications* 23: 467–468.

Harby A, Olivier J-M, Merigoux S, Malet E (2007). A mesohabitat method used to assess minimum flow changes and impacts on the invertebrate and fish fauna in the Rhone River, France. *River Research and Applications* 23: 525–543.

Harris MB, Tomas W, Ao GM, Da Silva CJ, Aes EG, Sonoda F, Fachim E (2005). Safeguarding the Pantanal wetlands: threats and conservation initiatives. *Conservation Biology* 9: 714–720.

Hart BT, Pollino CA (2009). Bayesian modelling for risk-based environmental water allocations. Waterlines Report Series No 14. Canberra, Australia: National Water Commission. Available at: www.nwc.gov.au/www/html/1021-bayesian-modelling-report-no-14.asp

Hatton T, Evans, R (1998). *Dependence of Ecosystems on Groundwater and Its Significance to Australia*. Canberra, Australia: Land and Water Resources Research and Development Corporation.

Hawkes HA (1975). River zonation and classification. In *River Ecology,* Whitton BA (Ed), 312–374. Oxford, UK: Blackwell Science.

Haxton TJ, Findlay CS (2008). Meta-analysis of the impacts of water management on aquatic communities. *Canadian Journal of Fisheries and Aquatic Sciences* 65: 437–447.

Haycock NE, Pinay G (1993). Groundwater nitrate dynamics in grass and poplar vegetated riparian buffer strips during the winter. *Journal of Environmental Quality* 22: 273–278.

Hearne J, Johnson IW, Armitage PD (1994). Determination of ecologically acceptable flows in rivers with seasonal changes in the density of macrophyte. *Regulated Rivers: Research and Management* 9: 17–184.

Heiler G, Hein T, Schiemer F (1995). Hydrological connectivity and flood pulses as the central aspects for the integrity of a river-floodplain system. *Regulated Rivers: Research and Management* 11: 351–361.

Hemminga M, Duarte CM (2000). *Seagrass Ecology*. Cambridge, UK: Cambridge University Press.

Henley WF, Patterson MA, Neves RJ, Dennis-Lemley A (2000). Effects of sedimentation and turbidity on lotic food webs: a concise review for natural resource managers. *Reviews in Fisheries Science* 8: 125–139.

Hill M, Platts W, Beschta R (1991). Ecological and geomorphological concepts for instream and out-of-channel flow requirements. *Rivers* 2: 198–210.

Hirji R, Davis R (2009). *Environmental Flows in Water Resources Policies, Plans, and Projects: Findings and Recommendations.* Washington, DC: The World Bank.

Hobbs BF, Ludsin SA, Knight RL, Ryan PA, Biberhofer, Ciborowski JJH (2002). Fuzzy cognitive mapping as a tool to define management objectives for complex ecosystems. *Ecological Applications* 12: 1548–1565.

Hogan Z, Moyle P, May B, Vander Zanden J, Baird, I (2004). The imperiled giants of the Mekong: ecologists struggle to understand—and protect—Southeast Asia's large, migratory catfish. *American Scientist* 92: 228–237.

Howell TD, Arthington H, Pusey BJ, Brooks AP, Creese B, Chaseling J (2010). Responses of fish to experimental introduction of structural woody habitat in riffles and pools of the Hunter River, New South Wales, Australia. *Restoration Ecology.* 20: 43–55.

HRF (Hudson River Foundation) (2002). *Harbor Health/Human Health: An Analysis of Environmental Indicators for the NY/NJ Harbor Estuary.* New York, NY: Hudson River Foundation. Available at: www.harborestuary.org/reports/HEP_IndicatorReport02.pdf

Hubert WA, Gordon KM (2007). Great Plains fishes declining or threatened with extirpation in Montana, Wyoming, or Colorado. In *Status, Distribution, and Conservation of Native Freshwater Fishes of Western North America,* Brouder MJ, Scheurer JA (Eds), 3–13. Bethesda, MD: American Fisheries Society.

Hughes DA (Ed) (2004). SPATSIM, an integrating framework for ecological reserve determination and implementation: incorporating water quality and quantity components for rivers. Report No. 1160/1/04. Pretoria, South Africa: Water Research Commission.

Hughes DA, Hannart P (2003). A desktop model used to provide an initial estimate of the ecological instream flow requirements of rivers in South Africa. *Journal of Hydrology* 270: 167–181.

Hughes JM, Schmidt DJ, Finn DS (2009). Genes in streams: using DNA to understand the movement of freshwater fauna and their riverine habitat. *BioScience* 59: 573–583.

Humphreys WF (2006). Aquifers: the ultimate groundwater dependent ecosystems. *Australian Journal of Botany* 54: 115–132.

Humphries P (1996). Aquatic macrophytes, macroinvertebrate associations and water levels in a lowland Tasmanian river. *Hydrobiologia* 321: 219–233.

Humphries P, King AJ and Koehn JD (1999). Fish, flows and floodplains: links between freshwater fishes and their environment in the Murray–Darling River system, Australia. *Environmental Biology of Fishes* 56: 129–151.

Hynes HBN (1975). The stream and its valley. *Verhandlungen des Internationalen Verein Limnologie* 19: 1–15.

ICOLD (International Commission on Large Dams) (2003). *World Register of Dams, 2003.* Paris, France: International Commission on Large Dams.

Illies J, Botosaneanu L (1963). Problèmes et méthodes de la classification et de la zonation écologique des eaux courantes, considérées surtout du point de vue faunistique. *Verhandlungen des Internationalen Verein Limnologie* 12: 1–57 (cited in Thorp et al. 2008).

IPCC (2007). *Climate Change 2007: Synthesis Report; Intergovernmental Panel on Climate Change, Fourth Assessment Report.* Cambridge, UK: Cambridge University Press.

Jackson RB, Carpenter SR, Dahm CN, McKnight DM, Naiman RJ, Postel SL, Running SW (2001). Water in a changing world. *Ecological Applications* 11: 1027–1045.

Jacobson RA (2008). Applications of mesoHABSIM using fish community targets. *River Research and Applications* 24: 434–438.

Jacobson RB, Galat DL (2006). Flow and form in rehabilitation of large-river ecosystems: an example from the Lower Missouri River. *Geomorphology* 77: 249–269.

Jacobson RB, Galat DL (2008). Design of a naturalized flow regime: an example from the Lower Missouri River, USA. *Ecohydrology* 1: 81–104.

Jansson R, Nilsson C, Dynesius M, Andersson E (2000a). Effects of river regulation on river-margin vegetation: a comparison of eight boreal rivers. *Ecological Applications* 10: 203–224.

Jansson R, Nilsson C, Renöfält B (2000b). Fragmentation of riparian floras in rivers with multiple dams. *Ecology* 81: 899–903.

Jassby AD, Kimmerer WJ, Monismith SG, Armor C, Cloern JE, Powell TM, Schubel JR, Vendlinski TJ (1995). Isohaline position as a habitat indicator for estuarine populations. *Ecological Applications* 5: 272–289

Jelks HL, Walsh SJ, Burkhead NM, Contreras-Balderas S, Díaz-Pardo E, Hendrickson DA, Lyons J, Mandrak NE, McCormick F, Nelson JS, Platania SP, Porter BA, Renaud CB, Schmitter-Soto JJ, Taylor EB, Warren ML Jr (2008). Conservation status of imperiled North American freshwater and diadromous fishes. *Fisheries* 33: 372–407.

Jensen FV (1996). *An Introduction to Bayesian Networks.* London, UK: UCL Press.

Jiang X, Arthington A, Changming L (2010). Environmental flow requirements of fish in the lower reach of the Yellow River. *Water International* 35: 381–396.

Johnson BM, Saito L, Anderson MA, Weiss P, Andre M, Fontane DG (2004). Effects of climate and dam operations on reservoir thermal structure. *Journal of Water Resources Planning and Management* 130: 112–122.

Johnson WC (1992). Dams and riparian forests: case study from the upper Missouri River. *Rivers* 3: 229–242.

Jones MJ, Stuart IG (2008). Regulated floodplains: a trap for unwary fish. *Fisheries Management and Ecology* 15: 71–79.

Jorde K, Schneider M, Zoellner F (2000). Analysis of instream habitat quality: preference functions and fuzzy models. In *Stochastic Hydraulics,* Wang H (Ed). Rotterdam, Netherlands: Balkema.

Jowett IG (1989). River Hydraulic and Habitat Simulation, RHYHABSIM Computer Manual. Fisheries Miscellaneous Report 49. Christchurch, New Zealand: New Zealand Ministry of Agriculture and Fisheries.

Jowett IG (1997). Instream flow methods: a comparison of approaches. *Regulated Rivers: Research and Management* 13: 115–127.

Junk WJ, Bayley PB, Sparks RE (1989). The Flood-Pulse Concept in river-floodplain systems. *Canadian Journal of Fisheries and Aquatic Sciences Special Publication* 106: 110–127.

Karim F, Kinsey-Henderson A, Wallace J, Arthington AH, Pearson R (2011). Wetland connectivity during over bank flooding in a tropical floodplain in north Queensland, Australia. *Hydrological Processes.* doi: 10.1002/hyp.8364.

Katopodis C (2003). Case studies of instream flow modelling for fish habitat in Canadian Prairie rivers. *Canadian Water Resources Journal* 28: 199–216.

Kaushal SJ, Likens GE, Jaworski NA, Pace ML, Sides AM, Seekell D, Belt KT, Secor DH, Wingate R (2010). Rising stream and river temperatures in the United States. *Frontiers in Ecology and the Environment* 8: 461–466.

Kelly D, Davey A, James G (2006). "Like a fish out of water": life in a disappearing river. *Water and Atmosphere* 14: 18–19.

Kennard MJ, Olden JD, Arthington AH, Pusey BJ, Poff NL (2007). Multi-scale effects of flow regime and habitat and their interaction on fish assemblage structure in eastern Australia. *Canadian Journal of Fisheries and Aquatic Sciences* 64: 1346–1359.

Kennard MJ, Mackay SJ, Pusey BJ, Olden JD, Marsh N (2010a). Quantifying uncertainty in estimation of hydrologic metrics for ecohydrological studies. *River Research and Applications* 26: 137–156.

Kennard MJ, Pusey BJ, Olden JD, Mackay SJ, Stein JL, Marsh N (2010b). Classification of natural flow regimes in Australia to support environmental flow management. *Freshwater Biology* 55: 171–193.

Kennen JG, Kauffman LJ, Ayers MA, Wolock DM (2008). Use of an integrated flow model to estimate ecologically relevant hydrologic characteristics at stream biomonitoring sites. *Ecological Modelling* 211: 57–76

Kennish MJ (2002). Environmental threats and environmental future of estuaries. *Environmental Conservation* 29: 78–107.

Keyte PA (1994). *Lower Gwydir Wetland Plan of Management, 1994–1997.* Report for the Lower Gwydir Wetland Steering Committee. Sydney, Australia.

Kilgour BW, Neary J, Ming D, Beach D (2005). Preliminary investigations of the use and status of instream-flow-needs methods in Ontario with specific reference to application with hydroelectric developments. *Canadian Manuscript Report of Fisheries and Aquatic Sciences* 2723. Burlington, ON: Fisheries and Oceans Canada.

Kimmerer WJ (2002). Effects of freshwater flow on abundance of estuarine organisms: physical effects or trophic linkages? *Marine Ecology Progress Series* 243: 39–55.

King AJ, Humphries P, Lake PS (2003). Fish recruitment on floodplains: the roles of patterns of flooding and life history characteristics. *Canadian Journal of Fisheries and Aquatic Sciences* 60: 773–786.

King AJ, Ward KA, O'Connor P, Green D (2010). Adaptive management of an environmental watering event to enhance native fish spawning and recruitment. *Freshwater Biology* 55: 17–31.

King EG, Caylor KK (2011). Ecohydrology in practice: strengths, conveniences, and opportunities. *Ecohydrology* 4: 608–612.

King JM, Brown CA (2010). Integrated basin flow assessments: concepts and method development in Africa and South-East Asia. *Freshwater Biology* 55: 127–146.

King JM, Louw MD (1998). Instream flow assessments for regulated rivers in South Africa using the Building Block Methodology. *Aquatic Ecosystem Health and Management* 1: 109–124.

King JM, Pienaar, H (Eds) (2011). Sustainable use of South Africa's inland waters: a situation assessment of resource directed measures 12 years after the 1998 National Water Act. Water Research Commission Report No. TT 491/11. Pretoria, South Africa: Water Research Commission.

King JM, Tharme RE (1994). Assessment of the Instream Flow Incremental Methodology and initial development of Alternative Instream Flow Methodologies for South Africa. Report No. 295/1/94. Pretoria, South Africa: Water Research Commission.

King JM, Cambray JA, Impson DN (1998). Linked effects of dam-released floods and water temperature on spawning of the Clanwilliam yellowfish *Barbus capensis. Hydrobiologia* 384: 245–265.

King JM, Tharme RE, De Villiers M (Eds) (2000). Environmental flow assessments for rivers: manual for the Building Block Methodology. Technology Transfer Report No. TT131/00. Pretoria, South Africa: Water Research Commission.

King JM, Brown CA, Sabet H (2003). A scenario-based holistic approach to environmental flow assessments for rivers. *River Research and Applications* 19: 619–640.

King S, Warburton K (2007). The environmental preferences of three species of Australian freshwater fish in relation to the effects of riparian degradation. *Environmental Biology of Fishes* 78: 307–316.

Kingsford RT (2000). Ecological impacts of dams, water diversions and river management on floodplain wetlands in Australia. *Austral Ecology* 25: 109–127.

Kingsford RT (2011). Conservation management of rivers and wetlands under climate change: a synthesis. *Marine and Freshwater Research* 62: 217–222.

Kingsford RT, Lemly AD, Thompson JR (2006). Impacts of dams, river management and diversions on desert rivers. In *Ecology of Desert Rivers,* Kingsford RT (Ed), 336–345. Melbourne, Australia: Cambridge University Press.

Kingsford RT, Fairweather PG, Geddes MC, Lester RE, Sammut J, Walker KF (2009). *Engineering a Crisis in a Ramsar Wetland: The Coorong, Lower Lakes and Murray Mouth, Australia.* Sydney, Australia: Australian Wetlands and Rivers Centre, University of New South Wales.

Knight JT, Arthington AH, Holder GS, Talbot RB (2012). Conservation biology and management of the endangered Oxleyan pygmy perch *Nannoperca oxleyana* Whitley in Australia. *Endangered Species Research* 17: 169–178.

Koehler CL (1995). Water rights and the public trust doctrine: resolution of the Mono Lake controversy. *Ecological Law Quarterly* 22: 541–590.

Konikow LF, Kendy E (2005). Groundwater depletion: a global problem. *Hydrogeological Journal* 13: 317–320.

Konrad CP, Brasher AMD, May JT (2008). Assessing streamflow characteristics as limiting factors on benthic invertebrate assemblages in streams across the western United States. *Freshwater Biology* 53: 1983–1998.

Korbel KL, Hose GC (2010). A tiered framework for assessing groundwater ecosystem health. *Hydrobiologia* 661: 329–349.

Kotlyakov VM (1991). The Aral Sea basin: a critical environmental zone. *Environment* 33: 4–38.

Kottek M, Grieser J, Beck C, Rudolf B, Rubel F (2006). World map of the Köppen-Geiger climate classification updated. *Meteorologische Zeitschrift* 15: 259–263.

Krapu GL, Facey DE, Fritzell EK, Johnson DH (1984). Habitat use by migrant sandhill cranes in Nebraska. *Journal of Wildlife Management* 48: 407–417 (cited in Poff et al. 1997).

Krause S, Hannah DM, Fleckenstein JH, Heppell CM, Kaeser D, Pickup R, Pinay G, Robertson AL, Wood PJ (2010). Inter-disciplinary perspectives on processes in the hyporheic zone. *Ecohydrology* 4: 481–499.

Krchnak K, Richter B, Thomas G (2009). *Integrating Environmental Flows into Hydropower Dam Planning, Design, and Operations.* World Bank Water Working Notes No. 22. Washington, DC: World Bank Group.

Labbe L, Fausch KD (2000). Dynamics of intermittent stream habitat regulate persistence of a threatened fish at multiple scales. *Ecological Applications* 10: 1774–1791.

Lake PS (2011). *Drought and Aquatic Ecosystems: Effects and Responses.* Chichester, UK: John Wiley and Sons.

Lake PS, Marchant M (1990). Australian upland streams: ecological degradation and possible restoration. *Proceedings of the Ecological Society of Australia* 16: 79–91.

Lamberts D (2006). The Tonle Sap Lake as a productive ecosystem. *International Journal of Water Resources Development* 22: 481–495.

Lamberts D (2008). Little impact, much damage: the consequences of Mekong River flow alterations for the Tonle Sap ecosystem. In *Modern Myths of the Mekong,* Kummu M, Keskinen M, Varis O (Eds), 3–18. Espoo, Finland: Helsinki University of Technology, Water and Development Publications.

Lamouroux N, Souchon Y, Herouin E (1995). Predicting velocity frequency distributions in stream reaches. *Water Resources Research* 31: 2367–2376.

Land and Water Australia (2009). A framework to provide for the assessment of environmental water requirements of groundwater dependent ecosystems. Canberra, Australia: Land and Water Australia.

Larned ST, Datry T, Arscott DB, Tockner T (2010). Emerging concepts in temporary-river ecology. *Freshwater Biology* 55: 717–738.

Leigh C, Sheldon F, Kingsford RT, Arthington AH (2010). Sequential floods drive 'booms' and wetland persistence in dryland rivers: a synthesis. *Marine and Freshwater Research* 61: 896–908.

Leopold LB (1968). *Hydrology for urban land planning: a guidebook on the hydro-*

logic effects of land use. US Geological Survey 554: Reston, VA (cited in Poff et al. 1997).

Le Quesne T, Kendy E, Weston D (2010). *The Implementation Challenge: Taking stock of Government Policies to Protect and Restore Environmental Flows.* WWF-UK and The Nature Conservancy.

Leslie DJ, Ward KA (2002). Murray River environmental flows 2000–2001. *Ecological Management and Restoration* 3: 221–223.

Lessard JL, Hayes DB (2003). Effects of elevated water temperature on fish and macroinvertebrate communities below small dams. *River Research and Applications* 19: 721–732.

Leung GY (1996). Reclamation and Sediment Control in the Middle Yellow River Valley. *Water International* 21: 12–19.

Lévêque C, Balian EV (2005). Conservation of freshwater biodiversity: does the real world meet scientific dreams? *Hydrobiologia* 542: 23–26.

Limburg KE, Hattala KA, Kahnle A (2003). American shad in its native range. *American Fisheries Society Symposium* 35: 125–140.

Linke S, Turak E, Nel J (2011). Freshwater conservation planning: the case for systematic approaches. *Freshwater Biology* 56: 6–20.

Livingston RJ, Niu XF, Lewis FG, Woodsum GC (1997). Freshwater input to a gulf estuary: long-term control of trophic organization. *Ecological Applications* 7: 277–299.

Lloyd N, Quinn G, Thoms M, Arthington A, Gawne B, Humphries P, Walker K (2003). *Does Flow Modification Cause Geomorphological and Ecological Response in Rivers? A Literature Review from an Australian Perspective.* Technical Report 1/2004, Cooperative Research Centre for Freshwater Ecology: Canberra, Australia.

Loneragan NR, Bunn SE (1999). River flows and estuarine ecosystems: implications for coastal fisheries from a review and a case study of the Logan River, southeast Queensland. *Australian Journal of Ecology* 24: 431–440.

Lorenzen K, Enberg K (2002). Density-dependent growth as a key mechanism in the regulation of fish populations: evidence from among-population comparisons. *Proceedings of the Royal Society of London Biological Sciences* 269: 49–54.

Lorenzen K, Smith L, Nguyen Khoa S, Burton M, Garaway C (2007). *Management of Irrigation Development Impacts on Fisheries: Guidance Manual.* Colombo, Sri Lanka: International Water Management Institute; Penang, Malaysia: WorldFish Center; London, UK: Imperial College.

Lotze HK (2010). Historical reconstruction of human-induced changes in U.S. estuaries. *Oceanography and Marine Biology: An Annual Review* 48: 265–336.

Lowe-McConnell RH (1985). *Ecological Studies In Tropical Fish Communities.* Cambridge University Press: London, England.

Lucas MC, Baras E (2001). *Migrations of Freshwater Fishes.* Blackwell Science: Oxford, UK.

Lyon JP, Nicol SJ, Lieschke JA, Ramsey DSL (2009). Does wood type influence the colonisation of this habitat by macroinvertebrates in large lowland rivers? *Marine and Freshwater Research* 60: 384–393.

Lytle DA, Merritt DM (2004). Hydrologic regimes and riparian forests: a structured population model for cottonwood. *Ecology* 85: 2493–2503.

Lytle DA, Poff NL (2004). Adaptation to natural flow regimes. *Trends in Ecology and Evolution* 19: 94–100.

MacKay H (2006). Protection and management of groundwater-dependent ecosystems: emerging challenges and potential approaches for policy and management. *Australian Journal of Botany* 54: 231–237.

Mackay SJ, Arthington AH, Kennard MJ, Pusey BJ (2003). Spatial variation in the distribution and abundance of submersed aquatic macrophytes in an Australian subtropical river. *Aquatic Botany* 77: 169–186.

Mackay SJ, James C, Arthington AH (2010). Macrophytes as indicators of stream condition in the Wet Tropics region, Northern Queensland, Australia. *Ecological Indicators* 10: 330–340.

Magurran AE (2009). Threats to freshwater fish. *Science* 324: 1215–1216.

Maheshwari BL, Walker KF, McMahon TA (1995). Effects of regulation on the flow regime of the River Murray, Australia. *Regulated Rivers* 10: 15–38.

Malan H, Bath A, Day J, Joubert A (2003). A simple flow concentration modeling method for integrating water quality and water quantity in rivers. *Water SA* 29: 305–312.

Malard F, Tockner K, Dole-Olivier MJ, Ward JV (2002). A landscape perspective of surface–subsurface hydrological exchanges in river corridors. *Freshwater Biology* 47: 621–640.

Margules CR, Pressey RL (2000). Systematic conservation planning. *Nature* 405: 243–253.

Marsh N (2003). River Analysis Package: User Guide; Sofware Version V1.0.1. Melbourne, Australia. Cooperative Research Centre for Catchment Hydrology. More recent versions available at: www.toolkit.net.au/Tools/RAP

Martell KA, Foote AL, Cumming SG. (2006). Riparian disturbance due to beavers (*Castor canadensis*) in Alberta's boreal mixedwood forests: implications for forest management. *Ecoscience* 13: 164–171.

Marzliff JM, Ewing K (2008). Restoration of fragmented landscapes for the conservation of birds: a general framework and specific recommendations for urbanizing landscapes. *Urban Ecology* 2008: 739–755.

Maser C, Sedell JR (1994). *From the Forest to the Sea.* St Lucia Press: Delray Beach, Florida.

Matson PA, Parton WJ, Power AG, Swift MJ (1997). Agricultural intensification and ecosystem properties. *Science* 277: 504–509.

Matthews RC Jr, Bao Y (1991). The Texas Method of preliminary instream flow determination. *Rivers* 2: 295–310.

Matthews WJ (1998). *Patterns in Freshwater Fish Ecology.* Chapman and Hall: New York.

Mattson RA (2002). A resource-based framework for establishing freshwater inflow requirements for the Suwannee River Estuary. *Estuaries* 25: 1333–1342.

Mauclaire L, Gibert J (1998). Effects of pumping and floods on groundwater quality: a case study of the Grand Gravier well field (Rhone, France). *Hydrobiologia* 389: 141–151.

Mawdsley J (2011). Design of conservation strategies for climate adaptation. *WIREs Climate Change* 2: 498–515.

Mazzotti FJ, Ostrenko, Smith AT (1981). Effects of the exotic plants *Melaleuca quinquenervia* and *Casuarina equisetifolia* on small mammal population in the eastern Florida Everglades. *Florida Scientist* 44: 65–71.

McCartney M (2007). *Decision Support Systems for Large Dam Planning and Operation in Africa.* IWMI Working Paper 119. Colombo, Sri Lanka: International Water Management Institute.

McCartney M (2009). Living with dams: managing the environmental impacts. *Water Policy* 11 (Suppl. 1): 121–139.

McCosker RO (1998). Methods addressing the flow requirements of wetland, riparian and floodplain vegetation. In *Comparative Evaluation of Environmental Flow Assessment Techniques: Review of Methods,* Arthington AH, Zalucki JM (Eds), 47–65. Occasional Paper No. 27/98. Canberra, Australia: Land and Water Resources Research and Development Corporation.

McCosker RO, Duggin JA (1993). Gingham watercourse management plan. Department of Ecosystem Management Final Report. Armidale, Australia: University of New England (cited in McCosker 1998).

McCully P (2001). *Silenced Rivers: The Ecology and Politics of Large Dams.* Enlarged and updated edition. London: ZED Books.

McDowall RM (2006). Crying wolf, crying foul, or crying shame: alien salmonids and a biodiversity crisis in the southern cool-temperate galaxioid fishes? *Reviews in Fish Biology and Fisheries* 16: 233–422.

McKay J (2005). Water institutional reforms in Australia. *Water Policy* 7: 35–52.

McMahon TA, Finlayson BL (2003). Droughts and anti-droughts: the low flow hydrology of Australian rivers. *Freshwater Biology* 48: 1147–1160.

MDBMC (Murray-Darling Basin Ministerial Council) (1995). An audit of water use in the Murray-Darling Basin. Canberra, Australia: Murray-Darling Basin Ministerial Council.

MEA (Millennium Ecosystem Assessment) (2005). *Ecosystems and Human Well-Being: General Synthesis*. Washington, DC: Island Press.

Medeiros ESF, Arthington AH (2010). Allochthonous and autochthonous carbon sources for fish in floodplain lagoons of an Australian dryland river. *Environmental Biology of Fishes* 90: 1–17.

Merritt DM, Scott ML, Poff NL, Lytle DA (2010). Theory, methods, and tools for determining environmental flows for riparian vegetation: riparian vegetation-flow response guilds. *Freshwater Biology* 55: 206–225.

Meybeck M, Vörösmarty CJ (Eds) (2004).The integrity of river and drainage basin systems: challenges from environmental change. In *Vegetation, Water, Humans and the Climate: A New Perspective on an Interactive System,* Kabat P, Claussen M, Dirmeyer PA, Gash JHC, Bravo de Guenni L, Meybeck M, Pielke Sr. RA, Vörösmarty CJ, Hutjes RWA, Lutkemeier S (Eds), 297–479. Heidelberg, Germany: Springer.

Micklin PP (1988). Desiccation of the Aral Sea: a water management disaster in the Soviet Union. *Science* 241: 1170–1176.

Minckley WL, Meffe GK (1987). Differential selection by flooding in stream-fish communities of the arid American Southwest. In *Community and Evolutionary Ecology of North American Stream Fishes,* Matthews WJ, Heins DC (Eds), 93–104. Norman, OK: University of Oklahoma Press.

Mitsch WJ, Gosselink JG (2007). *Wetlands*. Hoboken, NJ: John Wiley and Sons.

Mitsch WJ, Day JW, Zhang L, Lane R (2005). Nitrate-nitrogen retention in wetlands in the Mississippi River basin. *Ecological Engineering* 24: 267–278.

Molden D (Ed) (2007). *Water for Food, Water for Life*. London, UK: Earthscan; Colombo, Sri Lanka: International Water Management Institute.

Molden D, Oweis T, Steduto P, Bindraban P, Hanjra MA, Kijne J (2010). Improving agricultural water productivity: between optimism and caution. *Agricultural Water Management* 97: 528–535.

Molles MC, Crawford CS, Ellis LM (1995). Effects of an experimental flood on litter dynamics in the Middle Rio Grande riparian ecosystem. *Regulated Rivers: Research and Management* 11: 275–281.

Monk WA, Wood PJ, Hannah DM, Wilson DA (2007). Selection of river flow indices for the assessment of hydroecological change. *River Research and Applications* 23: 113–122.

Montgomery DR (1999). Process domains and the River Continuum Concept. *Journal of the American Water Resources Association* 35: 397–410.

Moore M (2004). Perceptions and interpretations of environmental flows and implications for future water resource management: a survey study. Master's thesis, Department of Water and Environmental Studies, Linköping University, Sweden.

Morrice JA, Valett HM, Dahm CN, Campana ME (1997). Alluvial characteristics, groundwater–surface water exchange and hydrological retention in headwater streams. *Hydrological Processes* 11: 253–267.

Mouton A, Meixner H, Goethals PLM, De Pauw N, Mader H (2007). Concept and application of the usable volume for modelling the physical habitat of riverine organisms. *River Research and Applications* 23: 545–558.

Moyle PB (1986). Fish introductions into North America: patterns and ecological impact. In *Ecology of Biological Invasions of North America and Hawaii*, Mooney HA Drake JA (Eds), 27–43. New York, NY: Springer-Verlag.

Moyle PB, Baltz DM (1985). Microhabitat use by an assemblage of California stream fishes: developing criteria for instream flow determinations. *Transactions of the American Fisheries Society* 114: 695–704.

Moyle PB, Light T (1996a). Biological invasions of fresh water: empirical rules and assembly theory. *Biological Conservation* 78: 149–161.

Moyle PB, Light T (1996b). Fish invasions in California: do abiotic factors determine success? *Ecology* 77: 1666–1670.

MRC (Mekong River Commission) (1995). Agreement on the Cooperation for the Sustainable Development of the Mekong River Basin, 5 April 1995. Chieng Rai, Thailand: Mekong River Commission.

Muir WD, Smith SG, Williams JG, Sandford BP (2001). Survival of juvenile salmonids passing through bypass systems, turbines, and spillways with and without flow deflectors at Snake River dams. *North American Journal of Fisheries Management* 21: 135–146.

Munn MD, Brusven MA (1991). Benthic invertebrate communities in non-regulated and regulated waters of the Clearwater River, Idaho, USA. *Regulated Rivers: Research and Management* 6: 1–11.

Murchie KJ, Hair KPE, Pullen CE, Redpath TD, Stephens HR, Cooke SJ (2008). Fish response to modified flow regimes in regulated rivers: research methods, effects and opportunities. *River Research and Applications* 24: 197–217.

Murray BR, Zeppel MJB, Hose GC, Eamus D (2003). Groundwater dependent ecosystems in Australia: it's more than just water for rivers. *Ecological Management and Restoration* 4: 110–113.

Murray BR, Hose GG, Eamus D, Licari D (2006). Valuation of groundwater-dependent ecosystems: a functional methodology incorporating ecosystem services. *Australian Journal of Botany* 54: 221–229.

Murray-Darling Basin Authority (2011). Proposed basin plan. MDBA Publication No. 192/11. Canberra, Australia: Murray-Darling Basin Authority. Available at: www.mdba.gov.au/draft-basin-plan/draft-basin-plan-for-consultation

Næsje T, Jonsson B, Skurdal J (1995). Spring flood: a primary cue for hatching of river spawning Coregoninae. *Canadian Journal of Fisheries and Aquatic Sciences* 52: 2190–2196.

Nagrodski A, Raby GD, Hasler CT, Taylor MK, Cooke SJ (2012). Fish stranding in freshwater systems: Ssources, consequences, and mitigation. *Environmental Management* 103: 133–141.

Naiman RJ, Décamps H (1997). The ecology of interfaces: riparian zones. *Annual Review of Ecology and Systematics* 28: 621–658.

Naiman RJ, Dudgeon D (2010). Global alteration of freshwaters: influences on human and environmental well-being. *Ecological Research* 26: 865–873.

Naiman RJ, Magnuson JJ, McKnight DM, Stanford JA (1995). *The Freshwater Imperative: A Research Agenda*. Washington, DC: Island Press.

Naiman RJ, Bilby RE, Bisson PA (2000). Riparian ecology and management in the Pacific coastal rain forest. *BioScience* 50: 996–1011.

Naiman RJ, Bunn SE, Nilsson C, Petts GE, Pinay G, Thompson LC (2002). Legitimizing fluvial ecosystems as users of water: an overview. *Environmental Management* 30: 455–467.

Naiman RJ, Décamps H, McClain MC (2005). *Riparia*. San Diego, CA: Academic Press.

Naiman RJ, Latterell JJ, Pettit NE, Olden JD (2008). Flow variability and the vitality of river systems. *Comptes Rendus Geoscience* 340: 629–643.

National Water Act (1998). National Water Act, Act No. 36 of 1998, Republic of South Africa. Available at: ftp://ftp.hst.org.za/pubs/govdocs/acts/1998/act36.pdf

Navarro RS, Stewardson M, Breil P, García de Jalón D,Eisele M. (2007). Hydrological impacts affecting endangered fish species: a Spanish case study. *River Research and Applications* 23: 511–523.

Nel J, Turak E, Link S, Brown C (2011). Integration of environmental flow assessment and freshwater conservation planning: a new era in catchment management. *Marine and Freshwater Research* 62: 290–299.

Nelson K, Palmer MA, Pizzuto J, Moglen G, Angermeier P, Hilderbrand R, Dettinger M, Hayhoe K (2009). Forecasting the combined effects of urbanization and climate change on stream ecosystems: from impacts to management options. *Journal of Applied Ecology* 46: 154–163.

Nesler TP, Muth RT, Wasowicz AF (1988). Evidence for baseline flow spikes as spawning cues for Colorado squawfish in the Yampa River, Colorado. *Transactions of the American Fisheries Society Symposium* 5: 68–79.

Nestler J, Latka D, Schneider T (1998). Using RCHARC to evaluate large river restoration alternatives (abstract). In *Engineering Approaches to Ecosystem Restoration,* Proceedings of Wetlands Engineering and River Restoration Conference. Reston, VA: American Society of Civil Engineers.

Newson M (1994). *Hydrology and the River Environment*. Oxford, UK: Clarendon.

Nichols FH, Cloern JE, Luoma SN, Peterson, DH (1986). The modification of an estuary. *Science* 231: 567–648.

Nielsen, DL, Brock, MA, Rees, GN, and Baldwin DS (2003). The effect of increasing salinity on freshwater ecosystems in Australia. *Australian Journal of Botany* 51: 655–665.

Nilsson C, Renöfält BM (2008). Linking flow regime and water quality in rivers: a challenge to adaptive catchment management. *Ecology and Society* 13: 18–38.

Nilsson C, Svedmark M (2002). Basic principles and ecological consequences of changing water regimes: riparian plant communities. *Environmental Management* 30: 468–480.

Nilsson C, Reidy CA, Dynesius M, Revenga C (2005). Fragmentation and flow regulation of the world's large river systems. *Science* 308: 405–408.

Nilsson C, Brown RL, Jansson R, Merritt DM (2010). The role of hydrochory in structuring riparian and wetland vegetation. *Biological Reviews* 85: 837–858.

Nixon SW (2003). Replacing the Nile: are anthropogenic nutrients providing the fertility once brought to the Mediterranean by a great river? *Ambio* 32: 30–39.

Northcote TG (2010). Controls for trout and char migratory/resident behaviour mainly in stream systems above and below waterfalls/barriers: a multi-decadal and broad geographical review. *Ecology of Freshwater Fish* 19: 487–509.

NSW (New South Wales) Department of Primary Industries, Fishing and Aquaculture (2012). Cold water pollution. Cronulla, NSW, Australia: NSW Department of Primary Industries. Available at: www.dpi.nsw.gov.au/fisheries/habitat/threats/cold-water-pollution

NWC (National Water Commission) (2011). The National Water Initiative—securing Australia's water future: 2011 assessment. Canberra, Australia: National Water Commission. Available at: www.nwc.gov.au/__data/assets/pdf_file/0018/8244/2011-BiennialAssessment-full_report.pdf

Ogden JC, Davis SM, Jacobs KJ, Barnes T, Fling HE (2005). The use of conceptual ecological models to guide ecosystem restoration in South Florida. *Wetlands* 25: 795–809.

Ogden RW, Thoms MC, Levings P (2002). Nutrient limitation of plant growth on the floodplain of the Narran River, Australia: growth experiments and a pilot soil survey. *Hydrobiologia* 489: 277–285.

Ohio DNR (Ohio Department of Natural Resources) (n.d.). *Removal of Lowhead Dams*. Video. Available at: www.dnr.state.oh.us/tabid/21463/Default.aspx

O'Keeffe JH, Hughes DA (2002). The Flow Stress Response Method for analysing flow modifications: applications and developments. In *Proceedings of International Conference on Environmental Flows for Rivers*. Cape Town, South Africa: University of Cape Town.

Olden JD, Naiman RJ (2010). Broadening the science of environmental flows: managing riverine thermal regimes for ecosystem integrity. *Freshwater Biology* 55: 86–107.

Olden JD, Poff NL (2003). Redundancy and the choice of hydrological indices for characterising streamflow regimes. *River Research and Applications* 19: 101–121.

Olden JD, Poff NL, Bestgen KR (2006). Life-history strategies predict fish invasions and extirpations in the Colorado River basin. *Ecological Monographs* 76: 25–40.

Olden JD, Lawler JJ, Poff NL (2008). Machine learning methods without tears: a primer for ecologists. *Quarterly Review of Biology* 83: 171–93.

Olden JD, Kennard MJ, Lawler JJ, Poff NL (2011). Challenges and opportunities in implementing managed relocation for conservation of freshwater species. *Conservation Biology* 25: 40–47.

Olden JD, Kennard MJ, Pusey BJ (2011). A framework for hydrologic classification with a review of methodologies and applications in ecohydrology. *Ecohydrology* doi: 10.1002/eco.251

Olsen M, Boegh E, Pedersen S, Pederson MF (2009). Impact of groundwater abstraction on physical habitat of brown trout *(Salmo trutta)* in a small Danish stream. *Hydrological Research* 40: 394–405.

Orlins JJ, Gulliver JS (2000). Dissolved gas supersaturation downstream of a spillway, II: computational model. *Journal of Hydraulic Research* 38: 151–159 (cited in Ran et al. 2009).

Ormerod SJ, Dobson M, Hildrew AG, Townsend CR (2010). Multiple stressors in freshwater ecosystems. *Freshwater Biology* 55 (Suppl. 1): 1–4.

Orth RJ, Carruthers TJB, Dennison WC, Duarte CM, Fourqurean JW, Heck KL Jr, Hughes AR, Kendrick GA, Kenworthy WJ, Olyarnik S, Short FT, Waycott M, Williams SL (2006). A global crisis for seagrass ecosystems. *BioScience* 56: 987–996.

Overton IC (2005). Modelling floodplain inundation on a regulated river: integrating GIS, remote sensing and hydrological models. *River Research and Applications* 21: 991–1001.

Overton IC, Jolly ID, Slavich PB, Lewis MM, Walker GR (2006). Modelling vegetation health from the interaction of saline groundwater and flooding on the Chowilla floodplain, South Australia. *Australian Journal of Botany* 54: 207–220.

Palmer MA, Bernhardt ES, Allan JD, Lake PS, Alexander G, Brooks S, Carr J, Clayton S, Dahm C, Follstad Shah J, Galat DJ, Gloss S, Goodwin P, Hart DH, Hassett B, Jenkinson R, Kondolf GM, Lave R, Meyer JL, O'Donnell TK, Pagano L, Srivastava P, Sudduth E (2005). Standards for ecologically successful river restoration. *Journal of Applied Ecology* 42: 208–217.

Palmer MA, Reidy-Liermann C, Nilsson C, Florke M, Alcamo J, Lake PS, Bond N (2008). Climate change and the world's river basins: anticipating management options. *Frontiers in Ecology and the Environment* 6: 81–89.

Palmer MA, Lettenmaier DP, Poff NL, Postel SL, Richter B, Warner R (2009). Climate change and river ecosystems: protection and adaptation options. *Environmental Management* 44: 1053–1068.

Palmer RW, O'Keeffe JH (1989). Temperature characteristics of an impounded river. *Archiv für Hydrobiologie* 116: 471–485.

Parasiewicz P (2001). MesoHABSIM: A concept for application of instream flow models in river restoration planning. *Fisheries* 26: 6–13.

Parasiewicz P (2007). The mesoHABSIM model revisited. *River Research and Applications* 23: 893–903.

Paton DC, Rogers DJ, Hill BM, Bailey CP, Ziembicki M (2009). Temporal changes to spatially-stratified waterbird communities of the Coorong, South Australia: implications for the management of heterogeneous wetlands. *Animal Conservation* 12: 408–417.

Payne TR (2003). The concept of weighted usable area. IFIM Users Workshop, 1–5 June 2003, Fort Collins, CO.

Peake P, Fitzsimons J, Frood D, Mitchell M, Withers N, White M, Webster R (2011). A new approach to determining environmental flow requirements: sustaining the natural values of floodplains of the southern Murray-Darling Basin. *Ecological Management and Restoration* 12: 128–137.

Pearce F (2007). *When the Rivers Run Dry: What Happens When Our Water Runs Out?* London, UK: Transworld Publishers.

Pearlstine L, McKellar H, Kitchens W (1985). Modelling the impacts of a river diversion on bottomland forest communities in the Santee River floodplain, South Carolina. *Ecological Modelling* 29: 283–302 (cited in Merritt et al. 2010).

Peel MC, Finlayson BL, McMahon TA (2007). Updated world map of the Köppen-Geiger climate classification. *Hydrology and Earth System Sciences* 11: 1633–1644.

Peterson BJ, Wollheim WH, Mulholland PJ, Webster JR, Meyer JL, Tank JL, Marti E, Bowden WB, Valett HM, Hershey AE, McDowell WH, Dodds WK, Hamilton SK, Gregory S, Morrall DJ (2001). Control of nitrogen export from watersheds by headwater streams. *Science* 292: 86–90.

Petrosky CE, Schaller HA (2010). Influence of river conditions during seaward migration and ocean conditions on survival rates of Snake River chinook salmon and steelhead. *Ecology of Freshwater Fish* 19: 520–536.

Petts GE (1989). Perspectives for ecological management of regulated rivers. In *Alternatives in Regulated River Management,* Gore JA, Petts GE (Eds), 3–24. Boca Raton, FL: CRC Press.

Petts GE, Amoros C (1996). *Fluvial Hydrosystems.* London, UK: Chapman and Hall.

Petts GE, Calow P (1996). *River Flows and Channel Forms.* Oxford, UK: Blackwell Science.

Petts GE, Gurnell (2005). Dams and geomorphology: research progress and future directions. *Geomorphology* 71: 27–47.

Petts GE, Moller H, Roux AL (Eds) (1989). *Historical Change of Large Alluvial Rivers: Western Europe.* Chichester, UK: John Wiley and Sons.

Petts GE, Bickerton MA, Crawford C, Lerner DN, Evans D (1999). Flow management to sustain groundwater-dominated stream ecosystems. *Hydrological Processes* 13: 497–513.

Petts GE, Morales Y, Sadler J (2006). Linking hydrology and biology to assess the water needs of river ecosystems. *Hydrological Processes* 20: 2247–2251.

Phillips PJ (1972). *River Boat Days*. Melbourne, Australia: Lansdowne Press.

Phillips W, Muller K (2006). Ecological character of the Coorong, Lakes Alexandrina and Albert Wetland of International Importance. Adelaide, Australia: Department for Environment and Heritage.

Pierson WL, Bishop K, Van Senden D, Horton PR, Adamantidis CA (2002). Environmental water requirements to maintain estuarine processes. Environmental Flows Initiative Technical Report No. 3. Canberra, Australia: Commonwealth of Australia.

Pinay G, Clément JC, Naiman RJ (2002). Basic principles and ecological consequences of changing water regimes on nitrogen cycling in fluvial system. *Environmental Management* 30: 481–491.

Pizzuto J (2002). Effects of dam removal on river form and process. *BioScience* 52: 683–691 (cited in Poff and Hart 2002).

Poff NL (1996). A hydrogeography of unregulated streams in the United States and an examination of scale-dependence in some hydrological descriptors. *Freshwater Biology* 36: 71–91.

Poff NL (1997). Landscape filters and species traits: towards mechanistic understanding and prediction in stream ecology. *Journal of the North American Benthological Society* 16: 391–409.

Poff NL, Hart DD (2002). How dams vary and why it matters for the emerging science of dam removal. *BioScience* 52: 659–738.

Poff NL, Ward JV (1990). Physical habitat template of lotic systems: recovery in the context of historical patterns of spatiotemporal heterogeneity. *Environmental Management* 14: 629–645.

Poff NL, Zimmerman JK (2010). Ecological impacts of altered flow regimes: a meta–analysis to inform environmental flow management. *Freshwater Biology* 55: 194–205.

Poff NL, Allan JD, Bain MB, Karr JR, Prestegaard KL, Richter BD, Sparks RE, Stromberg JC (1997). The natural flow regime: a paradigm for river conservation and restoration. *BioScience* 47: 769–784.

Poff NL, Allan JD, Palmer MA, Hart DD, Richter BD, Arthington AH, Rogers KH, Meyer JL and Stanford JA (2003). River flows and water wars: emerging science for environmental decision making. *Frontiers in Ecology and the Environment* 1: 298–306.

Poff NL, Bledsoe BP, Cuhaciyan CO (2006a). Hydrologic variation with land use across the contiguous United States: geomorphic and ecological consequences for stream ecosystems. *Geomorphology* 79: 264–285.

Poff NL, Olden JD, Vieira NKM, Finn DS, Simmons MP, Kondratieff BC (2006b). Functional trait niches of North American lotic insects: trait-based ecological applications in light of phylogenetic relationships. *Journal of the North American Benthological Society* 25: 730–755.

Poff NL, Richter BD, Arthington AH, Bunn SE, Naiman RJ, Kendy E, Acreman M, Apse C, Bledsoe BP, Freeman MC, Henriksen J, Jacobson RB, Kennen JG, Merritt DM, O'Keeffe JH, Olden JD, Rogers K, Tharme RE, Warne A (2010). The ecological limits of hydrologic alteration (ELOHA): a new framework for developing regional environmental flow standards. *Freshwater Biology* 55: 147–170.

Ponce VM (1995). *Hydrologic and Environmental Impact of the Paran and Paraguay Waterway on the Pantanal of Mato Grosso, Brazil: A Reference Study.* San Diego, CA: San Diego State University.

Poole GC (2002). Fluvial landscape ecology: addressing uniqueness within the river discontinuum. *Freshwater Biology* 47: 641–660.

Possingham HP, Ball IR, Andelman S (2000) Mathematical methods for identifying representative reserve networks. In *Quantitative Methods for Conservation Biology,* Ferson S, Burgman M (Eds), 291–305. New York, NY: Springer-Verlag.

Postel S, Richter B (2003). *Rivers for Life: Managing Water for People and Nature.* Washington, DC: Island Press.

Postel SL, Daily GC, Ehrlich PR (1996). Human appropriation of renewable fresh water. *Science* 271: 785–788.

Powell GL, Matsumoto J, Brock DA (2002). Methods for determining minimum freshwater inflow needs of Texas bays and estuaries. *Estuaries* 25: 1262–1274.

Power G, Brown RS, Imhof JG (1999). Groundwater and fish: insights from northern North America. *Hydrological Processes* 13: 401–422.

Power ME, Sun A, Parker G, Dietrich WE, Wootton JT (1995). Hydraulic food-chain models. *BioScience* 45: 159–167.

Preece RM, Jones HA (2002). The effect of Keepit Dam on the temperature regime of the Namoi River, Australia. *River Research and Applications* 18: 397–414.

Pringle CM (2001). Hydrologic connectivity and the management of biological reserves: a global perspective. *Ecological Applications* 11: 981–998.

Pringle CM, Scatena FN (1999). Freshwater resource development: case studies from Puerto Rico and Costa Rica. In *Managed Ecosystems: The Mesoamerican Experience,* Hatch LU, Swisher ME (Eds), 114–121. New York, NY: Oxford University Press.

Pringle CM, Naiman RJ, Bretschko G, Karr JR, Oswood MW, Webster JR, Welcomme RL, Winterbourn MJ (1988). Patch dynamics in lotic systems: the stream as a mosaic. *Journal of the North American Benthological Society* 7: 503–524.

Puckridge JT, Sheldon, F, Walker KF, Boulton AJ (1998). Flow variability and the ecology of large rivers. *Marine and Freshwater Research* 49: 55–72. Available at: www.publish.csiro.au/nid/126/paper/MF94161.htm

Pusey BJ (1998). Methods addressing the flow requirements of fish. In *Comparative Evaluation of Environmental Flow Assessment Techniques: Review of Methods,* Arthington AH, Zalucki JM (Eds), 66–105. Occasional Paper No. 27/98. Canberra, Australia: Land and Water Resources Research and Development Corporation.

Pusey BJ, Arthington AH (2003). Importance of the riparian zone to the conservation and management of freshwater fish: a review. *Marine and Freshwater Research* 54: 1–16.

Pusey BJ, Storey AW, Davies PM, Edward DHD (1989). Spatial and temporal variation in fish communities in two south-western Australian river systems. *Journal of the Royal Society of Western Australia* 71: 69–75.

Pusey BJ, Arthington AH, Read MG (1993). Spatial and temporal variation in fish assemblage structure in the Mary River, south-east Queensland: the influence of habitat structure. *Environmental Biology of Fishes* 37: 355–380.

Pusey BJ, Kennard MJ, Arthington AH (2000). Discharge variability and the development of predictive models relating stream fish assemblage structure to habitat in north–eastern Australia. *Ecology of Freshwater Fish* 9: 30–50.

Pusey BJ, Kennard MJ, Arthington AH (2004). *Freshwater Fishes of North-Eastern Australia.* Melbourne, Australia: CSIRO Publishing.

Pusey BJ, Kennard M, Hutchinson M, Sheldon F (2009). Ecohydrological classification of Australia: a tool for science and management. Technical Report. Canberra, Australia: Land and Water Australia.

Rabalais NN, Turner RE, Díaz RJ, Justić D (2009). Global change and eutrophication of coastal waters. *ICES Journal of Marine Science* 66: 1528–1537.

Ramsar Convention (2005). A Conceptual Framework for the Wise Use of Wetlands and the Maintenance of Their Ecological Character. Resolution IX.1 Annex A. Available at: www.ramsar.org/lib.lib_handbooks2006_e.htm

Ramsar Convention Secretariat (2010). Ramsar Handbooks for the Wise Use of Wetlands, 4th ed. Available at: www.ramsar.org/cda/en/ramsar-pubs-handbooks/main/ramsar/1-30-33_4000_0__

Ran LI, Jia LI, KeFeng LI, Yun D, JingJie F (2009). Prediction for supersaturated total dissolved gas in high-dam hydropower projects. *Science in China Series E: Technological Sciences* 52: 3661–3667.

Reckhow KH (1999). Water quality prediction and probability network models. *Canadian Journal of Fisheries and Aquatic Sciences* 56: 1150–1158.

Reed MS (2008). Stakeholder participation for environmental management: a literature review. *Biological Conservation* 41: 2417–2431.

Reguero MA, Marenssi SA, Santillana SN (2002). Antarctic Peninsula and South America (Patagonia) Paleogene terrestrial faunas and environments: biogeographic relationships. *Palaeogeography, Palaeoclimatology, Palaeoecology* 179: 189–210.

Reidy Liermann CA, Olden JD, Beechie TJ, Kennard MJ, Skidmore PB, Konrad CP, Imaki H (2011). Hydrogeomorphic classification of Washington State rivers to support emerging environmental flow management strategies. *River Research and Applications*. doi: 10.1002/rra.1541

Renöfält BM, Jansson R, Nilsson C (2010). Effects of hydropower generation and opportunities for environmental flow management in Swedish riverine ecosystems. *Freshwater Biology* 55: 49–67.

Reyes-Gavilan FG, Garrido R, Nicieza AG, Toledo MM, Brana F (1996). Fish community variation along physical gradients in short streams of northern Spain and the disruptive effect of dams. *Hydrobiologia* 321: 155–163.

Richardson BA (1986). Evaluation of instream flow methodologies for freshwater fish in New South Wales. In *Stream Protection: The Management of Rivers for Instream Uses,* Campbell IC (Ed), 143–167. Melbourne, Australia: Chisholm Institute of Technology, Water Studies Centre.

Richter BD (2010). Re-thinking environmental flows: from allocations and reserves to sustainability boundaries. *River Research and Applications* 26: 1052–1063.

Richter BD, Thomas GA (2007). Restoring environmental flows by modifying dam operations. *Ecology and Society* 12: 12. Available at: www.ecologyandsociety.org/vol12/iss1/art12/

Richter BD, Baumgartner JV, Powell J, Braun DP (1996). A method for assessing hydrologic alteration within ecosystems. *Conservation Biology* 10: 1–12.

Richter BD, Baumgartner JV, Wigington R, Braun DP (1997). How much water does a river need? *Freshwater Biology* 37: 231–249.

Richter BD, Mathews R, Harrison DL, Wigington R (2003). Ecologically sustainable water management: managing river flows for ecological integrity. *Ecological Applications* 13: 206–224.

Richter BD, Warner AT, Meyer, JL, Lutz K (2006). A collaborative and adaptive process for developing environmental flow recommendations. *River Research and Applications* 22: 297–318.

Richter BD, Postel S, Revenga C, Scudder T, Lehner B, Churchill A, Chow M (2010). Lost in development's shadow: the downstream human consequences of dams. *Water Alternatives* 3: 14–42.

Rieman BE, McIntyre JD (1995). Occurrence of bull trout in naturally fragmented habitat patches of varied size. *Transactions of the American Fisheries Society* 124: 285–296.

Riis T, Biggs BJF (2001). Distribution of macrophytes in New Zealand streams and lakes in relation to disturbance frequency and resource supply: a synthesis and conceptual model. *New Zealand Journal of Marine and Freshwater Research* 35: 255–267.

Ritche S (2003). *Management Cues: State of the Estuary; CALFED and S.F. Estuary Project, 2001 Conference and 2002 Report*. Sacramento, CA: CALFED Science Program. Available at: www-csgc.ucsd.edu/POSTAWARD/POSTAWD_PDF/soemgmtcues.pdf

Roberts J, Young WJ, Marston F (2000). Estimating the water requirements for plants of floodplain wetlands: a guide. Report No. 99/60. Canberra, Australia: CSIRO Land and Water.

Roberts T (2001). On the river of no returns: Thailand's Pak Mun Dam and its fish ladder. *Natural History Bulletin of the Siam Society* 49: 189–230.

Robins JB, Halliday IA, Staunton-Smith J, Mayer DG, Sellin MJ (2005). Freshwater-flow requirements of estuarine fisheries in tropical Australia: a review of the state of knowledge and application of a suggested approach. *Marine and Freshwater Research* 56: 343–360.

Robins J, Mayer D, Staunton-Smith J, Halliday I, Sawynok B, Sellin M (2006). Variable growth rates of the tropical estuarine fish barramundi *Lates calcarifer* (Bloch) under different freshwater flow conditions. *Journal of Fish Biology* 69: 379–391.

Rodriguez MA, Lewis WM Jr (1997). Structure of fish assemblages along environmental gradients in floodplain lakes of the Orinoco River. *Ecological Monographs* 67: 109–128.

Rogers KH (2006).The real river management challenge: integrating scientists, stakeholders and service agencies. *River Research and Applications* 22: 269–280.

Rolls RJ, Wilson GG (2010). Spatial and temporal patterns in fish assemblages following an artificially extended floodplain inundation event, northern Murray-Darling Basin, Australia. *Environmental Management* 45: 822-833.

Rood SB, Mahoney JM (1990). Collapse of riparian poplar forests downstream from dams in western prairies: probable causes and prospects for mitigation. *Environmental Management* 14: 451–464.

Rood SB, Samuelson GM, Braatne JH, Gourley CR, Hughes FMR, Mahoney JM (2005). Managing river flows to restore floodplain forests. *Frontiers in Ecology and the Environment* 3: 193–201.

Rørslett B, Mjelde M, Johansen SW (1989). Effects of hydropower development on aquatic macrophytes in Norwegian rivers: present state of knowledge and some case studies. *Regulated Rivers: Research and Management* 3: 19–28.

Rosenfeld JS, Hatfield T (2006). Information needs for assessing critical habitat of freshwater fish. *Canadian Journal of Fisheries and Aquatic Sciences* 63: 683–698.

Ruhl JB, Salzman J (2006). Ecosystem services and the public trust doctrine: working change from within. *Southeastern Environmental Law Journal* 15: 223–239.

Rutherford DA, Kelso WE, Bryan CF, Constant GC (1995). Influence of physicochemical characteristics on annual growth increments of four fishes from the Lower Mississippi River. *Transactions of the American Fisheries Society* 124: 687–697.

Ryder DS, Tomlinson M, Gawne B, Likens GE (2010). Defining and using "best available science": a policy conundrum for the management of aquatic ecosystems. *Marine and Freshwater Research* 61: 821–828.

Sanborn SC, Bledsoe BP (2006). Predicting streamflow regime metrics for ungauged streams in Colorado, Washington, and Oregon. *Journal of Hydrology* 325: 241–261.

Sanderson EW, Jaiteh M, Levy MA, Redford KH, Wannebo AV, Woolmer G (2002). The human footprint and the last of the wild. *BioScience* 52: 891–903.

Sand-Jensen K, Madsen TV (1992). Patch dynamics of the stream macrophyte, *Callitriche cophocarpa*. *Freshwater Biology* 27: 277–282.

Santoul F, Figuerola J, Mastrorillo S, Céréghino R (2005). Patterns of rare fish and aquatic insects in a southwestern French river catchment in relation to simple physical variables. *Ecography* 28: 307–314.

Scheffer M, Carpenter SR, Foley J, Folke C, Walker BH (2001). Catastrophic shifts in ecosystems. *Nature* 413: 591–596.

Schellnhuber HJ (2009). Tipping elements in earth systems Special Feature. *Proceedings of the National Academy of Sciences* 106: 20561–20621.

Scholz M (2007). Expert system outline for the classification of sustainable flood retention basins (SFRBs). *Civil Engineering and Environmental Systems* 24: 193–209.

Schwarz HE, Emel J, Dickens WJ, Rogers P, Thompson J (1990). Water quality and flows. In *The Earth as Transformed by Human Action,* Turner BL, Clark WC, Kates RW, Richards JF, Mathews JT, Meyer WB (Eds), 253–270. Cambridge, UK: Cambridge University Press.

Scruton DA, Katopodis C, Pope G, Smith H (2004). Flow modification assessment methods related to fish, fish habitat, and hydroelectric development: a review of the state of the science, knowledge gaps, and research priorities. Report for Fisheries and Oceans Canada (DFO) and the Canadian Electricity Association (CEA) (cited in Kilgour et al. 2005).

Sculthorpe CD (1967). *The Biology of Vascular Plants.* Arnold: London.

Sedell JR, Ritchie JE, Swanson FJ (1989). The River Continuum Concept: a basis for expected ecosystem behaviour of very large rivers. *Canadian Journal of Fisheries and Aquatic Sciences* 106: 49–55.

Semeniuk CA, Semeniuk V (1995). A geomorphic approach to global classification for inland wetlands. *Plant Ecology* 118: 103–124.

Shafroth PB, Wilcox AC, Lytle DA, Hickey JT Andersen DC, Beauchamp VB, Hautzinger A, McMullen LE, Warner A (2010). Ecosystem effects of environmental flows: modelling and experimental floods in a dryland river. *Freshwater Biology* 55: 68–85.

Shaikh M, Green D, Cross H (2001). A remote sensing approach to determine the environmental flows for wetlands of the Lower Darling River, New South Wales, Australia. *International Journal of Remote Sensing* 22: 1737–1751.

Sheldon F, Bunn SE, Hughes JM, Arthington AH, Balcombe SR, Fellows CS (2010). Ecological roles and threats to aquatic refugia in arid landscapes: dryland river waterholes. *Marine and Freshwater Research* 61: 885–895.

Sheng Y, Gong P, Xiao Q (2001). Quantitative dynamic flood monitoring with NOAA AVHRR. *International Journal of Remote Sensing* 22: 1709–1724.

Sherman B, Todd CR, Koehn JD, Ryan T (2007). Modelling the impact and potential mitigation of cold water pollution on Murray cod populations downstream of Hume Dam, Australia. *River Research and Applications* 23: 377–389.

Shields FD, Simon A, Steffen LJ (2000). Reservoir effects on downstream river channel migration. *Environmental Conservation* 27: 54–66.

Shuman JR (1995). Environmental considerations for assessing dam removal alternatives for river restoration. *Regulated Rivers* 11: 249–261.

Sidle JG, Carlson DE, Kirsch EM, Dinan JJ (1992). Flooding mortality and habitat renewal for least terns and piping plovers. *Colonial Waterbirds* 15: 132–136 (cited in Poff et al. 1997).

Simon A, Rinaldi M (2006). Disturbance, stream incision, and channel evolution: The roles of excess transport capacity and boundary materials in controlling channel response. *Geomorphology* 79: 361–383.

Skelton PH (1986). Fish of the Orange-Vaal system. In *The Ecology of River Systems*, Davies BR, Walker KF (Eds), 353–374. Dordrecht, Netherlands: Dr W. Junk, Publishers.

Sklar FH, Browder JA (1998). Coastal environmental impacts brought about by alterations to freshwater inflow in the Gulf of Mexico. *Environmental Management* 22: 547–562.

Smakhtin VU, Anputhas M (2006). *An Assessment of Environmental Flow Requirements of Indian River Basins.* IWMI Research Report 107. Colombo, Sri Lanka: International Water Management Institute.

Smart MM, Lubinski KS, Schnick RA (Eds) (1986). *Ecological Perspectives of the Upper Mississippi River.* Dordrecht, Netherlands: Dr W. Junk Publishers.

Smith VH, Schindler DW (2009). Eutrophication science: where do we go from here? *Trends in Ecology and Evolution* 24: 201–207.

Snelder TH, Biggs BJF (2002). Multi-scale river environment classification for water resources management. *Journal of the American Water Resources Association* 38: 1225–1240.

Sobrino I, Silva L, Bellido JM, Ramos F (2002). Rainfall, river discharges and sea temperature as factors affecting abundance of two coastal benthic cephalopod species in the Gulf of Cádiz (SW Spain). *Bulletin of Marine Science* 71: 851–865.

Song BY, Yang J (2003). Discussion on ecological use of water research. *Journal of Natural Resources* 18: 617–625.

Soulsby C, Malcolm IA, Tetzlaff D, Youngson AF (2009). Seasonal and inter-annual variability in hyporheic water quality revealed by continuous monitoring in a salmon spawning stream. *River Research and Applications* 25: 1304–1319.

Sowden TK, Power G (1985). Prediction of rainbow trout embryo survival in relation to groundwater seepage and particle size of spawning substrates. *Transactions of the American Fisheries Society* 114: 804–812.

Sparks RE (1995). Need for ecosystem management of large rivers and floodplains. *BioScience* 45: 168–182.

Stalnaker CB, Arnette SC (Eds) (1976). *Methodologies for the Determination of Stream Resource Requirements: An Assessment.* Logan, UT: Utah State University.

Stalnaker CB, Lamb BL, Henriksen J, Bovee K, Bartholow J (1995). The Instream Flow Incremental Methodology: a primer for IFIM. Biological Report 29. Fort Collins, CO: US Department of the Interior, National Biological Service.

Stanford JA, Ward JV (1986a). The Colorado River system. In *The Ecology of River Systems,* Davies BR, Walker KF (Eds), 353–374. Dordrecht, Netherlands: Dr W. Junk Publishers.

Stanford JA, Ward JV (1986b). Fish of the Colorado system. In: *The Ecology of River Systems,* Davies BR, Walker KF (Eds), 385–402. Dordrecht, Netherlands: Dr W. Junk Publishers.

Stanford JA, Ward JV (1993). An ecosystem perspective of alluvial rivers: connectivity and the hyporheic corridor. *Journal of the North American Benthological Society* 12: 48–60.

Stanford JA, Ward JV, Liss WJ, Frissell CA, Williams RN, Lichatowich JA, Coutant CC (1996). A general protocol for restoration of regulated rivers. *Regulated Rivers: Research and Management* 12: 391–413.

Stanley EH, Doyle MW (2002). A geomorphic perspective on nutrient retention following dam removal. *BioScience* 52: 693–701.

Stanley EH, Doyle MW (2003). Trading off: the ecological effects of dam removal. *Frontiers in Ecology and the Environment* 1: 15–22.

Statzner B, Gore JA, Resh VH (1988). Hydraulic stream ecology: observed patterns and potential applications. *Journal of the North American Benthological Society* 7: 307–360.

Staunton-Smith J, Robins JB, Mayer DG, Sellin MJ, Halliday IA (2004). Does the quantity and timing of freshwater flowing into a dry tropical estuary affect year-class strength of barramundi *(Lates calcarifer)? Marine and Freshwater Research* 55: 787–797.

Steube C, Richter S, Griebler C (2009). First attempts towards an integrative concept for the ecological assessment of groundwater ecosystems. *Hydrogeology Journal* 1: 23–35.

Stewardson MJ, Cottingham P (2002). A demonstration of the Flow Events

Method: environmental flow requirements of the Broken River. *Australian Journal of Water Resources* 5: 33–48.

Stewardson MJ, Gippel CJ (2003). Incorporating flow variability into environmental flow regimes using the Flow Events Method. *River Research and Applications* 19: 459–472.

Stewardson MJ, Howes E (2002). The number of channel cross-sections required for representing longitudinal hydraulic variability of stream reaches. In *Proceedings of the Hydrology and Water Resources Symposium* (CD ROM). Melbourne, Australia: Institution of Engineers Australia.

Stewart-Koster B, Kennard MJ, Harch BD, Sheldon F, Arthington AH, Pusey BJ (2007). Partitioning the variation in stream fish assemblages within a spatio-temporal hierarchy. *Marine and Freshwater Research* 58: 675–686.

Stewart-Koster B, Bunn SE, Mackay SJ, Poff NL, Naiman RJ, Lake PS (2010). The use of Bayesian networks to guide investments in flow and catchment restoration for impaired river ecosystems. *Freshwater Biology* 55: 243–260.

Stoch F, Artheau M, Brancelj A, Galassi DMP, Malard F (2009). Biodiversity indicators in European ground waters: towards a predictive model of stygobiotic species richness. *Freshwater Biology* 454: 745–755

Strayer DL (2008). *Freshwater Mussel Ecology: A Multifactor Approach to Distribution and Abundance.* Berkeley, CA: University of California Press.

Strayer DL (2010). Alien species in fresh waters: ecological effects, interactions with other stressors, and prospects for the future. *Freshwater Biology* 55 (Suppl. 1): 152–174.

Strayer D, Downing JA, Haag WR, King TL, Layer JB, Newton TJ, Nichols SJ (2004). Changing perspectives on pearly mussels, North America's most imperilled animals. *BioScience* 54: 429–439.

Streng DR, Glitzenstein JS, Harcombe PA (1989). Woody seedling dynamics in an East Texas floodplain forest. *Ecological Monographs* 59: 177–204.

Stringer C, McKie R (1996). *African Exodus: The Origins of Modern Humanity.* New York, NY: Henry Holt.

Stromberg JC, Lite SJ, Marler R, Paradzick C, Shafroth PB, Shorrock D, White JM, White MS (2007). Altered stream-flow regimes and invasive plant species: the Tamarix case. *Global Ecology and Biogeography* 16: 381–393.

Stubbington R, Wood PJ, Boulton AJ (2009). Low flow controls on benthic and hyporheic macroinvertebrate assemblages during supraseasonal drought. *Hydrological Processes* 23: 2252–2263.

Stubbington R, Wood PJ, Reid I, Gunn J (2010). Benthic and hyporheic invertebrate community responses to seasonal flow recession in a groundwater dominated stream. *Ecohydrology* 4: 500–511.

Suren AM, Riis T (2010). The effects of plant growth on stream invertebrate communities during low flow: a conceptual model. *Journal of the North American Benthological Society* 29: 711–724

Tennant DL (1976). Instream flow regimens for fish, wildlife, recreation and related environmental resources. *Fisheries* 1: 6–10.

Tharme RE (2003). A global perspective on environmental flow assessment: emerging trends in the development and application of environmental flow methodologies for rivers. *River Research and Applications* 19: 397–441.

Thieme ML, Abell R, Stiassny MLJ, Lehner B, Skelton P, Teugels G, Dinerstein E, Kamden Toham A, Burgess B, Olson D (2005). *Freshwater Ecoregions of Africa and Madagascar: A Conservation Assessment*. Washington, DC: Island Press.

Thorp JH, Thoms MC, Delong MD (2006). The Riverine Ecosystem Synthesis: biocomplexity in river networks across space and time. *River Research and Applications* 22: 123–147.

Thorp JH, Thoms MC, Delong MD (2008). *The Riverine Ecosystem Synthesis*. San Diego, CA: Elsevier.

Thrush SF, Hewitt JE, Cummings VJ, Ellis JI, Hatton C, Lohrer A, Norkko A (2004). Muddy waters: elevating sediment input to coastal and estuarine habitats. *Frontiers in Ecology and Environment* 2: 299–306.

Tickner DP, Angold PG, Gurnell AM, Mountford OJ (2001). Riparian plant invasions: hydrogeomorphological control and ecological impacts. *Progress in Physical Geography* 25: 22–52.

TNC (The Nature Conservancy) (2009). Conserve Online: ELOHA Case Studies. Available at: http://conserveonline.org/workspaces/eloha/documents/template-kyle

Tockner K, Bunn S, Gordon C, Naiman RJ, Quinn GP, Stanford JA (2008). Flood plains: critically threatened ecosystems. In *Aquatic Ecosystems,* Polunin NVC (Ed), 45–61. Cambridge, UK: Cambridge University Press.

Tockner KA, Lorang MS, Stanford JA (2010). River flood plains are model ecosystems to test general hydrogeomorphic and ecological concepts. *River Research and Applications* 26: 76–86.

Todd CR, Ryan T, Nicol SJ, Bearlin AR (2005). The impact of cold water releases on the critical period of post-spawning survival and its implications for Murray cod *(Maccullochella peelii peelii):* a case study of the Mitta Mitta River, southeastern Australia. *River Research and Applications* 21: 1035–1052.

Tomlinson M, Boulton AJ (2010). Ecology and management of subsurface groundwater dependent ecosystems in Australia: a review. *Marine and Freshwater Research* 61: 936–949. Available at: www.publish.csiro.au/nid/126/paper/MF09267.htm

Tooth S (2000). Process, form and change in dryland rivers: a review of recent research. *Earth-Science Reviews* 51: 67–107.

Toth LA (1995). Principles and guidelines for restoration of river/floodplain ecosystems: Kissimmee River, Florida. In *Rehabilitating Damaged Ecosystems*, Cairns J (Ed), 49–73. Boca Raton, FL: Lewis Publishers/CRC Press.

Townsend CR (1989). The patch dynamics concept of stream community ecology. *Journal of the North American Benthological Society* 8: 36–50.

Townsend PA, Walsh SJ (1998). Modelling floodplain inundation using an integrated GIS with radar and optical remote sensing. *Geomorphology* 21: 295–312.

TRPA (Thomas R. Payne and Associates) (n.d.). RHABSIM Version 3.0. Available at: http://trpafishbiologists.com/rindex.html

UNESCO (1972). Convention Concerning the Protection of the World Cultural and Natural Heritage, the General Conference of the United Nations Educational, Scientific and Cultural Organization Meeting in Paris from 17 October to 21 November 1972. Available at: http://whc.unesco.org/en/about

UN General Assembly (2000). UN Millennium Declaration 55/2. Resolution adopted by the General Assembly, United Nations Headquarters, New York. Available at: www.un.org/millennium/declaration/ares552e.htm

United Nations (2002). The Johannesburg Declaration on Sustainable Development. World Summit on Sustainable Development, 26 August–4 September 2002, Johannesburg, South Africa. Available at: www.johannesburgsummit.org/html/documents/summit_docs/131302_wssd_report_reissued.pdf

UN-WWAP (UN World Water Assessment Programme) (2003). *Water for People: Water for Life*. UN World Water Development Report 1. Paris, France: UNESCO.

UN-WWAP (UN World Water Assessment Programme) (2009). *Water in a Changing World*. UN World Water Development Report 3. Paris, France: UNESCO; London, UK: Earthscan.

Valentine LE (2006). Habitat avoidance of an introduced weed by native lizards. *Austral Ecology* 31: 372–375.

Vannote RL, Minshall GW, Cummins KW, Sedell JR, Cushing CE (1980).

The River Continuum Concept. *Canadian Journal of Fisheries and Aquatic Sciences* 37: 130–137.

Vitousek PM, Mooney HA, Lubchenco J, Melillo JM (1997). Human domination of Earth's ecosystems. *Science* 277: 494–499.

Vörösmarty CJ, Meybeck M, Fekete B, Sharma K (1997). The potential impact of neo-Cartorization on sediment transport by the global network of rivers. In *Proceedings of the Rabat Symposium,* IAHS Publication No. 245, 261–273. Wallingford, Oxfordshire, UK: International Association of Hydrological Sciences.

Vörösmarty CJ, Meybeck M, Fekete B, Sharma K, Green P, Syvitski JPM (2003). Anthropogenic sediment retention: major global impact from registered river impoundments. *Global and Planetary Change* 39: 169–190.

Vörösmarty CJ, Lettenmaier D, Lévêque C, Meybeck M, Pahl-Wostl C, Alcamo J, Cosgrove W, Grassl H, Hoff H, Kabat P, Lansigan E, Lawford R, Naiman RJ (2004). Humans transforming the global water system. *EOS, American Geophysical Union Transactions* 85: 509–514.

Vörösmarty CJ, Lévêque C, Revenga C (2005). Fresh water. In *Millennium Ecosystem Assessment,* vol. 1, *Ecosystems and Human Well-Being: Current State and Trends.* Washington, DC: Island Press.

Vörösmarty CJ, McIntyre PB, Gessner MO, Dudgeon D, Prusevich A, Green P, Glidden PS, Bunn SE, Sullivan CA, Reidy Liermann C, Davies PM (2010). Global threats to human water security and river biodiversity. *Nature* 467: 555–561.

Wagener T, Wheater HS, Gupta HV (2004). *Rainfall-Runoff Modeling in Gauged and Ungauged Catchments.* London, UK: Imperial College Press.

Walker KF, Thoms MC, Sheldon F (1992). Effects of weirs on the littoral environment of the River Murray, South Australia. In *River Conservation and Management,* Boon PJ, Calow P, Petts GE (Eds), 272–292. Chichester, UK: John Wiley and Sons.

Walker KF, Sheldon F, Puckridge JT (1995). An ecological perspective on dryland river ecosystems. *Regulated Rivers: Research and Management* 11: 85–104.

Walling DE (2006). Human impact on land-ocean sediment transfer for the world's rivers. *Geomorphology* 79: 173–191.

Walsh CJ, Fletcher TD, Ladson AR (2005). Stream restoration in urban catchments through re-designing stormwater systems: looking to the catchment to save the stream. *Journal of the North American Benthological Society* 24: 690–705.

Walters CJ (1986). *Adaptive Management of Renewable Resources.* New York, NY: Macmillan.

Ward JV (1989). The four-dimensional nature of lotic ecosystems. *Journal of the North American Benthological Society* 8: 2–8.

Ward JV, Stanford JA (1979). *The Ecology of Regulated Streams.* New York, NY: Plenum Press.

Ward JV, Stanford JA (1983). The Serial Discontinuity Concept of lotic ecosystems. In *Dynamics of Lotic Ecosystems,* Fontaine TD, Bartel SM (Eds), 29–42. Ann Arbor, MI: Ann Arbor Science.

Ward JV, Stanford JA (1995). Ecological connectivity in alluvial river ecosystems and its disruption by flow regulation. *Regulated Rivers: Research and Management* 11: 105–119.

Waycott M, Duarteb CM, Carruthers TJB, Orth RJ, Dennison WC, Olyarnick S, Calladine A, Fourqurean JW, Heck KL Jr, Randall Hughes A, Kendrick GA, Judson Kenworthy W, Short FT, Williams SL (2009). Accelerating loss of seagrasses across the globe threatens coastal ecosystems. *Proceedings of the National Academy of Sciences, USA* 106: 12377–12381.

WCD (World Commission on Dams) (2000). *Dams and Development: A New Framework for Decision-Making.* London, UK, and Sterling, VA: Earthscan.

WCD (World Commission on Dams) (2005). *The Wealth of the Poor: Managing Ecosystems to Fight Poverty.* Washington, DC: UN Environmental Programme and World Bank.

Webb AJ, Stewardson MJ, Koster WM (2010). Detecting ecological responses to flow variation using Bayesian hierarchical models. *Freshwater Biology* 55: 108–126.

Wedderburn S, Barnes T (2009). *Condition Monitoring of Threatened Fish Species at Lake Alexandrina and Lake Albert (2008–2009).* Adelaide, Australia: University of Adelaide.

Wei Q, He D, Yang D, Zhang W, Li L (2004). Status of sturgeon aquaculture and sturgeon trade in China: a review based on two recent nationwide surveys. *Journal of Applied Ichthyology* 20: 321–332.

Weisberg SB, Janicki AJ, Gerritsen J, Wilson HT (1990). Enhancement of benthic macroinvertebrates by minimum flow from a hydroelectric dam. *Regulated Rivers: Research and Management* 5: 265–277.

Weitkamp DE, Katz M (1980). A review of dissolved gas supersaturation literature. *Transactions of the American Fisheries Society* 109: 659–702.

Welcomme RL (1985). *River Fisheries.* FAO Fisheries Technical Paper 262. Rome, Italy: Food and Agriculture Organization of the United Nations.

Welcomme RL, Hagborg D (1977). Towards a model of a floodplain fish population and its fishery. *Environmental Biology of Fishes* 2: 7–24.

Welcomme RL, Bene C, Brown CA, Arthington A, Patrick Dugan P, King JM, Sugunan V (2006). Predicting the water requirements of river fisheries. In *Wetlands and Natural Resource Management,* Verhoeven JTA, Beltman B, Bobbink R, Whigham DF (Eds), 123–154. Berlin, Germany: Springer-Verlag.

Werren G, Arthington AH (2002). The assessment of riparian vegetation as an indicator of stream condition, with particular emphasis on the rapid assessment of flow-related impacts. In *Landscape Health of Queensland,* Playford J, Shapcott A, Franks A (Eds), 194–222. Brisbane, Australia: Royal Society of Queensland.

Wetzel RG (1990). Land-water interfaces: metabolic and limnological regulators. *Verhandlungen der Internationalen Vereinigung für Limnologie* 24: 6–24.

White DS (1993). Perspectives on defining and delineating hyporheic zones. *Journal of the North American Benthological Society* 12: 61–69.

White DS, Hendricks SP, Fortner SL (1992). Groundwater–surface water interactions and the distribution of aquatic macrophytes. In *Proceedings of the First International Conference on Ground Water Ecology,* Stanford JA, Simons JJ (Eds), 247–256. Bethesda, MD: American Water Resources Association (cited in Boulton and Hancock 2006).

Wilcock RJ, Nagels JW, Mcbride GB, Collier KH (1998). Characterisation of lowland streams using a single-station diurnal curve analysis model with continuous monitoring data for dissolved oxygen and temperature. *New Zealand Journal of Marine and Freshwater Research* 32: 67–79 (cited in Suren and Riis 2010).

Wilding TK, Poff NL (2008). *Flow-Ecology Relationships for the Watershed Flow Evaluation Tool.* Denver, CO: Colorado State University for the Colorado Water Conservation Board.

Wild Rivers Act (2005). Wild Rivers Act of 2005, Queensland Parliamentary Counsel. Available at: www.legislation.qld.gov.au/LEGISLTN/CURRENT/W/WildRivA05.pdf

Winemiller KO (2004). Floodplain river food webs: generalizations and implications for fisheries management. In *Proceedings of the Second International Symposium on the Management of Large Rivers for Fisheries,* vol. 1, Welcomme R, Petr T (Eds), 285–312. Bangkok, Thailand: FAO Regional Office for Asia and the Pacific.

Winemiller KO, Rose KA (1992). Patterns of life history diversification in North American fishes: implications for population regulation. *Canadian Journal of Fisheries and Aquatic Sciences* 49: 2196–2218.

Winterbourn MJ, Rounick JS, Cowie B (1981). Are New Zealand stream eco-systems really different? *New Zealand Journal of Marine and Freshwater Research* 15: 321–328.

Wishart MJ (2006). Water scarcity: politics, populations and the ecology of desert rivers. In *Ecology of Desert Rivers,* Kingsford RT (Ed), 76–99. Melbourne, Australia: Cambridge University Press.

Wolanski E (2007). *Estuarine Ecohydrology.* Amsterdam, Netherlands: Elsevier.

Wood PL, Armitage PD (1997). Biological effects of fine sediment in the lotic environment. *Environmental Management* 21: 203–217.

Woodward G (2009). Biodiversity, ecosystem functioning and food webs in fresh waters: assembling the jigsaw puzzle. *Freshwater Biology.* 54: 2171–2187.

Wootton JT, Parker MS, Power ME (1996). Effects of disturbance on river food webs. *Science* 273: 1558–1561.

Worrall F, Burt TP (1998). Decomposition of river nitrate time-series. Comparing agricultural and urban signals. *The Science of the Total Environment* 210/211: 153–162.

Worster D (1985). *Rivers of Empire: Water, Aridity, and the Growth of the American West.* New York, NY: Pantheon.

Wright JP, Jones CG (2006). The concept of organisms as ecosystem engineer ten years on: progress, limitations, and challenges. *BioScience* 56: 203–209.

Wu J, Loucks OL (1995). From balance of nature to hierarchical patch dynamics: a paradigm shift in ecology. *Quarterly Review of Biology* 70: 439–466.

Xenopoulos M, Lodge DM, Alcamo J, Märker M, Schulze K, Van Vuuren DP (2005). Scenarios of freshwater fish extinctions from climate change and water withdrawal. *Global Change Biology* 11: 1557–1564.

Xue Z, Liu JP, Ge Q (2011). Changes in hydrology and sediment delivery of the Mekong River in the last 50 years: connection to damming, monsoon, and ENSO. *Earth Surface Processes and Landforms* 36: 296–308.

Young WJ, Kingsford RT (2006). Flow variability in large unregulated dry-land rivers. In *Ecology of Desert Rivers,* Kingsford RT (Ed), 11–46. Melbourne, Australia: Cambridge University Press.

Zachos JC, Dickens GR, Zeebe RE (2008). An early Cenozoic perspective on greenhouse gas warming and carbon-cycle dynamics. *Nature* 451: 279–283.

Zalasiewicz J, Williams M, Smith AG, Barry TL, Coe AL, Bown PR, Brenchley P, Cantrill D, Gale A, Gibbard P, Gregory FJ, Hounslow MW, Kerr AC, Pearson P, Knox R, Powell J, Waters C, Marshall J, Oates M, Rawson P, Stone P (2008). Are we now living in the Anthropocene? *GSA Today* 18: 4–8.

Zhang Y, Arthington AH, Bunn SE, Mackay S, Xia J, Kennard M (2011). Classification of flow regimes for environmental flow assessment in regulated rivers: the Huai River basin, China. *River Research and Applications* doi: 10.1002/rra.1483

Zhong YG, Power G (1996). Environmental impacts of hydroelectric projects on fish resources in China. *Regulated Rivers: Research and Management* 12: 81–98.

INDEX

aquatic vegetation
exotic, increased with urbanization, 80
as factor in holistic assessments, 150
response to flow alteration, 114, 196,
202–203
as "target habitat," 168
aquifers
freshwater stored in, 223–224
overview of, 214–215
saltwater infiltration into, 227–228
uncoupling river baseflow system
from, 225
Arachnocampa luminosa, 215
Aral Sea (Uzbekistan and Kazakhstan),
122, 248
Arkansas River (U.S.), 226
Arnette, S. C., 134
artesian springs, 214–215
Arthington, A. H., 60, 64, 185, 192,
207
Asian rhinoceros, one-horned, 306
assets. *See* ecosystem services
Aswan High Dam (Egypt), 100,
110–111, 264
Atlantic salmon, 227
Australia
application of ELOHA framework,
196–197, 197 (table)
flow regime types, 27, 29–30, 31
(table), 32 (fig.)
legislation for water reform, 308–309
Australian lungfish, 93, 281, 300
Australian swamp paperbark, 115
avoiders, 69
Azov, Sea of, 264

Baltz, D. M., 143
Bangladesh, 208
Barbus capensis, 108 (table), 120
Barcelona Convention and Statute
on the Regime of Navigable
Waterways of International
Concern, 301

barramundi, 269
Barron River (Australia), 157, 158 (fig.),
159 (table)
basins
effect of shape on hydrographs, 39
(fig.), 39
variability of flow regimes within,
40, 41 (fig.), 42
water-allocation approach focused
on, 282–284
See also catchments; *specific river
basins*
bass, striped, 179
Bayesian network (BN) models, 182,
208–210, 210 (fig.)
beavers, 88, 104
Beerling, D. J., 313
Benchmarking Methodology, 136,
155–160, 158 (fig.), 159 (table)
Bennett, M., 252
Bidyanus bidyanus, 108 (table)
billabongs, 36, 244
Bill Williams River (U.S.), 204
biodiversity
freshwater biodiversity crisis, 1–2, 7,
273–274
See also aquatic biodiversity
birds
benefiting from floods, 65, 253–254,
289, 297
impacted by flow alteration, 121,
248, 249
migratory bird agreements, 279,
297, 300, 319
threatened by oil spill, 250
blackflies, 50, 117
simuliid blackflies, 123
Black Sea, 264
bluntnose shiner, Pecos, 115
Booker, D. J., 148
Boulton, A. J., 221–224, 232–235, 237,
241, 321
Bovee, K. D., 142

estuaries *(continued)*
    land-based threats to, 261–263
    methods to determine inflow
        requirements for, 267–271, 270
        (table)
estuarine turbidity maximum (ETM),
    264–265
Euastacus armatus, 93
Eucalyptus camaldulensis, 118–119, 253,
    297
Euphrates River (Mesopotamia), 88
Europe
    flow regime types, 27
    Water Framework Directive
        (WFD), 129, 274, 304–305
European Aquatic Modelling Network
    (EAMN), 148
eutrophication, 227, 246, 261, 262
Everglades National Park (U.S.), 173,
    267–268, 307
exotic species
    flow alterations favoring, 116, 281,
        291
    hydroecological principle on altera-
        tion of flow and, 61 (table), 65
    impact on indigenous species,
        93–94, 182
    invasion by, 78, 115, 116
experiments, flow restoration projects
    established as, 173–176, 175 (fig)
extinctions
    due to groundwater abstraction, 225
    fish vulnerable to, 93, 94, 206, 248, 249
    freshwater species, 2

Fairbridge, R. W., 259
fine particulate organic matter
    (FPOM), 50
fish
    barrier effects of dams, 94–97, 96
        (table)
    benefits of upwelling groundwater,
        219–221

effects of hydroelectric dams, 110,
    117
effects of stabilized flows below
    dams, 115–116
effects of thermally or chemically
    altered flow releases from dams,
    107–109, 108 (table), 109 (fig.)
exotic vs. indigenous, 93–94
flood pulses' influence, 52, 53
groundwater abstraction's impact,
    226–227
impacts of altered flows on life
    history, 119–120
integrated approach to EFA frame-
    work for, 208–209, 210 (fig.)
models of response to flow altera-
    tion, 205–208
responses to changes in flow magni-
    tude, 183–184
zonation schemes, 49
See also specific fish
fish assemblage structure, 206–207
fisheries
    climate change and, 315–316
    floodplains and, 52, 53, 207, 208
    impact of wetlands altered by dams,
        248, 264
    response to river inflow in estuaries,
        265–266, 269–270
fish population models, 207–208, 209,
    210 (fig.)
Fitzroy River (Australia), 160
Flaming Gorge Dam (U.S.), 100–101
flashiness, 21
    See also rate of change of flows
floodplain inundation model, 252–253
floodplain rivers, 121–122
floodplains
    altering management of, to enhance
        resilience to climate change,
        319–320
    Flood Pulse Concept (FPC), 51
        (fig.), 52–53

Froend, F., 231–233
Functional Flows Model (FFM),
    147–148, 204

Galat, D. L., 137
Galaxias
    maculatus, 249
    occidentalis, 97
galaxias, common, 249
Gambusia holbrooki, 116
Gan, K. C., 142, 145
gangetic dolphin, 306
Garrison Dam (U.S.), 105
gas supersaturation, 109–110
Gavialis gangeticus, 306
geographical areas
    climate types for, 17 (table)
    levels of threat for human water
        security and/or freshwater
        biodiversity, 7
    See also specific countries
geomorphic features, interacting with
    flow regimes, 34
geomorphic gradients
    longitudinal profile, 38–39, 39 (fig.)
    longitudinal zones, 36–38, 37 (fig.),
        49
geomorphic processes, influencing
    ecological responses, 204
gharial crocodile, 306
Ghassemi, F., 123
giant catfish, 94
Gibert, J., 235
Gila cypha, 115–116
Gippel, C. J., 137, 140
Glen Canyon Dam (U.S.), 115–116
Global Water System Project, 274
glowworm, 215
gobies, desert, 215
golden perch, 108 (table), 109 (fig.), 160
Gordon, N., 36
Grand Canyon Monitoring and
    Research Center, 174

Great Artesian Basin (Australia), 215
Great Fish River (South Africa), 123
Great Man-Made River Project
    (Libya), 224
Great Miami River (U.S.), 290
Great Plains (North America), 121, 226
Green, J., 252
greenhouse gases, 94, 311, 312, 313
Green River (Kentucky, U.S.), 176
Green River (Utah, U.S.), 100–101
green sea turtles, 263
Groffman, P. M., 80
Groot River (South Africa), 293
Grossman, G. D., 207
groundwater
    abstracted for irrigation, 224, 225,
        226, 227, 292–293
    defined, 213
    fauna in, 235–236
    freshwater held as, 13, 14 (fig.)
    "sustainable yield" approach to
        managing, 238–239
    upwelling, benefits to fish, 219–221
groundwater-dependent ecosystems
    (GDEs)
    defined, 215
    defining and assessing health of,
        236–237
    ecological stress on, 238–239
    identifying and evaluating, 229–233,
        230–231 (table)
    rivers as, 216–222, 217 (fig.), 218
        (table), 220 (fig.)
    subsurface groundwater-dependent
        ecosystems (SGDEs), 222, 223
        (fig.), 234, 237
    threats to, 223–228
    valuing and prioritizing, 239–241
groundwater systems
    human activities altering, 224–225,
        226, 227–228
    management of, 237–239
    overview of, 213–215, 214 (fig.)

on flow and nitrogen cycling,
65–69, 67 (table), 68 (fig.)
on flow regimes and riparian
vegetation, 69–73, 70 (fig.), 71–73
(tables)
on flow regime's governance of
aquatic biodiversity, 60–65, 61
(table), 62 (fig.), 63 (table), 64
(table), 66 (table)
origin of, 60
hydroelectric power dams. *See* hydropower dams
hydrogeomorphic variability, as
gradients vs. patches, 42–44, 45
(fig.)
hydrographs
impact of basin shape on, 39 (fig.),
39
impact of longitudinal profile on,
38–39, 39 (fig.)
vegetation cover as influencing, 39
hydrological character, determined
from stream gauges, 40, 41 (fig.),
42
hydrological classification
as foundation of ELOHA, 33
role in water management, 32–33
hydrological methods, 131–137
flow duration curve (FDA) analysis
methods, 134–135
Flow Translucency Approach, 137
Montana (or Tennant) Method,
132–134, 133 (table)
overview of, 131–132
Range of Variability Approach
(RVA), 135–136
hydrologic alteration, setting limits on,
274–276, 276 (fig.)
hydrologic cycle
accelerated by climate change, 8
environmental flow and, 11
overview of, 13, 14 (fig.)
Hydrologic Engineering Center's

Ecosystem Functions Model
(HEC-EFM), 204
"hydrologic sponges," 247
hydropower dams
effects on habitat and aquatic
biodiversity, 116–117
gas supersaturation below, 109–110
modifying releases from, 289
natural flow regimes altered by,
102–103, 103 (fig.)
hyporheic flow paths, 233–234
hyporheic zone
defined, 216–217, 217 (fig.)
groundwater dependencies in, 218
(table), 219–221, 220 (fig.)
groundwater-dependent ecosystems
and, 222, 223 (fig.)
permeability of, 225
hypoxia, 264

Indicators of Hydrologic Alteration
software, 195
indigenous people/tribes, 87–88, 179,
320–321
Indigirka River (Russia), 27
Indus River (India), 88
insects, aquatic, 107, 119–120
Instream Flow Incremental Methodology (IFIM), 131, 142–146, 143
(fig.)
in-stream flow methods, 9
integrated river basin assessment
(IBFA), 282, 283 (table)
interbasin transfers (IBTs), 122–124,
124 (fig.)
Intergovernmental Panel on Climate
Change (IPCC)
on evidence of global warming,
311–312
greenhouse gas forecast, 312
river runoff and water availability
prediction, 313–314
temperature increase prediction, 8